ORGANIZING INFORMATION
Principles of Data Base and Retrieval Systems

LIBRARY AND INFORMATION SCIENCE

CONSULTING EDITORS: *Harold Borko and G. Edward Evans*
GRADUATE SCHOOL OF LIBRARY SCIENCE
UNIVERSITY OF CALIFORNIA, LOS ANGELES

ORGANIZING INFORMATION
Principles of Data Base
and Retrieval Systems

Dagobert Soergel

College of Library and Information Services
University of Maryland
College Park, Maryland

1985

ACADEMIC PRESS, INC.

(Harcourt Brace Jovanovich, Publishers)

Orlando   San Diego   New York   London
Toronto   Montreal   Sydney   Tokyo

ACADEMIC PRESS, INC.
Orlando, Florida 32887

United Kingdom Edition published by
ACADEMIC PRESS INC. (LONDON) LTD.
24–28 Oval Road, London NW1 7DX

LIBRARY OF CONGRESS CATALOGING-IN-PUBLICATION DATA

Soergel, Dagobert.
    Organizing information.

    (Library and information science)
    Bibliography: p.
    Includes index.
    1. Information storage and retrieval systems.
I. Title.   II. Series.
Z699.S539   1985   025'.04   83-15741
ISBN 0-12-654260-0 (alk. paper)
ISBN 0-12-654261-9 (paperback)

PRINTED IN THE UNITED STATES OF AMERICA

85 86 87 88   9 8 7 6 5 4 3 2 1

Contents

II
OBJECTIVES OF ISAR SYSTEMS

V

ISAR SYSTEMS OPERATION AND DESIGN

Preface

This book gives a theoretical base and a perspective for the analysis, design, and operation of information systems, particularly their information storage and retrieval (ISAR) component, whether mechanized or manual. Information systems deal with many types of entities: events, persons, documents, business transactions, museum objects, research projects, and technical parts, to name a few. Among the purposes they serve are to inform the public, to support managers, researchers, and engineers, and to provide a knowledge base for an artificial intelligence program. The principles discussed in this book apply to all these contexts. The book achieves this generality by drawing on ideas from two conceptually overlapping areas—data base management and the organization and use of knowledge in libraries—and by integrating these ideas into a coherent framework. The principles discussed apply to the design of new systems and, more importantly, to the analysis of existing systems in order to exploit their capabilities better, to circumvent their shortcomings, and to introduce modifications where feasible.

This book is intended for use in an introductory course on organizing and retrieving information (called, for example, "Introduction to the Organization of Information," "Introduction to Information Storage and Retrieval," or "Introduction to Information Science") offered in a school of library and information science, a business school, or a more broadly based information studies or information management program. Beyond that, it is meant to inspire a modernization and integration of the library/information science curriculum. The book can be used for a broadly based course that teaches the general principles of ISAR and treats cataloging and reference service as specific areas of application. Such a course not only overcomes the artificial separation of cataloging and reference but also gives students wide flexibility in choosing their first position and a sound base from which to strike out in many directions in the further development of their careers. It can be offered as a package of designated sections of the cataloging and reference course, without changing any course numbers. Such a course can be extended to include students from business information systems, journalism, and cognate areas: The theoretical base is common to all, but the application areas are different. This book is also suitable for self-study by practitioners who are looking for a sounder theoretical base for their daily work. A workbook with exercises and discussion of additional examples is in preparation; a draft is available from the author.

Information studies is a nascent field. It shows considerable confusion in its terminology, partly due to the lack of a prevalent conceptual framework: The same term is used for different concepts; different terms are used for the same concept. This book follows the terminology of major writers in the field but sometimes introduces a new term for a new concept or to replace an existing term that reflects a faulty concept analysis.

Throughout the book the development of ideas proceeds from the point of view that information specialists are professionals who cooperate with the user in determining information needs and who use their knowledge to design systems or to do searches to meet these needs, as opposed to merely looking for what the user thinks is needed.

Organization of the Book. Part I places information systems in context; it discusses the nature and structure of information and lays out the overall structure of an information system. Part II provides the basis for considering the design and use of ISAR systems in light of the objectives to be achieved, allowing for a discussion of the merits of design alternatives in Parts III through V. Part III deals with the logical representation of data and with structures for providing access to these data. It deals on a general level with the rules and conventions necessary in an ISAR system. Part IV focuses attention on subject retrieval (but many of the principles have more general application). It discusses the nature of index languages—terminological control, basic functions, and conceptual structure. Part V discusses indexing and searching and, in conclusion, testing and design of the system.

Acknowledgments. This book was developed from lectures given at the University of Maryland; the students' many questions forced me to sharpen my thinking, and their comments on successive versions of the manuscript were extremely useful. Norman Roberts, Harold Borko, and Raya Fidel all gave good advice, which, among other things, was instrumental in reducing this book to a manageable size. Jane Bergling and Marie Somers typed the manuscript many times over, somehow managing to interpret my scribbled revisions. My wife Lissa was always ready to examine and discuss ideas and to make suggestions concerning both content and form; she also spent hours editing and proofreading. I owe an intellectual debt to many in the field but above all to the pioneering spirit of Calvin Mooers.

PART I

The Systems Approach
to Information Transfer

CHAPTER I

Information Systems for Problem Solving

Information systems are all around us: management information systems, message distribution systems, information and referral centers, libraries, abstracting/indexing services, legal data bases, employment agencies, stores and store catalogs (merchandise information systems), to name a few. Information systems grow in response to problems; information is for problem solving. The more complex the world in which we live, the more information we need to solve our problems. Figure 1.1 shows some of the problems and information needs arising from these problems.

An information system identifies problems, acquires helpful information, and delivers this information to those who need it. An information system may also identify and deliver helpful entities, such as merchandise, technical parts, or even people (as in an employment agency). See the following diagram.

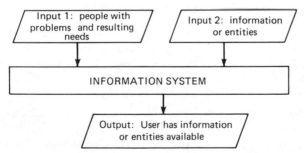

An information system deals with many problems and thus must answer many requests for information; it acquires large amounts of information and thus must deal with many entities; and it must find just the right information in response to a request—just the information needed for solving the problem at hand. Matching available information with an information need is the task of the information storage and retrieval (ISAR) component of an information system.

Problem	Information need
Many children do not achieve their full potential because parents use improper techniques of child-rearing, particularly during the first three years of life.	Information on child-rearing, how to stimulate a child's development in various areas. Some parents obtain the information needed from a bookstore or a public library, but those parents who are not aware of their information needs will not be served by either.
Among people in the inner city, unemployment is much above average. Partly this is due to lack of training.	Information on training needed to gain employment, on training programs, and on government assistance for participants in such programs. Without at least a general idea that opportunities are available, there will be no motivation to seek that information on the part of the unemployed. The public library could fill this need.
Decide whether a chemical should be permitted as a new food additive.	Information on the toxicity of the chemical and on the patterns of consumption of the foods for which the new additive is to be used. Such information can be obtained from the literature, as found in a bibliographic information system, from an information system that stores results of animal experiments (toxicity), and from an information system that stores data from consumption surveys.
An engineer needs an electronic component for an engine ignition system that will perform reliably under voltage variations.	For each make of the electronic component in question the engineer needs data on actual use in various circumstances and data on failures. Failure reports can be obtained from the information system GIDEP (Government-Industry Data Exchange Program).
Study the relationship between insects and plants, specifically between bees and squashes. (Some species of bees live only on certain species of squash which, in turn, need these bees for pollination.)	Time series data on the geographical distribution of plants and insects. Through analysis one could detect cases where the geographical area of a plant species co-varies with the geographical area of an insect species, suggesting a relationship.

In each of these examples it is the function of the information system to supply the user with the information needed so that the problem can be solved. The information system should do this even if the user is not aware of his or her information need.

Fig. 1.1   Problems and information needs.

This selection function occurs in many types of information systems. An information system for parents must not only distribute material of general interest but also retrieve literature, toys, organizations, or people who might be helpful in solving a specific problem of child rearing. An employment agency must find the job openings appropriate for the skills of a job seeker or, conversely, find a job seeker who fits the requirements of a job. To help an unemployed person, the public library must find a training program for which he or she is eligible and which is suited to his or her interests and abilities. An information and referral center must find a human services agency that meets the needs of the client, will accept him or her, and is reasonably nearby. A bibliographic information system, such as *Chemical Abstracts,* must find from among several million journal articles and other documents the few (perhaps 20–100) that deal with the toxicity of a given chemical. A store catalog should enable the prospective customer to find the needed item quickly. A management information system must provide each manager with those data about the organization's performance that are pertinent to the decisions he or she must make. A message distribution system must route an internal or external message to all whose work may be affected by it. A legal data base must find sections of laws and prior decisions that are applicable to the case at hand.

The following examples illustrate further the wide range of information systems and the retrieval tasks within them:

- an encylopedia with its index, printed or on-line, accessible from computer terminals (an idea whose time has come!),
- computer-stored set of data for use by an artificial intelligence program (e.g., a program for understanding a piece of text and answering questions about it),
- a library and its catalog on cards or microfilm, or on-line,
- the filing system in an agency (records management),
- a handbook of physical data, printed or on-line, and
- an information system matching inventions with companies that could utilize and market them.

The study of ISAR systems covers the intertwined aspects of intellectual organization and technological implementation. Retrieval requires an organization of the data or entities that allows selection by the characteristics of interest. Often such an organization is created through intellectual work specifically for the ISAR system: an indexer examines the entities (jobs, persons, organizations, merchandise, documents) with respect to the characteristics of interest. With documents we may be able to use their inherent organization and operate directly on their text, either through full text searching or through automated indexing—that is, using a program that reads the text and assigns index terms.

It is often advantageous to organize the characteristics of interest into a logically coherent framework, a classification. Classification may be crucial to the success of an ISAR system. Whether a person finds the right job may depend on whether the employment agency's ISAR system uses the right characteristics to index both jobs and job openings. The intellectual organization of the information, with classification at the center, should reflect the structure of the problems to be solved and should be in tune with the organi-

zation of knowledge and the pattern of thought in the minds of the users.
Classification theory is a central part of ISAR.

There are many technologies that can be used for ISAR. The older technologies are still important: arranging merchandise, parts, or books on shelves, possibly in a meaningful order based on an appropriate classification; or providing an index (entries printed on a page or a card catalog) for human searching. However, computers are more suitable for most retrieval tasks. How to organize large amounts of data for rapid access from a computer terminal is an important research problem in computer science. Technology advances; today some machines can search with a speed of one million characters (500 pages) per second, so that we can search through the entire text of many documents and exploit their internal organization for retrieval to an extent not possible before. Microcomputers and telecommunication make possible small personal information systems linked to large public information systems. On the other hand, we must not become so preoccupied with technology that we lose sight of the intellectual problems. Some search topics are so complex that judging the relevance of a document requires an understanding of the document as a whole, which is beyond present computer programs.

Information storage and retrieval overlaps, meshes, and coincides with data base management, decision support, and artificial intelligence. A *data base management system* (DBMS) is a computer program that can organize large collections of interrelated data according to a well-defined schema and produce reports by extracting and reformatting data. Reformatting may range from rearrangement or simple totaling to complex statistical analysis. Thus a DBMS is a system for information storage, retrieval, and analysis with emphasis on formatted data.

A *decision support system* (DSS) retrieves and processes information to suit the style of the manager for whom it was customized. Developing forecasts (for example, of sales or profits) under varying assumptions (what-if analysis) is a particularly important DSS function. Thus a DSS must be capable of economic and other modeling using the data in its data base. Decision support systems often deal with narrow subject domains. Some have been implemented on personal computers that store often-used data locally and access other computers to obtain additional data as needed.

Artificial intelligence (AI) is concerned with sophisticated applications of computers, such as optical character recognition, voice recognition and synthesis, image interpretation, natural language understanding, and expert systems. Knowledge representation, pattern recognition, and theorem proving are general methods of artificial intelligence.

AI research has led to exciting developments in information storage and retrieval. An *expert system*—for example, a system for medical diagnosis—

is an information system that incorporates in its retrieval process procedures that simulate expert reasoning. A diagnosis system retrieves diseases when given a set of symptoms. Other systems have been developed to analyze geological data for the occurrence of mineral deposits or to analyze oil rig mechanical problems, for example. Expert systems usually deal with narrow, well-defined subject domains.

Processing of natural language (as opposed to artificial languages such as programming languages or mathematical notation) is useful for retrieval of documents or passages from documents. *Natural language understanding* can be used to prepare a summary of a text, to determine whether a document contains anything new as compared with an existing collection of data, or to construct a human–computer interface that can understand a query phrased in natural language.

Many AI applications require large amounts of semantic and real-world knowledge. For example, in interpreting the sentence "He went to the shelf for milk, took it to the cashier, and paid for it," a computer program would consult its list of things normally bought in a supermarket, find *Milk* but not *Shelf* and conclude that the person took the milk rather than the shelf. AI researchers have given a good deal of thought to methods of representing and storing such knowledge in a way suitable for AI programs. This is an information storage and retrieval problem, but AI researchers have developed their schemes independently from the ISAR community. More exchange of ideas would benefit both.

As the name implies, information storage and retrieval has two aspects: storage and organization of information, on the one hand, and retrieval, on the other. In library work these are known as cataloging and reference. These two aspects cannot be separated from each other: retrieval requirements dictate how the store should be organized; conversely, the organization of the store determines its usability for retrieval, its searchability.

It is important that we know how well an ISAR system functions so that we can change its design and operation if necessary. But how do we know how well an ISAR system helps its users solve their problems? Evaluation of performance and impact is an important area in the study of ISAR systems.

Information storage and retrieval is important for problem solving. It is a challenging field, both in the area of intellectual organization and in the area of implementation technology. This book provides an introduction with emphasis on the problems of intellectual organization.

CHAPTER 2

The Nature of Information

OBJECTIVES

The objectives of this chapter are to introduce the concept of information in a very informal way, using the notion of a mental image, and to show the central importance of information for problem solving or decision making.

2.1 THE ROLE OF THE IMAGE

You are driving a car in a 40 miles-per-hour zone. From the speed limit signs you have an image of the desired speed; from the speedometer you have an image of the actual speed. If there is a difference, you have a problem you must solve. In developing a solution you are guided by your image of the car's behavior when you press the accelerator or step on the brake. You take appropriate action. By observing the speedometer, you update your image of the actual speed and compare it again with the desired speed. You go through this feedback cycle until the actual speed is at the proper value (see Fig. 2.1). If the actual speed changes—for example, because you are going up a hill—the whole process starts over. So far we have considered only reactive regulation. When you approach a hill, your mental image tells you that the car will need more power to maintain speed. So you take anticipatory action by pressing down the accelerator a little harder.

This very simple example shows how the mental image that we hold guides us in problem solving and decision making. The image need not cover everything. As the driver of a car you need not know the details of the functioning of the car's engine, or the variety of the trees lining the street, or the names of the people passing by; but your image must contain the essential elements described in the example, lest you press the accelerator when you want to slow down. The mental image is a model of the state of affairs; we can manipulate the image—run through various scenarios in our minds—to find out what would happen in reality.

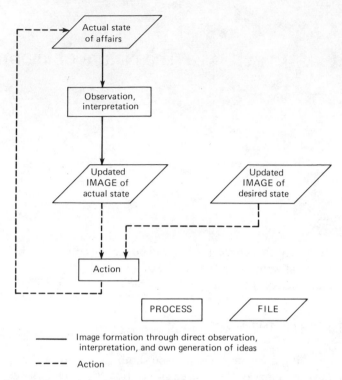

Image formation through direct observation, interpretation, and own generation of ideas

－ － － Action

Fig. 2.1   Information and regulation: overview.

Since the concept of a mental image is central, we give three more examples. A rocket is sent toward Venus, its artificial eye focused on a bright star. The angle between eye direction and rocket axis indicates the actual direction. The onboard computer also has an image of the rocket's planned trajectory; at any moment it can give the desired flight direction expressed as an angle. When actual and desired direction do not agree—either because the actual direction changes for some reason or because the desired direction changes (the rocket must turn)—the computer figures out which engines to fire to bring the rocket on course. The American government and its objective to achieve peace in the Middle East provides another example. To take proper action toward this objective, a very complex and intricate image is required: the military and economic stance of the actors (nations, factions, movements), the alliances in which the actors are involved with other actors both within and outside the Middle East, the channels of influence, the religious and other feelings of the people, the psychology of the leaders. The third example is much simpler: A man who is hungry and wants to go to a restaurant needs a mental map of the city. The map need not be overly detailed, just sufficient for the person to find his way to a restaurant.

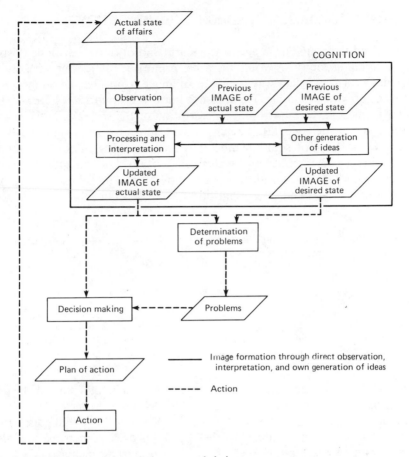

Fig. 2.2   Information and regulation: expanded view.

2.2 IMAGE FORMATION BY A SOLITARY INDIVIDUAL

A person who is all alone forms an image based on the processing of signals received from the environment or from his or her own body (e.g., a feeling of hunger). There is an overwhelming mass of signals in the environment; the image guides the selection of important signals and their interpretation, resulting in an updated image. A person might also generate ideas not directly traceable to any input signal; such ideas organize observations and update the image of the desired state. The whole process of image formation, also called cognition, is a complex interaction of several components, as shown in simplified form in Fig. 2.2.

2.3 IMAGE FORMATION THROUGH COMMUNICATION

If we had to create our image of the world and of ourselves alone as solitary individuals, our lives would be rather primitive. Interacting with others provides a more efficient way to create an image. Consider the hungry man from the previous example. He does not know the way to a restaurant. He therefore asks A, who gives him a description of the way. An outsider can observe just the behavior: B, the hungry man, looks worried, approaches A, and utters a string of sound symbols; A utters a string of sound symbols back, whereupon B smiles and walks in a certain direction, turns certain corners, enters the restaurant, and eats something. The following diagram presents an analysis and interpretation of these observations.

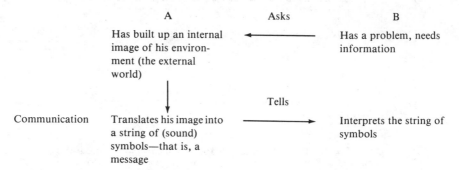

After receiving the message, B shares enough of A's mental map of the city to find his way to the restaurant (see Fig. 2.3). Without the message from A, without the benefit of "picking A's brain," B would have had to spend a long time to form a mental map of the city on his own. A message may also be a graphic representation, such as a picture, diagram, or map.

B's updated image enabled him to solve his problem and to take proper action. Successful action that is dependent on an updated image is an indicator of successful information transfer. But the updated image does not always result in action; it may result in avoiding an action that would be unwise. An update in the image may also increase a person's confidence in taking an action he or she would have taken anyway or just change his or her attitudes or feelings.

The interpretation of a message requires a previous image, namely, knowledge of the language or code in which the message is phrased and a background to which the message can be related. For example, A may say: "Go to Christ Church, there turn right, ..." This does B no good unless he knows where Christ Church is. If B does not know, the message must be changed in order to result in a proper update of B's image: "Go in this direction [A points] until you see a church on the left; then turn right, ..."

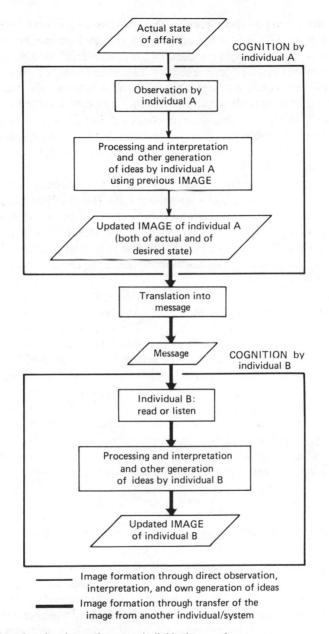

Fig. 2.3 Transfer of an image from one individual to another.

This will do as long as B can recognize a building as a church—that is, if B has grown up in Western culture and has internalized the concept of a church building (not at all a simple concept). This principle of the necessary background is important in reference service: One must find out the user's background before selecting messages that might update the user's image. For example, if a user needs to learn about statistics, the reference librarian should ask if he or she knows calculus. If the user does, a statistics text using calculus is best, because statistics can be treated more elegantly this way. On the other hand, if the user does not know calculus, a more elementary statistics text is indicated.

The discussion so far has centered on the message from A to B which updates B's image. But there is also a message from B to A: B communicates an empty spot or deficiency in his image, thereby updating A's image of B and causing A to send a message. If B does not understand A's message, he asks for clarification, thereby updating A's image of B further and enabling A to adapt the message sent to B. This kind of exchange is often essential in successful communication.

These examples illustrate messages that add to B's image elements that are used for deriving a solution to the problem at hand. Such messages are *substantive*. (It is quite possible that a substantive message will not update B's image completely. For example, A might direct B to a certain point, advising him to ask again there.) There is also another type of message, as can be seen from the following variation of the example. B asks A, but A does not know the way to a restaurant. However, A does know that C across the street knows the city and thus points to C, advising B that he should ask her. B's mental map of the city is not updated at all by this message; the transmitted element does not figure as such in finding the right way. But B is further along in his search: he now knows of a source who can give him a message to update his mental map. A's message points to another source; it is *directional*.

2.4 A MODEL OF INFORMATION TRANSFER AND USE

Figure 2.4 presents an overall model of information transfer that combines Figs. 2.2 and 2.3. As an example, consider parents who have a certain expectation of how well their child should read, an image of the desired state. They observe their child reading and form an image of the actual state. They compare the two and determine that their child does not read as well as they think he or she should. This constitutes a problem. They think about ways to solve the problem, ways to help their child improve reading skills, and discover that they do not know enough about the process of learning to read. Thus they have a gap in their image, an information need. Because it would

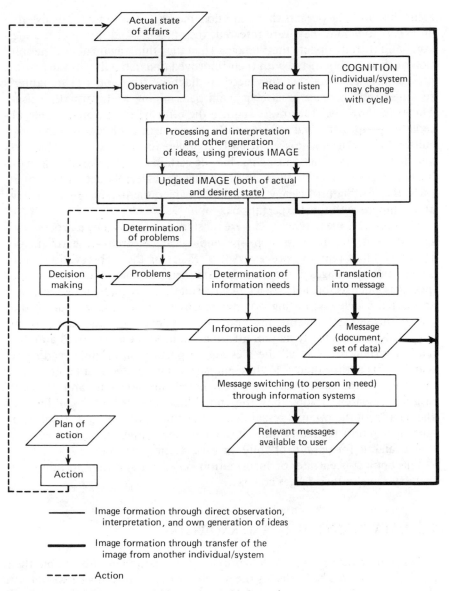

Fig. 2.4 below the diagram:

Image formation through direct observation,
interpretation, and own generation of ideas

Image formation through transfer of the
image from another individual/system

----- Action

Fig. 2.4   A model for the acquisition and use of information.

take much too long for them to form an image of the learning process through their own direct observation, they decide to look for a message that could update their image. They make the information need known to an information system, which selects from the many available messages a few that seem suitable. The parents then read documents, listen to tapes, or listen to an expert to whom they were referred; they process and interpret the messages and thereby update their image. Then they think again about the solution of their problem, and with their improved understanding of the reading process they discover that they need to diagnose their son's or daughter's reading problem more precisely, again determining an information need. This time, however, they must acquire the information through direct observation—updating and refining their image of their child's reading difficulties. Finally the image is sufficiently complete for them to make a decision and devise a plan of action, such as buying certain reading materials and doing reading exercises with their child. The actions affect the actual state of affairs, the reading proficiency of the child, which the parents again observe and compare with their expectations.

The messages the parents read were most likely produced by a process with several steps. In the first step—psychological research—researchers observed children reading, processed the results of their observations, produced updated images in their minds, and then translated those images into messages, such as journal articles. As a result there are many messages, such as journal articles, reporting original research. Then an author decided to pull all this research together in a book that would also include advice to parents. This author clearly had an information need; he or she used an information system to select all the messages reporting on original reading research. This author then read these messages, interpreted them and formed an image of the total reading process based on many bits and pieces of original research. (Note that the individual involved in cognition has changed from the original researcher to the author of the book.) The book author then translated this image into a message, namely the book, which is now available for parents of children with reading problems.

This book concentrates on information systems, but it is important to see these systems in their larger context.

2.5 DATA, INFORMATION, AND KNOWLEDGE

The terms *data* and *information* are easily understood intuitively, but their precise definition is bedeviled by the problem of distinguishing between form and content. This section provides an explanation without giving formal definitions. Earlier *message* was defined as a string of symbols or a graphic representation. But consider two symbol strings with the same meaning—that is, two symbol strings that produce the same result in updating a recipient's image; do we have two messages or one message in two different forms? The common use of the term *message* is often ambiguous in this respect. In the following *message* is used in the form-oriented sense—different strings of symbols are different messages. The data content or information content of a message is the effect it has on the image of a person who can understand the message and who has no elements in his existing image that are duplicated in the message (so that the message has its greatest possible effect). *Data* and *information* could likewise be defined in a form-oriented sense, making them synonymous with *message*. In common usage, content orientation prevails in some contexts, form orientation in others. In data processing, the term *data* is used in a form-oriented sense; *data* refers to a string of symbols. On the other hand, an economist considers wheat sale data from two sources the same, even if one source reports them in pounds and the other in tons. Information is perhaps more often used in the content-oriented sense. On the other hand, an information system cannot retrieve information as content, but only messages that provide such content. For the purposes of this book the ambiguity between a form-oriented and a content-oriented definition of *data* and *information* need not be resolved, but understanding the difference is important.

Substantive data are data that are used in deriving a solution to the problem at hand and developing a plan of action (or data that affect attitudes or feelings), whereas *pointer data (directional data)* are data that point or direct the recipient to other sources of data. The distinction between substantive data and pointer data hinges on use. For example, a researcher searching a library catalog for publications by a certain author in order to learn about a topic for which that author is a known expert uses the catalog data as pointer data. On the other hand, an administrator searching for publications by a person in order to judge that person's qualifications uses the same data as substantive data.

Information is often defined as "data useful for decision making"—for example, per capita sales, broken down by state. Information is contrasted with *raw data*—for example, data on individual sales transactions. The term *data* is used with many different connotations; for example, to a data-processing person any machine-readable message, be it substantive or directional, is data. To a scientist, data are empirical findings—data that result from observation—rather than theoretical statements. Both empirical data and theories are substantive data as defined here. The information stored in an information system is called a *data base*.

The last concept in this series is *knowledge*. Knowledge has structure that ties together and integrates individual pieces of an image. For example, a theory in science relates many observations by explaining one observation in terms of another. Knowledge is the basis for action. For example, Mark Twain, in his *Life on the Mississippi,* describes how a tree root sticking out of the water signifies that a shortcut several miles up the river cannot be taken because the water level is too low. To be acted upon, knowledge must be an integral part of an active system, such as a person or a computer system. Knowledge can also be recorded in a message. Expressions like "the universe of knowledge" or "the knowledge contained in all the books in a library" refer to recorded knowledge.

2.6 CLASSIFICATION OF INFORMATION SYSTEMS BY SERVICES DELIVERED

The users of an information system are ultimately interested in obtaining substantive data. Some information systems supply the user directly with a tailor-made package of substantive data, perhaps even presented in a way adapted to his or her background. Other systems provide only assistance in locating documents—that is, premade packages of substantive data—in which the user may look for the specific substantive data needed. Most information systems provide both types of services in varying degrees.

To make these ideas more concrete, consider the following problem: The director of a library working on the budget determines that with $30,000 she could do one of the following:

- Improve the subject catalog, subscribe to more printed abstracting–indexing services, such as *Chemical Abstracts,* provide on-line searching, or hire a reference librarian to do literature searches.
- Subscribe to 200 more serials and take care of their housing and reshelving as they are used.
- Hire a reference librarian to provide users with the substantive data they need, so that users need not wade through many documents to gather the data needed.

What should the library do? The answer depends on the needs of the clientele. Do they have sufficient knowledge of relevant documents, and is their main problem obtaining these documents? Or must they first find the documents relevant for a problem? Do they have the ability and time to compile the substantive data they need in a way that is appropriate for the problem at hand? These questions should be addressed very explicitly in the planning and budgeting process.

This example leads to the following classification of services an information system might provide.

1. *Providing access to documents,* more generally, providing intellectual and physical access to premade packages of substantive data, which may include, for example, knowledgeable persons. This involves *document storage and retrieval* in the broad sense. Once the documents have been provided, it

is up to the user to extract the specific substantive data he needs. This service includes two components:

(a) *Intellectual access to documents or other sources (reference storage and retrieval).* This involves assisting the user in identifying relevant documents; the service should cover documents available anywhere, not just those available in the library's collection. The information storage and retrieval system is essential for this service.

(b) *Physical access to documents*—more specifically, to primary documents (documents containing substantive data, not bibliographies) and other primary sources known to the user. This involves *document storage and retrieval* in the narrow sense. The information system must acquire the actual documents, either permanently for its collection or temporarily through interlibrary loan, and make them accessible through circulation, through a machine for rapid selection and display of microfiche, or through a videodisc player. Alternatively, the library can provide a terminal for accessing documents stored in a remote computer. The information storage and retrieval system can be minimal; access by author and title or by document identifiers such as ISBN (International Standard Book Number) or report number is sufficient.

2. *Providing tailor-made packages of substantive data.* This can be accomplished through direct retrieval of substantive data (called *data storage and retrieval* or *question-answering*). The information storage and retrieval system deals directly with the entities of interest (such as commodities and their production, or federal programs and expenditures for them) or with properly formatted small chunks of substantive data, rather than with entire documents (premade large packages of data). This service can also be provided by extracting the pertinent substantive data from documents obtained from a document storage and retrieval system. To a limited degree this can be done by computer programs, but in general it requires an information specialist.

An information system is characterized by the mix of services that it provides; listing all the services and giving for each the level of effort (in absolute dollars and in percentage of the total effort) results in a *service profile*. This gives a much more meaningful picture of the nature of an information system than simply classifying it into one of the customary categories: library, special library, abstracting–indexing service, information analysis center, daily transaction information system, or management information system.

The discussion so far has been limited to systems that deal with information or data. However, the principles to be discussed in this book apply also to systems that deal with finding any type of entity, such as museum objects, technical parts, groceries or other merchandise, or people. As long as such a system merely indicates the existence and whereabouts of entities that might be helpful in solving a given problem, it is an information system in the strict definition. But in a broader view, an information system includes also the function of physical access to such entities. A grocery store helps customers find the products they need through its arrangement and often through an index. Thus a grocery store is an information system in the broader definition; the problems of providing access to groceries or any other type of entity are basically the same as the problems of providing access to documents.

2.7 SUMMARY AND EVOLVING PRINCIPLES

Three important principles evolve from our discussion:

- The information provided by an information system should help the user to solve his problems and to direct his actions to a desired end.
- The information should be as close as possible to the substantive data needed and should allow the user to obtain these substantive data with minimum effort. A tailor-made package of substantive data is better than a package of five journal articles from which the substantive data can be extracted, which in turn is better than a bibliography in which such journal articles could be identified. This principle has an important consequence for the objective of reference storage and retrieval systems: The aim of reference storage and retrieval is *not* to retrieve all relevant references but to retrieve the smallest subset of references or documents that among them contain all substantive data needed by the user.
- The substantive data at which the user finally arrives must relate to his previous knowledge.

CHAPTER 3

The Structure of Information

OBJECTIVE

The objective of this chapter is to explain how information can be represented by a set of *entities* connected by *relationships*. This provides the basis for the mastery of essential functions in information handling, namely: analyzing a search topic; analyzing a data base or reference tool so as to better exploit it in searching; and designing the logical structure of a data base—for example, a company data base or a university data base.

INTRODUCTION

There are several approaches to structuring data in a data base. The most appropriate approach for purposes of this book is the relational approach. This chapter provides a first introduction to this approach through an example (Section 3.1), a more general discussion of the evolving concepts (Section 3.2), and an illustration of how this approach can be used in the analysis of reference tools, such as biographical dictionaries (Section 3.3). The approach to information structure presented in this chapter is the basis for much of the remainder of the book.

3.1 THE UNIVERSITY DATA BASE: AN EXAMPLE

The best way to design or understand a data base is to consider the topics for which the data base is to be searched. In the example, development of the data base structure proceeds from the list of search topics and their analysis shown in Fig. 3.1. The examples in Fig. 3.1 suggest the entity types:

Who were the students in the Fall 1979 offering of the course Vegetable Pickling?
Entity types involved: *Course offering*
                                      Person
Relationship: ⟨has student⟩

Who taught the Fall 1979 offering of the course Vegetable Pickling?
Entity types involved: *Course offering*
                                      Person
Relationship: ⟨has instructor⟩

What are the prerequisites of the course Vegetable Pickling?
Entity type involved: *Course*
Relationship: ⟨has prerequisite⟩

What grade did J. Doe get in Vegetable Pickling in Fall 1979?
Entity types involved: *Course offering*
                                      Person
                                      Grade
   However, the situation in this example is more complex: a grade does not pertain to a person alone nor to a course offering alone but rather to a person–course offering combination. We consider such a combination as a new, composite entity. Thus, we revise the entity types as follows:
Revised entity types: (*Course offering* ⟨has student⟩ *Person*)
                                      Grade
Relationship: ⟨has attribute⟩
Answer contains: A list of grade values (one value in the example)
Selection criteria: Grade value is assigned to the combination entity
             (Fall 1979 offering of Vegetable Pickling ⟨has student⟩ J. Doe)

Fig. 3.1 Sample search topics and their analysis

- *Course* (an intellectual entity listed in the university catalog);
- *Course offering* (a course offered in a given semester at a given time and place as listed in the appropriate schedule of classes);
- *Person, Grade,* and *Semester.*

They also suggest the relationship types:

> < has prerequisite >, < is offered as >, < takes place in >, < has instructor >, < has student >, and < has attribute > (referring to *Grade).*

Figure 3.2a shows in graphic form the *conceptual schema* of a data base containing these entity and relationship types and an instance of this schema with actual entity and relationship values. Figure 3.2b shows the same data base; all relationships of the same type are grouped into a table called a *relation.*

Figure 3.3a shows a much expanded version of the same data base, introducing many more entity and relationship types. They form an intricate network of relationships from which many questions can be answered. For example, we might ask which instructors use their own textbooks. To answer this, we would start with *Course offering 1* (COF1) and follow the arrow labeled <text used> to document *D3* and from there the arrow labeled <authored by> to *J. Kolb*. Starting again from *COF 1*, we would also follow the arrow labeled <has instructor> to *L. Kahn*. In this case the instructor is not the author of the textbook. But if we do the same analysis starting from *COF 2*, we come to *L. Kahn* as an author (via document *D2*) and also to *L. Kahn* as an instructor.

Figure 3.3b shows the same data base in tabular form.

3.2 ELEMENTS OF INFORMATION STRUCTURE

A data base consists of *entities* which are connected through *relationships*. Entity is understood very broadly. Examples of entity types are:

Person
Organization
Course
Course offering
Test (e.g., Graduate Record
    Exam)
Test scores
Grade
Document, intellectual work
Document, physical volume
Technical object, type
Technical object, individual
    piece
Geographical location
Date
Subject, concept, idea
Process
Event (an instance of a process;
    for example, a shipment or
    a fire)
Statement (as defined later in
    this section)
Relation (as defined later in
    this section)

(*Text continues on p. 30.*)

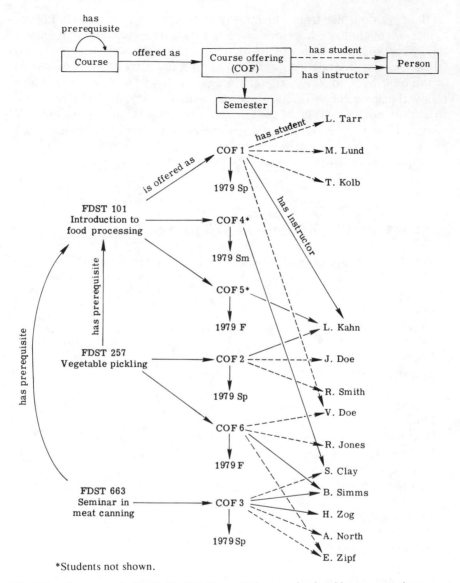

*Students not shown.

Fig. 3.2a   Structure of a University Data Base. Basic example. Graphic representation

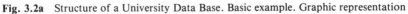

Fig. 3.2b   Structure of a University Data Base. Basic example. Tabular representation

Entities

Entity 1. Course

FDST 101	Introduction to food processing
FDST 257	Vegetable pickling
FDST 663	Seminar in meat canning

Entity 2. Course offering

COF 1
COF 2
COF 3
COF 4
COF 5
COF 6

Entity 3. Semester

1979 Spring
1979 Summer
1979 Fall

Entity 4. Person

S. Clay
J. Doe
V. Doe
R. Jones
L. Kahn
A. Kim
T. Kolb
M. Lund
J. Manet
A. North
N. Phillip
B. Simms
R. Smith
L. Sprotto
L. Tarr
E. Zipf
H. Zog

Relations

Relation 1. ⟨has prerequisite⟩

Course	⟨has pre⟩	*Course*
FDST 257		FDST 101
FDST 663		FDST 101

Relation 2 included in Fig. 3.3b.

Relation 3. ⟨is offered as⟩

Course	⟨is offd⟩	*Course offering*
FDST 101		COF 1
FDST 257		COF 2
FDST 663		COF 3
FDST 101		COF 4
FDST 101		COF 5
FDST 257		COF 6

Relation 4. ⟨takes place in⟩

Course offrg	⟨t pl in⟩	*Semester*
COF 1		1979 Sp
COF 2		1979 Sp
COF 3		1979 Sp
COF 4		1979 Sm
COF 5		1979 Fall
COF 6		1979 Fall

Relation 5. ⟨has instructor⟩

Course offrg	⟨has inst⟩	*Person*
COF 1		L. Kahn
COF 2		L. Kahn
COF 3		B. Simms
COF 3		H. Zog
COF 4		S. Clay
COF 5		L. Kahn
COF 6		B. Simms

Relation 6. ⟨has student⟩

Course offrg	⟨has stu⟩	*Person*
COF 1		L. Tarr
COF 1		M. Lund
COF 1		T. Kolb
COF 1		V. Doe
COF 2		J. Doe
COF 2		R. Smith
COF 3		S. Clay
COF 3		A. North
COF 3		E. Zipf
COF 4		J. Manet
COF 4		A. Kim
COF 4		N. Phillip
COF 5		L. Sprotto
COF 5		R. Jones
COF 6		V. Doe
COF 6		R. Jones
COF 6		E. Zipf

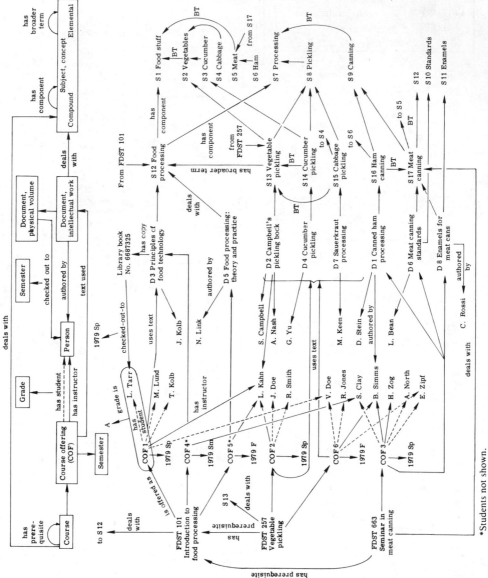

Fig. 3.3a Structure of a University Data Base. Expanded example. Graphic representation

*Students not shown.

26

Entities

Entity type 1. Course

FDST 101	Introduction to food processing
FDST 257	Vegetable pickling
FDST 663	Seminar in meat canning

Entity type 2. Course offering

COF 1
COF 2
COF 3
COF 4
COF 5
COF 6

Entity type 3. Semester

1979 Spring
1979 Summer
1979 Fall

Entity type 4. Person

L. Bean	J. Manet
S. Campbell	A. Nash
S. Clay	A. North
J. Doe	L. O'Hara
V. Doe	N. Phillip
R. Jones	C. Rossi
L. Kahn	B. Simms
Y. Kalaf	R. Smith
M. Keen	L. Sprotto
A. Kim	D. Stein
J. Kolb	L. Tarr
T. Kolb	G. Yu
N. Link	E. Zipf
M. Lund	H. Zog

Entity type 5. Grade

A
B
C
D
F
I

Entity type 6. Document, intellectual work

D1 Canned ham processing
D2 Campbell's pickling book
D3 Principles of food technology
D4 Cucumber pickling
D5 Food processing: theory and practice
D6 Meat canning standards
D7 Sauerkraut processing
D8 Enamels for meat cans

Entity type 7. Document, physical volume

Library book no. 6687325

Entity type 8. Subject, concept

S 1 Food stuff
S 2 Vegetables
S 3 Cucumber
S 4 Cabbage
S 5 Meat
S 6 Ham
S 7 Processing
S 8 Pickling
S 9 Canning
S10 Standards
S11 Enamels
S12 Food processing
S13 Vegetable pickling
S14 Cucumber pickling
S15 Cabbage pickling
S16 Ham canning
S17 Meat Canning

S1–S11, Elemental subject, concept

S12–S17, Compound subject, concept

Fig. 3.3b Structure of a University Data Base. Expanded example. Tabular representation

Relations

Relation 1. ⟨has prerequisite⟩

Course ⟨has pre⟩	Course
FDST 257	FDST 101
FDST 663	FDST 101

Relation 2. ⟨deals with⟩

Course ⟨deals w⟩	Subject
FDST 101	S12
FDST 257	S13
FDST 663	S17

Relation 3. ⟨is offered as⟩

Course ⟨is offd⟩	Course offering
FDST 101	COF 1
FDST 257	COF 2
FDST 663	COF 3
FDST 101	COF 4
FDST 101	COF 5
FDST 257	COF 6

Relation 4. ⟨takes place in⟩

Course offrg ⟨t pl in⟩	Semester
COF 1	1979 Sp
COF 2	1979 Sp
COF 3	1979 Sp
COF 4	1979 Sm
COF 5	1979 Fall
COF 6	1979 Fall

Relation 5. ⟨has instructor⟩

Course offrg ⟨has inst⟩	Person
COF 1	L. Kahn
COF 2	L. Kahn
COF 3	B. Simms
COF 3	H. Zog
COF 4	S. Clay
COF 5	L. Kahn
COF 6	B. Simms

Relation 6. ⟨has student⟩ (CS = Course offering–Student combination)

CS#	Course offrg	⟨has stu⟩ Person
CS 1	COF 1	L. Tarr
CS 2	COF 1	M. Lund
CS 3	COF 1	T. Kolb
CS 4	COF 1	V. Doe
CS 5	COF 2	J. Doe
CS 6	COF 2	R. Smith
CS 7	COF 3	S. Clay
CS 8	COF 3	A. North
CS 9	COF 3	E. Zipf
CS10	COF 4	J. Manet
CS11	COF 4	A. Kim
CS12	COF 4	N. Phillip
CS13	COF 5	L. Sprotto
CS14	COF 5	R. Jones
CS15	COF 6	V. Doe
CS16	COF 6	R. Jones
CS17	COF 6	E. Zipf

Relation 7. ⟨has attribute⟩

CS#	⟨has attr⟩ Grade
CS 1	A
CS 2	C
CS 3	B
CS 4	F
CS 5	A
CS 6	A
CS 7	B
CS 8	B
CS 9	D
CS10	I
CS11	A
CS12	B
CS13	C
CS14	A
CS15	A
CS16	A
CS17	B

Fig. 3.3b (continued)

Relation 8. ⟨uses as text⟩

Course offrg	⟨uses txt⟩	Document intel. work
COF 1		D3
COF 2		D2
COF 2		D4
COF 2		D7
COF 3		D1
COF 3		D6
COF 3		D8
COF 4		D3
COF 5		D5
COF 6		D2
COF 6		D4
COF 6		D7

Relation 9. ⟨is authored by⟩

Document, intel. wrk ⟨is by⟩	Person
D1	B. Simms
D1	D. Stein
D2	S. Campbell
D2	L. Kahn
D2	A. Nash
D3	J. Kolb
D4	G. Yu
D5	N. Link
D6	L. Bean
D7	M. Keen
D8	C. Rossi

Relation 10. ⟨deals with⟩

Document	⟨deals w⟩	Subject
D1		S16
D2		S13
D3		S12
D4		S14
D5		S12
D6		S10
D6		S17
D7		S15
D8		S11
D8		S17

Relation 11. ⟨has copy⟩

Document, intel. wrk ⟨has copy⟩	Document, phys. volume
D3	#6687325

Relation 12. ⟨is checked out to⟩

Document, phys. vol.	⟨is chkd out to⟩	Person
#6687325 (this pair is DP# 1)		L. Tarr

Relation 13. ⟨takes place in⟩

DP#	⟨t pl in⟩	Semester
1		1979 Sp

Relation 14. ⟨has component⟩

Subject	⟨has comp⟩	Subject
S12		S1
S12		S7
S13		S2
S13		S8
S14		S3
S14		S8
S15		S4
S15		S8
S16		S6
S16		S9
S17		S5
S17		S9

Relation 15. ⟨has broader term (BT)⟩

Subject	⟨has BT⟩	Subject
S 2		S 1
S 3		S 2
S 4		S 2
S 5		S 1
S 6		S 5
S 8		S 7
S 9		S 7
S13		S12
S14		S13
S15		S13
S16		S17
S17		S12

Fig. 3.3b (continued)

Each entity type has associated with it a set of entity values, called its *domain*. The domain defines the scope of the entity type in the data base at hand. Entity values are represented by symbols; for example, FDST101 represents a value of the entity type *Course,* it is a course *identifier.* To give another example, the identifier for a *Person* could be a social security number or a name; in this data base we use the name. The identifier for a *Document, intellectual work* could be a number or the title; for a *Document, physical volume* it might be a circulation number. Identifiers used in a computerized data base should be unique and short. Identifiers used externally (to be read by humans) should be unique and short while still easily understood. The domain for each entity type determines what entity identifiers are allowed in the data base. The domain can be defined by simply listing the admissible values, such as S1–S17 for *Subject, concept.* Alternatively, the domain can be defined by giving a format that identifiers must follow. For example, the format of person identifiers could be an initial followed by a space followed by a character string, the first character of which must not be a digit; the system managing the data base then checks this format whenever a person identifier is expected.

A *statement* is an association between two or more entities, in which the entities are in a given *relationship* or, in other words, in which each participating entity has a given role.

Example

Entity 1	Relationship	Entity 2
Principles of food technology	⟶	J. Kolb
	< is authored by >	
	⟵	
	< is author of >	
Role: authored work		Role: author

The statement connecting both entities can be read with focus on the book. With this focus, the statement gives information about the book—namely, that the entity *J. Kolb* is related to the book in the role of author. Put differently, *Author: J. Kolb* is an attribute of the book. The statement can also be read with focus on the person. The statement then gives information about the person *J. Kolb*—namely, that she has written the book *Principles of Food Technology.* Put differently, *Authored work: Principles of Food Technology* is an attribute of the person *J. Kolb.* An entity value, such as *J. Kolb,* occurring in a statement is called an *entity occurrence. J. Kolb* may occur in many statements.

Other examples of statements arc

FDST257   FDST101
                            ————————————————▶
                                < has prerequisite >

                        ◀————————————————
                                < is prerequisite of >
COF1   ————————————————▶   L. Tarr
                                < has student >

                        ◀————————————————
                                < is enrolled in >

A statement informs about the relationship between two entities, for example, *Course offering* COF 1 < has student > *Person* L. Tarr, without emphasizing one or the other entity. A set of statements informs about many pairs. A request may introduce a focus on one entity type; for example, it may focus on a *Student* and ask in what *Course offerings* he or she is enrolled. Such a request is easy to answer when the statements are arrayed by student, but it is difficult otherwise. Conversely, to facilitate finding all students in a course offering, the statements should be arranged by course offering. While order in a set of statements does not affect the information given, it does affect access to that information from a particular point of view. The problem of arrangement for access will be discussed in Chapter 11, "Data Structures and Access."

A set of statements that agree in the entity types and the relationship type (e.g., a set of statements of the form *Course offering* < has student > *Person*) can be represented in the form of a table, as illustrated in Figs. 3.2b and 3.3b. Each column heading specifies the entity type and the role played by the entity of this type in a statement, and each row gives a pair of entity occurrences. Such a table (a set of pairs) is also called a binary or dyadic *relation*.

Higher-order relations can be represented as tables with three or more columns. In particular, several two-column tables that have the same first column can be compressed into one multicolumn table. For example, the three tables with the column headings:

1. Authored work: Book   Author: Person
2. Published work: Book   Publisher: Organization
3. Published work: Book   Publishing time: Date

can be compressed into one four-column table with the headings (given in simplified format):

Book	Author	Publisher	Date
D3 Principles of food technology	J. Kolb	Academic Press	1983

Book now assumes different roles depending on the other column with which it is paired. Each row in the four-column table is a quadruplet. In general, a table is a set of *n-tuples*. A data base, then, is a collection of statements that express relationships between entities. Suitable subsets of statements may be organized in relations or tables with two or more columns for more succinct representation.

3.3 ANALYZING REFERENCE TOOLS: AN EXAMPLE

The principles of information structure discussed here can be used to advantage for the analysis of reference tools. Analyzing the entities and relationships covered makes explicit the information given in the reference tool; the analysis may suggest uses for which the reference tool was not originally intended. Consider *Chamber's Biographical Dictionary,* a reference tool intended to give information about persons. It contains the following entry:

> HANSOM, Joseph Aloysius (1803–82), English inventor and architect, born at York, invented the 'Patent Safety (Hansom) Cab' in 1834 and designed Birmingham town hall and the R.C. cathedral at Plymouth.

This entry covers entities of many types:

Person, Profession, Place, Date, Technical product, Building.

It establishes many relationships between these entities, such as:

Person < was born on > *Date,*
Person < designed > *Building,* and
Technical product < was invented in > *Date.*

Thus this short paragraph contains the information to answer questions not just about Hansom but also about the other entities with which he is related, such as "Who invented the patent safety cab?" or "What English inventors lived in the nineteenth century?". There are even answers to questions that do not involve Hansom, such as "When was the patent safety cab invented?" or "When was the Roman Catholic Cathedral at Plymouth built?". The latter question can be answered only approximately: From the plausible assumptions that Hansom probably did not design the cathedral before he was 25 years of age and that it was built shortly after he designed it, one can deduce a building date between 1828 and 1882.

The ideas on information structure presented in this chapter will be used and expanded upon throughout the book, particularly in Chapter 9, "Data Schemas and Formats," and in the discussion of query formulation (definition of search topics) in Chapter 17.

CHAPTER 4

The Information Transfer Network

OBJECTIVES

The objectives of this chapter are to show that an information system is a node in a large information transfer network and that it should be designed to fill its role in this network, and to introduce the variables that describe information transfer transactions and influence their success.

INTRODUCTION

The two previous chapters developed a micro-view of information, its nature and structure. This chapter gives a macro-view of the total network in which information is transferred. Understanding the overall information transfer network is important for designing an individual information system and its services. Few information systems can be self-contained; users are better served if an information system is seen as an access point to many other sources of information. The transfer of information to practitioners is often accomplished best not through direct transactions from an information system to the practitioner, but rather through a chain, from the information system to a person and then from that person to the practitioner. (A person who often transmits information to others, for example, an especially well-informed member of a research and development laboratory, is called a _gatekeeper_.) An information system is usually not the only source of information for a user; it should be designed to augment rather than to duplicate information available just as easily elsewhere. Sections 4.1 and 4.2 describe elemental transactions and configurations of such transactions through which information is transferred.

To understand the functioning of the overall information transfer network and to design an individual information system for a given clientele, one must describe information transfer transactions in terms of the variables that influence their success. Section 4.3 gives a list of pertinent variables with a brief discussion.

4.1 TRANSACTIONS IN THE INFORMATION TRANSFER NETWORK

An information transfer network consists of many nodes. A node can be any of the following: a person, an organization or agency, a machine system, or a record. Information transactions are the atomic elements of information transfer. In a transaction from node A to node B, node A either sends a message to node B or gives node B physical access to another source:

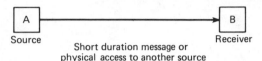

Examples of messages transmitted in a transaction are: speech produced by a person or computer system, images played from a videotape, or a visual image "played" from a printed page while the eye scans over it. They are all of limited duration; they are *short-duration messages*. The videotape and the printed page themselves are permanent; they are *long-duration messages* or *records*. In our model, records are nodes in their own right. The act of writing or printing is a short-duration message from the source—a person or machine system—to the receiver—a record on paper, magnetic tape, or another medium.

A node participating in a transaction can play any of the following roles:

- *Source*—provides information (substantive data or pointer data or both) or physical access to other sources.
- *Receiver*—receives information or physical access to other sources.
- *Original source*—produces information through direct observation or original ideas and then transmits it.
- *Final receiver*—receives information and uses it in problem solving, decision making, or actions.
- *Intermediate receiver, intermediate source*—receives information only to pass it on to another node. Information systems fall into this category.

Often these roles are mixed. For example, a node may receive information, modify it (thereby adding new information, as in writing a state-of-the-art report), and then send it. Thus the role of a node in a transaction can be characterized by the degree to which it performs the following functions:

producing information
selecting and sending information
receiving information
storing information
using information

The total role of a node in the information transfer network is derived by considering all transactions in which it participates. For example, an information system usually receives, stores, and selects and sends information; to a limited extent it might also produce information through original ideas applied to the organization of the information received. It does not use the information it stores and sends out.

4.2 CONFIGURATIONS OF TRANSACTIONS

The information transfer network consists of a large number of nodes. Sometimes information is transferred directly from the original source to the final receiver, but more often information transfer involves a *chain of transactions* as in the following example:

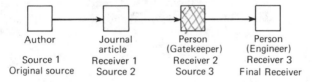

Author	Journal article	Person (Gatekeeper)	Person (Engineer)
Source 1	Receiver 1	Receiver 2	Receiver 3
Original source	Source 2	Source 3	Final Receiver

Each node makes its unique contribution to the chain: the author produces the information, the journal article makes it possible for anybody to receive a short-duration message without the need of talking to the author, the gatekeeper selects from the information acquired through the journal article those parts that are helpful for solving a problem that the engineer is facing, and the engineer uses the information to solve the problem.

There are also *series of transactions* with the same receiver where several nodes work together to finally give the user the information needed. The following diagram gives an example:

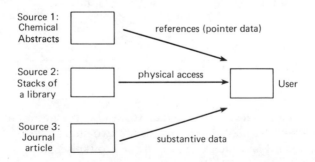

Chemical Abstracts provides references to documents, the stacks of a library provide physical access to such documents, and the documents finally provide substantive data, all to the same user.

These two diagrams can be combined into one more complex diagram:

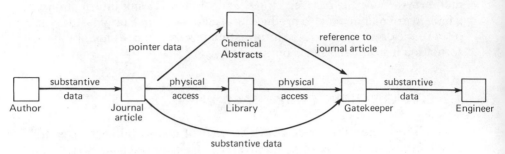

Many transactions are initiated by the receiver: there is a request for information (an auxiliary message) from the receiver to the source, which is then followed by the main message from the source to the receiver, giving the information requested. The following diagram illustrates this situation.

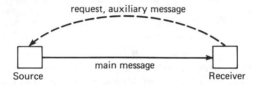

If the information transmitted is not satisfactory, another auxiliary message may be needed, and so on. That is, information transfer may be improved through feedback.

Interlibrary loan involves a two-step chain. First, two auxiliary messages go backwards—from the user to his or her library and then from the user's library to the lending library. Then there are two transactions of physical access—from the lending library to the user's library and then from the user's library to the user. We can show this graphically:

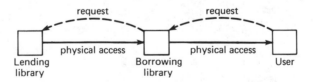

Information transfer from one person to another can be accomplished in a one-step chain with a spoken message. But a two-step chain—from the first person to a record and then from the record to the second person—is also possible. In some cases the two-step and one-step chains may be completely equivalent—as in leaving a note for a person who is not at her desk at the moment and thus cannot receive a spoken message. But there is a difference: the note is a record that might be read by somebody else or introduced as evidence in a trial. Thus, the note takes on a life of its own as an information source independent from the person who wrote it.

There are internal information transfer transactions in the brain, from the processing unit of the brain, which includes the short–term memory, to the long-term memory and from long-term memory back to the processing unit. The long-term memory is functionally equivalent to external sources. Much of the information a person needs may be already available from his or her long-term memory. In the analysis of information needs, the long-term memory should be treated as a source among others.

4.3 CHARACTERISTICS OF TRANSACTIONS

A transaction can be described in terms of its source, its receiver, and their relationship; its substance; and the medium used. These characteristics are independent variables that influence the dependent variables, namely, the quality of the results and cost–benefit aspects. Figure 4.1 gives some examples of variables (it is *not* a complete listing).

Most of these variables are self-explanatory. We shall discuss just a few of them. The variable *Type of node* (for both the source and the receiver) has many values. For example, a record could be a book, a periodical, or a report, in hard copy or microform, or it could be an audio record. The type makes a difference in the frequency and success of transactions where such a record serves as a source. A person (more precisely, the role a person plays) could be a scientist (distinguished by field), an engineer (again distinguished by field), or a "man in the street"/consumer/citizen. Information needs vary with the role of a person, and so do the types of nodes most suitable as sources. For example, scientists, particularly in chemistry, tend to rely on printed documents, particularly journals. On the other hand, engineers and other practitioners tend to prefer, at least for some types of information, another person as a source, because the person can select just the information needed to solve a practical problem at hand and can present the information in a way suited to the background of the engineer.

Motivation is an extremely important variable. Knowing the motivation of a source is important in judging the information from the source. For example, knowing that a radio station established for the continuing education of physicians is supported heavily by contributions from the pharmaceutical industry instills a measure of caution when interpreting the contents of its programs. It is well known from learning theory how important proper motivation of the receiver is for comprehending information. One factor influencing motivation is the stage of decision making in which a person finds himself. While a person is looking for alternatives and trying to find out about advantages and disadvantages, he is open to all kinds of information.

1. The source

   1.1   Original versus intermediary source
   1.2   Type (person, organization, machine, record)
   1.3   Capabilities (scope and size of store, searchability)
   1.4   Accessibility (place, time)
   1.5   Language, code in which information is stored
   1.6   Intellectual level of presentation
   1.7   Motivation
   1.8   Role of system in the social-political-organizational context

2. The receiver

   2.1   Final versus intermediary
   2.2   Type (as above)
   2.3   Information needs (e.g., general orientation versus need for specific substantive data). Previous knowledge
   2.4   Location, mobility (place, time)
   2.5   Languages, codes the receiver can understand
   2.6   Intellectual level of understanding
   2.7   Motivation
       2.7.1   Strongly self-motivated, scientific curiosity
       2.7.2   Outside motivated, needs information for job
   2.8   Role of system in the social-political-organizational context

3. Source–receiver relationship

   3.3   Match of source capabilities with receiver needs (derived from 1.3 and 2.3)
   3.4   Communication distance (derived from 1.4, 2.4, and 5)
   3.5   Language or code compatibility (derived from 1.5 and 2.5)
   3.6   Intellectual compatibility (derived from 1.6 and 2.6)
   3.7   Who is active (source-initiated versus receiver-initiated transaction) (related to 1.7 and 2.7)
   3.8   Social or institutional relationship (related to, but not entirely derivable from, 1.8 and 2.8). Sample values:
       3.8.1   Two persons are friends or colleagues
       3.8.2   Two systems have a cooperative agreement
       3.8.3   A person is a staff member of the agency served by an information system
   3.9   Who controls what is transferred (receiver, source, or third party, as in privacy)

4. The substance of the transaction

   4.1   Substantive or pointer data versus physical access to another source
   4.2   Subject field involved
   4.3   Theory versus methodology versus empirical data. Raw versus analyzed data

5. The medium used

   5.1   The medium used for storage in the source
   5.2   The medium used for transmission from the source
   5.3   The medium used for perception by the receiver
   5.4   The medium used for storage in the receiver

6. Quality of results and cost–benefit aspects

   6.1   Quality of selection and presentation of information
   6.2   Comprehension of information by the receiver
   6.3   Impact of the information on problem solving

Fig. 4.1 Variables for analyzing information transfer transactions.

Once the person leans toward a particular alternative and is close to making a decision, he tends to look for information favoring that alternative and to discount information militating against that alternative, even if such information is highly relevant. It is important to keep this in mind when considering users' judgments of relevance in evaluating information systems.

The *role of a person in the social-political-organizational context* influences very heavily the extent to which messages from that person are received and acted upon; it also influences what information a person receives, both from the information center and from other sources. A management information system must be properly embedded in the social-political-organizational context of an organization, or it will not receive the information input necessary for its functioning; nor will it be used as an information source, no matter how good it may be technically.

Even more important than the variables characterizing the source or the receiver individually are the variables that characterize the source–receiver relationship. Some of these variables, such as language compatibility, are derived by merely matching the source variable with the receiver variable. Others—especially, social or institutional relationships—are characteristic of the source–receiver pair and are constant across all transactions within this pair. For example: two persons are friends or colleagues; two systems have a cooperative agreement; a person is a staff member of the agency served by an information system. The influence of this variable on the frequency and success of transactions is obvious.

Communication distance is a measure of the amount of effort a receiver must expend to receive information from a source or, conversely, the amount of effort a source must expend to transmit information to a receiver. Physical distance influences communication distance; studies suggest, for example, that use of a special library, particularly for minor information needs, is heavily dependent on the distance between the library and the potential user's office. Physical distance also influences public library use, but availability of transportation, either one's own car or public transportation, also makes a big difference; the real variables are travel time and affordability. An information source can be far away yet easily accessible through telephone or computer terminals.

Who is active has an effect on motivation. If the receiver initiates an information transfer transaction, he is more likely to pay attention to the information being transferred. On the other hand, in many situations the receiver is not aware of her own information need, so the source must take the initiative for the benefit of the receiver; information transfer in schools is an example of this, but by no means the only one. There are also cases in which the source has a strong interest in the receiver's having certain information that may or may not be beneficial to the receiver also—for example, in advertising.

A closely related variable is the *locus of control over what is being trans-ferred*. If a receiver puts a very specific request to an information system, the receiver is in control. On the other hand, in elementary and high school and in many college or university courses the source is in control of what is transferred, even if the receiver initiated the transaction in the first place, for example, by registering for a course. There are also cases of third party control: An individual (the third party) controls what information his doctor (the source) may give to an insurance company (the receiver); the United States government controls what technical information American companies can give to companies in Eastern European countries.

The network model presented in Sections 4.1 and 4.2 and the classification of variables provide a framework for the analysis of information transfer, particularly for studies to uncover the effects of source and receiver characteristics on the success of transactions. For example, a topic of interest in education is how subject matter, type of presentation, and cognitive style of the learner influence the degree of comprehension achieved. In scientific or technical information transfer one studies what kinds of information sources are most effective in transmitting certain types of information to engineers. To study information use by a certain group of users—for example, engineers—one examines a sample of transactions that have these particular users as their receiver. However, such a study would give only a very superficial picture of the information sources of importance for engineers. A more thorough analysis must account for the complete information transfer chains that lead from original sources to engineers as final receivers. It has been found that engineers do not read extensively in the scholarly literature of their fields but prefer to get information from persons. However, many of these persons, called gatekeepers, get their information from scholarly journals, so that scholarly journals and special libraries that provide access to them, while not used directly by engineers, are important for the transmission of information to engineers.

To get a true picture of the importance of an information source, such as the public library, one should assess its use and impact by studying all the information transfer chains in which the source participates and following these chains to the final receivers. Such a study would give a good idea of the role of the source in the overall information transfer network.

CHAPTER 5

The Structure of Information Systems

OBJECTIVE

The objective of this chapter is to provide a framework for the detailed discussion in later chapters by outlining the individual components of an information system and the ISAR system within it.

5.1 THE OVERALL STRUCTURE OF INFORMATION SYSTEMS

This book often uses a "divide and conquer" approach to problem solving, dividing a problem into subproblems and dealing with each subproblem in turn, using "divide and conquer" again until the resulting subproblem can be solved immediately. To apply this technique of *stepwise refinement,* proceed as follows:

First, identify the major functional components. In an information system these components are acquisition of needs, acquisition of information or entities, ISAR, and making information or entities available. Next, determine the input and output of each functional component in the overall system. At this stage treat each component as a *black box:* do not consider the component's inner workings lest consideration of the trees obscure the view of the forest. Next, consider each functional component in turn. Starting from its purpose as defined by inputs and outputs, analyze or design its inner workings (how it transforms inputs to outputs), again using stepwise refinement. Continue this process until the desired level of detail is reached.

This divide-and-conquer process started with the consideration of information system functions in the overall context of information transfer for problem solving (Section 2.6—"A model for the acquisition and use of information," and Chapter 4—"The Information Transfer Network"). At-

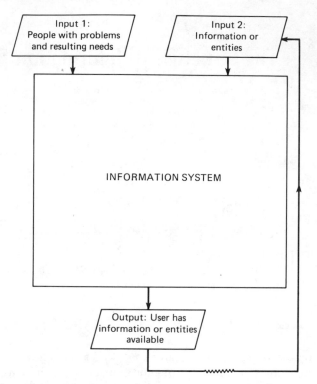

Fig. 5.1a   Information systems: inputs and outputs.

tention now turns to the functional component *information system*. Section 5.2 concentrates on the *information storage and retrieval (ISAR) system*.

Figure 5.1a shows a segment of the overall model shown in Fig. 2.3. This segment shows the inputs and outputs of an information system, considering the system itself as a black box. An information system has two inputs:

- People with problems and resulting needs
- Information and entities to be found outside the system.

The output of an information system is a change in the state of the person in need: The user has the needed information or entities.

This result may lead to a change in the need and thus influence input 1, and to the production of new information and new entities and thus influence input 2. Figure 1.1 gave examples of information for problem solving that should be transmitted through an information system.

The review of the overall role of an information system sets the stage for an examination of its internal structure. What are the functions that an information system must perform to achieve its objectives? Figure 5.1b is a

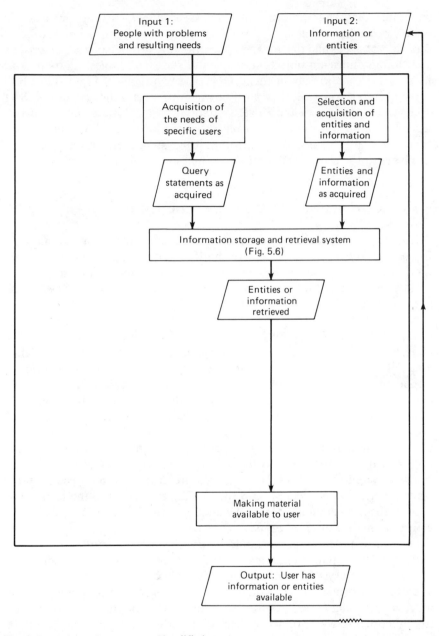

Fig. 5.1b   Information systems. Simplified structure.

simplified diagram, showing only the essential elements. An information system needs two components for the acquisition of inputs—one for the acquisition of needs and one for the acquisition of entities (such as persons, organizations, museum objects, documents, statistical tables, or food products) or information about them. Once the two types of inputs have been brought into the system, they must be matched; this is the task of the ISAR system. The output of the ISAR system is, for each need, an actual collection of matching entities or a report giving information about such entities. The last function of an information system is making this material available to the user, usually a person, but sometimes a machine system.

5.1.1 IDENTIFYING THE NEEDS OF SPECIFIC USERS

Knowing about the user's needs, actively identifying them, is among the foremost responsibilities of an information professional. Some users make their needs known, but others with needs just as important or more so remain silent; unless the information system actively seeks out these people and their needs, it fails in its mission to serve them. Some parents may not be aware that they need more information on child rearing; by actively identifying these parents and supplying them with the information and materials (e.g., toys) they need, the information system can help them to raise brighter and better adjusted children. Some inner city residents may not be aware of opportunities for training and subsequent employment; by actively identifying unemployed persons and giving them the information they need, the public library might help them find a job. The scientist examining a food additive petition may think she has all the information necessary to evaluate it (the petitioning food company is supposed to submit a complete bibliography) and may not check with the information center. By actively keeping track of incoming petitions, conducting a literature search for each without waiting for a formal request, and forwarding the results to the scientist involved, the information center may contribute to a better informed decision affecting the health of all of us.

Of course, potential users should be encouraged to submit requests (see Section 5.1.7 on public relations). Identifying people who can benefit from the information system is the joint responsibility of these people themselves and of the information professional. Even if an information system receives more requests than it can handle, its management should still actively identify other people with problems; their needs may be more pressing. Management should participate in setting priorities among the needs to be served and should not relinquish this responsibility completely to the users.

Once the information professional has determined the existence of a need, he must work with the user to analyze the problem at hand and to determine the specific needs for information or entities. This is the purpose of the *reference interview*.

Determining needs and priorities is a process of joint problem solving. The contributions of the user and of the information professional to this process may vary widely from one situation to another. Scientists and engineers served by an information center may make most of their needs known through requests and may be able to state their remaining needs clearly when approached by the information professional. Contrariwise, students in elementary school (or even high school) know little about their own needs; their needs are determined almost exclusively by information professionals, namely, curriculum developers and teachers.

The statement of a need, the topic of a request, is called a *query*.

5.1.2 Acquiring Entities or Information about Them

The process of acquiring entities or information about them is much better understood than the acquisition of needs. It results in an unorganized collection of entities or of information about entities, such as descriptions of proposed new courses, books as they come from the publisher and are stored in the work area awaiting processing, or goods as they come from shippers or a warehouse, before they are organized properly on the shelves of a grocery store.

5.1.3 The ISAR System

The ISAR system *matches the two inputs,* that is, for each query statement it searches the collection of information or entities acquired and finds those that match.

5.1.4 Making Entities or Information Available to the User

To make available tangible objects, such as parts, groceries, or books, the system must physically retrieve them from the store. To make available information, the system must make available a physical object carrying a message and, if needed, a device to read the message, such as a tape player, a reading machine that converts printed text to spoken text, or a microform reader, or it must present a message through some output device, such as a computer terminal or a telephone, possibly over a long distance. The message presented may be any combination of visual and sound elements—visual text, graphics, spoken text, music, and sound effects. Information may be given through a premade message, such as a printed book or a talking book, or through a message specifically created for the user, such as a list of references or a tailor-made package of substantive data created in response to a request.

In addition to these four core functions of an information system there are three important supporting functions: further processing of information, identifying user needs in general, and public relations. They are shown in the complete diagram in Fig. 5.1c.

5.1.5 FURTHER PROCESSING OF INFORMATION

In many cases the documents or substantive data retrieved by an information system can be further processed to provide an information product more meaningful to the user. Alternatively, this processing can be done as an integral part of retrieval—for example, screening a list of cities to identify those with an average per capita income below $15,000. Or the processing can be done even earlier—after documents or substantive data are acquired, but before they are stored. Some systems store only processed substantive data; others store also the documents from which these data were extracted or the raw substantive data from which they were derived through analysis.

Figure 5.2 gives examples of further processing of information to aid in specific decision-making situations.

The distinctive mark of extracting substantive data from a document is the intellectual contribution. Merely copying an entire journal article is *not* extraction of substantive data; it just makes the article available to the user. Identifying a specific table in a journal article as useful and copying that table *is* extraction of substantive data. Preparing a simple list of references does not involve extracting substantive data. Preparing annotations may involve extracting substantive data, particularly if the annotations are done in response to a specific query.

5.1.6 IDENTIFYING NEEDS IN GENERAL: THE NEEDS DIRECTORY

Identifying user needs is an important information system function. It appears twice in the information system diagram in Fig. 5.1c: first, as the identification of needs of specific users, and second, as the identification of needs in general. Identifying specific needs, discussed in Section 5.1.1, serves the purpose of information delivery to specific users. Identifying needs in

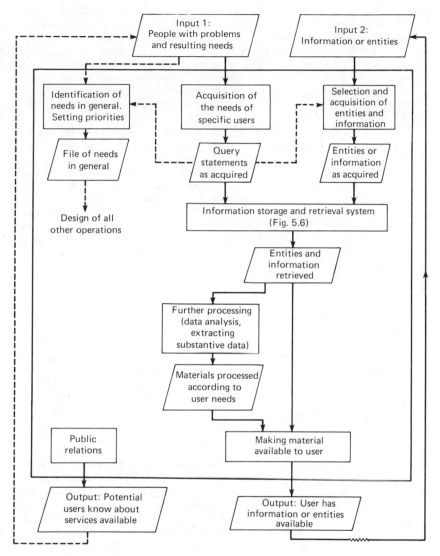

Fig. 5.1c Information systems. Complete structure.

general provides a basis for *designing* the information system in such a way that needs can be served properly.

Knowledge of the clientele to be served, their problems and needs, and of the search requests to be expected is extremely important in the design of

A *university administrator* must decide about the *reallocation of faculty positions* among departments according to their needs. Perhaps the most important consideration in such decisions is teaching load. A printout of course sections offered in the last three years and the students enrolled in them would be easy to produce but would be too bulky to be of any use in decision support. Through processing, this could be reduced to a printout giving just the number of students in each course offering. But this would still be too bulky. The administrator needs a report that gives for each department the number of weighted credit hours per faculty (one credit hour equals one student enrolled in one section for one credit). The credit hours should be weighted by the level of the course (undergraduate versus graduate), by the nature of the course (large lecture classes versus small seminars), adjusting for the fact that some subjects, by their nature, can be dealt with in large lecture classes whereas others do need small group instruction or laboratory experience under instructor supervision. But what the administrator is really interested in are not data about the past but projections for the future. Ingredients of such a projection are the analysis of trends in the past data, analysis of the number of students who wanted to take a course but were turned down for lack of seats, and developments in the job market. Thus the university administrator needs an information product produced by further processing internal and external data.

A *university administrator* must decide on *sites for extension courses*. Census data are helpful if processed properly: determine the criteria that define the people most likely to take extension courses; for each block or equivalent lowest unit in rural areas compute the *student potential*, the number of people meeting these criteria. Then, by computer program, create a *map* that shows each block in a color corresponding to its student potential and that also shows the possible sites for courses and the main traffic arteries. This map would be very useful in decision support; without such a map it would be very hard to properly consider census data in the decision.

The management of a *slide rule company* must make critical *investment decisions*: whether to replace old machinery, whether to expand, etc. (assume it's 1955). They need to know many things. For example: How are the prices of their materials going to develop? What about wages? What about price/demand curves as dependent on the overall economic situation (if people have lots of money, they may buy a slide rule even if it is expensive)? What about overall economic development? The answers to many of these questions lie in reams and reams of raw data. Company management needs processed data—for example, a curve of wood prices over the next ten years. Such a curve can be derived from the raw data using an econometric model (barring political upheaval in important supplier countries). Other areas in which the slide rule company needs information include: programs of schools influencing slide rule demand; emergence of competing technology (cheap pocket calculators).

An *engineer* needs reliable data on the *strength of a new material*. You find five documents that include measurements. Prepare one page that shows in tabular form the results of the various measurements, and possibly even add some judgment as to which might be the most reliable value. This serves the engineer much better than copies of the five articles, not to mention just the list of references.

A *superintendent* of a school system wants to improve *methods of reading instruction*. A literature search produces a large body of literature on the topic. Using this literature, produce a concise report outlining the major methods that would be appropriate for the situation at hand, their advantages and disadvantages. This is extracting substantive data followed by evaluation and synthesis.

Fig. 5.2 Further processing of data for decision support. Examples.

every function of the information system. It influences the method for identifying specific needs. It influences the collection development policy; if the acquisition process starts only when a user needs an entity, much delay results. Knowledge of needs should be a prime consideration in designing the ISAR system so that entities and information can be retrieved from the points of view of interest to the users. Knowledge of needs determines what, if any, capabilities for further processing should be available. Needs of the users should also be considered in the design of procedures and mechanisms for making material available (e.g., installing a reading machine for the blind). Finally, knowledge of needs influences the design of proper public relations operations. In short, knowledge of needs in general allows us to be preactive in designing a responsive system rather than merely reactive to individual specific needs.

Data on needs, both general and specific, should be organized in a *needs directory* or *user catalog,* which is organized in a hierarchy of organizational units—from the community to be served as a whole, to groupings within that community, and then to individuals. In an organization the subordinate groups are organizational subunits; in the general public they are specialized subgroups such as civic association officers, small businessmen, homemakers, or children. For each organizational unit the needs directory gives the following information:

- a statement of general background;
- a list of problems and, for each problem, needs for information or entities; a list of query statements.

The needs directory must be constantly updated. It can be combined with a directory of sources to form an *information directory.* For each "point" (organizational unit, individual, or subordinate information system) an information directory gives a description of the information to be fed to the point and a description of the information that the point can provide (often these two descriptions overlap considerably).

5.1.7 PUBLIC RELATIONS

If the clientele is small enough that the information system can initiate service to each member, no public relations effort is needed. However, often the clientele is so large that the information system must rely largely on the users to make their needs known. A user will not take such initiative unless he or she perceives that the information system can be of use. Designing an information system that is ideally suited to meet the needs of a given clientele is not sufficient. Users must be made aware of all the ways in which the system can be useful to them; this requires a public relations effort. On the other hand, the best public relations campaign will be in vain if the information system is not designed to meet the needs of the clientele. Public relations can create only an initial perception; good service must make this initial perception permanent.

5.1.8 FUNCTIONAL VERSUS ORGANIZATIONAL BREAKDOWN OF A SYSTEM

Fig. 5.1c presents a *functional breakdown* of an information system, or *what* is done; this contrasts with an *organizational breakdown,* or *who* does it. There is usually not a one-to-one correspondence between organizational units and functions: one organizational unit may perform several functions. For example, the reference department in a library is often involved in selection, an acquisitions function. Conversely, one function may be performed by several units. For example, in many libraries the interlibrary loan department orders documents from other libraries—an acquisitions function—and checks out these documents to users—the function of making material available to the users. The functional analysis may suggest reorganization: For example, one might integrate the ordering of documents from other libraries into the acquisitions process (acquiring a document through interlibrary loan or through purchase is often a choice that should be considered) and integrate the checkout function into the general circulation system.

5.2 THE RETRIEVAL PROBLEM: A VIEW FROM SCRATCH

The previous section gave an overall view of the structure of an information system and defined the functions of an ISAR system within that structure. Following the procedure of stepwise refinement, this section gives a close–up view of the internal structure of an ISAR system, the subsystem of major interest in this book. It develops the theme of designing an ISAR system responsive to requests through the example of an ISAR system for documents or other main entities. This example will illustrate the importance of a user-, request-, or problem-oriented approach to the design and operation of an ISAR system. A simple and seemingly obvious reassessment of the retrieval problem leads to important, but often neglected, consequences.

An ISAR system has two inputs:

1. Query statements expressing needs, submitted by the user, identified by the information specialist, or agreed upon in a reference interview.
2. A collection of information or entities as acquired; the unorganized

collection of courses, documents, paintings, materials, food products, job applicants, houses, or whatever, or of information about them.

The ISAR system must find the information or entities that are relevant to a query. In the following we discuss ways to accomplish this task.

Elementary Solution: Searching the Whole Unorganized Collection

This involves reading and understanding the query statement, then examining every entity in the collection with a view to the query and deciding whether it is relevant to the query at hand—whether a relationship between the entity and the query should be established. The information specialist acts as the user's agent, examining entities and making relevance judgments in the user's stead. To get a feel for the process, try it out on the very much simplified list of query statements and documents provided in Fig. 5.3, examining titles of documents instead of the documents themselves. Even this very much simplified example shows that making relevance judgments is not a trivial matter. For example, document 15 on *Oversea cables* may well be relevant for the search on *Pipes* because oversea cables are made in the form of a thin-walled pipe.

Sample query statements

a   All material on pipes of all kinds
b   Plastic pipes
c   Production and use of metal pipes

Sample list of documents

1   Copper tubes for air conditioning equipment
2   How to draw copper wire
3   Artificial arteries: Plastic helps surgeons
4   The production of steel pipes
5   The production of copper rods
6   The production of copper pipes
7   Vinyl hoses in appliances
8   Spiral copper tubes as cooling elements
9   Precision methods in wire drawing
10   The production of pipes
11   All about copper
12   The production of PVC capillaries
13   Polyvinylchloride reactions
14   On the background of Lindsay's cable to Rockefeller
15   Overseas cables change communication

Fig. 5.3   Query statements and document titles for examination.

With this method a search requires the following operations: understanding the query statement, examining entities, and assessing relevance. Examining entities is the most time-consuming of these operations. Attending courses to get a full understanding of their content, approach, and quality; reading and understanding documents; selecting paintings for an exhibit based on theme and artistic quality; or examining various types of steel for their suitability in a given product—all take time. The more thorough the examination required to make relevance judgments, the more time is needed.

In the elementary method every entity is examined anew for each individual search. This is inefficient and leads to two major disadvantages:

- The *user* must wait very long for the answer.
- The *information specialist* must spend many hours on any one search.

Fortunately, there are four ways for increasing efficiency.

First Economy Measure: Cutting Examination Time

This involves substituting an *entity representation* for the entity itself. For example, for documents one prepares an abstract that summarizes the essential aspects. This is a one-time investment. In every search the searcher needs to read only the abstract rather than the whole document. Other examples: preparing descriptions of courses, paintings, or food products.

This method cuts the waiting time for the user; it also cuts the working time of the information specialist, because the time saved in searching outweighs the time spent on preparing entity representations (unless there are only a few requests). Still more time could be saved by using existing representations, such as course descriptions, or titles or tables of contents of documents.

This cost–benefit analysis is based on the assumption that one can judge relevance just as well on the basis of a representation, such as an abstract, as on the basis of the entity itself. However, this may not be so. By its very nature a representation abridges and leaves out aspects of the entity. The representation must cover all aspects of the entity that may be important for judging its relevance for any query that might come up. How can the information specialist preparing the representations know beforehand what these aspects will be? How can the system designer know whether existing representations will be adequate?

Second Economy Measure: Batching Queries

If two queries arrive at the same time, the searcher deals with them simultaneously: she reads and understands both queries, examines each entity with both queries in mind, and, after examining an entity, makes two relevance judgments.

This method cuts the total hours spent on examination, the major time-eater, by almost one half (it may take a little longer to examine an entity with respect to two queries). It does not help the user at all; he still must wait until the searcher has gone through the entire collection. The savings in search time are even more dramatic if one lets a batch of queries accumulate (for example, 50 queries for a week). The searcher would read and understand all of them, and only then search through the whole collection, examining every entity, one at a time, and comparing it with each query in memory to judge its relevance for that query. Time for examination is now reduced to about one-fiftieth of the original. Time for relevance judgments is not reduced because the searcher still must judge each entity with respect to each query.

This method inconveniences the user, who must wait even longer. More importantly, this approach poses a fundamental intellectual problem: how can a searcher keep 50 queries in mind at once and analyze entities from 50 viewpoints simultaneously? The solution lies in bringing order and structure into the list of queries. A good method for doing this is to summarize each query in a brief caption or topic statement and to develop a coherent framework for organizing these captions. The resulting structured list of query captions serves as a checklist for the analysis of entities.

Third Economy Measure: Collecting Anticipated Queries and Examining Entities in Advance.

Neither cutting examination time nor batching queries alone is efficient enough for large ISAR systems. Using these two approaches simultaneously increases efficiency further. Figure 5.4 gives examples.

In each of these examples the following procedure is used:

Anticipate queries and make a list of anticipated query statements.

As entities arrive, examine them and judge their relevance with respect to each anticipated query, in advance of the actual search for that query. Put differently, examine every incoming entity with the list of anticipated queries as a guide. Note the queries for which the entity is relevant (establish relationships between entities and queries), thus creating an entity representation.

This method of anticipated queries is a logical development of batching queries—all anticipated queries are listed so that each entity is examined only once. The problem of keeping all the queries in mind is solved by listing them in a coherent, logical structure. This method is also a logical development of cutting examination time—when a query arrives, the searcher need only

In the *University Data Base, access to courses* can be improved by collecting query statements from students, and then examining each course and noting the queries for which it is relevant. When one of these queries comes up, retrieval is easy.

A *special librarian* serving, for example, 25 scientists, has a standing query or "interest profile" for each of them. As a new document arrives, the librarian examines it and notes the scientists for whose interest profile it is relevant; each scientist is then notified of new documents of interest. This is batching queries. But instead of examining documents in the collection retrospectively, the librarian examines the documents as they arrive.

A *librarian in a public library* who specializes in *programs for home computers* knows what kind of queries come in frequently. Thus, as she learns of a new program, she examines it, judges its relevance with respect to each of the frequent queries, and makes a note of the queries for which it is relevant, thus making future retrieval easier.

To write a *state-of-the-art report*, proceed as follows:

Think of all the topics to be dealt with in the report and arrange them in a systematic outline.

Read literature that might be useful; mark whole documents or sections of documents according to the topics for which they are relevant.

Write the report, using for each topic the documents or sections marked relevant for it.

This way you need to read each document only once and not each time you go on to a new topic. But now imagine that you realize later that you forgot a topic that must be covered in the report. Now you have no choice but to read all documents again to find out which ones are relevant for the new topic (or else rely on your memory for selecting relevant documents).

Fig. 5.4   The method of anticipated queries. Examples.

check each entity representation to see whether the query is listed in it. The entities have been *indexed* using the anticipated queries as *subject descriptors*. The aspects to be considered in writing the entity representations are rendered explicit by the list of anticipated query statements. The information specialist preparing entity representations now has the necessary guidance; the major problem associated with preparing entity representations is solved.

In reality, indexing is, of course, a process more complicated than noting the appropriate anticipated queries; likewise, searching is a process more complicated than just looking for a query number in an entity representation. More sophisticated procedures are needed to achieve efficiency of the ISAR system. But the principle illustrated by the examples is important: entities should be examined with a view to anticipated queries. Before organizing the collection, the designer must have a good idea of the queries that are going to be asked. A study of the needs of the potential users is essential for obtaining this knowledge. Combining the approach of cutting examination time with batching queries leads to a method far superior to both: the method of *request- or problem-oriented indexing*.

The method of anticipated queries fails whenever an unanticipated query arrives. If that happens, the searcher must go back, at least in principle, to the elementary method and examine all entities in the collection.

Fourth Economy Measure: Providing a Retrieval Mechanism

The retrieval procedure discussed so far is based on examining each entity or entity representation in turn, a process called *sequential scanning.* In most situations sequential scanning is inefficient. Retrieval efficiency can be improved still further by introducing a *retrieval mechanism,* cutting down both the waiting time of the user and the working time of the information specialist. On the other hand, resources are needed for establishing a retrieval mechanism. Again, there is a trade-off.

The oldest and perhaps the most obvious retrieval mechanism is grouping entities (e.g., documents or merchandise on shelves) such that one part of the file or shelf is a better place to look than other parts. In other words, the collection is divided in such a way that a search can be limited to the one part that is most likely to contain the relevant entities. For example, all the entities relevant to one query (one author, one subject) are grouped together; the relationships between entities and queries are expressed by arrangement. As a user comes in with a query, the searcher simply looks at all the groups until the pertinent group is found. This is much faster than looking at every individual entity.

Retrieval can be speeded up still further by arranging the *groups* in a logical order: authors alphabetically, or subjects in a meaningful order that *collocates* related subjects (and thus the corresponding entities), such as *Physics* and *Astronomy* or *Fresh beans* and *Fresh peas.* However, ordering the groups can get quite complicated. Even what would seem very simple—alphabetical ordering of authors—may require complicated filing rules. Finding a meaningful arrangement of subject groups is even more complex. A linear sequence can show only a fraction of the relationships between subjects. For example, the following two-dimensional diagram shows four related subject pairs:

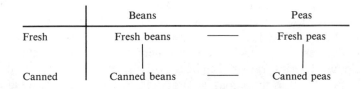

A linear arrangement can show only two of these pairs through collocation. The elements of the other two pairs would be dispersed.

Grouping entities or entity representations is useful for browsing but has intrinsic restrictions as a retrieval mechanism: Because each entity can be put into only one place, there is only one access point per entity. The one-access-point restriction is overcome by creating an additional file called *index* or *catalog* that allows for multiple entries. Each entry consists of an entity representation that, at the minimum, directs the user to the place where a more complete representation or the entity itself can be found. For example, a traditional card catalog contains multiple entries for each document to provide access by author, title, series, and subject. Other access points may be as useful or even more so, depending on the specific needs of the clientele. However, there are economic limits to the average number of entries per entity.

5.2.1 THE STRUCTURE OF INDEX LANGUAGES AND FILES: A PREVIEW

The following ISAR system structure emerges: A structured list of anticipated query statements is compiled from the study of needs. An indexer examines incoming entities from the point of view of the anticipated query statements and notes the queries for which the entity is relevant, thus establishing relationships between entities and queries. An index file then provides access to the entities from these queries. When a query arrives, the searcher identifies its number in the list of anticipated queries and then consults the index under that number. While this approach is a vast improvement over the elementary solution—examining all entities in the collection for every query that arrives—it is still not a feasible solution; in any real situation there are so many queries to consider that arranging them in a nice framework is not feasible.

A solution is suggested by the observation that most queries can be expressed as a combination of several conceptual components as shown for subject queries in the examples in Fig. 5.5.

Analyzing query statements into components reduces the impossible task of anticipating all queries to the smaller, but still difficult task of anticipating all components that might occur in query statements and arranging these components in a well-organized list. The number of components is very much smaller than the number of all anticipated queries. Thus, it is manageable for the indexer who uses it as a checklist in indexing. All components for which the entity being indexed is relevant are marked; they serve as *descriptors* for the entity. As a query arrives, the searcher does not find it as such in a list of anticipated queries; rather she checks the list of anticipated query components and identifies those that in combination express the query at hand; these form the *query formulation*. Accordingly, the index file should be set up to allow for rapid retrieval not only of all entities indexed by one descriptor but of all entities indexed by any combination of descriptors. This pro-

Query statement: I need material on canned beans
Components: *Canned* AND *Beans*
Query statement: I need a handbook on canned vegetables published after 1972
Components: *Canned* AND *Vegetables* AND *Handbook* AND *Date after 1972*
                     Documents exhibiting all four characteristics, and only those documents, are relevant.

The last example gives a more systematic analysis of a query statement into components, using a predetermined list of viewpoints or *facets* to be used in searching for food products.

Query statement: I need a list of all brands of frozen cut green beans
Components:

Product type:	Vegetable product
Food source:	Beans
Part of plant:	Pod with immature seeds
Physical state or form:	Cut into medium sized pieces
Degree of cooking:	(Any term acceptable)
Treatment applied:	(Any term acceptable)
Preservation method used:	Frozen
Packing medium:	(Any term acceptable)
Container type:	(Any term acceptable)
Food contact surface:	(Any term acceptable)
User group:	(Any term acceptable)

Fig. 5.5   Query formulations as combinations of subject descriptors.

cedure is much more flexible because it allows for the expression of queries that have not been anticipated as such as long as the appropriate components are available in the system.

The approach outlined in this section follows directly from the discussion of the role of information in problem solving in Chapter 2. It forms the basis for the analysis of index language structure, query formulation and indexing, and data base structure in the remainder of the book.

5.3 THE STRUCTURE OF AN ISAR SYSTEM

The structure of an ISAR system as shown in Fig. 5.6 provides the framework for the treatment of individual components in the remainder of the book; study the diagram carefully. The ISAR system is a subsystem of the total information system. It has two inputs: (1) query statements (descriptions of the needed information or entities couched in natural language) and (2) entities or information about entities as acquired. The output of the ISAR system consists of entities or information about entities and their relationships presumed relevant for a query—that is, helpful for solving the problem that gave rise to the query.

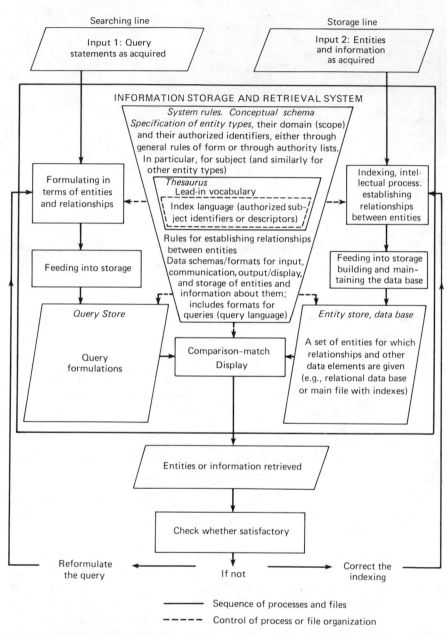

Fig. 5.6   The structure of an ISAR system.

5.3.1 THE ISAR SYSTEM AS A WHOLE

The ISAR system processes its inputs as follows.

For a query statement, the search unit (a human searcher or a computer program) determines the entities and relationships involved and expresses them in terms of the language used in the ISAR system, resulting in a *query formulation*. The following examples refer to the University Data Base, presented in Figure 3.3.

> List every *Course offering* that <has instructor> *Person* L. Kahn.
>
> List every *Document* that <is used as text in> *Course offering* COF2.
>
> List every *Document* that [<deals with> *Subject* Meat canning AND <deals with> *Subject* Standards] (both conditions must be met).

For a new entity to be added to the store, the indexing unit determines the relationships to other entities and then adds the entity and its relationships, integrating them into the data base. For example,

> *Course offering* COF5 <has instructor> *Person* L. Kahn
> *Course offering* COF5 <uses textbook> *Document* D5
> *Document* D5 <deals with> *Subject* S12

(The entity types are added for clarity; they need not be entered every time because the system knows that L. Kahn is a person and that D5 is a document.)

The entities and relationships included in the data base can now be matched against the query formulation and the entities or information meeting the specifications extracted; the result is a data base—a mini data base, as it were—displayed and formatted according to the specifications of the query formulation.

All processes are governed by the system rules and conventions, which are discussed in the next section.

5.3.2. SYSTEM RULES AND CONVENTIONS. THE CONCEPTUAL SCHEMA

The system rules and conventions consist of the *conceptual schema,* which defines the intellectual or logical content of the data base (the entity store of the ISAR system), and of rules for entering and extracting information or entities from the data base. The rules for extracting information form the *query language.*

Figure 3.3a gives the conceptual schema of the sample University Data Base. The conceptual schema of a data base does the following:

- It lists the entity types to be included, such as *Course, Course offering, Person,* and for each entity type the rules for entity identifiers (i.e., the names, terms, numbers, or other symbols that may be used to designate individual entity values).
- It lists the types of relationships between entities—such as *Prerequisite* (Course, course), *Offered as* (Course, Course offering), *Has student* (Course offering, Person), and *Deals with* (Course, Subject), and it gives rules that guide the indexer in deciding on specific relationships to be established, e.g., to how many subjects should a course be related through < deals with > .

An important part of the conceptual schema is the *index language.* It consists of all *subject identifiers,* which are also called *subject descriptors.* Most systems have a list of terms authorized as subject descriptors, an authority list; other terms may be included in a *lead-in vocabulary* with instructions for what term to use (e.g., *Lawyer* USE *Attorney*). Lead-in vocabulary and index language together are called *thesaurus.*

A query specifies information or entities to be extracted from the data base, and the format of the resulting mini data base. A query formulation is a combination of entities and relationships; the rules for writing query formulations make up the *query language.*

5.3.3 Notes on the Other Components of an ISAR System

The Searching Line (See Fig. 5.6)

Query formulation is an extremely important function. It involves choosing the entity values and the relationships between them that define the information or entities needed as described in the query statement. Query formulation can get quite complex, particularly if finding the information needed involves drawing inferences from the data stored. An example is the query "Which instructors use their own books as textbooks?" (see Chapter 3). For another example, consider the query statement "Who is the supervisor of L. Smith?" Assume the data base does not contain the answer directly but does contain the two statements:

> *Person* J. Tran < is manager of > *Department* Purchasing and
> *Person* L. Smith < works in > *Department* Purchasing.

From these a sophisticated ISAR system can infer

> *Person* J. Tran < is supervisor of > *Person* L. Smith.

Query statements and query formulations should be stored permanently for SDI (Selective Dissemination of Information), for a study of needs, or in case a request for the same topic comes up again.

The Storage Line (see Fig. 5.6)

To avoid duplication, the system should check whether the entity to be indexed is already in the store. In ISAR systems that focus on one type of entity, such as documents, persons, or food samples, checking for duplicates is done as part of the acquisition function outside the ISAR system. In ISAR systems with a more complex structure, this check is much more difficult, and may require that a statement be indexed first by expressing it in terms of entity identifiers and relationships. Even the definition of duplication becomes tricky: a new statement received for incorporation in the data base may not be stored as such but may be derivable through inference from data stored.

Comparison/match

Searching line and storage line converge in the comparison/match operation, which is performed by the retrieval mechanism. The structure of the retrieval mechanism is closely intertwined with the organization of the data base. It is important for the power, speed, and cost of the ISAR system.

Feedback Processes

If the search results are not satisfactory, reformulating the query and repeating the comparison with the new query formulation might help. This use of feedback helps the search at hand. Future searches benefit from tracing poor search performance to deficiencies in the ISAR system rules or in indexing and correcting these deficiencies. Irrelevant entities may have been retrieved due to incorrect indexing—indexing should be corrected if the ISAR system permits (most ISAR systems don't!). Perhaps the index language does not contain a subject descriptor that is important for the search. Or the organization of the data base may need improvement as in reorganizing books on shelves in accordance with changing user interests. ISAR systems that allow such changes based on experience from searching are called *dynamic*. Most existing ISAR systems are static: They do not allow changes. Developments in computer technology may make dynamic ISAR systems affordable. Correcting the content of the data base, such as subjects assigned to a document, is always beneficial. However, before making changes in the index language or other rules, the designer should consider the inconvenience this may cause to the users.

5.4 DEFINITIONS

5.4.1 DESCRIPTOR, LEAD-IN TERM, INDEX LANGUAGE, LEAD-IN VOCABULARY, THESAURUS

Assume the relationship:

Document D3 < deals with > *Subject* S12 Food processing.

This relationship causes document D3, Principles of food technology, to be retrieved in a search for the subject *Food processing; Food processing* is a descriptor for document D3. When we say that entity B (*Food processing*) is a *descriptor* for entity A (*Document* D3), we mean that B can be used to retrieve A; such retrieval is based on a relationship that exists between *A* and *B*. More precisely, the descriptor is the authorized identifier for entity *B*, such as an authorized subject term or the authorized name of an organization. A descriptor, then, is any authorized entity identifier that can be used for retrieving other entities. If the retrieving entities are concepts, we speak of *subject descriptors*. A *lead-in term* is any term or other symbol for which a relationship to a descriptor is established so that a user looking under the term is led to the descriptor.

The subject descriptors together form the *index language;* the lead-in terms constitute the *lead-in vocabulary*. Index language and lead-in vocabulary together form the (subject) *thesaurus*. A thesaurus in the broader sense can also be established for other types of entities (e.g., for corporate bodies) to control the variety of their names.

5.4.2 SEARCH REQUEST, QUERY, QUERY STATEMENT, QUERY FORMULATION

A *Search request* is a request for information or entities useful for solving a problem or relating to a topic. In this book we use the term *request* very broadly to include not only the case where a user puts the request to the information system but also the case where the information system anticipates a need on which action must be taken. A search request has a requester, a topic, and requirements as to the quality of the answer and deadline. The information system delivers an extract from its data base in response to the search request; the answer is in itself a data base, albeit a very small one; we call it a *mini data base*.

A retrospective search request has to do with a one-time need and often requires that the search be extended considerably back in time. An SDI (Selective Dissemination of Information) search request (also called current awareness search request, recurring search request, or standing search request) has to do with a continuing need and requires that a search be done at regular intervals—for example, once every month.

A *query* is the topic of the search request, perhaps qualified by formal criteria such as level of treatment or country of publication.

A *query statement* is a description of the need in ordinary language. It is often a paragraph, but it may range from a short phrase similar to a document title or a captionlike description of a patient's condition to a description of several pages. A query statement may be submitted by the user, worked out in cooperation between the user and the information specialist, or generated totally within the information system.

A *query formulation* is a precise formal definition of the mini data base containing the information which is described informally in the query statement. The mini data base is defined in terms of entities and relationships to be included.

5.4.3 INDEXING, CATALOGING, CODING

Indexing in its most encompassing sense refers to the total process of integrating new entities and relationships into a data base. This process consists of two steps. First comes an intellectual process which involves the following: assigning an identifier to a new entity (for example, assigning a course number to a new course and, if the instructor is new, determining the proper form of his or her name); determining any text associated with the new entity, such as a course title and course description; and determining relationships, for instance, between the course and the instructor, the course and an existing course needed as prerequisite, the course and a program of study in which it is required, and the course and the appropriate subject, and between a person (the instructor) and a rank. This intellectual process results in a representation of a new entity—in the example, the new course—and it may also add other new entities—for example, a new person (instructor)—or modify the representation of an existing entity (e.g., the program of study in which the new course is required). This intellectual process is also called indexing (in its narrow sense). It is followed by a clerical process which involves inputting the data generated into the data base and integrating them into its structure (for example, showing a new course under its subjects in a subject index of courses).

In preparing the index for a book, the intellectual process involves establishing for each page the relationships to subjects and introducing new subjects with their terms as necessary, and the clerical process involves typing and sorting entries. In indexing a library collection the intellectual process involves determining for each book the proper form of its title and the relationships to persons (author and other contributors), corporate bodies (document originators or publishers), date, number of pages, size, etc., resulting in the *document description*. The intellectual process also involves determining the book's relationships to subjects resulting in the *document representation*. The clerical process involves inserting a card for the title, each person, corporate body, and subject in the catalog and shelving the book in its proper place.

Particularly when indexing books and other documents, we distinguish between *descriptive indexing,* which is concerned with the document's or entity's description, and indexes that derive from it, such as an author–title index/catalog, and *subject indexing,* which is concerned with the document representation and the preparation of a subject index/catalog.

Common Usage of the Terms *Indexing* and *Cataloging*

Indexing is commonly used for the intellectual process of subject indexing: establishing relationships between an entity and appropriate subjects or, put differently, assigning subject descriptors to an entity. The term *indexing* in this meaning is used primarily in special libraries, especially if they are mechanized, and in abstracting and indexing services. The term *indexing* is also used for the total process of back-of-the-book indexing—preparing the index for a book as discussed earlier.

Cataloging is commonly used for the intellectual process of indexing in most library situations (except many special libraries). Accordingly, *descriptive cataloging* and *subject cataloging* are the terms used in most libraries. A *cataloger* is concerned only with the intellectual process, both descriptive and subject. The cataloging department, on the other hand, is concerned with the total process.

The terms *indexing* and *cataloging* are used for the same process depending on the context or on the type of entity to which the process is applied. This terminological divergence reflects the historical split of the information field into separate groups that are roughly reflected by the American Society for Information Science, the Special Libraries Association, and the American Library Association. There is a growing sense of commonality among these groups, and this should be expressed in a common use of terminology, which would make everybody's life easier. We have a slight preference for the term *indexing* as the term to be used.

The term *coding* is often used for the intellectual process of indexing, particularly if the identifiers for the subjects, corporate bodies, or other entities to which relationships are established are expressed by notations or codes, such as A1.1 (*Vegetable product*). For example, in a file of food products where notations are used to express subject descriptors, the term *coding* is used for the process of analyzing the products and assigning the appropriate subjects in code form. In survey research the term *coding* is used for the process of indexing the individual cases by the appropriate values of the variables used in the study at hand. The proper value may be seen, for example, from free answers the respondent gave. In all of these cases emphasis is on the intellectual process of determining the subjects to which an entity should be related. The term *coding* is also used for a merely clerical process: subjects are already assigned in the form of natural language terms, which must be converted into codes. This clerical process is part of indexing in the narrow sense, but it is of little interest in this book.

Request-oriented indexing or *problem-oriented indexing* is an approach to indexing that starts from anticipated problems and queries and establishes relationships between entities with a view to these anticipated queries. This very important principle was introduced in Section 5.2 and will be discussed in detail in Section 13.2.

Relation/file, data base, index, bibliography, bibliographic data base, substantive data base, catalog, and *directory* will be defined in Section 11.7.

PART II

Objectives of ISAR Systems

CHAPTER 6

Systems Analysis

OBJECTIVES

The objectives of this chapter are to enable the reader to apply the logical steps of systems analysis in practical situations, and to illustrate that some decision situations are quite complex and that sophisticated tools, such as operations research and decision theory, are available to deal with these situations, thus enabling the reader to recognize when to call in a systems analysis expert.

INTRODUCTION

Broadly defined, systems analysis is a formal approach to problem solving or decision making. It is used throughout this book and it is also useful in many other contexts.

Systems analysis consists of a step-by-step procedure, in which objectives are explicitly specified, the present situation is clearly described, and available alternatives are systematically explored and then evaluated with respect to the objectives. This procedure can be applied to any problem or decision, in particular to the design of systems, such as an urban mass transportation system, the arrangement of a kitchen, or a manual or computerized ISAR (information storage and retrieval) system.

Historically, analysis of information processing systems has been allied with electronic data processing and computer programming for two reasons:

- A computer requires very detailed specification of what it is to do. Humans, however, usually "muddle through" even if they are not given very explicit instructions.
- In the early days computers were very expensive, and, perhaps more importantly, the expense for computers was clearly visible "on the books."

Thus computerization had to be justified, whereas manual processing of the same information was taken for granted. However, one should not take for granted any task or any method for accomplishing the task. With prices for computer power falling and wages rising, the cost argument just presented may be reversed: A task that can *not* be computerized may be more expensive to perform and thus require more careful systems analysis.

6.1 APPROACHES TO DECISION MAKING

There are three basic approaches to problem solving or decision making:

- following tradition or authorities,
- making a decision through a political process, and
- applying the rational approach of common sense and systems analysis.

These approaches are not exclusive; all three operate, in varying degrees, in any decision-making process. A brief examination of these approaches will put systems analysis in context.

An example of following tradition—doing things the way they always have been done—is developing a budget simply by increasing last year's figures by 10%. An example of following an authority is designing a kitchen by consulting a designer's handbook and following the suggestions given there. Often this approach is quite reasonable. One cannot constantly examine and reexamine everything one is doing. If an organization were to constantly perform systems analyses of all the facets of its operation, it would get bogged down in analysis and never accomplish anything. Following authorities may be the best course available to the decision maker who does not have sufficient expertise to analyze the problem from scratch. On the other hand, this approach has dangers: Inefficient ways of doing things may be perpetuated; an authority's solution may be adopted even though the circumstances at hand require a different solution.

In decision making through a political process, the interests of the participants play a key role. For example, when Congress considers laws about the Merchant Marine, the interests of shipowners, maritime unions, businesses needing shipping capacity, and consumers are at stake. Often the interests of the group that can contribute most to the reelection of key congressional representatives will find primary consideration. A key point in the political process, then, is "Who stands to win and who stands to lose?". The picture is complicated because one issue is never considered alone; many deals are made. Personalities and organizations and their position in the power game form another ingredient of the political process. The most meritorious solution may not be accepted if it is suggested by a weak person and if its acceptance may detract from the ego of a strong person. The proponent of a solution being the nephew of the company president may have as much to do with the acceptance of that solution as its merits for the company's well-being.

In the rational approach the decision maker starts from objectives, considers various alternatives in the light of these objectives, and then chooses the alternative that promises the largest contribution toward the fulfillment of the objectives. The decision maker may rely on intuition and common sense; however, this may leave objectives and assumptions about the present situation largely implicit and hide them from close scrutiny. What is obvious at first sight often turns out to be erroneous under closer examination. Thus intuition and common sense may lead to solutions that are not optimal. Furthermore, intuition and common sense do not lend themselves very easily to decision making in groups. In systems analysis, objectives are formulated explicitly and assumptions are examined carefully. Furthermore, sophisticated procedures are used to determine the status quo; to determine, as far as possible, the outcomes of various alternatives under consideration; and to derive a total score for each alternative in the case where there are multiple and possibly conflicting objectives. Systems analysis comprises a number of *functions* to be performed when solving a problem or making a decision. Usually these functions are performed repeatedly in several cycles or *phases*. The precepts of systems analysis can be overdone; they should be followed to the extent warranted by the complexity of the problem at hand.

A political process envelops all other contributions to decision making. Systems analysis is not a method for determining ultimate objectives; it is only a method for finding out how such objectives, once determined, can best be achieved. Ultimate objectives must, by their nature, be determined by a political process. Once the ultimate objectives are determined, the political process should give way to systems analysis and sanction its results. In reality this very seldom happens. First, it is very difficult to formulate ultimate objectives explicitly, and thus discussion about these objectives will recur throughout the process of determining a solution. Often the ultimate objectives pursued by different participants in the decision-making process are hidden or at odds with each other. Second, the political environment sets constraints upon possible solutions. The results of systems analysis constitute one input into the political process. In some instances this input will be of overriding importance; in others it will be neglected.

6.2 FUNCTIONS IN THE SYSTEMS ANALYSIS PROCESS

Figure 6.1 shows a logical sequence of functions in formulating and solving a problem and in implementing the solution. This figure is not meant to suggest that systems analysis is a linear process in which one function neatly

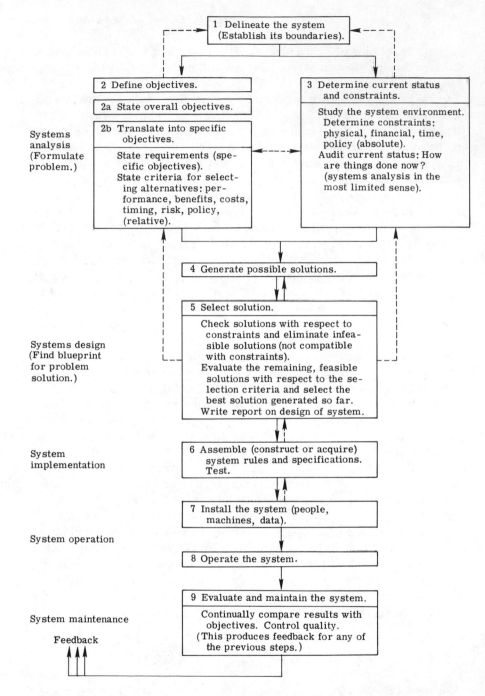

Fig. 6.1 Functions in systems analysis (in the broadest sense).

follows another from beginning to end. Functions 1–5 should be performed in several cycles, each time more thoroughly (see Section 6.3). One must often go back to an earlier point; for example, if no solution can be found to meet the stated objectives, the objectives must be reformulated. Function 4, Generate solutions, and function 5, Select solution, interact heavily. Moreover, while performing one function, the analyst considers one or more other functions as well; for example, when delineating the system, he already gives some thought to defining objectives.

Function 1: Delineate the System

Establishing from the outset what belongs and what does not belong to the system to be considered—establishing the system boundaries or the problem domain—provides a frame of reference for the other functions. System delineation requires much thought. If it is too narrow, the solution resulting from the analysis might be far from optimal in a wider context; if it is too broad, the problem might not be manageable. Four examples illustrate this.

A system to provide subject access to journal articles for the employees of one pharmaceutical company is too narrow in scope; the major investment of scanning many journals and indexing the relevant articles benefits only a limited number of people. Several companies should cooperate and establish an information system to serve all their employees.

A system to provide SDI (Selective Dissemination of Information) service based on machine-readable bibliographic data bases should include the function of physical access to the documents listed in SDI notices lest frustration result.

The delineation of an information system for the purpose of estimating the true cost must include user activities, such as user inquiry from a terminal and the working time spent on such activities.

On the other hand, a system that is to serve the information needs of all people in the world would be so broad as to be unmanageable.

The delineation of a system often results from the consideration of a higher level system. For example, cataloging operations may be delineated as a subsystem in the consideration of the total operations of a library system. This approach recognizes the close relationships of cataloging with acquisitions (the same bibliographical data that go into the catalog are needed for placing orders), with reference (the catalog is being used for reference), and with circulation (bibliographic data are needed for establishing the circulation file). Starting out by focusing exclusively on the cataloging activity as a system would leave these relationships hidden and lead to an inferior solution; the system delineation would be too narrow.

Function 2: Define Objectives

Before designing a new system or undertaking a meaningful analysis of an existing system, one must establish a clear sense of purpose. This is the theme of the following famous passage from *Alice in Wonderland*.

> "Come, it's pleased so far," thought Alice, and she went on. "Would you tell me, please, which way I ought to go from here?"
> "That depends a good deal on where you want to get to," said the Cat.
> "I don't much care where—" said Alice.
> "Then it doesn't matter much which way you go," said the Cat.

The same point is made in an old adage of systems analysis: "Never start at the beginning; always start at the end." It is very important that the objectives be clearly and explicitly spelled out, so that any solutions being considered (including a solution currently in effect) can be judged against these objectives. This leads to much clearer thinking, even if only one decision maker is involved. A group cannot engage in a rational decision-making process unless objectives are clearly defined.

Objectives can be divided into broad, overall objectives and specific objectives or requirements that are needed to achieve the overall objectives.

Examples of overall objectives are

- For a company: maximize profits.
- For the research and development (R and D) laboratory of a company: develop high quality products.
- For the information system of the research and development laboratory: make sure that the scientists and engineers have information conducive to the development of high quality products.
- For a circulation system: maximize availability of materials.
- For a public library: improve the standard of living in the community, help people to enrich their lives, help people to educate themselves, and so on.

Usually the broad objectives cannot be used by themselves as guides for design or analysis. They must be translated into specific objectives and requirements, which should be quantified when possible.

In the example of an *information system,* specific objectives might be

- Provide an SDI service covering journal articles and reports. A given level of quality should be stipulated.
- Respond to requests for data on the properties of materials within an hour or less.
- Provide high quality literature analyses.
- Provide access to material before the deadline set by the requester in 80% of all cases.

For a *circulation system* specific objectives might be

- Be able to find out where an item is at any given time.
- Be able to recall items needed urgently.
- Be able to see what a user has at any given time.
- Be able to supply users with a list of the items they have checked out (this may result in the user's returning the item more speedily and thus in increased availability).

A specific objective of a higher level system (the information system of a company research and development laboratory) can be the broad objective of a subsystem (e.g., the circulation system).

Specific objectives lead to *performance criteria;* these should be weighted with respect to their contribution to the overall objectives and, through the hierarchy of systems, to some ultimate benefit, such as the profit of a company. Further criteria to be used in selecting a solution are the following:

Cost. If a superior solution costs more, is it worth it? The improvement in performance may not be worth the cost.

Timing. How long will it take to implement a solution? Having the second best solution now might be better than having the best solution in 2 years.

Risk. Assume, for example, that a decision on the thoroughness of indexing must be made without knowing how many search requests to expect. On the one hand, indexing thoroughly and thus making searching easier is a good investment if many search requests come in; if there are only a few requests, it is a waste of money. On the other hand, superficial indexing causes much search effort if many requests come in, but it is appropriate if there are only a few requests. Not knowing the number of requests to be expected creates a quandary.

Policy. In an organization with a decentralized structure in which the heads of individual units are vigilant to protect their authority, a proposal for a centralized information system will not be looked upon very kindly. The proponents of such a proposal would have to demonstrate enormous advantages with respect to performance to have the proposal accepted.

The criteria developed through this function will be used in function 5 to select the best solution.

Function 3: Determine Current Status and Constraints

This function comprises studying the system's environment, especially user needs; determining constraints; and auditing the current status.

Studying the environment and user needs. How many people need to be served? What are their problems and what information do they need to solve them? How big must the data base be to provide useful service? (How many statistical data items? How many technical parts? How many documents?) How much is the monthly or annual increase?

Determining constraints. Like performance criteria, constraints deal with properties of possible solutions. But there is an important difference. Criteria are relative: a low score on one criterion may be compensated for by a high score on another criterion. Constraints, however, are absolute: if a constraint is not met, the solution is not feasible (unless some way to overcome the constraint can be found after all; see function 5). For example, consider the problem of finding the optimal place for a public library branch. If the city owns only three different lots in the area where the branch is to be built and there are no properties for sale, then any other location is not feasible, however suitable it may be with respect to accessibility by the prospective users. Or assume that top management has set a *cost ceiling* of $150,000 per year for an information system to be developed; no matter how much better a $175,000 system would be compared to all the cheaper solutions, it cannot be pursued.

A *time constraint* arises if a task has a deadline. A team that has been assembled to study the safety of nuclear power plants and directed to finish its report within a year needs information now; there is no time to develop a special index language and to index many documents—no matter how much better service could be achieved by this solution.

A *policy constraint* arises, for example, if the sentiment against centralized services within the organization is so strong that no proposal for a centralized information system has a chance of being accepted—no matter what its technical merits.

Auditing the current status. Is there a formal or informal system now serving the objectives? How well does it work? What procedures or methods are used? Even if the R and D laboratory of a company does not have a formally constituted information center, an information system does exist. The scientists, engineers, and other staff undertake activities through which they obtain information. A library may consider replacing its existing manual circulation system by an automated one, or improving the manual system. Many insights for the design of the new system, including the definition of objectives, can be gained from a careful analysis of the existing system; this is sometimes called systems analysis (in a narrow sense).

Functions 2 and 3, defining objectives and determining the current status, interact. On the one hand, the list of objectives and criteria serves as a guideline in the analysis of an existing system. On the other hand, knowledge of the system environment is necessary and knowledge of the operations of the present system is helpful in translating the overall objectives into specific objectives and criteria.

For example, planning an information system that will result in improved product design requires thorough knowledge of the nature of the products, the ways in which engineers go about developing these products, the type of information that might lead to improved product design, the sources in which such information is contained, and the method of information transfer that would be acceptable to the engineers.

To give another example, planning public library services that make a contribution to the improvement of the living standard in a community requires knowledge of the problems in the community. Is there high unemployment? This would call for information services that help people to educate themselves (either through educational programs in the library supported by appropriate materials or through referral to job training programs) and that assist in finding jobs. Or would improvement of living result from wiser use of existing resources, both public and private? Would the people in the community read suitable brochures or books, or should the information be channeled through community leaders to reach those who most need it?

Translating the broad objectives into specific objectives starts the process to be considered in function 4, Generate possible solutions. The specific objectives are the means to reach the overall objectives. In function 4, the means–end chain is worked out further.

The present situation, which is determined through function 3, and the desired future situation, which is defined by the objectives, combine to make up the problem to be solved.

Function 4: Generate Possible Solutions

There are many ways for achieving the specific objectives in the context of the system environment. There are existing solutions to be found, for example by reading the literature, and new solutions to be invented. Creativity should not be overly stifled by the constraints. Sometimes the best solution violates a constraint, but perhaps the constraint can be removed. On the other hand, it would not be wise to spend a great amount of time and money working out a solution violating a constraint that can clearly not be removed. Thus function 4 is primarily concerned with idea collection and generation, not with critical selection. Unusual ideas, even if they seem far out in the beginning, might lead to the best solution. Critical analysis of the ideas generated is the task of function 5.

Function 5: Select Solution

Any solution that violates a constraint can be eliminated right away unless it is expected to be far superior to any other solution considered, in which case it should be kept active. Such a judgment may be based on intuition or on a preliminary analysis that applies the selection criteria developed in function 2 and considers the severity of the constraint being violated. From the solutions that survive this feasibility test, the best one is selected by applying the selection criteria; if there are many criteria, this is a complex task. The process has given rise to a whole field, decision theory (see Section 6.5).

Function 4, Generate possible solutions, and function 5, Select solution, interact strongly. First, evaluation with respect to the selection criteria may generate ideas for improving a solution. Any quantitative parameter of a solution, such as the price to be charged for a service to maximize profit, can be computed in function 5 using methods of operations research. Second, there are two extreme patterns into which one can organize the conduct of functions 4 and 5. The first pattern is called *optimizing:* Here one generates all possible solutions in function 4 and then selects the best one through function 5. The second pattern is called *satisficing:* Here one generates one possible solution and evaluates it immediately. If it is acceptable, it is selected; if it is not acceptable, one goes back to function 4, generates another solution, and so forth, until an acceptable solution is found. With optimizing a great amount of effort is spent on generating and evaluating solutions. With satisficing much less effort is needed, and while the solution found may not be the best, the difference may not be very great. These two patterns are extremes on a continuous scale. Just how much effort should be spent on generating and evaluating solutions depends on how much is at stake. To most people it would not be worthwhile to spend three additional days shopping to save $20 in buying a car. On the other hand, if a $10 billion weapon system is being considered, it might be worthwhile to spend $500 million on a careful analysis of all available options.

The selection process may suggest that no satisfactory solution can be found; it then becomes necessary to go back and devise more realistic objectives or to go back a step further and redefine the system. It might also emerge that more information about the system environment is needed to make a meaningful selection decision; it then becomes necessary to go back to function 3 and collect more information.

Once a solution has been selected, it must be described in sufficient detail to produce a general systems design, a blueprint for function 6, Assembly of system rules and specifications.

Function 6: Assemble and Test System Rules and Specifications for Equipment and Personnel

This function continues function 4 on a much more specific level for the one solution selected. Examples are constructing or acquiring an index language, a cataloging code, filing rules, or a computer program, and testing them. Subtasks within this function may require a systems analysis of their own.

During the construction and testing, difficulties not foreseen previously may be discovered. It may also turn out that the performance is not as good as expected or that the cost is higher than expected. In each of these cases, one must go back to functions 5 and 4 or even further in the systems analysis process.

Function 7: Install the System

This function involves hiring and/or training the personnel who are to operate the system; getting ready any hardware and supplies that are needed (e.g., file drawers, microfilm machines, terminals, computers); and converting any old data to a new format (especially data from a manual system to machine-readable form). A real-life test, called pilot operation, may also be considered part of this function; it may be performed in parallel with existing procedures.

Function 8: Operate the System

This function involves carrying out the operations prescribed by the systems design.

Function 9: Maintain the System

This includes maintenance in the narrow sense as well as continuous evaluation and adaptation to new situations or other improvements. Both require continuous quality control by comparing the results of system operation continuously with the objectives. If deviations occur, one or more of the systems analysis functions must be repeated. Deviations may be the result of internal system malfunction or of changes in the system environment that require modifications in the system.

Both management or policy-makers and systems analysts or staff participate in the decision-making process. Management should take the deciding role in functions 1 and 2, System delineation and definition of objectives, and in function 5, Selection of solution. The other functions should be left primarily to the systems analysts.

6.3 PHASES IN SYSTEMS ANALYSIS: SYSTEM LIFE CYCLE

One outcome of the systems analysis process described in Section 6.2 is a decision whether

- a new system should be installed (to replace an existing system or to perform an entirely new function),

- an existing system should be modified or left as is, or
- an existing system should be discontinued without replacement.

In the rational approach such decisions are based on a comparison of expected benefits with expected costs. But a systems analysis requires considerable resources in itself, and this expense should be incurred only if there is a reasonable chance that a beneficial change in the status quo can be found. Unwarranted expense can be avoided by organizing the systems analysis process into several *phases:* The process starts with a very brief preliminary analysis (phase A); if things look promising, the process moves on to an intermediate analysis (phase B) and, if warranted, to a more costly detailed analysis (phase C). If things still look good, the process continues with design (phase D) and, if all goes well, assembly (phase E), installation (phase F), and operation and maintenance (phase G). Phases A–C constitute a spiral of three consecutive cycles of performing systems analysis functions 1–5 with increasing thoroughness. Phase C deals very thoroughly with functions 1–3, assessing the problem, and phase D covers functions 4 and 5, specifying a solution. From then on each phase deals with one or two functions in the sequence given in Fig. 6.1. Phase E deals with function 6, assembly; phase F with function 7, installation; and phase G with functions 8 and 9, operation and maintenance. The functions to be performed in each phase are shown in Fig. 6.2.

The outcome of the deliberation of phase A is *not* a decision whether to go ahead with the system but merely a decision whether to go ahead with phase B of the deliberation. Likewise, at the end of phase B, a decision is made whether to proceed with phase C, and so on. Only completion of phase E leads to the final decision on system installation and operation. Whereas much of the work in each phase is done by systems analysts, the decision to proceed to the next phase is for management to make.

In the following we discuss each phase.

Phase A: Conception of Idea

Somebody, either a manager/policy-maker or a systems analyst, has the idea that a new system should be created, that an existing system should be modified, or that an existing system should be abolished. A very preliminary analysis, implicitly or explicitly performing systems analysis functions 1 through 5 in a superficial way, will show whether the idea is worth pursuing.

Example 1.

The director of the information center of a company has the idea of establishing an in-house bibliographic data base dealing with documents produced in-house and with published documents of particular interest to

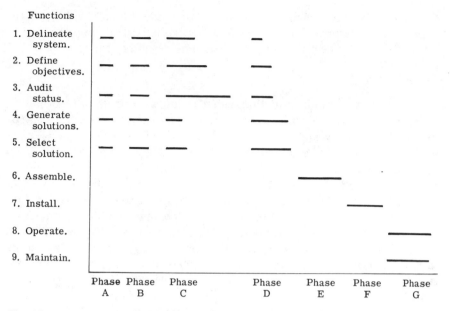

Fig. 6.2   Functions performed in each phase of systems analysis.
(Line length represents the amount of effort spent.)

the company. The data base could be updated as literature searches are done. She thinks that such a data base could improve information support significantly and that it would be of a manageable size. She decides to pursue the idea further.

Example 2.

A university administrator has the idea that a machine-readable file of course descriptions could be established to produce course catalogs, to provide on-line access for students and faculty, and to support the information needs of curriculum committees. He thinks that such a data base would lead to better curriculum planning and to better course selection by students. The data base is of manageable size and catalog production could be cheaper in the long run. Thus he decides to pursue the idea further.

Phase B: Initiation

This phase repeats functions 1 through 5, but somewhat more thoroughly. It should lead to enough insight for deciding whether a full-fledged systems analysis is appropriate while using the minimum of resources possible. Consulting experts is a quick way to get preliminary information on various aspects of the envisioned system. A rough cost estimate (with an error margin of 100% upwards or 50% downwards) is part of this phase. This phase ends with a decision whether to commit resources for phase C.

Example 1.

The director of the information center examines records of information needs, including records of past search requests, to develop a clearer sense of the specific objectives of the in-house bibliographic data base: How many search requests should be answerable from the in-house data base alone? To what types of in-house documents should it provide access? What quality of performance in individual searches should one aim at? She also looks at costs: How many document records would be included? How many would need to be indexed and input from scratch? How many could be transferred from other machine-readable bibliographical data bases? Are royalties to be paid? What savings could be achieved by running search requests against the in-house data base rather than using a commercial search service? What are possible ways to set up the system? Is there an existing ISAR program or a data base management system that would make writing a new program easier? How thoroughly should the indexing be done? From all these considerations evolves a preliminary image of the costs and benefits of the system being considered. If the costs are much out of line, the idea is abandoned at this stage. If the rough cost estimate is $110,000 and the savings to be achieved and the benefits to be reaped from the system are expected to total $100,000, a detailed systems analysis is warranted because the real cost may turn out to be only $80,000 and a better estimate of savings and benefits might be $150,000. Of course, the detailed analysis may also show that the real cost is $150,000, in which case the process would stop after phase C.

Example 2.

The university administrator calls in an information systems expert and a data-processing expert to discuss his idea. He obtains a preliminary estimate of the volume of data and the resulting costs for input and storage. Using this information, he considers the possibility of printing fewer catalogs and providing on-line access to the machine-readable catalog data base instead. With this option, costs arise for installing the computer program and converting all the cataloging data (initial costs), adding new data, storing the data base, computer time for on-line access and computer typesetting, and printing. (Assume terminals are already available on campus.) If the total cost promises to be lower than the cost of the existing catalog production and the cost (mostly hidden) that curriculum committees incur in gathering the information they need, a more detailed systems analysis is warranted, based on cost alone. If the new option is more expensive, improvements in expected performance may still warrant further exploration. On the other hand, the preliminary analysis might indicate that the new system is not expected to function as well as the old one, and that expected savings are not sufficient to offset the loss in quality, or that the new system is far too expensive to be considered.

Phase C: Detailed Analysis

This phase repeats systems analysis functions 1 through 3 (Define the system, Determine objectives, and Audit the current status) in much more detail and with enough anticipation of functions 4 and 5 (Generate and Select solution) to make a decision whether it is worthwhile to move on to the costly design phase. The cost estimate can be refined (perhaps to an error margin of 50% upward and 33% downward). This phase ends with a decision whether to commit resources to the design phase.

Phase D: Design

This phase repeats systems analysis functions 4 and 5, Generate and Select solutions, in detail. The final design is reviewed with respect to its internal logic as well as its relationship to other systems and its conformance to general policies. The cost estimate can be refined (perhaps to an error margin of 10%). Benefits are also known more precisely once the system is designed. The additional information available now may show that the proposed system is not worthwhile after all; the preliminary judgments made in previous phases were wrong, and the process stops. On the other hand, if all turns out as expected, one proceeds to phase E, Assemble and test the system rules and specifications. This is not yet a decision to install the system. It is quite possible that unexpected snags will be encountered during the assembly. The installation decision, therefore, should wait until the assembly is finished.

Phase E: Assembly and Testing of System Rules and Specifications

This phase involves systems analysis function 6. After testing is completed, the cost estimate for installing and operating the system should be fairly precise. Now a well-founded decision can be made whether to go ahead with the installation of the system. A system should never be installed simply on the grounds that much effort has been spent in assembling it. If installing and operating the system cost more than its benefits are worth, then it is better for the organization to abandon the effort at this point and write off the system analysis and assembly costs. One objective of the phased approach to systems analysis is to minimize the chances of this happening. However, in some cases, only actual assembly and testing can give enough information about the system being considered.

Phase F: Installation

This phase involves systems analysis function 7.

Phase G: System Operation and Maintenance

This phase involves systems analysis functions 8 and 9.

Continuous monitoring of system performance triggers ideas for adaptations and improvements (fine tuning) while leaving the basic design intact. Ideas for adaptations or improvements can arise from several sources:

- Better insight into user needs or changes in user needs, resulting in a change of objectives. Often users recognize the full potential of a new system, particularly an information system, only after a period of use; they may find additional ways in which the system can be useful and demand additional system features. Or circumstances change; for example, a company may start a new product line, or a school may put heavy emphasis on independent study, which redefines the role of the media center.
- Changes in the environment, particularly in the constraints.
- Changes in solutions: New technology or simply better solution ideas, perhaps stimulated through the experience with the system, may appear.

Any one of these factors may also lead to the idea that the search for a better system or a major system overhaul should begin: The whole process starts all over again with phase A, Conception of idea. Such reassessments are part of the *system life cycle.* Any system should be analyzed "from scratch" at regular intervals. In the political arena this is exemplified by laws that must be reviewed every 5 or 10 years; unless they are reenacted, they are discontinued.

Changes may also occur during the process of systems analysis. The new system may be fully designed, or even assembled and ready for installation, when a new technology becomes available and makes the chosen solution obsolete. Phase D or perhaps even phase C must be repeated.

6.4 INFORMATION AND DATA COLLECTION IN SYSTEMS ANALYSIS

Function 3, Determine current status and constraints, *is* data collection. It involves collecting data on the user's tasks or problems, on needs, and on information-seeking behavior. Chapter 7 discusses how such studies can be done. It also involves collecting data on how the existing system works, determining

- what is done
- using what *input,*
- with what *resources,*
- achieving what *results (output).*

One can form a good image of the system being studied by identifying all processes or subsystems, dividing each process into its component steps, and examining each step with respect to its function in the overall process and its costs. Some steps may not be needed at all. Determining the costs often involves detailed time studies.

Various methods exist for data collection:

Examining records created in the system (e.g., the catalog, any forms used in acquisitions and cataloging operations, circulation records, and records of reference requests).

Observing people and noting everything that they are doing. One can observe one person, thus capturing data about one part of a process, or one can follow, for example, a book from acquisition to cataloging to shelving. In the latter example, one observes in each step what records enter the step, who does what to them during the step, what additional records are produced as a result of the step, and what records are passed on to later steps. Furthermore, one observes the sources of all data that are entered into records.

Interviewing people about what they are doing and how long it takes them to do it. This method is not very reliable because it relies on people's memories. On the other hand, one might find out more about the rationale behind the activities in the existing system.

Data may be needed for all units—which means examining all records in the system, following all books processed in a given month, interviewing all staff members—or for a suitable sample.

In *function 2* the formulation of broad objectives may be determined, or at least aided, by a survey of those affected by the system; this may involve a very large effort (e.g., holding a referendum). Because broad objectives are based on value judgments, such a survey is often the only acceptable way. However, the translation into specific objectives is more technical in nature, requiring careful analysis by a knowledgeable expert. If we were to survey those affected by the system with respect to their preferences in order to determine specific objectives, we would supplant the expert systems analyst by the aggregate judgement of the system users, who usually have neither the time nor the expertise to study the problem carefully. We must ask, then, whether the aggregation of many partially considered judgments is better than the result of a careful analysis.

Nevertheless, the survey method is sometimes used to determine specific objectives. The service mix to be offered by the information center of a company is an example. One could ask the scientists and engineers how important various services are to their work, presenting them with a list such as the following (this is a partial list for illustration only):

• Provide SDI service
• Provide retrospective search service
• Have core journals in own, separate collection (for routing or browsing)
• Provide fast interlibrary loan
• Provide reading space
• Provide microform readers for office use
• Provide terminals for office use
• Provide tailor-made packages of substantive data

Each scientist or engineer would be asked to indicate the importance of each of these services by points, using 100 points total. Again, the validity of this method is questionable.

Determining the service mix to be offered by an information system could also be considered as the design blueprint resulting from functions 4 and 5, Generate and Select solution, in a high level analysis of the system.

Function 4, Generate possible solutions, *function 6,* Assemble system rules and specifications, and *function 7,* Install the System, require information about solutions to the same or similar problems reported elsewhere and about ideas and technologies that might help in generating solutions and later in assembling the new system; they also require information about available personnel and equipment, such as computer hardware and software. Suggestions from those affected by the system can also be helpful.

Function 5, Select solution, requires much information about the system environment and about the outcomes of each of the possible solutions with respect to the selection criteria. Again, the selection of a solution could be achieved by an aggregate judgment derived from a survey, but this would be even more questionable here than in determining specific objectives.

Function 9, Maintenance, requires data on system performance collected during system operation, data on changes in the system environment and in user needs, and data on new solution possibilities.

6.5 SELECTION DECISIONS

The selection decision is very easy if only one criterion must be considered and if the outcome is predictable, that is, if

- there is one specific objective—only one performance criterion;
- costs and the other criteria mentioned in function 2b need not be considered;
- for each solution under consideration, performance is predictable with certainty.

In this ideal situation one simply selects the solution that scores highest on the one criterion. In reality none of these conditions holds and the decision-making situation can become quite complex. In the following, we will introduce this complexity step by step.

First assume that cost does matter so that there are two selection criteria, performance and cost, both predictable with certainty. In this situation we can use the following selection process: Some solutions can be rejected out of hand. Assume solution C has a performance score of 8 and costs $50,000 and solution F has a performance score of 5 and costs $100,000. C is better in both selection criteria—performance and cost—and so F can be eliminated right away. In this pair, C is called the *dominant* solution—C has only advantages—and F is called the *dominated* solution. In the first selection step, then, all dominated solutions are eliminated. Next comes the difficult part. How does one decide between solution C (performance score 8, cost $50,000) and solution H (performance score 10, cost $75,000)? For this decision we must know how the performance differential affects ultimate benefits (e.g., company profits). If an increase in performance score from 8 to 10 leads to an increase in company profits by $30,000, then the net profit increase achieved by choosing solution H is $5000. Thus we should choose solution H over solution C unless we can invest $5000 more profitably. This type of decision making is called cost–benefit analysis. It requires prediction of costs, performance, and, most difficult, ultimate benefits.

Matters are further complicated if multiple performance criteria as well as the additional criteria of timing and policy must be considered. A first selection can be made by applying the idea of dominance generalized to many criteria. Solution A dominates solution B if it is better than or at least as good as solution B on *all* of the selection criteria; conversely, B is a dominated solution. All dominated solutions can be eliminated. This may leave only one solution. If several solutions remain, advantages must be traded off against disadvantages. This can be done through a formula that combines the various performance criteria into a single measure, weighting them with respect to their contribution to ultimate benefits. This leaves four criteria (total performance score, cost, timing, and policy). At this point additional solutions may turn out to be dominated and thus dispensable. If there are still several solutions left, the best can be selected in one of three ways: (1) by intuitively trading off the scores on the four criteria; (2) by developing a formula that combines performance, timing, and policy into a single score and trading that score off against cost; or (3) by combining all four criteria into one single score and selecting the solution that scores highest.

Most real-life situations are too complex for a straightforward prediction of the scores on the selection criteria as required for the selection process just discussed. Examples of such complex situations are

Predicting the performance of an ISAR system depending on the type of index language chosen

Predicting performance of one national interlibrary loan center compared with a configuration of four regional centers with respect to speed of delivery and availability of materials (Added question: Where should those four regional centers be placed? Their locations affect the comparison with one national center!)

Predicting the development of the number of users of an on-line search service as a function of resource allocation between public relations and providing a high quality service

Predicting how variations in the loan period affect the availability of books

These problems can be addressed through system testing (e.g., with respect to the effects of an index language) and through the methods of *operations research.* An operations researcher develops models that yield the required predictions of system performance given data on the system environment obtained from actual data collection or, in a pinch, from an educated guess.

For example, predicting the effect of various configurations of resource libraries requires data on the interlibrary loan load generated in different regions of the country. Predicting the amount of use of an on-line search service requires knowledge of the following:

- the effect of publicity on first-time use of the service;
- the effect of word-of-mouth on first-time use; and
- the effect of search quality on the "return rate" of people who have used the search service once and on word-of-mouth propagation.

This knowledge of the systems environment is then fed into a mathematical model or a simulation model, which takes into account the numerous relationships between the variables involved in the system and predicts an outcome for each possible solution. The quality of the prediction depends on the adequacy of the model and on the accuracy of the data fed into it.

We have not reached the end of complexity yet. Very often the outcome of a solution depends on future developments in the system environment that cannot be predicted with certainty (decision-making under risk). An example is the quandary of how thoroughly to index in the face of uncertainty about the number of search requests to be expected. With some oversimplification it can be described as follows: There are two solutions, thorough indexing and superficial indexing. There are two possible developments in the environment, many search requests and few search requests. Thorough indexing is good if there are many search requests, but it is a waste of money if there are only a few search requests. Superficial indexing causes tremendous search effort if there are many search requests, but it is fine if there are only a few search requests. The choice of indexing method hinges on the probability of there being many or few search requests, respectively, and on the amounts of money involved (How much does thorough indexing cost? How much does it cost to do many searches if indexing is superficial?). Assume the probability of many requests is only 20%; thorough indexing is inadvisable, particularly if the cost for doing many searches—in the unlikely event they had to be done—would not be exorbitant. Now assume many requests and few requests are both equally likely and search effort outweighs indexing effort; now thorough indexing is better: while there is a 50% chance of wasting money on indexing, with superficial indexing there is a 50% chance of having to spend even more money on searching. The *theory of games* offers methods to solve such problems quantitatively. (These methods are often illustrated through the example of a player in a game who must decide on a move when he or she is not certain about the opponent's move.) The amount of risk due to uncertainties in the environment may vary from one solution to another.

6.6 RESOURCE-ORIENTED VERSUS PROCEDURE-ORIENTED SYSTEMS ANALYSIS

In systems analysis oriented toward resource allocation the emphasis is on questions like

- Should this system be built?
- Should this function be performed?
- Should this program be funded?

In short, emphasis is on the question *whether something should be done at all* or whether resources could be better spent elsewhere.

In procedure-oriented systems analysis emphasis is on *how a certain function should be performed.* The question is not whether to have an information system but how to organize it, what functions are needed in the system (functional analysis), and who should do them (organizational analysis). In a lower level example, the question is not whether books should be cataloged, but rather what is the most efficient way of cataloging books. For example,

- Should a worksheet be filled out before original cataloging is done at a computer terminal, or should the cataloging data be keyed directly from the book?
- Should books be cataloged by library assistants with subsequent check and revision or by professional catalogers without revision?

Devising a computer program is another example of procedure-oriented systems analysis.

These two aspects of systems analysis interact: Whether or not a function should be performed may depend on its cost, and the cost may be substantially reduced if a clever way of performing the function is found. Furthermore, there is no clear-cut borderline. As the functions considered become smaller and smaller, the question of whether to perform them becomes less and less a matter of resource allocation and more and more a matter of determining procedure. Nevertheless, it is useful to distinguish between these two aspects of systems analysis.

6.7 PERFORMANCE VERSUS IMPACT OF INFORMATION SERVICES

The *performance* of an information system refers to its role in the transfer of information from an information source to a user. It does not refer to the use of that information by the user. The term *effectiveness* has come to be used in the same limited sense. Examples of performance criteria are

- What fraction of the needs in its domain does the system fill?
- How complete are the answers the system gives?
- How well are the answers adapted to the user's background?

The information transferred has *impact* if the user arrives at a better decision or solution with the information than without it. Another impact of information might be that a person feels more sure about a decision, or happier about something, or more secure in his or her role. In each case a monetary or other *benefit* is associated with the information impact. (Misinformation or incomplete information may have a negative impact.)

Information may be transferred effectively but not be put to use and thus have no impact. Effective information transfer is a necessary but not sufficient condition for information use and impact. One could take the position that information use and impact are outside the purview of the information system designer and that the designer's responsibility is limited to ensuring effective information transfer. But this is a rather limited view. The ultimate objective of an information system is to achieve impact. The specific objectives or performance requirements must be formulated in such a way that this ultimate objective is supported. If the information being transferred through a system is not used or has no impact, perhaps the information system should not exist at all or perhaps it transfers information that is not helpful in making the decisions or solving the problems at hand. Or perhaps the information receivers do not have incentives for using the information to advantage. The information system designer should be very much concerned with these issues.

CHAPTER 7

Assessment of Users' Problems and Needs

OBJECTIVES

The objectives of this chapter are to emphasize the importance of studying user needs as a basis for information system evaluation and design and to sketch some approaches to studying needs, especially problem analysis.

INTRODUCTION

This book emphasizes information systems that have as their general objective assistance in problem solving. Through a study of user needs, this general objective is translated into more specific objectives and requirements. Such a study analyzes the information or entities that the users need for solving their problems and the benefits to be expected. It is also concerned with the ways in which the people to be served presently obtain information or entities and with existing sources and chains or paths that might be used to get information or entities to potential users (see the discussion in Chapter 4). Lastly, such a study collects data about the environment in which the information system is to work. All these data provide a solid basis for designing a cost-beneficial information system that delivers the information or entities needed for problem solving in a form suitable for the user and thus contributes to the general objective. A study of actual information use and impact (benefits) is also useful for monitoring the information system to see whether it lives up to expectations.

System design requires a general picture of needs, system operation requires specifics about the needs of individual users. A sample survey is sufficient to obtain the general picture, but each potential user must be studied to determine specific needs.

All information about needs should be organized in an *information direc-*

tory. If a one-time large study of needs is not feasible, the information directory can be created through an incremental process. Clarifying the need of a user submitting a search request (e.g., through a reference interview) is part of this total process of studying user needs. The information directory should be updated as needs change.

In many information systems, particularly in many libraries, the extremely important function of general study of needs is carried out in a very cavalier manner. It may be said, for example, that the head librarian of the public library is "in touch with the community." With what part of the community? The head librarian cannot help but associate with those members of the community with whom she feels most comfortable, and who share her beliefs and values. For example, it is difficult for a middle-class white librarian to intuit the needs of a predominantly black and predominantly poor community. The resulting picture of needs may be very biased indeed. A more systematic effort, preferably a scientifically designed sample survey, is needed to obtain an unbiased picture.

Assessing a client's problems and then putting a technical apparatus to work to solve these problems is the hallmark of professionalism. Thus, this chapter is central to an understanding of information workers as professionals.

7.1 USER STUDIES AS A BASIS FOR SYSTEM DESIGN

A user study should answer the following questions:

Who Are the People, Organizations, or Systems To Be Served?

How important are their decisions or problem solutions?

How valuable is their time?

What are their characteristics, backgrounds, and skills? What are their physical abilities to communicate? What language abilities do they have? What kind of information or entities are they able to assimilate and use? Would training be possible to improve their skills?

How well can they articulate their needs?

What are their searching skills with respect to general principles of searching, with respect to searching specific types of sources (e.g., on-line searching), and with respect to specific sources? Do they want to do their own searches?

Where are they located? What means of communication do they have now (e.g., telephone, terminal, reading machine for the blind, transportation)? (When establishing the system, we may add to these.)

Do they themselves use the information or entities, or do they pass it on to others?

How homogeneous is the community to be served?

What Are Their Problems?

Which of these problems are to be addressed by the information system? Is there a wide variety of problems? How important are the problems? How urgent are they when they arise?

What Information Or Entities Are Needed to Solve These Problems?

What is the scope of the information or entities needed?

What concepts or other criteria are needed in searching? (As detailed a list as possible)

What Needs Are Met Now?

From what sources? Through what paths? How well? At what cost? How do users go about seeking for information or entities?

What Searches Are To Be Expected?

How many searches (per day, per week, per month)? Spread out equally or in bunches? (Searches may be requested by the user or done on the initiative of the system; they may be recurring for SDI or retrospective.)

How many of the searches will be broad, how many specific? How many of the searches will be ill defined?

How much variation among searches? (A few often-repeated standard topics or every search topic different?)

What are the requirements for answer quality? What about deadlines and other search requirements?

What Is the Present or Expected Impact of the Information?

What improvements could occur in solutions or decisions? What benefits could result?

The answers to these questions have direct consequences for system design: If users cannot apply the information or entities to their problems, the information system must provide for further processing and analysis of data (e.g., through a computerized decision support system or through a person serving in a counselor role). If many users can and want to do their own searching on an on-line system, and if analysis shows that user's own searching is at least as cost-effective as searching by an intermediary, then the system should be easy to use: an index language with concepts and terms the user can understand, a set of search commands that is easy to use, and special error diagnosis and user assistance. (This emphasis on ease of use may detract from system power and efficiency of use by professional searchers.) The more important the users' problems, the more money is justified to increase answer quality.

The problem analysis leads to a determination of information and entities needed. The concepts and other criteria needed for searching lead directly to the conceptual schema, particularly the index language.

A new information system should concentrate on unmet needs unless needs met now can be served better. Sometimes an indirect path is best for getting information or entities to the users; information may be more effective when filtered through an intermediary or gatekeeper.

The effort spent on building the ISAR system should be commensurate with the number and complexity of searches expected. If searches are specific and require precise answers that do not contain a lot of irrelevant material, a specific index language is needed. If search topics are often ill defined, the system must provide for interaction (e.g., browsing in the shelves; user doing, or being present during, an on-line search). If there are only a few standard search topics, the ISAR system can be simple; if search topics vary widely, the ISAR system must allow for retrieval with any combination of concepts and other search criteria. Short deadlines require an ISAR system that can pinpoint needed material quickly.

The design of information systems and services must be based on the assessed *need for substantive data or entities,* not on a stated need for access to sources. For example, the statement that users need better access to journals refers *not* to a need for substantive data but to a *means* for obtaining substantive data. Determining means is part of system design, not of needs assessment.

Design must not be based solely or even primarily on present information habits and/or the desires or preferences for additional or modified information services expressed by users. Both habits and preferences are biased by the user's preconceived notion of what an information system can do. It is the information professional's responsibility to design information sources and services that will meet the needs for substantive data or entities in the most efficient fashion.

The following example illustrates both points. Assume the users of a library would prefer a larger journal collection; in a preference-based design, the library would try to increase the journal collection without first investigating the following points.

- Would the substantive data to be obtained from the journals indeed fill the most pressing information needs? (No needs assessment.)

- If the answer is yes: Are journals the best source for these substantive data? (Let user preferences, rather than analysis, determine the choice of means.)
- If journals are the best source, is increasing the journal collection the best way to improve access to journals?

Consider another example. In many subject areas users now rely much more on informal interpersonal information transfer than on formal mechanisms such as the literature and systems providing access to the literature. One might conclude that fewer resources should be spent on the formal information transfer system. However, a properly organized formal information transfer system (e.g., one relying heavily on on-line access to information) might well perform more efficiently many functions now performed by informal information transfer. This possibility should be considered before decisions on the design of the formal information transfer system are made. Furthermore, the formal system is vital for information transfer to *gatekeepers* (as discussed in Chapter 4).

User attitudes and preferences are important in design decisions. The best information service is useless if it is not used. In some cases, user attitudes are so strong that they establish constraints for design. In other cases, user attitudes might be changed by user education, but then the costs for the user education program must be included in the costs for the design alternatives being considered. In summary, user attitudes and preferences are important ingredients of system design but should not be translated directly into a design. On the other hand, the principles advocated here are not an excuse for design decisions that go against justified user preferences while serving the convenience of the information professional.

7.2 PRINCIPLES FOR THE STUDY OF NEEDS

7.2.1 SETTING PRIORITIES

Resource limitations usually preclude investigating everybody's needs; management must set priorities as to whose needs are most urgent and should therefore be investigated. It is not uncommon to take the most convenient road and investigate the needs of present users (e.g., administering questionnaires or interviews to people as they enter a public library). However, this is an extremely biased sample; it neglects the people who do not come to the library but who nevertheless may have more pressing needs. The situation is akin to a counseling department in a high school that concentrates its resources on those students who take the initiative to seek counseling. These are probably *not* the students who need counseling most. The counseling department should find other means for identifying students who should be counseled first.

Not all the problems of the people selected are of equal importance; management must decide next what problems and needs to investigate. Like acquisition of books and other entities, acquisition of needs requires selection and value judgments.

7.2.2 SHARED RESPONSIBILITY— USER AND INFORMATION PROFESSIONAL

Assessment of the needs for information or entities is the joint responsibility of the (potential) user and the information professional. To rely solely on the user's statement about his or her needs means to abdicate professional responsibility and would be akin to a doctor's relying on a patient's assessment of necessary treatment. Some users do not fully understand their own problems, much less the information or entities that could be used to solve them. Other users may not be aware of available information and therefore may not articulate a need for it; or they may not follow a systematic problem-solving strategy which would make the connection between available information or entities and the problem to be solved. The information professional must probe much more deeply, study the problems to be solved, and, together with the user, draw inferences about the information or entities needed.

7.2.3 NEED, WANT, DEMAND OR RECOGNIZED NEED, USE, AND IMPACT

Distinguishing the following concepts contributes much to the clarity of user studies:

- need for information or entities as perceived by others ("objective" assessment based on problem analysis, commonly referred to as *need*)
- need as perceived by self, commonly referred to as *want*
- need as articulated by the (potential) user (*demand*) or by an information system (*recognized need*)
- information *use*
- information *impact* on achievement or problem solving

Not all needs are translated into wants; the user may not be aware that available information or entities could help to solve the problem at hand or may, perhaps subconsciously, perceive the cost of obtaining such information or entities as so high as to suppress even the thought of getting the information or entities. Conversely, not all wants correspond to real needs. Articulation of wants into demands is subject to the same barriers as described for needs into wants. Demand results in use only if, in the user's judgment, benefits from using the information exceed the costs. The user makes this cost–benefit analysis on the basis of his perception of present information sources.

These considerations show clearly how important it is that the information system actively recognize needs. As an example, consider environmental impact statements used by federal agencies, such as the Department of Energy, in making decisions about projects, such as nuclear power plants. Many of these agencies would be perfectly satisfied to make such decisions without considering environmental impact, yet the resulting decisions would often be far from optimal. A real information need is not translated into a want, much less a demand. In this case, Congress acted in the role of the information professional, determining an information need and writing it into legislation. This example also highlights the distinction between user satisfaction and the impact of information on achievement.

The impact of information is hard to measure, yet knowing the impact is crucial for a cost–benefit analysis. It is difficult enough to trace the impact of a single chunk of information on a problem solution or decision; it is even more difficult to estimate the impact of an information system, that is, the impact of all the chunks of information transferred with its help to the users (final receivers). Figure 7.1 outlines the possible kinds of effects of an information system. The impact of a given information system can be assessed

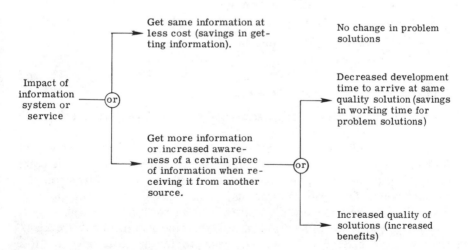

Fig. 7.1 Impact of an information system.

only in the context of the total information transfer network. The user receives information from many sources; analysis must determine the unique contribution of the system under consideration.

7.2.4 UNENCUMBERED ASSESSMENT OF NEEDS

The assessment of needs for information or entities, be it general for system design or specific for system operation, must not be encumbered by the limitations of any present or future information system, lest the assessment of needs be biased and result in a less than optimal system design or search. The user's perception of his or her own needs, as well as of the best means to satisfy them, is too often strongly influenced by what presently exists. It is the information professional's task to free the user from these encumbrances.

7.3 APPROACHES TO STUDYING NEEDS

There are three approaches to the study of needs:

- analyze the problems or decisions the users face;
- collect the users' statements about their needs; or
- examine past use and assume that it reflects future needs.

A combination of these with emphasis on problem analysis gives a good base for designing an information system with high impact.

There are three sources of information on needs:

- records of tasks, functions, problems, and decisions;
- records of past use; and
- the users themselves who can describe their problems, their past use, and their own assessment of their needs.

We will first discuss these approaches and sources in general and then add specifics in Sections 7.3.1–7.3.3.

From the premise that information is for problem solving, it follows that problem analysis is the most basic approach to studying needs. There are many records that can give information about a user's problem domain: organization charts, job descriptions, project descriptions, and publications. The information professional must immerse himself in the subject area and the structure of its problems. (This is true also for the reference interview, as we shall see in Chapter 17.) Each problem identified gives rise to a list of needs, and each need leads to a list of sources suitable to fill the need. This can serve as a yardstick in analyzing present information-seeking behavior.

A limited picture of needs emerges from an analysis of past and present use, particularly requests submitted to an information service; the answers given; and the reactions of or the effect on the users. The results of such an analysis are limited by two factors: Some people (maybe the majority) never submit requests. Even those who do, submit only requests that *in their perception* can be handled by the information system.

Since it is much easier to collect data on requests than to actually seek out people and study their problems and needs, there is always the temptation to use this information as the only or primary evidence on user needs. However, if an information system is designed primarily on the basis of the requests that are submitted, a mismatch between the service and real needs can develop; many needs that may be more important than those submitted may go unmet. As an example, consider an inner city area and a newly developed suburban area, both served by bookmobiles. Assume both bookmobiles are stocked with essentially the same collection and that the collection is geared to middle-class problems, tastes, and values. Circulation statistics show that the inner city bookmobile is used very little, the suburban bookmobile very heavily. Based on these data, the library system may decide to discontinue the inner city bookmobile and build a new branch in the suburban area. This example illustrates a vicious circle: An information system as designed initially serves a certain segment of the clientele, which indeed uses the system. Other segments, whose needs may be more pressing, do not use it because it does not serve their purposes. In 3 years a study of information needs based on the present users is undertaken; it shows only a part of the real needs of the clientele. The system will be modified to serve these needs still better while neglecting others even more.

Since users tend to submit requests that, in their experience, can be answered satisfactorily by the system, the *kind of requests* submitted may not reflect real needs. For example, archives receive few subject requests, most of them submitted by inexperienced users. Experienced users submit mostly requests for specifically identified documents or document groups, documents produced by a given organization, or documents mentioning certain names, which are all requests that can be answered reasonably well from a system organized by standard archival methods. One might conclude that the experienced users do not need to ask subject requests, since they already know the documents needed for their research or at least know the organization that produces such documents, and that, therefore, there is no need to do subject indexing in archives. But it is equally possible that the experienced users have learned not to submit subject requests because the results would not be satisfactory anyway.

In addition to shedding light on needs, request analysis allows for an operational test of the information system. Compared with retrieval experiments, analysis of requests has the disadvantage of diminished controls but the advantage of closer relationship to real life. Analysis of information use can also be helpful in assessing impact by following the user's problem-solving process and asking about the role of pieces of information that the user has seen, as known from request records.

If at all possible, the results of independent problem analysis and of information use studies should be checked, augmented, and put in perspective by querying the users themselves. This can be done through interviews or questionnaires about the users' own perception of their problems and needs and of their present ways of obtaining needed information or entities, about their preferences, and about their perceived competence in seeking information or entities. Ideally, the interview is a joint problem-solving session between the user and the information professional. The information professional must be well prepared in order for this to happen.

7.3.1 PROBLEM ANALYSIS BASED ON RECORDS

Various types of records provide data on the tasks or functions of (potential) users within an organization, within the community, or in other contexts. The analyst prepares a list of actual problems to be solved or decisions to be made by the user (a special form, one for each problem, may be useful). For each problem identified she derives a list of needs, indicating the importance of information or entities and their potential impact on achievement. Each need gives rise to a list of sources suitable to fill the need.

For a needs study in an organization, the results of a systems analysis of the whole organization, especially accurate job descriptions, are helpful. Superiors can also give information about the tasks or functions and resulting needs of their staff.

For a study of the needs of the poor living in the inner city, a socio-economic analysis of the community and its problems can provide useful insights. In a study of scientists and engineers much can be learned from their publications and descriptions of past and present projects. Curricula and course outlines are a good source for determining information needs of students and teachers.

A typology of data adapted to the particular context, such as the one shown in Fig. 7.2, is useful as a framework for developing the list of needs of an individual user.

Chemical structure data and similar scientific data

Data on methods
    Data on analytical methods in chemistry
    Data on methods for cell cultures and animal experiments

Data on results of laboratory experiments

Data on food samples

Data on food poisonings

Data on food consumption

Data on food production

Legal data

Fig. 7.2   Sample types of data (Bureau of Foods).

7.3.2 ANALYSIS OF REQUESTS AND SEARCHING BEHAVIOR

Figure 7.3 gives an illustrative list of items of information that can be collected for each request (or a sample of requests) and indicates how each item of information is linked to system design. Some items are included to pinpoint problem requests that have poor results or require much effort. A careful analysis of these problem requests can reveal weaknesses in the ISAR system—in particular, missing descriptors. Many of the items listed are important not just for analysis but also for doing the search (see Chapter 17).

The information can be collected reasonably well for requests submitted to an information specialist in a public or special library or information center. For an on-line system it is more difficult; at least some of the information can be collected by displaying a presearch and a postsearch questionnaire at the terminal. It is particularly important to capture the query statement. If—as is common—only the query formulation is entered, the investigator analyzing the search protocol has no way of knowing whether this formulation, or more generally, the overall search strategy, is adequate for the information need at hand. The investigator also cannot draw any conclusions on the adequacy of the ISAR system, particularly its index language, with respect to the information need. Simple usage statistics about descriptors do not reveal when a descriptor was misused, when a descriptor is not used when it should be (and thus shows low frequency of use), or when a descriptor needed for expressing the query topic is not available. Essential feedback is thus lost. Personal interviews uncover information about requests of end users searching a card or book catalog.

Beyond this static analysis of requests we should look at the dynamics of the search process. How do information professionals and end users approach the information system? Does the ISAR system support the searcher's approach? Is the searcher able to exploit the power of the system?

Item

1. User and user background; importance of user

2. Date received/deadline/date answered

3. Statement of the problem; the purpose of the search. Importance of the problem

4. Query statement (statement of the information or entities needed) as presented by the user or as written by an information specialist recognizing a need. This statement must in no way be encumbered by any limitation of the ISAR system, especially the ability of the index language to express topics. Otherwise such limitations do not become apparent.

5. Query formulation in terms of the index language

5.1 Field of request

5.2 Main viewpoint of the request: geographical area versus subject (e.g., economics)

6. Type of information (e.g., theories, methods, empirical data)

7. Type of request (e.g., specific data or general orientation; subject or author/title/date request)

8. Requirements for answer quality, especially recall (percentage of relevant entities correctly retrieved) and discrimination (percentage of irrelevant entities correctly rejected)

9. Manhours spent on processing the request

10. Special comments (e.g., number of places looked, concepts for which no descriptor is available, obtaining further clarification from the user)

11. Number of items found

12. User evaluation, especially assessment of discrimination and estimate of recall; independent evaluation

13. Impact of the answers on the user's work, including missed benefits due to *not* obtaining information or entities needed.

Fig. 7.3   Sample items for a request analysis form.

In a limited way such an analysis can be done by studying transaction logs of on-line searches, particularly if the query statement is available. Much preferable—and, for manual ISAR systems, mandatory—is observation of a searcher who at the same time verbalizes the rationale for her actions.

7.3.3 QUERYING (POTENTIAL) USERS ABOUT THEIR NEEDS

Interviews with (potential) users or data collection through questionnaires are an important source of information on needs. They complement the in-

Purpose or importance

Interpret the other data collected about the request.

Identify problem requests (answered after the deadline).

Interpret other data about the request. Introduce descriptors for problems and purposes; such descriptors are useful for request-oriented indexing.

Identify descriptor candidates; compare query statement and query formulation (topic expressed in terms of the index language) to reveal limitations of the ISAR system, especially in the ability of the index language to express the search topic. Concentrate on requests that were difficult to process (2 and 10) or had poor results (12). Also check on the ability of the information specialist (who is part of the ISAR system) to formulate queries; he or she may need more training.

For example, identify fields with many problem requests.

Data base organization. For example, arrange a file either by country first and then within country by subject or in the opposite order.

Identify types of information that lead to problem requests.

Identify types with many problem requests.

Compare with recall and discrimination actually achieved to test the ability of the ISAR system to respond to specified recall and discrimination requirements.

Identify problem requests that take an inordinate amount of time.

Identify problem requests; identify descriptor candidates; identify problems in the user-system interface.

Compare with expectations to spot problems.

Compare with requirements, see 8.

In combination with 1 and 3, put problem requests in perspective; investigate especially problem requests of high priority. Assess the benefits derived from the information system totaled over all requests (see Section 8.2 for elaboration).

Fig. 7.3 (*continued*)

formation gathered through independent problem analysis and through the study of past and present use, and they put this information in perspective. Since users' time is valuable, interviews should be conducted after all other sources have been consulted so that the interviewer need not ask questions that could be answered from another source (such as a curriculum vitae, an organization chart, or a journal routing list) and so that the interviewer has the background to ask pertinent questions and can make the most of the interview time.

The user interviewed may be a person, a work team, or an organizational unit represented by one or more persons knowledgeable about its work. Group interviews are useful for problem analysis because the participants stimulate each other's thinking.

The interviewer should concentrate on expanding and deepening her knowledge of the user's problems, needs, and interests. Drawing on the background gained through independent problem analysis, she should discuss the user's tasks, current projects, and problems encountered in these.

Discussing each problem or problem type in turn, interviewer and user explore ways to solve the problems with emphasis on the information or entities needed. A list of types of data, as in the example given in Fig. 7.2, might be helpful to jog the mind of all participants. Imagination is important, leading to questions like "Wouldn't it be useful to know about X?" or "Would not source Y contain useful information for this problem?" The interview should cover both primary and secondary interests.

Interviewer and user agree on a term, phrase, or statement for each need, resulting in a statement of interests that can serve as a basis for SDI service to the user. These statements of interest are perhaps the most important source for the development of the conceptual schema, particularly the index language.

As an example of the exploration of problems and resulting needs, consider an interview with an entomologist. The interviewer knew from reading the entomologist's papers that he studied the dependence of certain species of bees on certain species of squash. The entomologist used, among other techniques, an analysis of how geographical extension of squash growing led to geographical extension of occurrence of the appropriate species of bee. The interviewer concluded that the entomologist needs access to a botanical collection classified by when and where plant specimens were found. With a big enough data base covering both insects and plant distribution over time, insect–plant relationships could be studied on a much larger scale by computer analysis. This information need was not articulated by the entomologist but brought up during the second half of the interview by the interviewer. The entomologist considered this to be too expensive to be feasible; therefore he suppressed the need. But feasibility assessment must come later and must be based on a cost–benefit analysis considering *all* possible applications of such a data base and considering the adaptation of available data bases.

The interview now turns to the individual needs for information or entities. What needs are being met? From what sources? Sources may be listed by type, but specific names are preferable. How did the user find out about a source? How satisfactory are the information or entities received? Would more processing be useful? What needs go unmet? How essential are the information or entities? Does the user know of any source that could provide the information or entities if other arrangements were made? Why does the user neglect sources known to the interviewer from her preparation?

The interviewer may also explore, in more general terms, sources the user is using, including those prepared by the user, such as personal or departmental files. (The study of needs becomes intertwined with the study of available resources.) This may uncover further needs. If the user maintains a personal file, he or she needs information to put in the file. If a user is on the routing list for a journal that does not deal with any of his previously stated interests, why does he receive it? Having the user give the five most important items of information received in the last year and inquiring how he or she received them may also be illuminating; besides shedding light on interests, it can serve as a check on the information system (if none of the five came to the user, directly or indirectly, through the information system, something is wrong). The same purpose is served by questions about occasions when the user was looking for information but could not find it, when he or she found it too late, or when the user found a valuable piece of information by accident. These occasions are more serious if the information was important.

The interviewer should also discover what materials are more difficult to find than others. For example, most users might feel that they are reasonably well informed about new monographs from reviews in journals but that they are missing a lot of the newly appearing reports. If this feeling is validated through some objective assessment, an SDI service should concentrate on report literature.

The interviewer should get a feel for the user's sophistication in selecting and using sources.

This concludes the discussion of needs assessment as a step from the general objective of an information system to more specific objectives. The next chapter develops still more specific objectives and performance measures for ISAR systems.

CHAPTER 8

Objectives of ISAR Systems

OBJECTIVES

The objectives of this chapter are to show the importance of formulating explicit objectives for the design or selection and day-to-day operation of ISAR systems, the difficulties in measuring these objectives, and the application of insights into objectives to the design or selection of ISAR systems, to the evaluation of personnel, particularly in reference, to the formulation of search strategies, and to the quality control of reference services.

INTRODUCTION

This chapter deals with defining objectives and establishing performance measures (functions 2a and 2b of systems analysis). Chapter 18 deals with methods for measuring the performance of an operating ISAR system or predicting the performance of an ISAR system yet to be installed or built (function 5) and the applications to ISAR system design.

Definition of objectives and performance evaluation serve to improve system design and operation:

1. *ISAR system design and maintenance.* Changes in an existing system or design or selection of a new system should be based on prediction of how various design features and their combinations affect *global performance* (performance over all search requests). This area includes decisions on the *acquisition of reference tools* and on the *subscription to search services,* such as SDC, LEXIS, or DRI. Since indexers and reference librarians are vital components of an ISAR system, *personnel selection and training* is part of system design.

2. *Search strategy.* Decisions on an information source and on search

strategy should be based on a prediction of the *local performance* (the performance that can be achieved for the request at hand).

3. *Search monitoring and postsearch actions.* The searcher must continuously evaluate the results of an ongoing search to keep the search on track and to know when a satisfactory result is reached. The user must know the quality of the final search results so that she can judge whether they are satisfactory or whether additional effort is needed.

Monitoring and postsearch actions require only performance measurement after the fact. Search strategy and system design or selection require performance *prediction* for operating ISAR systems or, even more difficult, for ISAR systems yet to be built or installed. For operating ISAR systems, future performance can be extrapolated from present performance, but the context in which the ISAR system operates might change. For ISAR systems yet to be built, performance can be estimated from previous tests that explore systematically the effects of various design features on performance, and from insight into the functioning of ISAR systems.

The distinction between local and global performance (our terms) points to a two-step process in developing performance measures for ISAR systems:

1. First develop a measure (or measures) of ISAR system performance for one individual request (*local performance*); this in turn consists of two steps:
   a. Develop measures for individual aspects of answer quality (see Section 8.1.1);
   b. Combine these measures into one measure of total answer quality (see Section 8.1.2).
2. Then develop a measure (or measures) that aggregates performance over a set of requests (*global performance*).

The decision situations in the design of information systems, specifically, their ISAR subsystems, given in Fig. 8.1 provide a good starting point for developing performance measures. This chapter develops a general approach in the context of bibliographic systems; for other contexts the specific measures must be modified.

Ideally, one would like to measure directly the impact of ISAR design features on user achievement (Fig. 8.2a, p. 113). In the case of the information system for children, this can be done. The children's task can be well defined: to become knowledgeable about the daily life in a Pueblo village. Achievement can be measured quite well: At the end of the learning period we can ask each child to give a description of Pueblo life to a peer; then we can tape this description and analyze it carefully with respect to the aspects covered, the depth of coverage, and accuracy.

An *information system for children* that contains slides on all aspects of the daily life in a Pueblo village. The child asks a question, receives a pertinent set of slides, views them, asks another question, and so forth, and thus learns about the Pueblo culture. Design question: Should we use a broad classification, resulting in a broad answer set even if the question is specific, or a detailed classification, resulting in specific answer sets for specific questions? Which is more conducive to learning?

The *information center of the research and development laboratory of a company;* more specifically, the ISAR system for books. Design question: Which classification scheme should we use for shelving—Dewey Decimal Classification (DDC) or Library of Congress Classification (LCC)? Which will result in better information support and, ultimately, in better work by scientists and engineers and in increased profits?

An *ISAR system for technical reports* within a company information center. Design question: Should we produce an index based on words in titles or do thorough indexing based on a carefully structured index language? Which will lead to better work by company employees?

The *index to the yellow pages* (advertising section) of a telephone book. Design question: Should there be an index classified by subject in addition to the alphabetical index? Would users more often find a suitable merchant?

A *system for matching job applicants with job openings.* Design question: Which classification of skills will lead to the most satisfactory placements?

Fig. 8.1   Examples of information systems for evaluation.

Such a study was indeed done, using a broad classification for one half of the children and a detailed classification for the other half. Children with a high IQ did better with the detailed classification; children with a low IQ did better with the broad classification. It seems that children with a high IQ are able to think of enough topics for specific questions to cover all aspects of Pueblo life and that they can gather information more efficiently if they are able to obtain specific sets of slides. On the other hand, children with a low IQ miss important aspects if they receive specific answers. They get a full picture of Pueblo life only through serendipity (i.e., accidental finds) in the broad sets of slides given to them when the broad classification was used. This illustrates a very important point: The effect of an ISAR system design feature on achievement depends on the capabilities of the user. Different subgroups in a user population are best served by different ISAR systems (or by one ISAR system that can be used in different modes).

The situation in this example is well-defined. Neither ultimate benefits nor costs are at issue. Achievement can be defined and measured. The information used by the subjects comes from a single source that can be manipulated easily for purposes of the study, and factors other than information that influence achievement (in the example, IQ) can be controlled. The effect of the information provided is almost immediate.

In the case of the company information center—the decision between Library of Congress Classification (LCC) and Dewey Decimal Classification

(DDC)—none of these conditions holds. The designer must consider ultimate benefits, namely, the profit earned by the company as a result of the quality of product design, which, in turn, is affected by the ISAR system serving the R and D staff. When selecting an ISAR system, the designer must weigh the cost of each alternative against its effect on profit.

Profit can be measured, but it depends on many factors beside quality of product design and is therefore not suitable as a criterion for the impact of the R and D ISAR system. Thus it is necessary to measure quality of design directly, which is a much more difficult task. Moreover, that is not the end. How can the effects of the information system be isolated from the many other factors influencing accomplishment in product design? These other factors include the nature of the task; the background, intelligence, and creativity of the engineers; other information sources; the organizational climate; and sheer luck (of two equally qualified engineers, one may happen to have a good idea within a month and the other might not). Isolating information system effects would require an experiment with two R and D laboratories that are exactly alike in the factors mentioned and in the collection covered by their information centers, using DDC in one and LCC in the other. Differences observed in the quality of product design would allow some conclusions on the relative merit of these two classifications in the provision of information to engineers working in the subject area and having the qualifications and working conditions prevailing in the experiment. Since information often has a "sleeper effect" (information acquired today might help solve a problem 3 years from today), the experiment would need to extend over at least 5 years. Even if we had 5 years to decide, the experiment is clearly not feasible.

Given that the impact of an ISAR system cannot be measured directly, how does one choose intelligently between options in ISAR system design—for example, between two classification schemes? One must divide the big step from ISAR system design feature to impact into two smaller steps: from design feature to the *quality of answers* the ISAR system produces and from answer quality to impact (Fig. 8.2b). But how does one measure answer quality? The requirement for any measure is that the better answer should contribute more to user achievement. But there is again the problem of tracing the impact of information. However, the step from answer quality to impact is smaller than the step from design feature to impact; one can rely more on plausibility and intuition. The criteria developed in this way are tenuous, but they provide a better basis for system design and operation than arbitrary choices.

The requirement that any measure for answer quality be related to impact has an important consequence: The criteria for answer quality depend on the

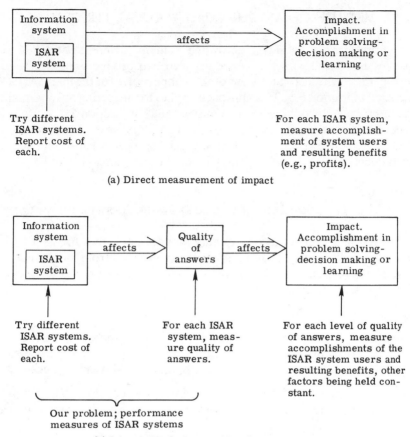

(a) Direct measurement of impact

(b) Intervening factor: quality of answers

Fig. 8.2   Approaches to measuring ISAR system performance.

information need resulting from the task at hand and thus vary from one situation to the next.

ISAR system performance cannot be measured in isolation. The quality of answers is determined by the total information system of which the ISAR system is but a part. The quality of answers depends also on the collection, the type of requests, and the interaction among these factors.

Answer quality refers to one individual request; it is a *local* performance measure (Section 8.1). However, decisions on ISAR system design or selection should be based on performance over a set of requests, that is, *global* performance (Section 8.2).

8.1 A MEASURE OF ANSWER QUALITY (LOCAL PERFORMANCE)

Any product can be judged according to many different criteria. A prospective user faced with the choice between two products decides by considering these criteria to the extent of their importance for the intended use as discussed in Section 6.5. This approach applies to measuring answer quality: Measures for individual aspects of answer quality (Section 8.1.1) are combined into a total figure of merit of the ISAR system response to one individual request (Section 8.1.2). The way this figure of merit should be computed depends entirely on the purpose to which the answer is to be put.

8.1.1 Measures for Individual Aspects of Answer Quality

Identifying aspects of answer quality that are important for the user is a complex task. As always in systems analysis, one starts from the end purpose to which the references retrieved are to be put and then works back the causal chain that leads to this purpose:

a	b	c	d	e
Collection and ISAR system	$\rightarrow$ Answer quality, references	Answer quality, substantive data	$\rightarrow$ Updated image of user	$\rightarrow$ Benefits, postsearch costs

Figure 8.3 shows the factors and the many steps of causal relationships involved. In the following we discuss these factors and relationships, considering first the chain

$c \rightarrow d \rightarrow e$ (working backwards from e) and then the chain
$a \rightarrow b \rightarrow c$ (working backwards from c)

Chain: answer quality, substantive data $\rightarrow$ image of user $\rightarrow$ ultimate benefits

An answer has two outcomes:

(e1) the *impact* on problem solving or decision making and resulting *benefits* and
(e2) the *cost for screening, reading, and understanding documents.*

What factors influence impact and cost?

The *impact of the information received on problem solving* (e1) comes about through the *updated mental image* of the user, its *completeness* (Does the updated image cover all aspects that are important for solving the problem at hand?), *structure* (Does the updated image represent all the relationships that exist in actuality, and is the image structured in such a way that it can be used easily to draw inferences necessary for problem solving?), and *timeliness* (factors d1–d3).

The *completeness of the updated image* (d1) depends on the *previous image* and on the *completeness of substantive data* contained in the documents found (factors c0 and c1).

The *structure of the updated image* (d2) depends on the *completeness of the updated image* (a missing piece of information may well preclude the formation of a lucid structure), the *previous image* and its structure, and the *appropriateness of the substantive data* (if the user cannot assimilate the substantive data contained in a document—e.g., for lack of background—then he or she cannot form a well-structured image) (factors d1, c0, and c2).

The *timeliness of the updated image* (d3) depends on the *speed of the answer* (the time elapsed between putting the request and obtaining the set of documents retrieved) and the *working time to read and understand the documents found* (factors b3 and d4). Answer speed, in turn, is determined by the *speed of retrieving references to relevant documents* and the *speed of physical access* to these documents (factors a3.2 and a3.1). This finishes the discussion of impact.

The *cost for screening, reading, and understanding* the documents found depends primarily on the time needed for these functions—the *working time to update the image* (d4).

The *working time* depends on the three factors influencing the structure of the updated image—namely, the *previous image, completeness,* and *appropriateness*—and a new factor, *conciseness* (factors c0–c4). The more a user knows already and the faster he can read and comprehend, the less time he needs to read and understand a document. The *completeness of the substantive data* contained in documents found may work both to increase and to decrease working time. It increases working time to the extent that completeness, everything else being equal, means more to read and think about. On the other hand, greater completeness may lead to better understanding and thereby decrease working time. The more appropriate the substantive data found in the documents, the less time is needed to assimilate them into the updated image. Conciseness is discussed below.

This finishes the discussion of the right side of Fig. 8.3; we now move on to the left side.

> Chain: ISAR system abilities → answer quality, references → answer quality, substantive data

The *completeness of substantive data* (c1) depends on the *completeness of the set of documents delivered* (b1). The user is interested in completeness in

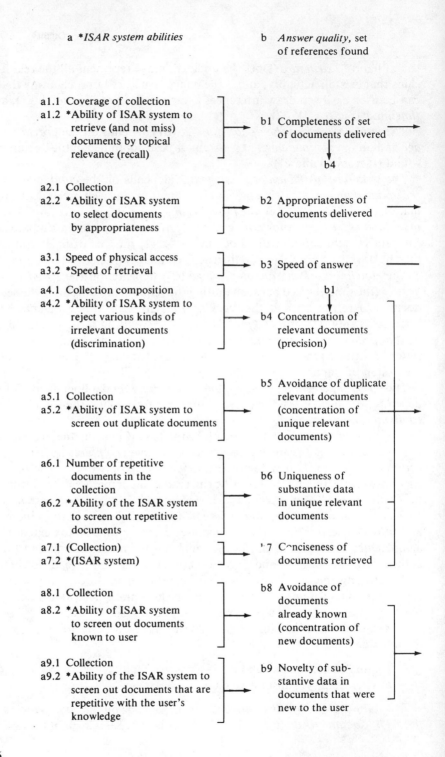

a *ISAR system abilities

b *Answer quality*, set
of references found

a1.1 Coverage of collection
a1.2 *Ability of ISAR system to
retrieve (and not miss)
documents by topical
relevance (recall)

b1 Completeness of set
of documents delivered

b4

a2.1 Collection
a2.2 *Ability of ISAR system
to select documents
by appropriateness

b2 Appropriateness of
documents delivered

a3.1 Speed of physical access
a3.2 *Speed of retrieval

b3 Speed of answer

a4.1 Collection composition
a4.2 *Ability of ISAR system to
reject various kinds of
irrelevant documents
(discrimination)

b1

b4 Concentration of
relevant documents
(precision)

a5.1 Collection
a5.2 *Ability of ISAR system to
screen out duplicate documents

b5 Avoidance of duplicate
relevant documents
(concentration of
unique relevant
documents)

a6.1 Number of repetitive
documents in the
collection
a6.2 *Ability of the ISAR system
to screen out repetitive
documents

b6 Uniqueness of
substantive data
in unique relevant
documents

a7.1 (Collection)
a7.2 *(ISAR system)

b7 Conciseness of
documents retrieved

a8.1 Collection
a8.2 *Ability of ISAR system
to screen out documents
known to user

b8 Avoidance of
documents
already known
(concentration of
new documents)

a9.1 Collection
a9.2 *Ability of the ISAR system to
screen out documents that are
repetitive with the user's
knowledge

b9 Novelty of sub-
stantive data in
documents that were
new to the user

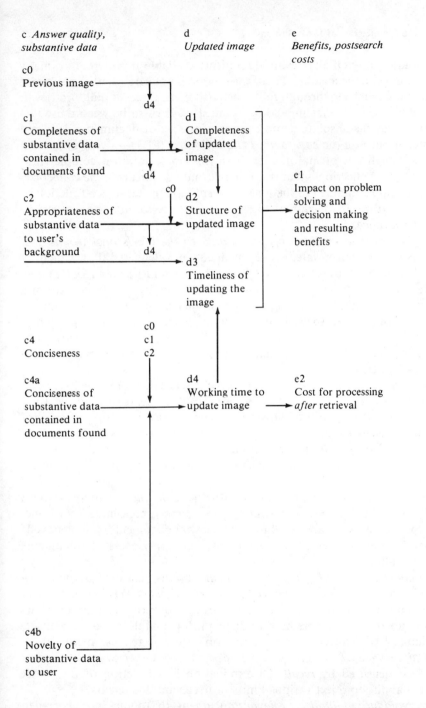

Fig. 8.3 Derivation of a local performance measure for a bibliographic ISAR system.

an absolute sense: Of all relevant documents available anywhere, how many are contained in the answer? Thus, the user does not care whether a relevant document was missed through faulty acquisition or through faulty retrieval. But for purposes of system testing we must distinguish between these two factors. Thus the absolute completeness of the set of documents delivered depends in turn on the *coverage of the collection* (a1.1)—a very important factor, though not of major interest in this book—and on completeness relative to the collection—that is, of all relevant documents *in the collection,* how many are contained in the answer (*recall,* a1.2). Recall is a function of the *ability of the ISAR system to retrieve (and not to miss) documents by topical relevance.*

The *appropriateness of substantive data to the user's background* (c2) depends on the appropriateness of the documents delivered (b2), which, in turn, depends on the *collection* (a2.1) and on the *ability of the ISAR system to select documents by appropriateness* (a2.2). A collection developed for a specific user group, such as high school students, may exclude documents clearly inappropriate to their background. Selection by appropriateness from a more varied collection can be achieved by indexing documents or document sources, such as journals and series, with a descriptor expressing their level of treatment.

Conciseness of substantive data delivered (c4) has two components: *intrinsic conciseness* of substantive data in the set of documents without regard to the user (c4a), and *novelty* of substantive data to the user (c4b). The case for conciseness is very simple: A user wants to obtain just the substantive data that are needed to solve the problem and that are new to her. She wants to obtain these data with a minimum of effort, avoiding repetition and wordiness.

The *intrinsic conciseness of substantive data in the set of documents delivered* (c4a) is influenced by four factors, namely, concentration of relevant documents, avoidance of duplicate relevant documents, uniqueness of substantive data contained in documents, and conciseness of documents (factors b4–b7).

The *concentration of relevant documents* (b4) as measured by *precision* depends on three factors: the *collection composition* (a4.1) (How many relevant documents are in the collection? Does the collection contain many irrelevant documents that are hard to distinguish from relevant documents?), the number of irrelevant documents correctly rejected as measured by *discrimination* (a4.2), and the completeness of the set of relevant documents found as measured by *recall.* Discrimination is a function of the ISAR system's ability to reject various kinds of irrelevant documents.

The *avoidance of duplicate relevant documents* (b5) comes into play when the same journal article is retrieved from *Chemical Abstracts* and from MEDLINE or, more subtly, when a technical report and a journal article or book based on it are both retrieved. Avoidance of duplicates is determined by the *collection* (How many duplicates are in the collection in the first place?) (a5.1) and by the *ability of the ISAR system to screen out duplicate documents* (for example, through a screening process following retrieval from multiple data bases) (a5.2).

Uniqueness of substantive data in unique relevant documents (b6) presents a problem that is as important as it is difficult to solve. The problem can be addressed in collection building by not acquiring a document that would merely repeat substantive data contained in documents already in the collection, or, if a new document is better, discarding the old one. The problem can also be addressed through the ISAR system by expressly noting repetitive documents in indexing (for example, "repeats Smith 1982a"). The case of a technical report and a journal article based on it could be subsumed here also because the two documents are not strictly duplicates. These considerations lead to the formulation of two factors determining the uniqueness of substantive data, namely, *number of repetitive documents in the collection* (a6.1) and *ability of the ISAR system to screen out repetitive documents* (a6.2).

The *intrinsic conciseness of documents retrieved* (b7) depends on the *collection* (a7.1) and the *ISAR system* (a7.2). Was an effort made to select concise documents for the collection? Having found two documents that contain the same relevant substantive data (and that are equally appropriate), is the ISAR system able to choose the one that requires less reading, either by being shorter or by providing the user with a mechanism to pick out just the substantive data wanted? Another consideration is the proportion of substantive data in a document that are actually relevant for the question at hand. Furthermore, this point is closely intertwined with avoidance of repetitive documents (b6) and novelty of substantive data (c4b). A human information analyst could screen documents for conciseness.

The *novelty of substantive data to the user* (c4b) depends on avoiding documents already known to the user (assuming the user knows the data contained in them or at least knows the document and would consult it if it were useful) and avoiding documents that tell the user nothing new (factors b8 and b9). These factors depend both on the collection and on the ISAR system. The importance of novelty for the user's working time and therefore for system evaluation has now been widely recognized.

This finishes the derivation of criteria for answer quality and corresponding ISAR system abilities. We now develop quantitative measures for these criteria.

Quantitative Measures

The most basic measures are *recall* and *discrimination*. Beware of un-critical use of these measures; they are only as good as the judgments of document relevance on which they are based (see Section 8.4). In spite of the fact that relevance is a matter of degree, the most common formulas deal with the simplest case: Documents are considered either relevant or not relevant and either retrieved or not retrieved. In this case retrieval performance can be analyzed based on the following 2 × 2 table (contingency table). (Fictitious figures for a sample request put to a sample collection of 10,000 documents are included for illustration.)

Judgment by ISAR system	Judgment by evaluator		Total
	Relevant	Not relevant	
Retrieved	A (correctly retrieved) 30	B (falsely retrieved) 35	65
Not retrieved	C (missed) 20	C'(correctly rejected) 9,915	9,935
Total	50	9,950	10,000

Recall measures the ability of the system to retrieve relevant documents:

$$\text{recall } r = \frac{\text{relevant retrieved}}{\text{all relevant}} = \frac{A}{A + C} = \frac{30}{50} = .6$$

Sometimes the absolute number of relevant documents retrieved is used in place of recall.

Discrimination (our term) measures the ability of the system to reject irrelevant documents:

$$\text{discrimination } d = \frac{\text{irrelevant rejected}}{\text{all irrelevant}} = \frac{D}{B + D} = \frac{9915}{9950} = .9965$$

Small variations in discrimination make a big difference in the number of irrelevant documents retrieved, since the base number of all irrelevant documents is so large.

Fallout, the complement of discrimination, measures the same ability:

$$\text{fallout } f = \frac{\text{irrelevant retrieved}}{\text{all irrelevant}} = \frac{B}{B + D} = \frac{35}{9950} = .0035$$
$$= 1 - d$$

Recall and discrimination are measures of system success, fallout is a measure of system failure. Recall is a commonly used measure. Fallout is used occasionally, discrimination rarely; the measure used instead is *precision:*

$$\text{precision } p \ = \ \frac{\text{relevant retrieved}}{\text{all retrieved}} \ = \ \frac{A}{A + B} \ = \ \frac{30}{65} \ = \ .46$$

Precision is a useful measure from the point of view of the user. However, precision does not measure a single ISAR system ability, as do recall and discrimination; rather it measures the combined effect of three factors: (1) number of relevant documents in the collection; (2) recall, which together with the number of relevant documents in the collection determines A, the number of relevant documents retrieved; and (3) discrimination, which influences B, the number of irrelevant documents retrieved. Thus precision is not a good measure for analyzing individual ISAR system abilities, but discrimination is.

For an individual request put to a given information system (with a given collection and using a given ISAR system), recall can be enhanced by broadening the query formulation. If the query formulation was optimal for the level of recall achieved, broadening it results in a loss of discrimination, as illustrated in Fig. 8.4. The magnitude of the loss of discrimination at each broadening step, and thus the shape of the recall-discrimination curve, varies

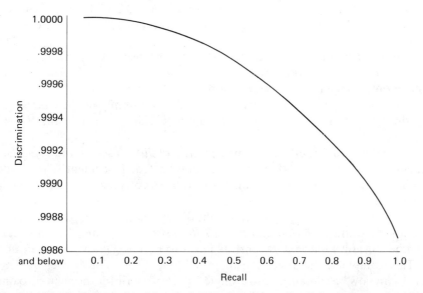

Fig. 8.4   Illustrative example of the relationship between recall and discrimination for an individual search.

widely from one request to the next. Usually the number of additional irrelevant documents retrieved exceeds the number of additional relevant documents retrieved; lower discrimination usually means lower precision. The qualification given at the beginning of this paragraph is often forgotten, and a universal inverse relationship between recall and discrimination is postulated. This *erroneous* postulate may take several forms, for example:

- When several requests are searched on the same ISAR system, the answers having high recall have low discrimination and vice versa.
- When the same request is searched on two different systems, the system giving higher recall gives lower discrimination.
- When two systems are compared with respect to average recall and average discrimination, the system having higher average recall has lower average discrimination.

In other words, ISAR system A is not better or worse than ISAR system B; the systems just differ in their emphasis in the trade-off between recall and discrimination. There is no credible evidence to support any of these generalizations. It is very well possible that a request is run on system A with both low recall and low discrimination and on system B with both high recall and high discrimination. System A may not work as well in general or may not be as suited for the search request at hand as system B. Fig. 8.5 shows results of searching many requests in a test of MEDLARS; each request is plotted according to its recall and discrimination value. Do you see a correlation?

Following recall and discrimination in importance is the *ability to select documents by their appropriateness to the user's background*. Measures are analogous to recall and discrimination.

The *ability to screen out duplicates* is measured simply by the fraction of all duplicate pairs detected over all duplicate pairs present in the "raw" retrieved set.

A similar measure can be defined for the *ability to screen out repetitive documents,* but the situation is more complicated. Document C may add nothing new once the contents of A and B are known; so it is not simply a matter of pairs of documents.

Novelty measures analogous to recall, discrimination, and precision arise from substituting *relevant and new to the user* for relevant. The absolute number of novel relevant documents has also been suggested as a measure.

This completes the discussion of individual criteria for answer quality. They can now be combined into a single figure of merit for the answer to one request.

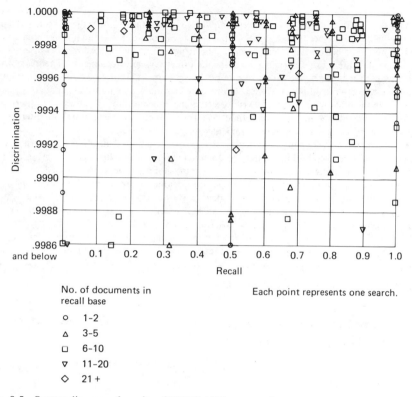

Fig. 8.5   Scatter diagram of results of MEDLARS test searches.

8.1.2 A SINGLE COMPOSITE MEASURE OF ANSWER QUALITY

A single measure of answer quality should be based on the importance of each answer quality criterion in the specific situation defined by the problem or request and the collection. The examples in Fig. 8.6 illustrate the point.

A formula for overall answer quality must consider the match between the requirements and the actual performance; a formula, such as the sum of recall and precision, that ignores differing user requirements is meaningless. If recall is not valued highly in a particular answer, the ISAR system should not get too many points for achieving high recall; if recall is valued highly, then high recall should count a lot. Thus a formula for answer quality should combine the individual criteria weighted by their importance for the search request at hand. For simplicity we combine just two measures, recall and the

A patent examiner needs very complete knowledge of the state of the art lest she award a patent erroneously; she needs high recall. If the search can be done with high discrimination as well, so much the better. But if high recall can be achieved only at the cost of lower discrimination, then the patent examiner must wade through the irrelevant documents. (There is a story that a patent for lifting sunken ships by pumping styrofoam balls into the hull was not granted because a character in a Mickey Mouse cartoon lifted a sunken ship by stuffing ping pong balls into it.) On the other hand, a student writing a term paper needs only a fraction of the literature on the topic but cannot afford to waste time with irrelevant material; emphasis is on discrimination and on rejecting inappropriate, if topically relevant, material.

A user may not be willing to examine more than 30 documents and may be less concerned with recall or precision; the absolute number of documents retrieved is the important criterion.

A user may be willing to examine many documents as long as at least every fourth one is relevant (precision at least 25%). The fewer relevant documents are found, the more important becomes discrimination: With 100 relevant documents, the user will tolerate 300 irrelevant ones; with only 10 relevant documents (fewer relevant documents in the collection), she will tolerate only 30 irrelevant ones. She needs higher discrimination.

Elapsed time, in minutes, is crucial in an emergency in a nuclear power plant; it is less important in the writing of a scholarly paper as long as it does not exceed one month.

Fig. 8.6   Importance weighting of answer quality criteria.

user-oriented precision, into a sample formula for overall answer quality, one for a patent examiner and one for a student.

Answer quality patent examiner $\quad q(\text{examiner}) = .8r + .2p$
Answer quality student $\qquad\qquad q(\text{student}) \;\; = .3r + .7p$

The coefficients are chosen to reflect roughly the priorities of each user.

Assume we run a query in three different ways, that is, conduct three searches, and evaluate the results from the point of view of the patent examiner and from the point of view of the student. The following table gives fictitious sample data.

	Individual criteria		Answer quality	
	Recall	Precision	For patent examiner	For student
search 1	$r = .8$	$p = .3$	$q(e) = .7$	$q(s) = .45$
search 2	$r = .2$	$p = .7$	$q(e) = .3$	$q(s) = .55$
search 3	$r = .8$	$p = .8$	$q(e) = .8$	$q(s) = .8$

For the patent examiner search 1 is better than search 2, but for the student it is just the reverse; their requirements differ. Search 3 is better for both; it was done on a more suitable ISAR system than either 1 or 2. Searches 1 and 2 might have been done on the same ISAR system—1 using a broad query formulation and 2 a narrow one. For one query searched on one ISAR system

there is a trade-off between recall and precision. The query should be formulated at the level of generality that gives the recall-precision combination
best suited for the user at hand, as seen from computing answer quality according to the user's specific formula. The flexibility of the ISAR system, its
ability to emphasize the criteria weighted heavily in the request, is important
here. While usually neither the exact shape of the recall-precision curve for
the request at hand nor the user's requirements are known in quantitative
form, the general approach still gives some guidance.

8.2 A MEASURE OF GLOBAL ISAR SYSTEM PERFORMANCE

Decisions on ISAR system selection or design must consider performance
in *all* requests. To do this, one could simply compute the average quality of
answers over all requests. This procedure is very simple, but it would ignore,
for example, the difference between a request for information needed for the
design of a vital part of a $2 billion rocket and a request on a topic that an
engineer pursues more or less as a hobby. A meaningful aggregate measure
must consider the importance of each request. Assume the total number of
requests is R. Each request has an *importance weight* $b(1)$, $b(2)$, . . . , $b(R)$;
these importance weights are used to compute a *weighted average answer
quality Q*, which is a measure of *overall performance* of the ISAR system.

$$Q = [b(1)q(1) + b(2)q(2) + \ldots + b(R)q(R)]/R$$

Where $b(1)$ is the importance of request 1,
$q(1)$ is the quality of answer to request 1, and
R is the total number of requests.
Q is a measure of the suitability of the ISAR system to the
situation defined by the search requirements and the collection.

Q can be seen as a direct measure of ultimate benefit by interpreting the
importance weight b as the amount of ultimate benefits from perfect information, and q as a fraction of this potential benefit that can actually be
realized; then Q is the average benefit, or payoff, per search. This can be
compared directly with average cost per search. An estimate of Q requires
estimates of the individual answer quality values q, or at least of the quality
values that can be achieved for certain classes of requests.

The formula given here is deliberately simplistic; a much more complex
formula would be required to express more precisely the complex relationship between the resources spent on a search, the answer quality achieved,
and the ultimate benefit. Moreover, in real life the data to put into any such

formula are seldom available. The purpose here is to introduce a way of thinking that might sharpen the common sense and intuition that are needed in decision making and that might guard against simplistic approaches of the kind mentioned in Section 8.3.

Based on estimates of the overall performance Q for all the ISAR systems under consideration, the designer can select the one that is most appropriate for the situation at hand (function 5 of the systems analysis process). First, she screens based on performance and cost alone without quantifying benefits; she eliminates dominated solutions as discussed in Section 6.5. In the remaining systems higher performance costs more; intelligent selection must take into account the benefits associated with a given level of performance to see whether these benefits outweigh the costs. Unfortunately, the estimation of the ultimate benefit is even more tenuous than the estimate of performance. For instance, imagine that information is needed to find the best routing for a subway line. Who knows how much the information system contributes to the decision? Who knows how much the better routing is worth to the population? However, somebody at some time will decide on an information system for the transit authority and on the amount of money to be spent on it; the person making this decision will, at least implicitly, if unknowingly, estimate all the quantities that we find so hard to measure. So we might as well try to make all factors explicit to the extent possible.

8.3 TESTING VERSUS EVALUATION

To test is not to evaluate. To test is to determine certain performance characteristics, such as recall, discrimination, and novelty. To evaluate is to assign value, to weight the performance characteristics in accordance with a given situation and value measure. In an ISAR system serving scientists evaluating the efficacy and safety of drugs, recall is of paramount importance; in an ISAR system serving practicing physicians who must make quick decisions, discrimination is what counts. In an ISAR system serving both groups, flexibility to emphasize either recall or discrimination in an individual search is at a premium. If most search requests are broad, the ability to do specific searches with good discrimination is not valued highly. If the collection is of medium size and covers many subject fields, the ISAR system need not be able to make subtle distinctions. If the users have varying backgrounds, the ISAR system should be able to select documents by appropriateness.

When evaluating an operating ISAR system, one must collect data in sufficient detail to compute the measure of overall quality Q. For each request, one must assess the importance of the ingredients of answer quality—namely, recall, discrimination, novelty, and other performance measures—

and measure the actual performance with respect to these criteria. Average recall and average discrimination and other average measures have little meaning in this situation: They ignore the differences between requests with respect to the user's requirements for recall, discrimination, and other aspects of answer quality and differences in the intrinsic importance of requests.

When evaluating an existing ISAR system for use in a specific situation or when considering the design features of an ISAR system yet to be built, one must estimate a future value of Q. This involves taking a sample of requests to be expected, attaching importance to each, and predicting performance for each, perhaps by class of requests. This calls for performance data in considerable detail, and studies of retrieval tests should report them this way. They should report data for each criterion separately, not for some composite function (such as the sum of recall and precision). They should differentiate between types of requests and between types of entities, which may vary with respect to ease of retrieval. Only such detailed data allow extrapolation to a given situation with its unique mix of types of requests and its unique mix of types of entities. Less detailed data, such as average recall and average discrimination, are less helpful but not completely useless if they are indicative in a general way of how the system would perform for a given request.

Sometimes ISAR systems are evaluated and ranked independently from any specific situation or purpose, using a total figure of merit, such as the sum (or some other function) of average recall and average precision achieved in a test. Such rankings are nearly worthless; the total figure of merit does not give the detailed information needed for evaluating an ISAR system with respect to a specific situation.

8.4 RELEVANCE AND RELEVANCE JUDGMENTS

Relevance judgments are the basis of all ISAR system evaluation. Any computations of recall, discrimination, and so on are only as reliable as the relevance judgments on which they are based. This section deals with three major issues: what standards should be applied in judging relevance, what information should be used, and who should make relevance judgments.

Figure 8.7 shows three *standards* that can be *used in judging relevance* and links them to the steps in request processing. Judging relevance against the query formulation is indicated for a study of ISAR system effects due to indexing (particularly indexing errors); it does not support a study of effects due to any previous steps. Judging relevance against the query statement is useful for detecting effects that are due to query formulation, or to indexing, or to both; it cannot isolate these effects. Judging relevance against the prob-

1. The problem. Can the document contribute to the solution of the problem? Real information need.

State specifications
for helpful documents.

2. The query statement. Does the document meet the specifications of the query statement?

Formulate in terms of
descriptors.

3. The query formulation. Does the document meet the specifications expressed through the descriptors and query logic used?

Indexing

Retrieval results. Documents actually retrieved or missed.

Fig. 8.7   Standards for relevance judgments and related retrieval operations.

lem brings into play the effects of all three steps, individually or combined. Thus the standard to be used depends on the purpose of the evaluation. Documents judged irrelevant with respect to the query statement may be judged relevant with respect to the problem and vice versa. Proper development of the query statement should minimize such discrepancies, and the ISAR system should aid in the development of the query statement (reference interview, computer system feedback). A thorough system evaluation may require independent relevance judgments against all three standards.

A closely related issue is whether appropriateness of the document to the user's background should be included in the requirements against which relevance is to be judged. In the interest of clarity, *topical relevance*—which is judged without regard to the user—should be distinguished from *appropriateness* to the user's background and present situation. Documents that are both topically relevant and appropriate may be called *pertinent*.

What *information* should be *used in judging relevance?* There is general agreement that titles provide but a scant basis for relevance judgments. In some retrieval experiments documents that were carefully indexed using the full text are rejected as irrelevant based on a brief examination of the title. A good abstract is sufficient most of the time, but depending on the request and on the document, the full text or even background information about the author may be needed.

Who should make the relevance judgments? Often it is accepted without further discussion that the user and the user alone should make the relevance judgments because it is he or she, after all, who is being served and who has to work with the documents or other entities. Relevance judgments by users bring two problems. First, users generally judge relevance against the problem, the information need, not the query statement. Hence, judging relevance against the query statement requires neutral experts as judges. On the other hand, if a test is to cover the system's ability to assist the user in elucidating a proper query statement, then user relevance judgments are appropriate from this point of view (but see the second point).

Second, a user may not recognize the relevance of a document because its title is misleading, because he or she does not take the time to examine the document carefully, or because he or she lacks the background needed to understand the document. The careful work of an indexer working in the request-oriented mode may thus be obviated by quick relevance judgments made with less care or less insight. To give another example, a user may fail to see how a part found by the ISAR system can be used in the machine she is building. Furthermore, the user may fail to recognize relevance for any number of reasons having to do with the entire decision-making process. For example, a user is likely to reject even highly relevant documents if they contradict a decision just made. Why, then, should an ISAR system in which insightful indexers work hard at request-oriented indexing be "punished" rather than "rewarded" because an unsophisticated user does not recognize the relevance of a document? In a test that concentrates on retrieval ability, one should use experts as judges. However, if the test is to cover also the system's ability to help the user to recognize relevant documents (see Section 8.5.3), then user relevance judgments are appropriate. A thorough system evaluation may need relevance judgments by an expert (or, better still, two experts who first judge independently and then resolve their differences) and the user.

8.5 IMPLICATIONS FOR ISAR SYSTEM DESIGN AND OPERATION

The reflection on objectives leads to practical suggestions for the improvement of information services. This section discusses a few such suggestions, emphasizing innovative features.

8.5.1 IMPLICATIONS FOR SYSTEM DESIGN: INNOVATIVE FEATURES

Selecting Documents by Appropriateness to the User's Background

Most bibliographic ISAR systems cannot use appropriateness to the user's background as a retrieval criterion since they do not index documents by level of treatment beyond the distinction between juvenile and adult nor by specific prerequisites. On the other hand, ISAR systems for instructional materials specify level of treatment in considerable detail and index specific prerequisites as well. This approach should also be explored in libraries and abstracting/indexing services; for heavily used systems (e.g., the *Reader's Guide*) it might be worth the cost.

Another approach to selection by appropriateness is indexing by quality (e.g., on a scale from 1 "excellent" to 5 "bad"). The user who trusts the judgment of the indexer could avail himself or herself of the option of selecting by quality, but nobody would be forced to do so. Note that quality judgments made in the acquisitions process are forced upon the user, since documents that are judged "bad" are not even included in the collection.

Appropriateness criteria can be added to the query formulation by the user or by the information specialist based on interviewing the user or on previous knowledge of the user's background. To some extent this process could be automated by keeping a record of users and their backgrounds in a computer file.

Eliminating Duplicate Documents

Eliminating duplicates becomes an important ISAR system ability as more and more searches are done on multiple data bases, for example, *Chemical Abstracts, Biological Abstracts,* and MEDLINE. It is quite annoying to the user, and wasteful of the user's time, if references are repeated in the separate printouts produced from the three data bases. A computer, even a microcomputer used as an intelligent terminal, can be programmed to combine the results from searching several data bases and to consolidate the information for duplicate documents. This produces consolidated records, which list author, title, and other descriptive information only once, but which preserve subject information (particularly abstracts) from the individual data bases.

Eliminating Documents Known to the User

While an information system cannot know precisely what a user has read, it can keep a record (1) of the documents it has provided to the user in the past and (2) of the journals that the user reads. It is then a simple matter to (1) screen out individual documents and (2) screen out articles appearing in journals that the user reads regularly. Eliminating an article based on the journal in which it appears is possible in most operating computerized ISAR systems; it is merely a matter of using available capabilities. Listing documents known to the user separately may be better than suppressing them completely; the user can then refresh her memory if she chooses.

Eliminating Repetitive Documents

This is essential for achieving the objective of retrieving the smallest subset of documents covering all substantive data needed. Unfortunately, eliminating repetitive documents is very difficult. Reference storage and retrieval systems deal with documents as entire packages; they can retrieve documents only for their relevance to the topic. They cannot open the packages, look at what is inside, and compare two documents with respect to the substantive data they contain. If a full ability to do so were added, we would have a data storage and retrieval system; the cost would be tremendous. The best we can hope for is indication of "repetition linkages" by the indexer. For example:

1. *A* is superseded by *B; B* supersedes A. Such a linkage could be used to suppress *A* if both *A* and *B* were retrieved.

Other types of linkages are

2. *A* is abridged version of *B; B* is full version of A.
3. *A* has same content as *B; B* has same content as A.
4. *A* content covered by content of *B; B* covers content of *A* and more.

When both *A* and *B* are retrieved, the ISAR system can select the document more appropriate to the user and the problem at hand. Thus these linkages serve to eliminate the most obvious (and perhaps most annoying) cases of repetitive documents. They still do not solve problems such as the following: *A* and *B* together contain all substantive data contained in *C.*

Still more difficult is the task of eliminating documents that, while not known to the user, tell the user nothing new.

8.5.2 IMPLICATIONS FOR SYSTEM OPERATION

Adapting the Search Strategy to the Individual Request

When a request is put to a system, the user and the reference librarian must jointly determine the importance of the individual criteria of answer quality. The reference librarian can then plan the search strategy and allocate the resources available in such a way as to emphasize good performance in those criteria that are important. ISAR systems that are flexible—for example, those that allow the searcher to emphasize either recall or discrimination as appropriate—are better able to meet the requirements of each specific search.

Allocating Resources to Requests to Maximize Overall Performance

Resources for conducting searches, such as the reference librarian's time and money for on-line searching, are limited. Reference librarians often allocate these resources equitably over all patrons (perhaps with the exception of upper level management), or they allocate resources in proportion to the difficulty of the search, so that the results of all the searches are of approximately equal quality. Neither approach maximizes overall performance because the importance of requests is neglected. The reference librarian must form an estimate of the importance of each request, seeking guidance from management. Then he can allocate resources so that the important searches yield high quality results. An important request that is difficult needs appropriate resources, even if that means not dealing at all with some unimportant request. An easy request, on the other hand, needs less resources even if it is important. The law of diminishing returns applies: The tenth hour spent on a very important difficult request (e.g., weight 10) may increase search quality by .01. The same hour spent as the second hour on a request of medium importance (e.g., weight 4) may increase the search quality by .3. The first alternative produces an increase of .1, the second produces an increase of 1.2 in the weighted average quality Q (Section 8.2). The searcher should notice when more effort does not promise a corresponding increase in quality. He can then decide whether to stop or to continue, considering the importance of the request at hand and of the other requests pending.

A passive stance on the part of the reference librarian often stands in the way of achieving maximum overall performance. Some of the requests that are initiated by the user may be less important than other requests that the reference librarian might find by actively going out to the potential users. This demonstrates the fallacy of the often heard argument "We get more requests than we can handle now, so why should we go out and actively solicit even more?"

8.5.3 RELEVANCE JUDGMENTS AND PROFESSIONALISM

The ultimate objective of an information system is to update the user's image of the problem and its context in order to promote better decisions or solutions. If the user misjudges the relevance of a document, he or she may miss important information. A user may fail to recognize the relevance of a document due to a misleading title, insufficient time spent on examining the document, lack of background or sophistication, or psychological state (see Section 8.4).

One may take the view that the responsibility of the information system ends with retrieving relevant documents and making them available to the user and that the utilization of the documents is entirely the responsibility of the user. But a proper match between user and available information has not been achieved until the user recognizes the relevance of documents that can help in solving the problem. Therefore, the responsibility of the information system, particularly the professional responsibility of the reference librarian or information specialist, extends into the utilization of the information. If a document is relevant but the user does not recognize it, the system should help him to recognize the relevance of the document. If a user, as a consequence of missing a piece of information, loses a $1 million contract, the library may point out that the information was indeed available in a document given to the user; but if the title of this document was misleading, this is a weak defense.

There are several ways in which the system can help the user recognize the relevance of documents. The indexers can annotate those documents that have misleading titles. The reference librarian can annotate documents that bear an indirect, yet important, relationship to the problem at hand; highlighting the descriptors that led to retrieval of the document may be sufficient. Where necessary, the system can repackage substantive data into a format that the user can understand or add documents that provide the background needed to understand a relevant document. In sophisticated data storage and retrieval systems, application of this principle leads to a marriage of ISAR techniques and computer-assisted instruction techniques to result in a complete system for the provision of information. The information specialist should encourage the user to ask why certain documents were included in the answer. This approach fully exploits the potential of the ISAR system to assist in solving the problem at hand.

Of course, there are limits in terms of both resources and expertise within the information system. Some users need assistance more than others, and some users do not want any assistance at all, whether they need it or not. But this does not invalidate the principle, and assisting one user in the utilization of the documents that have been found may be a better use of resources than doing a search for another.

In this way the information specialist acts as a true professional with independent judgment and does not merely react to the wishes and preferences of the user. This is true user orientation.

PART III

Data Schemas and Data Structures

CHAPTER 9

Data Schemas and Formats

OBJECTIVES

The objectives of this chapter are to enable the reader to analyze the conceptual schema underlying an ISAR system; judge the adequacy of this schema with respect to the queries to be answered and the entities to be covered; use the knowledge of the schema to exploit fully the possibilities for extracting information from the ISAR system; and design a conceptual schema and input/output record formats.

This requires an understanding of data schemas and record formats, their purpose and nature, their processing characteristics, and the criteria for their evaluation.

Some acquaintance with on-line data input (e.g., in OCLC) is helpful as background, particularly for the discussion of input record formats. Refer also to the examples in Section 9.6.

INTRODUCTION

Continuing the process of stepwise refinement, this chapter deals with the ISAR system rules and conventions, primarily the *conceptual schema;* the conceptual schema specifies the types of entities to be included in the data base and the types of relationships to be established between these entities. For each entity type the conceptual schema defines the *domain* (scope)— what entity values are covered. It indicates what entity identifiers to use, either by giving an authority list of all entities with their authorized identifiers or by giving general rules of form. It gives rules for establishing relationships. Figure 9.1 gives the conceptual schema for the University Data Base (see Chapter 3).

The conceptual schema serves as a guide for collecting and organizing the

137

Entity types		Relationship types	
E1	Course	R1	Has prerequisite (Course, Course)
E2	Course offering	R2	Deals with (Course, Subject)
E3	Semester	R3	Offered as (Course, Course offering)
E4	Person	R4	Takes place in (Course offering, Semester)
E5	Grade	R5	Has instructor (Course offering, Person)
E6	Document,	R6	Has student (Course offering, Person)
	intellectual	R7	Has attribute (CS, Letter grade)
	work	R8	Uses text (Course offering, Document,
E7	Document,		intellectual work)
	physical volume	R9	Authored by (Document, Person)
E8	Subject,	R10	Deals with (Document, intel. work, Subject)
	concept, idea	R11	Has copy (Document, intel. work, Document,
			physical volume)
For each of these entity		R12	Checked out to (Document, phys. volume, Person)
types, define the		R13	Checkout time (DP, Semester)
domain, that is, the set		R14	Has component (Subject, Subject)
of entity values per-		R15	Has broader Term (Subject, Subject)
missible in the system.			

Combination entities

CS	Course offering— Person (R6)
DP	Document, physical volume— Person (R12)

Fig. 9.1 Conceptual schema for the University Data Base.

information to be included in the ISAR system and as the basis for retrieving information or entities from the system. Thus, the conceptual schema is at the heart of ISAR system design. Its development must be based on user needs. The conceptual schema defines the *intellectual or logical content* of the entity store (data base). There are many ways to arrange the *physical organization* of this content for easy access; these are discussed in Chapter 11, 'Data Structures and Access.'

Communication with the store of data is through one or more input formats and one or more output formats.

9.1 DESIGNING A CONCEPTUAL SCHEMA

The design of a conceptual schema should proceed from an analysis of the needs to be served. This yields a list of entity types to be included in the ISAR system. Some of these entities are of interest in themselves and can occur as focal entities in queries; they are *main entities* (our term). Other entities are of interest only as they relate to main entities. In the University Data Base all entities except *Semester, Grade,* and *Subject* are main entities; each of them could be the focus of a query. For each entity type derived from the needs analysis, the designer must define the domain or scope and decide on the entity identifiers to be used.

The next step is to determine the types of relationships that should be established between entities. Each relationship gives information on both entities involved. For example, *COF3* < has instructor > *B. Simms* gives information about *COF3: B. Simms* is the instructor. It also gives information about *B. Simms;* she teaches *COF3.* Such an item of information about an entity is called a *data element.* There may still be additional information about an entity, such as a course title or course description; the title, the abstract, table of contents, or full text of a book; the statement of interest of an applicant to a doctoral program; or even the entity itself. These pieces of information (or the entity itself) are further data elements for the entity. Lastly, an entity identifier (ISBN or LC card number for a book, social security number or name for a person) is a data element. Thus, there are three types of data elements for an entity:

- the entity identifier;
- an item of information unique to the entity; also the entity itself;
- an item of information that arises from a relationship to another entity.

Including an entity type, main or otherwise, a relationship type, or a further data element type means costs for data collection, input, processing, storage, and retrieval. Are these costs justified by benefits to users? The designer needs an estimate of how often a candidate main entity type is the focus of a query. For each candidate relationship type (or other data element type), its importance for problem solving should be stated explicitly. Is it useful for retrieval and data analysis operations, does it give useful information about an entity once retrieved, or both? In retrieval a relationship may serve as a direct selection criterion for the focal entity of interest, or it may be involved indirectly, as in finding the students (focal entity) that received an A in any course offering of a course above the 600 level (the relationship *Course* < is offered as > *Course offering* is involved indirectly). The usefulness of an entity or relationship type can be judged from the estimated number and importance of queries in which it is involved; this is the principle of anticipated queries applied to the selection of relationship types. Usefulness should be weighed against the cost. As shown in Chapter 11, using a relationship or other data element type as access point for rapid retrieval costs extra. Therefore, the designer may want to include a relationship or other data element type only as an item of information. Figure 9.2 gives some examples of conceptual schema design.

Information system for a government agency dealing with international development

This system must serve a multitude of purposes: administration and evaluation of individual development projects (which includes the information need: find subject experts who can help in a project); research into factors that make projects successful; employment service for subject experts; information support for agency personnel, personnel in other agencies, and researchers working on development problems. From this analysis emerge four main entity types: *Project, Organization, Person,* and *Document.* There are important relationships between all four: a *Project* has associated with it official *Documents* (planning documents, progress reports, evaluation reports) and perhaps other documents about it, a sponsoring *Organization* and an implementing *Organization, Persons* in various relationships (administrator, field staff). *Organizations* are originators and/or publishers of *Documents. Persons* are members of *Organizations* and authors of *Documents. Persons* and *Organizations* are receivers of *Documents,* either on individual order or through selective dissemination of information (SDI). A user concerned with a project (which may have been retrieved in a subject search) may need to know the people involved or may need to look at the documents. A user may want to find all projects sponsored by a given organization or by all organizations in a given country. While assessing the qualifications of an expert, a user may want to look at the documents the expert has written or the projects in which he or she participated. When a direct search for experts in a given subject is not successful, one can search for documents on that subject and look at the authors of these documents.

There are some other candidates for main entities—for example, *Country* with relationships to *Project,* to *Organization,* to *Person* (< home country is >, < stationed in >, or < expert on >), and to *Document* (< deals with > and < published in >) and perhaps also socioeconomic data. There are many other entities important through their relationships with one or more of the main entities as well as other data elements that should be included in the conceptual schema.

Bibliographic retrieval system (excerpts; user needs assumed known)
Entity types
    Document, the only main entity type, identified by ISBN (International Standard Book Number)
    Person, identified by name, following precise rules of form
    Organization (corporate body), identified by name
    Place, Date
    Subject, identified by a term, as in subject headings, or by a class number as in a classification
Relationship types
    Document < authored by or contributed to by > *Person*
    Document < emanating from > *Organization*

    Document < published in > *Place*
    Document < published by > *Organization*
    Document < published in > *Date*

    Document < deals with > *Subject*
    Document < cites > *Document* (for a citation index)

Other data elements for documents
    ISBN, Title
Rules for establishing relationships
    Establish a relationship between a document and all contributing persons (author, compiler, editor, illustrator, and so on).

Establish a relationship between a document and an organization if the document is an official document of the organization, lists resources available through the organization, or represents the views of the organization.

Establish a relationship between a document and up to five subjects.

Information and referral center

The main entity type is *Organization* with scope *Social Service Agency.* There are obvious data elements such as subject area and eligibility requirements. But a sophisticated ISAR system should be able to use other selection criteria, such as *transportation distance* between a person and an agency. To do this, the conceptual schema must include the entity types *Public transportation routes, Stops, Times,* and *Geographical location* (for example, street intersections or large buildings, stored as points in a coordinate grid). Given an agency address and an inquirer address, the system can then compute the transportation distance using public transportation. If private transportation is to be considered as well, data on streets must be added. If the IR center cannot afford to include such data in its data base, it may make arrangements to tap into a separate data base maintained by the metropolitan transit authority.

Employment service

An employment service has two main entity types: *Person* (job applicant)—the entity type of interest to employers, and *Job opening*—the entity type of interest to job applicants. To decide on the data elements to be collected from job applicants, one must know the characteristics that employers use in selection and the characteristics that employment counselors use in matching applicants with job openings; at least some of these data elements must be available for searching. Information items about a job applicant must include name, address, and phone number. One may look beyond the obvious to such data elements as *Height, Weight, Size of shoes,* and so on. In some specialized situations these would be valid selection criteria. To decide elements for job openings, one must know the job characteristics that job seekers would like to use in selecting a job and the characteristics that employment counselors use. For both *Persons* (job applicants) and *Job openings* a list of data elements emerges; the two lists will show considerable overlap in the entities involved, for example, *Skills, Geographical area,* and *Date of availability.*

Fig. 9.2   Conceptual schemata: some sketchy examples.

Once a conceptual schema is constructed in this problem- or request-oriented mode, it serves as a guideline for data collection and storage. This guideline is communicated to the indexer through one or more input formats (Sections 9.2 and 9.4).

Contrast this request-oriented approach with the often used entity-oriented approach. In the latter approach one starts from the given entity type (e.g., document) and asks, What characteristics come to mind when examining this entity? What data elements are needed to describe it? These questions are asked without the guidance of a statement of user needs or anticipated requests.

The following two sections elaborate on rules and conventions in the conceptual schema and give more examples.

9.1.1 RULES AND CONVENTIONS FOR THE FORM OF ENTITY IDENTIFIERS

These rules specify for each entity type (1) its domain or scope—the set of the individual entities (entity values) allowed in the system, and (2) the form of the entity identifiers. The rules may be very liberal and restrict neither the entities admitted into the system nor their identifiers; for example, they may allow any person identified by a name in any form, or any subject designated by any term in any grammatical form. At a first level of standardization, the rules may still admit all entities of a given type but insist on *general rules of form* for their identifiers; examples are given below. Finally, at the highest level of standardization, the rules may consist of an *authority list* which explicitly specifies the entities that are allowed and the identifiers to be used for these entities.

General Rules of Form

Examples of general rules of form are:

- An International Standard Book Number (ISBN) consists of 10 digits with optional spaces or hyphens for legibility.
- For *Person* give last name, first name, and middle initial (not full middle name). Alternative rules: Give last name followed by two initials, which are separated by a space but not followed by a period (a frequent British practice). Or give last name, first name, full middle name, and date of birth (as in large library catalogs).
- For *Subject* prefer nouns in the nominative singular; if a phrase must be used, use natural word order.
- Give measures in centimeters.
- Give date in the form 790705; alternative rule: 1979 July 5.

Authority Lists

An authority list gives all entity values of a certain entity type, such as *Subject, Corporation, Person,* and the authorized form of the identifier for each entity value. As an example, consider the entity type *Subject.* Many ISAR systems have specified a set of subjects and identifiers of these subjects, the *subject descriptors* (e.g., *Attorney*). The set of subject descriptors is called the *index language;* it is a subject authority list. To aid the indexers and searchers, the designer may add a *lead-in vocabulary* consisting of additional terms, such as synonyms or spelling variants, with leads to the proper subject descriptors; for example, the lead-in vocabulary would contain the terms *Lawyer, Counsel, Solicitor,* and *Barrister* with an instruction that *Attorney* must be used to identify the subject wherever it occurs. Index language and lead-in vocabulary together form a subject *thesaurus*. The processes of query formulation and indexing depend on the entire thesaurus, but the resulting query formulations and entity representations contain only authorized subject descriptors, and data base organization and the comparison/match operation rely only on those.

A thesaurus in the wider sense—that is, an authority list with lead-in from variant forms—is used for other entity types as well; for example, there are thesauri giving the authorized names of corporate bodies and leads from variant forms. The rules for corporate names are so complex and require so much knowledge of the corporate body at hand that their application by the individual indexer or searcher would waste considerable effort and lead to low consistency.

An authority list should be consistent in itself and adhere to general rules of form, with exceptions made only for overriding reasons. The List of Library of Congress Subject Headings is a major sinner against this commonsense rule. For example: *Education of prisoners* but *Delinquents, education; Literature and science* but *Art and literature.*

Rules of form should be capable of being applied easily and consistently; the rules-of-form approach is indicated for entities for which new values arise all the time. For an entity type with a fairly closed domain and difficult rules of form, such as subjects, the thesaurus (authority list) approach is preferable.

9.1.2 GENERAL RULES FOR ESTABLISHING RELATIONSHIPS

A few sample rules illustrate this concept.

To what substances should a food product be related by <consists of>? Sample rules are as follows:

- Establish a relationship between a food product and its first ingredient as seen from the label.
- Establish a relationship between a food product and any ingredient above 5%.

To what subjects should a document be related through <deals with>, a person through <has skill in>, and so on? This is governed by rules for subject indexing. For example,

- Establish a relationship between a document and every chemical compound discussed in it. (From the point of view of the document: Index the document by every chemical compound discussed.)
- Establish a relationship between a job applicant and every subject in which he or she has a special skill.

- Establish a relationship between an object and its shape and an object and its material.

Under what circumstances should a document or other work be related to a person through < is authored by > ? (Some cases are quite difficult; for example, should a compiler of a bibliography be considered the author?)

9.2 RECORD FORMATS: GENERAL CONSIDERATIONS

9.2.1 FUNCTIONS OF RECORDS IN DATA BASE PROCESSES

Requests often deal with one focal entity type; the information for each focal entity of interest is output as a list of data elements. Such a list of data elements pertaining to the same focal entity is called a *record*. For example, information about a course offering requested from the University Data Base may be structured in a record as follows:

COF5 FDST 101 Introduction to food processing 1979F L. Kahn
Text used: D5 Food processing theory and practice By: N. Link

These data elements for *Course offering 5* are gleaned from the data base using the relationships from *Course offering* to other entities, such as *Documents,* and perhaps relationships starting from these, such as *Document–Person.* The students enrolled are not included in the record; this information was not requested. The *record format* specifies which data elements are to be included in the record, where each data element is to be placed in the record, and in what form it is to appear. The relationship < has instructor > between *COF5* and *L. Kahn* is implied by the position of the person identifier (name) in the record. Other examples of *output records* (also called display records) are a credit card statement, a schedule form for a student, a bibliographic record printed or displayed on a video terminal, and a bibliographic or other record on a catalog card found by a user.

We now turn to data input. To add data to the data base, one could just enter the entities and their relationships. For example, to add data on a course offering, one would enter the following:

COF5   (add entity)
COF5 < is offering of > FDST 101   (add relationship)
COF5 < offered in semester > 1979F   (add relationship)
COF5 < has instructor > L. Kahn   (add relationship)

Since this same sequence of relationships is entered often, it is more efficient to enter it as one *input record:*

COF5   FDST101   1979F   L. Kahn

Again the relationships of the other entities to *COF5* are implied by position. A computer can be programmed to take this input record, extract the component relationships, and add them to the data base. Other examples of input records are a credit card charge slip, a schedule request form, a drop/add slip, a bibliographic record input to the On-Line Computer Library Center (OCLC), a catalog card master, and a form filled in by a job applicant. The input record format determines the efficiency of the input task, which in computerized systems often takes the biggest chunk of total system cost.

Output and input formats derive from the conceptual data schema: Only entities and relationships covered in the schema can be displayed in output, and the entities and relationships required by the conceptual schema must be included in some input record. Output and input record formats are also called *external data schemas.*

In the tabular representation of the University Data Base (Chapter 3), each relationship between two entities is expressed as a pair in the appropriate table. This representation is extremely flexible but requires a suitable program—a data base management system—to assemble all the information on an entity of interest as specified in an output format. If such a program is not available, or if the data base at hand is written, typed, or printed, the designer must decide on one main entity type and store information in large, preassembled records pertaining to this one entity type, such as records for documents in a bibliography or for persons in a biographical handbook. These are called *internal records* or *storage records.*

Data are communicated from one data base to another by means of *communication records,* which are output from the sending data base in an agreed-upon format suitable for input to the receiving data base. These records can be transmitted on printed cards, on magnetic tape, or through direct computer-to-computer transmission.

From this discussion emerge the following data base processes and associated formats:

data input	input format
communication between systems	communications format
data storage	internal format or storage format
output for human readers	output format or display format

The conceptual schema (which may include internal record formats) is defined by the data base administrator and is in common to all users. Communication formats are often standardized across systems for compatibility. Input and output formats can be defined for an individual application.

In manual library operations the same format is used for input (typing data on a catalog card master), communication (through the Library of Congress card service), storage (in the catalog), and output (to a user reading a catalog card). In the OCLC system the MARC format, a widely used format for bibliographic records, is used for data input through original cataloging by participating libraries, for data communication on magnetic tape (from the Library of Congress to OCLC and from OCLC to participating libraries that have their own computer system), for storage, and for the display of bibliographic records on terminals. A different format serves for printing catalog cards for participating libraries.

In these examples the same format is used in several data base processes, but at least in computerized systems this is neither necessary nor always most efficient. The input format should be designed for ease of input, the data communications format for efficiency of transmission, the internal format for efficiency of storage and internal processing, and the display format for ease of comprehension. On the other hand, conversion from one format to another means added cost. In a manual system, conversion costs tend to be prohibitive.

Input formats and output formats are part of the human–system interface. In the design of these formats the characteristics of human beings as information processors must be considered just as much as or even more than the characteristics of computers as information processors. The design of input formats and output formats is thus much too important to be left to form designers or to computer programmers alone. That is one reason why it is so important for information specialists to understand the principles of record formats.

With the trend to data base management systems that can manipulate data stored in a relational data base as illustrated in the University Data Base, the importance of record structure for storage is decreasing, but record structure is still important for input and output.

The remainder of this section deals with record formats and their properties.

9.2.2 STRUCTURE AS A KEY CONCEPT

To comprehend a record, a human reader or a computer program must be able to identify the individual data elements in the total record. To some extent a human reader can identify data elements based on their form: In an address we can readily identify city name and street name, whether they are in the sequence street–city or city–street. In a bibliographic record we can identify the title and the author without regard to their placement in the record. But the three numbers for height, width, and depth of an object are identical in form, and we can tell which is which only if they are labeled or if they are put in a fixed order that we know. But even when it is possible, implicit identification of data elements by their form requires much background knowledge and processing of such knowledge. Computers cannot yet do this as well as humans. Thus computer programs can be simpler if the data elements are identified explicitly. One method is to assign to each data element a fixed position on a video terminal screen. The program can identify the data elements by position as they are entered; structure is introduced through position. For human readers this method is also used, particularly in the display of tables.

Fixed field records also make use of position. For example, the character string

    C5907321265961281300

as it appears in a file on magnetic disk or on a piece of paper, makes very little sense as such. A computer, as well as a human reader, needs a format—a pattern, a structure—to interpret this string. Here is such a format

    `TYPE|CIRC-NO|SOC-SEC-N|DUE`

With this pattern the character string becomes intelligible:

    `TYPE|CIRC-NO|SOC-SEC-N|DUE`
    `|C|5907321|265961281|300|`

The type *C* signals a record on the entity: *Document, physical volume,* identified through its circulation number. The record establishes the relationship < borrowed by> to a *Person,* identified through social security number, and the relationship < due on> between the composite entity (*Document* < borrowed by> *Person*) and a *Date* (day 300 of the present year). Each data element has a fixed position in the record.

Variable field records use a different principle for identifying data elements. For example, the character string

    $DE Bilingual education; Minorities; Federal programs

cannot be interpreted by a computer program unless it is instructed to consider $DE as a label for subject descriptors and ";" as a delimiter between subject descriptors. A delimiter is a designated character or character string (such as /-) that separates data elements.

These examples show how structure is used to "decode" the message given through the record. The structural information needed for interpretation is imbedded in the human mind or in a computer program and is used as the data are processed in the brain or in computer memory.

9.2.3 FIXED FIELD AND VARIABLE FIELD RECORDS

This section elaborates on the concept of record structure. *Data elements* are the elemental components of a record. A *group* consists of one or more data elements; a *segment* consists of one or more groups; a *record* consists of one or more segments. The four-level hierarchy (data element, group, segment, record) is convenient to simplify discourse, but more or fewer hierarchical levels (ever more comprehensive groupings of data elements) can be and are used. A *data field* is the space provided in a record structure for a data element, a group, or a segment. If a data field refers to a group, the portion of space provided for an individual data element within the group is called a *subfield*.

The structure of a record is determined by two characteristics of its components—*length* and *number of occurrences*. These characteristics can be applied to data elements, groups, segments, or the record as a whole.

Length	Fixed number of characters versus variable number of characters	
Number of occurrences	Maximum and minimum number of occurrences of the same type of	
	data elements	in a group (or in a segment or record);
	groups	in a segment (or in a record);
	segments	in a record.

For example, the format may specify at most five authors, exactly one title, (at most one and at least one), at most five and at least one subject descriptor. A data element, group, or segment that occurs at least once is called *required*. A data element, group, or segment that may occur a variable number of times is called *repeating*.

The following examples illustrate these concepts. *Social security number* for a person and *Title* for a document are usually required and are singly occurring data elements. For documents, *Subject descriptor* should be defined as repeating and required, *Author* and *Series* as repeating and optional. *Position held* is a repeating group in a personnel record; the group consists of the data elements *Time started, Time ended, Employer, Position title, Salary, Reason for quitting,* and *Performance.*

The simplest record structure is one in which all data elements are of fixed length and occur a fixed number of times; this is commonly referred to as a *fixed field record format.* The record as a whole is also of fixed length. Any variation from this format leads to a variable length record.

Example:

Data element	Length	Nature
Document number	3	For all data elements
Author-1	10	
Author-2	10	
Author-3	10	max 1, 1 required
Title	90	
Source	60	
Date	8	
Subject-descriptor-1	15	
Subject-descriptor-2	15	

```
1  3 4          13 14        23 24          33 34
001 Anderson,  Adam, S.J.              Copper tubes for air conditionin

                                123 124                                183
g equipment                          J. Copper Inst. 7(1): 98-102

184  191 192              206 207   221
197303  Air conditionin Pipes
```

The author names are truncated. Since there is no third author, space is wasted. Space is also wasted in the title field and in the source field. Only two out of four subject descriptors can be accommodated; both are truncated. Fixed field records have advantages for processing. They are easy to store, transfer, and access as a whole. A person or a computer program can pick out very rapidly any data field (e.g., the title field) and process it. If the data at hand fit easily into fixed field records, all is fine. But if the data are variable and unpredictable, such as medical or bibliographical data, the fixed field format becomes a "procrustean bed"—a rigid scheme in which data must be forced.

A first measure of flexibility is achieved by allowing *repeating data elements, groups,* or *segments* while keeping their fixed length for ease of processing. The following table is an example.

Data element or group	Length	Nature
Document-number	3	Max 1, 1 required
Author	10	Repeating, optional
Title	90	Max 1, 1 required
Source	50	Max 1, 1 required
Date	8	Max 1, 1 required
Subject-descriptor	15	Repeating, one required

1 3	4 13	14 23	24
001|Anderson,| Adam, S.J.|Copper tubes for air conditioning equipmen

113	114 173	174 181	
t   J. Copper Inst. 7(1): 98-102   197303

182 196	197 211	2 12 226	227 241	
Air conditionin|Pipes   Copper   Cooling

No space for a third author is wasted, and all four subject descriptors are accommodated. Authors and subject descriptors are still truncated, and the title field wastes space. The exact position of each field is no longer the same for each record. To know where the title field starts, the program or the human reader must know (e.g., from a record directory) how many authors occur in a particular record or scan the record to find the title.

Maximum flexibility is achieved in *variable field formats.* In these formats the length of the data fields and subfields may differ from one record occurrence to another, and thus position in the record can no longer be used to identify data fields. The data fields and subfields within a record must be marked through *field labels* and/or *delimiters.* Section 9.4 gives an example of a variable field input format. Variable field output formats are used in many on-line or printed data bases.

9.3 CRITERIA FOR THE DESIGN AND EVALUATION OF DATA SCHEMAS

In this section the term *schema* is used to refer both to the conceptual schema and to record formats (external schemas). A schema should be exhaustive, specific, flexible, hospitable, compact, efficient, and reliable in operation.

Exhaustivity

Does the conceptual schema include all entity and relationship types that are needed for retrieval and display in response to search requests? Do the input record formats among them cover all entities and relationships included in the conceptual schema? Does the output format for a request include all entity and relationship types needed by the user? The design of an exhaustive conceptual schema must draw on a thorough study of needs. The exhaustivity of the conceptual schema should be checked in day-to-day operation by examining requests and the answers given.

Specificity

Does the schema define the entities and relationships at the appropriate level of detail? For example, is the date given as year, year/month, or year/month/day? Is the precise nature of the contribution of a person to a work identified? Such identification would include producer, director, camera operator, and so on for a film; or author, compiler, editor, translator, illustrator, and so on for a book. Is *Level of treatment* given only as *Juveniles* and *Others,* or are finer distinctions made? Are concepts given only at a general level (e.g., *Vegetables*) or with more specificity (e.g., *Beans* or even *Garbanzo beans*).

Flexibility

Does the schema adapt to the variability between entities? For example, does a schema for courses allow for identifying both an instructor and a graduate assistant, or two instructors? Does it provide for free comments, thus allowing for information that does not fit into a schema that must be somewhat rigid. Exhaustivity, specificity, and flexibility all contribute to a schema's *expressiveness,* its ability to express the various characteristics of an entity.

Hospitality

Can entity and relationship types be added as the need for them becomes known? Can specificity be increased? Can all this be done without disturbing the usability of the existing data and without requiring major changes in the programs for input processing and data base creation and retrieval? Hospitality depends heavily on the data structure and associated programs for processing data.

Compactness

This quality refers to the storage space needed and its relation to the intellectual content of the data base. It depends on technical features of the storage organization but also on the identifiers used for entities and, with record-oriented storage, on the storage format. The number for a month is more compact than the name; an initial needs less space than a full first or middle name. Increased specificity means longer identifiers (e.g., 19720312 instead of just 1972) and thus less compactness. Including the same data element value twice, as is done for the author on many catalog cards and in the MARC format, wastes input time, storage space, and user time. The display of unneeded data elements in output records wastes communication time and user time.

Efficiency

This attribute refers to the relationship of quality to effort: effort needed for data collection and typing or keying, for processing of data recorded in the input format, for communicating data, for integrating new data into the data base, for assembling the data required by a display format from the internal organization of the data base, and finally, for reading and comprehending data in the output or display format. The more compact a format, the less data need to be keyed, processed, and read. Unless these operations become more difficult due to compactness, the more compact format is thus more efficient. Reading an author's name once is more efficient than reading it twice. On the other hand, human comprehension may be faster if the month is given by name, not number.

Reliability

This quality refers to the avoidance of error by humans or machines in the various data base processes.

9.4 INPUT FORMATS

An input record is used to update the data base; it usually centers on a focal entity and gives data elements about it, especially relationships to other entities. The input format serves the double function of communicating to the indexer the relationships and other data elements required by the conceptual schema and of providing structure so that the ISAR system staff or a computer program can recognize the individual data elements in the record. Query formulations are also input to an ISAR system, but we postpone discussion of query format until Chapter 17.

Input of both data and queries is a critical operation in terms of cost and of speed. The efficiency of input is determined in large measure by the input format: The time it takes to fill in a form depends largely on the design of the form; likewise, the time for keying the data on the form and for computer processing of the keyed data depends on the input format. Figure 9.3, a segment from the ISAR system diagram shown in Fig. 5.2, shows the functions of the input format in the ISAR process. This process can be applied in many contexts. For example, in a social science survey a questionnaire might be used for data collection, a coding sheet for data formatting, and keying from the coding sheet for data input. In cataloging, one often uses a worksheet on which data on a document are recorded in the proper format and from which they are then typed onto a catalog card or keyed. The steps following input processing—namely, data base building and maintenance, comparison/match, and display—are the subject matter of Chapter 11. Data base build-

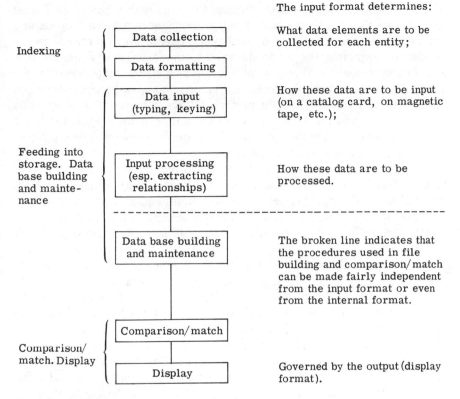

Fig. 9.3   The ISAR process.

ing uses the representation of data in the form of dyadic relationships that was introduced in Chapter 3. For example, the pair (Document 3, Medicine) represents a relationship between a document and a subject. The conversion of an input record into a set of pairs is the function of *input processing;* it requires knowledge of the input format. The programs for data base building and maintenance operate on the new representation and need no knowledge of the input format. Data base management systems exploit this fact to achieve efficiency. They allow the user to define his or her own input (and output) formats to meet the special requirements of the entities and queries to be processed but use a common core of programs to build data structures and search them.

As an example for the role of the input format in data collection for indexing, consider an employment service. The input format for a job applicant, usually presented as a printed form, tells what data about a job applicant are important and must be collected. If the value of a data element type cannot be seen easily, the indexer must take pains to determine it. For example, if

Typing speed is a required data element, the employment center staff must give the applicant a typing test. Bibliographic indexing also may require special effort. The author of a journal article may be given at the end rather than at the beginning; the precise date and volume number of a journal issue may appear not on the first page of a journal article but on the cover of the issue; the fact that a book represents the proceedings of a conference can sometimes be seen only from the preface. On the other hand, data elements that are not part of the input format should not be included even if they are easily available because they would only swamp the system. The input format serves as a checklist for these decisions.

Different subsets of data may be collected and input on different occasions; different input formats are needed. For instance, we can distinguish between input records that pertain to new main entities and input records used for updating the data on a main entity already in the data base.

The remainder of this section deals with bibliographic data to illustrate processing of variable field input records by computer program. A (much simplified) example is shown in Fig. 9.4. To a computer program a variable field record appears simply as one long string of characters. The record is structured using a divide-and-conquer approach. On the macro-level the record is subdivided into data fields, which are identified by field labels—in the example $NO, $AU, $TI, $SO, and $DE. Within a data field, special *delimiter characters* separate data elements: In the author field ';' separates several authors; in the imprint field for journal articles '1' separates the journal title from the date, ';' separates the date from the volume and issue, and ':' separates these from the page number; in the descriptor field ';' separates descriptors.

The input processing program uses a top-down approach, corresponding to the record structure. There is a main module for dealing with the overall record structure and many specific modules, each dealing with the structure of one data field. The main module looks for $ to determine the boundaries of a field and uses the two-character field label following $ for selecting the appropriate individual module. The individual modules use delimiter characters within the data field to be processed. For example, the module for processing the author field looks for ';' to determine the boundaries of one author. In this way the main module (and the programmer writing it) must contend only with the macro-structure of the record; it does not need to "know" anything about the micro-structure, that is, the structure of the individual data fields. Conversely, the module for a given field must contend only with the micro-structure of that field; it need not be concerned with either the macro-structure of the record or the micro-structure of other fields. This approach makes for ease of program creation and program modification; it introduces a greal deal of flexibility.

The Format

$NO *Document number*

$AU *Authors*   Personal name example: Anderson, Carter H.
           Corporate name example: *Metco (* is prefix)
           Several names separated by ;

$TI *Title*

$SO *Source* Books: New York: Wiley; 1968. 384 p.
           Articles: J. Copper Inst. 1973.3; 7(1): 98–102

$DE *Subject descriptors* separated by ;

Sample abstract to be processed

Copper tubes for air conditioning. Carter H. Anderson, S. J. Adam (Climate Technology, Inc.). J. Copper Inst. vol. 7, no. 1, March 1973, p. 98–102, 3 ill., 9 ref. Describes various kinds of copper tubing for air conditioning equipment and their specifications as to diameter and thickness. Discusses advantages over other types of tubing.

Input records

$NO 1 $AU Anderson, Carter H.; Adam, S.J. $TI Copper tubes for air conditioning equipment
  $SO J. Copper Inst. 1973.3; 7(1): 98–102 $DE Air conditioning; Pipes; Copper; Cooling
$NO 2 $AU Timm, S. T.; *Metco $TI How to draw copper wire $SO New York: Wiley; 1968.
  384 p. $DE Wire; Copper; Production
$NO 3 $AU Dunn, A. K.; Meter, S. R.; Smith, D. J. $TI Artificial arteries: plastic helps sur-
  geons $SO Medical Devices Quarterly. 1971.10; 15(4): 583–598 $DE Pipes; Plastic; Artificial;
  Medicine

Relationships produced through input processing

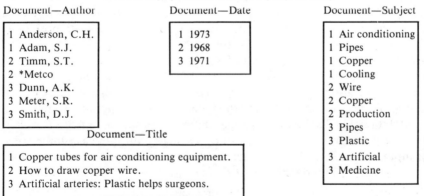

Document—Author

| 1 Anderson, C.H. |
| 1 Adam, S.J. |
| 2 Timm, S.T. |
| 2 *Metco |
| 3 Dunn, A.K. |
| 3 Meter, S.R. |
| 3 Smith, D.J. |

Document—Date

| 1 1973 |
| 2 1968 |
| 3 1971 |

Document—Subject

| 1 Air conditioning |
| 1 Pipes |
| 1 Copper |
| 1 Cooling |
| 2 Wire |
| 2 Copper |
| 2 Production |
| 3 Pipes |
| 3 Plastic |
| 3 Artificial |
| 3 Medicine |

Document—Title

| 1 Copper tubes for air conditioning equipment. |
| 2 How to draw copper wire. |
| 3 Artificial arteries: Plastic helps surgeons. |

Fig. 9.4   Processing of variable field records.

9.4.1 DESIGN CONSIDERATIONS FOR INPUT FORMATS

To save the time of the data typist and to minimize errors, field labels that occur in all or in a good portion of the input records should be supplied by machine, ideally in a workform displayed on a video screen as in OCLC. Workform input (also called menu-driven input) can be implemented easily on mini- or microcomputer-based input stations. If necessary, the input format can be divided into parts to be displayed one after the other. However, the ideal input format has only a few data fields, and each data field is required for every record. In this way all field labels can be included in the workform and completeness can be checked automatically, since every data field in the record must contain data. (The data value may be *Not applicable*—for example, for the rare case of a document without any author.) If the entities to be described vary a good deal in the data elements needed, this ideal cannot be achieved. As a rule of thumb, the workform should contain those data fields that are needed in more than 30% of all records; if they do not apply to the entity at hand, the data typist simply skips over them. The data typist must enter the labels for data fields that, due to their low frequency, are omitted from the workform.

Every occurrence of an infrequent data field causes extra work (if there are many infrequent data field types, there may be one or two occurrences in every record). Therefore, the data field definitions should be fairly broad. For example, there should be one data field to include both personal authors (and other contributors) and corporate entries (as in Fig. 9.3 but not in MARC II). Logically, the relationship of either personal authors or corporate entries to the document is very similar; only the type of entity to which the relationship is established is different. Corporate entries can be distinguished easily by prefixing the name with an asterisk. The one data field occurs in almost every record; if two data fields are defined, both must be included in the workform with the percentage of use going down. The data field $AU includes also compilers, editors, translators, illustrators, and other contributors who must be mentioned. The particular relation of a person or organization to the document can be shown through an indicator such as comp(iler) or ed(itor) following the name. Consider another example of a broad data field. The MARC I format defined separate data fields for place of publication, publisher, and date of publication. But this was cumbersome for input. These data elements occur in almost all document records, forming a standard group of three data elements; they are best combined in one data field with appropriate delimiters (as in MARC II). A repeating data element, such as subject descriptor, should have one data field with delimiters within so that the field label appears only once; in contrast, in the MARC format the field label 650 must be keyed for every subject heading (except the first when using a workform).

Delimiters can be single characters or character combinations. Single characters are easier for input and computer processing. However, it is very important that a delimiter never appear as part of a data value in the field at hand. For example, ',' is not a suitable delimiter in the author field because commonly ',' is used as part of the author's name, separating last name from first name. (Many bibliographic citations use ',' to separate names anyway.) Likewise, using '/' as delimiter in the subject descriptor field rules out descriptors such as *V/STOL aircraft.* In the format of the source field for journal articles, '.' is not a suitable delimiter after the journal title because '.' occurs in abbreviated titles; we can use '1' as a delimiter ('1' is the first digit of the date). If possible, delimiters should make sense not only to the computer system but also to the humans preparing, inputting, or proofreading data. The characters ; : . ( ) are very suitable from this point of view; ‡a, ‡b, and so on (used in the MARC II format) are less suitable. Proper choice of delimiters makes programs for output of data easier, since delimiters can be displayed as they are with no translation necessary.

9.5 OUTPUT FORMATS

The output format determines the completeness of the information given and the ease of scanning and comprehension by human readers and thus is an important factor in the quality of information transfer achieved through the information system.

An output format should be designed with the specific purpose and background of the user in mind. Many computer retrieval systems let the user design a tailor-made output format for the request at hand; others have a series of standard formats from which the user can choose. The specification of the output format is part of the query formulation (see Chapter 17). In written, typed, or printed retrieval tools the output format is designed once and for all; it cannot be adapted to a specific request. However, it may well be that one output format is appropriate in the author catalog and another in the subject catalog. In a computer-produced catalog such differentiation can be implemented easily.

The design of an output format should start with the consideration of its *exhaustivity*—what entities and relationships to include. Data that are not really needed are distracting and wasteful of space. Next comes the determination of the best *sequence of data elements,* considering the importance of each element and the logical flow of the total record. For example, bibliographic records found in response to a subject request might be displayed in the sequence

Title
Abstract (if any)
Subject descriptors assigned
Journal and date (indication of quality and up-to-dateness)
Author and author affiliation (again indication of quality)
Pointer to more information (abstract, full text, reviews).

If abstracts are subdivided into sections, such as

Problem
Method
Results
Conclusions

their inclusion and sequence may be varied in accordance with the purpose at hand; *Results* may be the most important section and therefore be displayed first (perhaps even before the title).

Next to be considered is *specificity;* for example, the conceptual schema may distinguish several *Levels of readability,* but the output format may distinguish only the easiest documents (marked by asterisk) and the rest. The *entity identifiers* used in output records should be the shortest identifiers that are easily comprehended by the user. For serials, ISSN (International Standard Serial Number), while short, will not do. An accepted very short abbreviation, such as JASIS (for *Journal of the American Society for Information Science*) or ARIST (for *Annual Review of Information Science and Technology*), will do for serials in the user's own discipline. Full titles or easily recognizable abbreviations, such as *J. Amer. Soc. Info. Sci.,* are needed outside the user's discipline. It may be advisable to indicate the type of data element explicitly, such as *Author* or *AU* and *Title* or *TI.* For data that can be displayed in a columnar format, labels on the top of each column establish a fixed field output format.

Typography may be quite important for speed of comprehension. The record structure can be made visual by using separate lines for groups of one or more data elements, line spaces, indentions, underline, boldface, or (on a video screen) black on white or flashing characters. Output in the form of a graph or map and audio output (including voice) can also be very effective.

Defining the output format is one aspect of query formulation. Another aspect is specification of the entities about which information is wanted, that is, specification of selection criteria. This aspect is treated on a very elementary level in the next chapter so as to provide the prerequisites for the discussion of data structures in Chapter 11. Query formulation is discussed much more fully in Chapter 17.

APPENDIX 9.1 EXAMPLES OF RECORD FORMATS

OCLC number	1933939
Record status	New
Date entered	76–01–19
Date used	79–05–30
Type	language material, printed
Bibliographic level	monograph
Government publication	not a government publication
Language	English
Source	non-LC cataloging
Illustrations	none
Form of reproduction code	not a reproduction
Encoding level	full cataloging input by OCLC
Conference publication	not a conference publication
Country of publication	California
Type of date designator	imprint contains one known or probable date of publication
Main entry in body of entry designator	main entry in body of entry
Index designator	index not present
Modified record designator	record not modified
Festschrift designator	not a festschrift
Form of contents designator	bibliographies, statistics
Descriptive cataloging code	record is in ISBD form
Intellectual level	not applicable
Date of publication	1975
Cataloging source	YHM (Hamilton College, Clinton, N.Y.)
Call number	HD6058. C38
Personal name	Cartter, Allan Murray
Title and author	The disappearance of sex discrimination in first job placement of new Ph.D's/by A.M. Cartter, W.E. Ruhter
Imprint	Los Angeles: Higher Education Research Institute, 1975
Collation	27p 23cm.
Series	HERI Research Report; 75–1
Bibliography note	Bibliography: p. 27
Subject headings	Women college graduates—Employment; Sex discrimination against women
Added entry Personal name	Ruhter, Wayne E., joint author

(a) full output record, field labels given explicitly

Cartter, Allan Murray
   The disappearance of sex discrimination in
first job placement of new Ph.D's/by Allan M.
Cartter and Wayne E. Ruhter.—Los Angeles:
Higher Education Research Institute, 1975.
     27 p.   23 cm.   (HERI Research Report; 75–1)
     Bibliography: p. 27.

     1.Women college graduates—Employment.
2.Sex discrimination against women. I.Ruhter,
Wayne E.

(b) catalog card

OCLC: 1933939   Rec Stat: n   Entrd: 760119   Used: 790530
Type: a   Bib lvl: m   Govt pub: Lang: eng   Source: d   Illus:
Repr: Enc lvl: I   Conf pub: 0   Ctry: cau   Dat tp: s   M/F/B: 10
Index: 0   Mod rec: Festschr: 0   Cont: bs
Desc: i   Int lvl: Dates: 1975,

```
010      ---
040      YHM ‡c YHM ‡d m. c.
090      HD6058 ‡b .C38
100 10   Cartter, Allan Murray. ‡w cn
245 14   The disappearance of sex discrimination in first job placement of new Ph.D.'s / ‡c by
         Allan M. Cartter and Wayne E. Ruhter.
260 0    Los Angeles: ‡b Higher Education Research Institute ‡c 1975
300      27p.;‡c 23 cm.
490 0    HERI Research Report;  ‡75–1
504      Bibliography: p. 27
650 0    Women college graduates ‡x Employment
650 0    Sex discrimination against women
700 10   Ruhter, Wayne E        , ‡e joint author
```

(c) OCLC terminal display

1 12	13 24	25 65
	Variable Control	Variable
Leader 12	Number 12	Fixed Fields 41
00511nƀamƀƀ	ƀƀ76225678ƀ	ƀƀƀ760119a1975ƀƀƀƀcauƀƀƀƀƀƀƀbsƀ000100eng

Variable Fields

040ƀƀ YHM‡cYHM ‡d m.c. 090ƀƀHD6058‡b.C38 10010 ‡aCartter Allan Murray 24514
‡aThe disappearance of sex discrimination in first job placement of new PhDs‡cby Allan
M. Cartter and Wayne E. Ruhter 2600ƀ ‡aLos Angeles:‡bHigher Education Research Inst
itute, ‡c1975 300ƀƀ ‡a27 p.; ‡c23 cm. 4900ƀ ‡aHERI Research Report; ‡v75–1 504ƀƀ
‡aBibliography: p.27 650ƀ0 ‡aWomen college graduates‡xEmployment 650ƀ0 ‡aSex discri
mination against women 70010 ‡aRuhter Wayne E‡ejoint author

(d) modified internal MARC format.

Fig. 9.5 Bibliographic records in several formats.

<u>print full indented</u>

AUTHOR	Kandel RF
TITLE	A selective survey of national legislation on foods for infants and young children.
LANGUAGE	Eng
MESH HEADING	Advertising/STANDARDS
MESH HEADING	Age Factors
MESH HEADING	Breast Feeding
MESH HEADING	Child, Preschool
MESH HEADING	Food Handling/STANDARDS
MESH HEADING	Food Labeling/STANDARDS
MESH HEADING	Human
MESH HEADING	Infant Food/*STANDARDS
MESH HEADING	Infant Nutrition
MESH HEADING	Infant
MESH HEADING	Infant, Newborn
MESH HEADING	International Cooperation
MESH HEADING	Legislation
MESH HEADING	United Nations
MESH HEADING	World Health Organization
SOURCE	Food Nutr (Roma) 1981;7(1):28–31

<u>print</u>

AU - Kandel RF
TI - A selective survey of national legislation on foods for infants and young children.
SO - Food Nutr (Roma) 1981;7(1):28–31

<u>print ti,au</u>

TI - A selective survey of national legislation on foods for infants and young children.
AU - Kandel RF

<u>print au,ti</u>

AU - Kandel RF
TI - A selective survey of national legislation on foods for infants and young children.

Fig. 9.6   MEDLINE output formats. The command requesting each format is underlined.

FILE26:FOUNDATION DIRECTORY 1979 ED.
(CORP. FOUNDATION CTR.)

ID No. 003174 EI No. 396084804
 TRANE COMPANY FOUNDATION, INC., THE
 3600 PAMMEL CREEK ROAD, LA CROSSE, WI 54601 (608) 782-8000
 INCORPORATED IN 1964 IN WISCONSIN
 PURPOSE AND ACTIVITIES: GENERAL GIVING, WITH EMPHASIS ON COMMUNITY
FUNDS, THE PERFORMING ARTS, YOUTH AGENCIES, AND HIGHER EDUCATION
 FINANCIAL DATA (YR. ENDING 12/31/77):
 ASSETS: $426,224 AM GIFTS RECEIVED: $200,000 EXPENDITURES: $113,282
 GRANTS AMOUNT: $112,990
 OFFICERS: RICHARD R. GRIFFITHS/ PRESIDENT, JAMES C. WORKMAN/SECRETARY, CHARLES
 H. BENTZEL/TREASURER
 WRITE: RICHARD R. GRIFFITHS, PRESIDENT
 APPLICATION INFORMATION: GRANT APPLICATION GUIDELINES AVAILABLE; INITIAL AP-
PROACH BY LETTER; APPLICATION FORM REQUIRED; SUBMIT 2 COPIES OF PROPOSAL IN AUGUST OR
SEPTEMBER; APPLICATION DEADLINE OCTOBER 15; BOARD MEETS AS REQUIRED

Fig. 9.7   Foundation directory record format.

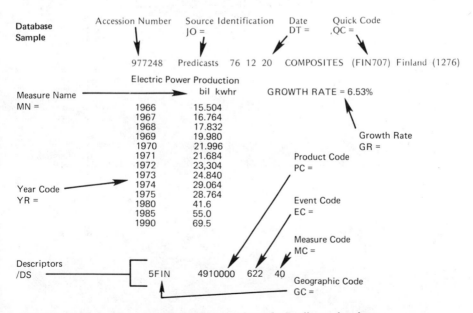

Fig. 9.8   Numerical data record: A time series from the Predicasts data base.

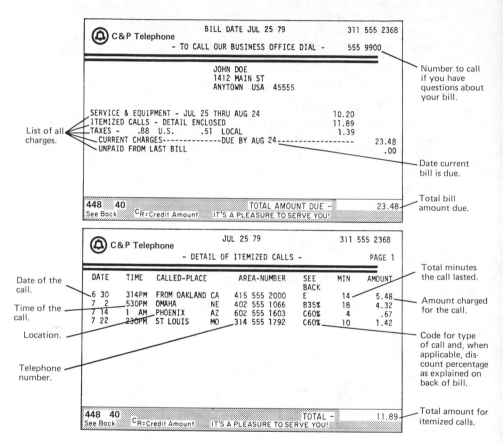

Fig. 9.9 Telephone bill record format.

CHAPTER 10

Elementary Query Formulation

OBJECTIVES

The objectives of this chapter are to explain the use of AND and OR and the problems of NOT in query formulation.

10.1 LOGICAL AND

This and the following sections all start from an illustrative query put to a bibliographic ISAR system.

Query statement: I need documents on airports in New York

Consider which of the following documents are relevant:

Airports	Airports in Washington, DC	
Noise control at airports	The PanAm terminal in New York	New York
Principles of airport design	Subway access to New York airports	The finances of New York
A new London airport for traffic on airways from the East	Capacity of New York airports for handling traffic on new airways	Entertainment in New York
		The New York Subway
		Bus terminals in New York
	Airways starting from New York	

For a document to be relevant, *both* aspects of the query statement—*Airports* and *New York*—must be present. This is the meaning of logical *AND;* thus the query formulation

Airports AND New York

AND is a *logical operator* or *Boolean operator*. It corresponds to the *set operator intersection*. Let us call the set of all documents dealing with *Airports* the *Airports* set. The intersection of the *Airports* set and the *New York* set is defined as the set of all documents that belong to both, that is, all documents relevant to the sample query. The schema shows the intersection as a *Venn diagram*.

10.2 LOGICAL OR

Query statement: Documents on airports and documents on airways

Consider which of the following documents are relevant:

Airports	Airports in Washington, DC
Noise control at airports	The PanAm terminal in New York
Principles of airport design	Subway access to New York airports
A new London airport for traffic on airways from the East	Capacity of New York airports for handling traffic on new airways
Airways between the East and West Coast	Airways starting from New York
Airways in the Northeastern United States	Airways

A document is relevant if it deals with at least one of the two concepts (1) *Airports* and (2) *Airways*. In other words, a document is relevant if it deals with *Airports* or *Airways* or both. This is the meaning of logical OR (inclusive OR). Thus the query formulation

Airports OR Airways

Logical OR corresponds to the set operator *union*. The union of the *Airports* set and the *Airways* set is defined as the set of all documents that belong to at least one of the two original sets; that is, the union consists of all documents relevant to the sample query.

10.3 LOGICAL AND WITH LOGICAL OR

Query statement: Documents on airports in and airways to New York

This is more specific than query 2. The requester is interested in the same overall topic *Airports* OR *Airways* but restricted to the city of New York.

<u>Airports</u>	Airports in Washington, DC	
Noise control at airports	The PanAm terminal in New York	
Principles of airport design	Subway access to New York airports	<u>New York</u>
A new London airport for traffic on airways from the East	Capacity of New York airports for handling traffic on new airways	The finances of New York Entertainment in New York The New York Subway
Airways between the East and West Coast	Airways starting from New York	Bus terminals in New York
Airways in the North-eastern United States	<u>Airways</u>	

The subject condition of the query is satisfied if a document deals with at least one of the concepts (1) *Airports* or (2) *Airways*. The geographical condition is satisfied if a document deals with *New York*. A document is relevant if *both* conditions are met. Thus the query formulation

(Airports OR Airways) AND New York

The first condition is a compound condition.

In terms of sets one should form the union of the *Airports* set and the *Airways* set (as in query 2) and then form the intersection of this new set with the set of all documents dealing with *New York*.

In the example there are two *facets* (types of conditions)—a subject and a place. It is good practice to discern facets in query formulation. Another good method is to find the individual concepts that are mandatory—without which the entity would not be relevant (in the example this is *New York*) and then proceed to more complex conditions (in the example *Airports* OR *Airways*).

Some equivalences:

- Airports OR Airways is the same as Airways OR Airports.
- New York AND (Airports OR Airways) is the same as
- (New York AND Airports) OR (New York AND Airways)

More generally, the following formula holds:

A AND $(B$ OR $C) = (A$ AND $B)$ OR $(A$ AND $C)$

The two sides are logically equivalent and lead to the same search results, but execution time, for example, in a computer search, might be quite different. This is why the formula is important.

Parentheses are needed to avoid ambiguity as in *New York* AND (*Airports* OR *Airways*). The parentheses indicate to a human searcher or to a computer program: First form the OR combination, then AND the result with *New York*. This is very different from (*New York* AND *Airports*) OR *Airways:* One condition for retrieval of a document is that it be indexed by *New York* and by *Airports;* but *Airways* alone would also suffice for a document to be retrieved. In

New York AND Airports AND Planning

all three concepts must be ANDed. The result is the same no matter in which sequence the operations are performed. Parentheses are not needed.

10.4 THE AMBIGUITY OF NATURAL LANGUAGE "AND"

Query statement: Pollution and Wildlife in the U.S. and Canada

Clearly, the effect of *Pollution* on *Wildlife* is meant, so both must be present. Therefore, the correct operator is AND. An individual document is relevant if it deals with one of the two countries. Therefore, the correct operator is OR. Thus

Pollution AND Wildlife AND (US. OR Canada).

If "and" connects two interacting concepts, such as *Pollution* and *Wildlife,* the correct logical operator is AND. If "and" connects two parallel concepts as, in this example, *U.S.* and *Canada,* the correct logical operator is OR. However, the query statement

Economic relations between the U.S. and Canada

clearly requires the formulation

Economic relations AND U.S. AND Canada.

What logical operator should be used for

Steel corrosion in hot and humid climate?

Consider that corrosion is influenced by the *joint* action of high temperature and humidity. Corrosion in hot and dry climate would be quite different.

Thus, the query formulation should be

Corrosion AND Steel AND Hot climate AND Humid climate

Often "and" is inherently ambiguous and the reference librarian must seek clarification from the requester, either by asking directly or by inventing some document titles (or job descriptions or whatever) such that some would be retrieved only by the OR interpretation, not by the more specific AND interpretation. If the user rejects these sample titles, then AND is intended. Consider query statement 2,

References on airways and airports.

If the requester rejects the documents

Airways in the northwestern U.S. and
Principles of airport design

but accepts the document

A new London airport for traffic on airways from the East,

then the query formulation should be

Airways AND Airports

Even in the first example

Pollution and wildlife in the U.S. and Canada

the requester may have in mind documents that compare the situation in the two countries. If so, the parallel concepts *U.S.* and *Canada* must both be present; in this case, logical AND is the correct operator.

10.5 LEVELS OF PARENTHESES

Query statement: Rapid traffic connections between Houston and Dallas on the one hand and New York and Boston on the other.

In query 3, parentheses were needed in the query formulation to avoid ambiguity. In this query formulation several levels of parentheses are needed. By first looking for individual concepts that must be present to make a document relevant, one finds that *Rapid traffic connections* is a necessary condition—without it a document cannot be relevant. Thus the query formulation starts

Rapid traffic connections AND

However, this condition is not sufficient. What are sufficient conditions? If the document deals, in addition, with both Houston and Dallas, that is, with

Houston AND Dallas

it is relevant. However, that condition is not necessary.

New York AND Boston

will do just as well. The two AND pairs must be joined by OR. This results in the final query formulation

Rapid traffic connections AND
[(Houston AND Dallas) OR (New York AND Boston)]

10.6 LOGICAL NOT AND ITS PITFALLS

Query statement: Freight transport not using rails

Many people (and many textbooks) suggest the query formulation

(1) Freight transport AND NOT Rail transport

This is straightforward and simple enough. However, on second thought problems appear. Consider the document *Comparative cost data for freight transport on inland waterways and on rails.* Is it relevant? The answer is clearly yes. However, the document would *not* be retrieved because AND NOT *Rail transport* means that a document that deals with *Rail transport* will be excluded. Some more examples are found in the diagram where the bold-framed area corresponds to the initial query formulation.

Freight transport		
The role of freight transport in the economy		
Shipping freight on the Mississippi	Truck–rail competition	
Freight ships on the Great Lakes	Comparative cost data for freight transport on inland waterways and on rails	
Jumbo airplanes for military freight	Pipelines versus rail for coal transport	AMTRAK: The first five years
The economics of trucking	The freight trains are rolling again	The railway networks in the United States and Europe
Transportation of coal slurry through pipelines	The performance of U.S. railways in freight transport	
		Airlines versus super-trains
		Rail transport

Many relevant documents are excluded by the condition AND NOT *Rail transport*. A better query formulation would be

(2) Freight transport AND
     (Water transport OR Air transport OR Road transport OR
     Hovercraft transport)

This query formulation retrieves most of the documents that were missed by the first one, and it correctly excludes, as does the first one, those documents that deal only with *Rail transport* and with no other mode of transportation. The fallacy of AND NOT is that somebody naively employing the first query formulation means to exclude only the documents that deal *exclusively* with *Rail transport*. But he or she is not aware that documents dealing with *Rail transport among other modes of transportation* are also excluded.

The second query formulation also has a problem. How well it works depends on the searcher's ability to think of all the possible modes of transportation. In the example, the document *Transportation of coal slurry through pipelines*—found by formulation (1)—is missed because the searcher overlooked pipelines as a mode of transportation. Combining (1) and (2) with OR leads to more complete retrieval:

(3) Query 2 OR (Freight transport AND NOT Rail transport)

However, this formulation still misses the document *Pipelines vs. rails for coal transport;* it does not contain any of the ORed concepts from query formulation (2) and thus is not retrieved by query 2, and it *does* contain rail transport and thus is excluded by AND NOT *Rail transport*.

If the searcher cannot think of the various modes of transportation, and if *Freight transport* alone would be too broad, formulation (1) must do. Any of these query formulations can be improved by adding

OR (Freight transport AND Review/comprehensive treatment)

If every entity is concerned with at most one mode of transportation, then AND NOT can be used without problems. While this is very unlikely for documents, it may well be true for other types of entities (e.g., products), and in that case one should certainly take advantage of the convenience of AND NOT.

CHAPTER 11

Data Structures and Access

OBJECTIVES

The objectives of this chapter are to enable the reader to (1) take a data base and analyze its data structure with respect to searchability and effort needed for creation and maintenance and determine the optimal way for searching a given query, and (2) design a new data structure given data base content and query characteristics.

11.1 EXPLORATION OF DATA STRUCTURES

The intellectual content of the entity store of an ISAR system (Fig. 5.6) is determined by the conceptual schema. The data structure is concerned with actual access to the data. It serves two purposes: (1) to find all entities that meet the query conditions; (2) for each entity found, to assemble the data required by the output format.

We shall analyze several data structures to see how well they serve the two purposes, considering also the cost for processing and storage space needed to create and maintain each data structure. A small data base dealing with documents on material objects serves as example. Its conceptual schema is simple. The main entities are *documents,* identified by a number; they are related to other entities as follows: *Document* < is authored by > *Person, Document* < is published in > *Date,* and *Document* < deals with > *Subject.* All data structures discussed implement this one conceptual schema. Queries are also simple; each asks for the documents (the focal entities) that fit a Boolean combination of data element values; the sample queries are shown in Fig. 11.1. For each data structure, we present an example on the right (odd) page and explanation on the facing left (even) page.

Data base 1. *One file of document records arranged by number*

Searching

Query 1: Pipes AND Copper

The searcher or computer program must examine each document record in turn to see whether it has both subject descriptors, *Pipes* and *Copper*. The structure gives no assistance in pinpointing the relevant documents faster. Examination for the two descriptors is easy because all subject descriptors are right there in the record. Examining all records in a file is slow unless the file is small or the scanning mechanism extremely fast.

Query 3: Pipes AND (Copper OR Plastic)

Again one must examine every document record checking for *Pipes* and at least one of *Copper* or *Plastic*.

Queries 4–6 are searched the same way: Date and author are just as much a part of the records as subject descriptors.

Assembling Data about a Document Found

All data are already assembled in the record.

Creating and Maintaining the Data Base

This step is simple: Document records can be entered in any sequence; new records can be added anywhere—at the end, at the beginning, or randomly in the middle. *Space requirements* are minimal since each entity identifier and each of the data element values occur only once.

```
Query 1: Pipes          AND   Copper
Query 2: Pipes          AND   Copper  AND   Production
Query 3: Pipes          AND   (Copper  OR   Plastic)
Query 4: Pipes          AND   Date 1971 or later
Query 5: Pipes          AND   Copper AND Date 1971 or later
Query 6: Simon,L.A.           (Author)
```

Fig. 11.1   Sample queries for examining data structures.

Data base 1. *One file of document records arranged by number*

File 1.0. *File of document records*

1	Adam, S. J. 1973. *Copper tubes for air conditioning equipment.* Pipes; Copper; Cooling.
2	Timm, S. T. 1968. *How to draw copper wire.* Wire; Copper; Production.
3	Dunn, A. K. 1970; Elm, B.C.; Hut, D.D.. *Artificial arteries: Plastic helps surgeons.* Pipes; Plastic; Artificial; Medicine.
4	Kerr, J. L. 1970. *The production of steel pipes.* Pipes; Steel; Production.
5	Ruth, E. F. 1969. *The production of copper rods.* Rods; Copper; Production.
6	Gill, M. C. 1965. *The production of copper pipes.* Pipes; Copper; Production.
7	Hut, D. D. 1972. *Vinyl hoses in appliances.* Pipes; Plastic; Appliances.
8	Irk, H. R. 1973; Simon, L. A.. *Spiral copper tubes as cooling elements.* Pipes; Copper; Plastic; Cooling.
9	Elm, B. C. 1971; Timm, S. T.. *Precision methods in wire drawing.* Wire; Copper; Steel; Production; Precision.
10	Mann, M. M. 1971; Jackson, T. R.. *The production of pipes* Pipes; Production.
11	Ford, H. X. 1965; Simon, L. A.. *All about copper.* Copper.
12	Simon, L. A. 1973. *The production of PVC capillaries.* Pipes; Plastic; Production.
13	Berry, W. K. 1970. *Polyvinylchloride reactions.* Plastic; Reactions.

Data base 2. *A set of dyadic relations with pairs arranged in document order* (for computerized ISAR only)

Searching

The relations of data base 2 consist of pairs—for example, (1 Pipes), which is short for *Document* 1 <deals with> *Subject* Pipes. As in data base 1 one must examine data for each document in turn; the structure is no help in pinpointing the relevant documents faster. Queries 1–3 use only subject descriptors; the search requires only relation 2.4. To see whether a document has the requisite subject descriptors, one examines all its pairs.

Query 4: Pipes AND Date 1971 or later

The search process begins with scanning relation 2.4 and finding the pair (1 *Pipes*). Consulting relation 2.2 for document 1 shows the date 1973, so document 1 is relevant. For document 2, there is no pair with *Pipes* in relation 2.4. For document 3, there is a pair with *Pipes,* but accessing relation 2.2 gives the date 1970; document 3 is not relevant. The salient point is that relation 2.4 does not have enough information to decide about relevance of a document; to obtain the information needed, one must access relation 2.2 for each document found in relation 2.4. Since relation 2.2 is arranged by document number (the document number is the *primary key*), the appropriate pair can be found quickly. Accessing a relation with a given primary key value is in itself an important problem of data structure design, but we ignore it here.

Assembling Data about a Document Found

The program must access all four relations to assemble the data. This requires more effort than in data base 1.

Creating and Maintaining the Data Base

This data base is created by converting each document input record into a set of pairs and then rearranging the pairs into relations. It is updated by adding each new pair to the appropriate relation; it does not matter where in the relation the new pair is added. *Space requirements* are slightly increased, since the document numbers are stored several times, not just once as in data base 1.

As long as the focus is on documents, data base 2 is worse than data base 1. But in an integrated data base that gives equal weight to all entity types and their various relationships, dyadic relations are easier to handle. Furthermore, data base 2 is a step from data base 1 to 3 and finally 4.

Data base 2. *A set of dyadic relations with pairs arranged in document order*

Relation 2.1. *Document—Author*

1	Adam, S. J.
2	Timm, S. T.
3	Dunn, A. K.
3	Elm, B. C.
3	Hut, D. D.
4	Kerr, J. L.
5	Ruth, E. F.
6	Gill, M. C.
7	Hut, D. D.
8	Irk, H. R.
8	Simon, L. A.
9	Elm, B. C.
9	Timm, S. T.
10	Mann, M. M.
10	Jackson, T. R.
11	Ford, H. X.
11	Simon, L. A.
12	Simon, L. A.
13	Berry, W. K.

Relation 2.2. *Document—Date*

1	1973	8	1973
2	1968	9	1971
3	1970	10	1971
4	1970	11	1965
5	1969	12	1973
6	1965	13	1970
7	1972		

Relation 2.3. *Document—Title*

1	Copper tubes for air conditioning equipment.
2	How to draw copper wire.
3	Artificial arteries: Plastic helps surgeons.
4	The production of steel pipes.
5	The production of copper rods.
6	The production of copper pipes.
7	Vinyl hoses in appliances.
8	Spiral copper tubes as cooling elements.
9	Precision methods in wire drawing.
10	The production of pipes.
11	All about copper.
12	The production of PVC capillaries.
13	Polyvinylchloride reactions.

Relation 2.4. *Document—Subject*

1	Pipes
1	Copper
1	Cooling
2	Wire
2	Copper
2	Production
3	Pipes
3	Plastic
3	Artificial
3	Medicine
4	Pipes
4	Steel
4	Production
5	Rods
5	Copper
5	Production
6	Pipes
6	Copper
6	Production
7	Pipes
7	Plastic
7	Appliances
8	Pipes
8	Copper
8	Plastic
8	Cooling
9	Wire
9	Copper
9	Steel
9	Production
9	Precision
10	Pipes
10	Production
11	Copper
12	Pipes
12	Plastic
12	Production
13	Plastic
13	Reactions

Data base 3. *A set of dyadic relations with pairs arranged in descriptor order* (for computerized ISAR only)

Searching

Query 1: Pipes AND Copper

To find the relevant documents, access relation 3.4 under *Pipes* and under *Copper.* For each document that occurs in a pair with *Pipes,* check whether it also occurs in a pair with *Copper;* if so, retrieve the document. There is no need to examine any more data about the documents; the structure of the data base allows for quick retrieval of the relevant documents.

Query 3: Pipes AND (Copper OR Plastic)

Retrieval follows the same pattern. For each document that occurs in a pair with *Pipes,* check whether it also occurs in a pair with *Copper* or, if that check fails, with *Plastic.*

Query 4: Pipes AND Date 1971 or later

Following the same principle, use relation 3.4 (for *Pipes*) and 3.2 (for *Date*).

Query 6: Simon, L. A. (author)

Access relation 3.1 under *Simon, L. A.* and find the numbers of all relevant documents.

Assembling Data about a Document Found

This now requires examination of *every* pair in relations 3.1 and 3.4 to find all authors and subject descriptors for a given document, and examination of relations 3.2 and 3.3 until the *one* pair with the number of the document is found. (There is only one date and only one title for each document.)

Creating and Maintaining the Data Base

This data base is created by sorting each relation in data base 2 by descriptor. It is updated by inserting each new pair in the appropriate relation *in the right place;* this requires extra effort to find the right place. The *space requirements* are the same as in data base 2.

Data base 3. *A set of dyadic relations with pairs arranged in descriptor order*

Relation 3.1. *Author—Document*

Adam, S. J.	1
Berry, W. K.	13
Dunn, A. K.	3
Elm, B. C.	3
Elm, B. C.	9
Ford, H. X.	11
Gill, M. C.	6
Hut, D. D.	3
Hut, D. D.	7
Irk, H. R.	8
Jackson, T. R.	10
Kerr, J. L.	4
Mann, M. M.	10
Ruth, E. F.	5
Simon, L. A.	8
Simon, L. A.	11
Simon, L. A.	12
Timm, S. T.	2
Timm, S. T.	9

Relation 3.2. *Date—Document*

1965	6	1971	9
1965	11	1971	10
1968	2	1972	7
1969	5	1973	1
1970	3	1973	8
1970	4	1973	12
1970	13		

Relation 3.3. *Title—Document*

All about copper	11
Artificial arteries: Plastic helps surgeons	3
Copper tubes for air conditioning equipment	1
How to draw copper wire	2
Precision methods in wire drawing	9
Polyvinylchloride reactions	13
The production of copper pipes	6
The production of copper rods	5
The production of pipes	10
The production of PVC capillaries	12
The production of steel pipes	4
Spiral copper tubes as cooling elements	8
Vinyl hoses in appliances	7

Relation 3.4. *Subject—Document*

Appliances	7
Artificial	3
Cooling	1
Cooling	8
Copper	1
Copper	2
Copper	5
Copper	6
Copper	8
Copper	9
Copper	11
Medicine	3
Pipes	1
Pipes	3
Pipes	4
Pipes	6
Pipes	7
Pipes	8
Pipes	10
Pipes	12
Plastic	3
Plastic	7
Plastic	8
Plastic	12
Plastic	13
Precision	9
Production	2
Production	4
Production	5
Production	6
Production	9
Production	10
Production	12
Reactions	13
Rods	5
Steel	4
Steel	9
Wire	2
Wire	9

Data base 4. *A set of files containing one record per descriptor (index files)*

This data base derives from data base 3: All pairs wih the same descriptor are consolidated into one record. The resulting files are *indexes.*

Searching

Searching works just as in data base 3. For example, when searching for *Pipes* AND *Copper,* find all document numbers that are listed both under *Pipes* and under *Copper.* There is no need to examine any other data. To search for *Copper* OR *Plastic,* find all document numbers that are listed under at least one of these two descriptors.

Assembling Data about a Document Found

This step is just as cumbersome as in data base 3, perhaps even more so.

Creating and Maintaining the Data Base

The data base is created by compressing the relations of data base 3. It is updated by inserting document numbers in the appropriate records. This is slightly more complex than inserting new pairs in the relations of data base 3. *Space requirements* for file 4.3 are the same as for relation 3.3, but files 4.1, 4.2, and 4.4 need less space than the corresponding relations since the descriptors are listed only once. Thus, data base 4 needs least space of all.

Implementation

Computers are ideally suited to implement data base 4, since they can manipulate the sets of document numbers at high speed; a computerized system can easily handle AND, OR, and any combination in a query for- mulation. Optical coincidence cards (peek-a-boo cards) provide another im- plementation. There is one card per descriptor; each card may have 1000 positions, one for each document. If document 6 deals with *Pipes,* hole 6 in the corresponding card is punched. Putting the cards for *Pipes* and *Copper* on top of each other reveals the holes punched in both, that is, the documents dealing with *Pipes* AND *Copper.* OR is not easily implemented this way. A printed index is not very practical for this data base, because manipulating large sets of document numbers is not a task at which humans excel, particularly if the two sets are on different pages.

Data base 4. *A set of files containing one record per descriptor (index files)*

File 4.1. *Author index*

Adam, S. J.	1
Berry, W. K.	13
Dunn, A. K.	3
Elm, B. C.	3,9
Ford, H. X.	11
Gill, M. C.	6
Hut, D. D.	3,7
Irk, H. R.	8
Jackson, T. R.	10
Kerr, J. L.	4
Mann, M. M.	10
Ruth, E. F.	5
Simon, L. A.	8,11,12
Timm, S. T.	2,9

File 4.4. *Subject descriptor index*

Appliances	7
Artificial	3
Cooling	1,8
Copper	1, 2, 5, 6, 8, 9, 11
Medicine	3
Pipes	1, 3, 4, 6, 7, 8, 10, 12
Plastic	3, 7, 8, 12, 13
Precision	9
Production	2, 4, 5, 6, 9, 10, 12
Reactions	13
Rods	5
Steel	4, 9
Wire	2, 9

File 4.2. *Date index*

1965	6,11
1968	2
1969	5
1970	3,4,13
1971	9,10
1972	7
1973	1,8,12

File 4.3. *Title index*

All about copper	11
Artificial arteries: Plastic helps surgeons	3
Copper tubes for air conditioning equipment	1
How to draw copper wire	2
Precision methods in wire drawing	9
Polyvinylchloride reactions	13
The production of copper pipes	6
The production of copper rods	5
The production of pipes	10
The production of PVC capillaries	12
The production of steel pipes	4
Spiral copper tubes as cooling elements	8
Vinyl hoses in appliances	7

The discussion so far has shown two *search modes:*

1. *Examination*—examining data about a document to see whether the document meets the query specifications.
2. *Look-up*—using the structure of the data base to select a subset containing all documents worthy of further examination; further searching can be restricted to the subset.

Data structures support these search modes in varying degrees. Data bases 1 and 2 support only examination. Data bases 3 and 4 support look-up so well that it can be used as the only search mode: All documents in the subset selected meet the query specifications. Data bases 3 and 4 are good for searching, but they are very inefficient for assembling the data about a document found; for data bases 1 and 2, it is just the other way around. A mixed data base for easy searching by subject and easy assemblage of other data could be created from data base 2 as follows. Instead of sorting *all* relations, one sorts only relation 2.4, resulting in three relations in document order and the subject descriptor relation in descriptor order. This leads to data base 5.

Data base 5. *One file of document records without subject descriptor, subject descriptor index*

Searching

Queries 1–3 are pure subject queries and are searched just as in data base 4 by look-up in the subject index.

Query 4: Pipes AND Date 1971 or later

This is a mixed query requiring two retrieval steps in data base 5.

Step 1: Look up in subject index under *Pipes;* find a list of document numbers.
Step 2: For each document number found, access file 5.0 and examine the document record to check the date.

Step 1 uses the structure of the file to find a subset of documents that contains the relevant documents. Step 2 examines each document in the subset to see whether it meets the query criteria. In short, look-up is used for a first screening, and examination for final selection. In this data base, look-up alone is not sufficient to pinpoint the documents meeting the query specifications because there is no index by date.

Data base 5. *One file of document records without subject descriptors, subject descriptor index*

File 5.0. *Document records without subject descriptors*

1	Adam, S. J. 1973. *Copper tubes for air conditioning equipment.*
2	Timm, S. T. 1968. *How to draw copper wire.*
3	Dunn, A. K. 1970; Elm, B. C.; Hut, D. D. *Artificial arteries: Plastic helps surgeons.*
4	Kerr, J. L. 1970. *The production of steel pipes.*
5	Ruth, E. F. 1969. *The production of copper rods.*
6	Gill, M. C. 1965. *The production of copper pipes.*
7	Hut, D. D. 1972. *Vinyl hoses in appliances.*
8	Irk, H. R. 1973; Simon, L. A. *Spiral copper tubes as cooling elements.*
9	Elm, B. C. 1971; Timm, S. T. *Precision methods in wire drawing.*
10	Mann, M. M. 1971; Jackson, T. R. *The production of pipes.*
11	Ford, H. X. 1965; Simon, L. A. *All about copper.*
12	Simon, L. A. 1973. *The production of PVC capillaries.*
13	Berry, W. K. 1970. *Polyvinylchloride reactions.*

File 5.4. *Subject descriptor index*

```
Appliances   7
Artificial   3
Cooling   1, 8
Copper   1, 2, 5, 6, 8, 9, 11
Medicine   3
Pipes   1, 3, 4, 6, 7, 8, 10, 12
Plastic   3, 7, 8, 12, 13
Precision   9
Production   2, 4, 5, 6, 9, 10, 12
Reactions   13
Rods   5
Steel   4, 9
Wire   2, 9
```

Query 5: Pipes AND Copper AND Date 1971 or later

The structure of the data base allows for narrowing retrieval to *Pipes* AND *Copper,* but then one must resort to examination.

Query 6: Simon, L. A. (author)

The structure provides no assistance in pinpointing relevant documents. One must examine every record in file 5.0.

Assembling Data about a Document Found

This is easy for the data elements *author, date,* and *title.* For subject descriptors, one must examine every record in file 5.4; if the number of a document is listed with a descriptor, that descriptor belongs to the document.

Creating and Maintaining the Data Base

There is less processing than for data base 4, since only one relation must be created and sorted. *Space requirements* are about the same as for data base 4.

Implementation.

This data structure can be implemented on a computer. File 5.0 could also be implemented in print; file 5.4, the subject index could be a printed file, a peek-a-boo file, or a file on a microcomputer (which may lack space for file 5.0). In a printed index, searching for descriptor combinations is cumbersome and often impractical. Examination cannot be used to make up for this, since the records in file 5.0 do not give the subject descriptors for the document (compare data base 6).

The data structures discussed so far are all nonredundant; each relationship is stored only once. In a nonredundant data structure one can arrange a relation either in document order for ease of assembling all data about a document, or in descriptor order for ease of look-up; there is a trade-off. Facilitating both assembling data and look-up requires a *redundant data structure,* in which some or all relationships are stored twice or even more often. Data base 6 illustrates a structure that is often used, particularly in bibliographic retrieval.

Data base 6. *File 1.0 (main file of full entity records) plus the index files 4.1–4.4* (display not repeated)

This data base is very similar to data base 5 but has the following differences.

Searching

It is now fairly easy to search for query 1: *Pipes* AND *Copper,* even if implementation is through printing on paper. Access the subject index under *Pipes* and obtain a list of document numbers. For each document number in turn, access the main file and examine the records for the presence of *Copper.* (In data base 5 this was not possible since the subject descriptors were not part of the record.) This procedure is faster than examining every record in the main file (an impossible task in a manual system). One could also look for *Copper* and examine for *Pipes;* in the example this would be slightly less work since there are fewer documents on *copper.*

Assembling Data about a Document Found

All data are already assembled in the main file record.

Creating and Maintaining the Data Base

The discussion for data base 4 applies. *Space requirements* are much higher, since file 1.0 is stored in addition to the index files.

This often-used data structure is discussed more fully in Section 11.3

The remainder of this section gives other examples of data structures in which redundancy reduces the processing required in searching and in assembling all data about a document. These are particularly important for data bases implemented by writing, typing, or printing on paper (or microform), since humans are not good at the kind of clerical manipulations required in searching. All data bases discussed have a main file of full document records, so that assembling data about a document is not a problem.

Data base 7. *File 1.0 as main file, indexes 4.1–4.3 and subject index by descriptor pairs*

Searching for descriptor combinations in a printed index is often cumbersome to the extent of being impractical. Yet many queries combine descriptors, particularly subject descriptors, with AND. An index by descriptor pairs solves this problem. This index originates from a triadic relation of the following form.

Pipes, Copper, 1	Pipes, Plastic, 3
Pipes, Cooling, 1	Pipes, Artificial, 3
Copper, Pipes, 1	Pipes, Medicine, 3
Copper, Cooling, 1	Plastic, Pipes, 3
Cooling, Pipes, 1	Plastic, Artificial, 3
Cooling, Copper, 1	Plastic, Medicine, 3
Wire, Copper, 2	Artificial, Pipes, 3
•	•
•	•
•	•

In this relation the relationship between a document and a descriptor is stored several times; for example, the relationship between document 1 and *Copper* is stored 4 times. Sorting by descriptor pairs and consolidation results in the subject index file 7.4.

Searching

Query 1: Pipes AND Copper

The index allows for a two-step look-up: First look under *Pipes,* and then within *Pipes* under *Copper.*

Query 2: Pipes AND Copper AND Production

Looking under *Pipes-Copper* and under *Pipes-Production,* the searcher locates two short lists of document numbers in proximity in the index; comparing these to identify the numbers in common is easy in this index. One can also look under *Pipes-Copper,* find a list of document numbers, and examine the corresponding document records in file 7.0 for *Production.*

Queries 4 and 5 involve date; one can look in the subject index, then examine for date in the main file.

Creating and Maintaining the Data Base

We have already discussed the processing necessary. *Space requirements* exceed those for a subject index for single descriptors (file 4.4).

Data base 7. *File 1.0 as main file and subject index by descriptor pairs*

File 7.0 Main file = File 1.0; Files 7.1–7.3 = 4.1–4.3 (not repeated)
File 7.4 *Subject index by descriptor pairs*

Appliances
  –Pipes   7
  –Plastic   7

Artificial
  –Medicine   3
  –Pipes   3
  –Plastic   3

Cooling
  –Copper   1, 8
  –Pipes   1, 8
  –Plastic   8

Copper   11
  –Cooling   1, 8
  –Pipes   1, 6, 8
  –Plastic   8
  –Precision   9
  –Production   2, 5, 6, 9
  –Rods   5
  –Steel   9
  –Wire   2, 9

Medicine
  –Artificial   3
  –Pipes   3
  –Plastic   3

Pipes
  –Appliances   7
  –Artificial   3
  –Cooling   1, 8
  –Copper   1, 6, 8
  –Medicine   3
  –Plastic   3, 7, 8, 12
  –Production   4, 6, 10, 12
  –Steel   4, 10

Plastic
  –Appliances   7
  –Artificial   3
  –Cooling   8
  –Copper   8
  –Medicine   3
  –Pipes   3, 7, 8, 12
  –Production   12
  –Reactions   13

Precision
  –Copper   9
  –Production   9
  –Steel   9
  –Wire   9

Production
  –Copper   2, 5, 6, 9
  –Pipes   4, 6, 10, 12
  –Plastic   12
  –Precision   9
  –Rods   5
  –Steel   4, 9
  –Wire   2, 9

Reactions
  –Plastic   13

Rods
  –Copper   5
  –Production   5

Steel
  –Copper   9
  –Pipes   4
  –Precision   9
  –Production   4, 9
  –Wire   9

Wire
  –Copper   2, 9
  –Precision   9
  –Production   2, 9
  –Steel   9

Data base 8. *File 1.0 as main file and indexes giving number and year in each document entry* (redundant but convenient)

Searching

For the pure subject queries 1-3, this index works just like the index 4.4, but for query 4 it is better.

Query 4: Pipes AND Date 1971 or later

Step 1, Look-up: Accessing the index under *Pipes* locates a list of entries—document number and date.
Step 2, Examination: Each entry in this list can be examined for the date; there is no need to access a different file to obtain the date.

Creating and Maintaining the Data Base

In index creation the date is carried along with the document number. The extra *space* needed for the date can be minimized by using document numbers of the form 76-1593, where 76 stands for the year 1976. The number within each year is shorter than a plain sequence number.

File 8.1. *Author index*

Adam, S. J.	1/1973	Irk, H. R.	8/1973
Berry, W. K.	13/1970	Jackson, T. R.	10/1971
Dunn, A. K.	3/1970	Kerr, J. L.	4/1970
Elm, B. C.	3/1970, 9/1971	Mann, M. M.	10/1971
Ford, H. X.	11/1965	Ruth, E. R.	5/1969
Gill, M. C.	6/1965	Simon, L. A.	8/1973, 11/1965, 12/1973
Hut, D. D.	3/1970, 7/1972	Timm, S. T.	2/1968, 9/1971

File 8.4. *Subject descriptor index*

Appliances	7/1972
Artificial	3/1970
Cooling	1/1973, 8/1973
Copper	1/1973, 2/1968, 5/1969, 6/1965, 8/1973, 9/1971, 11/1965
Medicine	3/1970
Pipes	1/1973, 3/1970, 4/1970, 6/1965, 7/1972, 8/1973, 10/1971, 12/1973
Plastic	3/1970, 7/1972, 8/1973, 12/1973, 13/1970
Precision	9/1971
Production	2/1968, 4/1970, 5/1969, 6/1965, 9/1971, 10/1971, 12/1973
Reactions	13/1970
Rods	5/1969
Steel	4/1970, 9/1971
Wire	2/1968, 9/1971

Data base 9. *File 1.0 as main file and indexes giving in each entry the document number and subject descriptors*

We show only part of index file 9.1 and index file 9.4

File 9.1. Author Index

```
Adam, S. J.
    1   Pipes; Copper; Cooling
    •
    •
    •

Simon, L.A.
    8   Pipes; Copper; Plastic; Cooling
   11   Copper
   12   Pipes; Plastic; Production
    •
    •
    •
```

File 9.4. Subject descriptor index

```
              Pipes; Plastic; Appliances 7
              Pipes; Plastic; Artificial; Medicine 3
              Pipes; Copper; Cooling 1
     Pipes; Copper; Plastic; Cooling 8
                         Copper 11
              Pipes; Copper; Cooling 1
              Pipes; Copper; Plastic; Cooling 8
              Pipes; Copper; Production 6
              Rods; Copper; Production 2
              Wire; Copper; Steel; Production; Precision 9
Pipes; Plastic; Artificial; Medicine 3
                 Pipes; Copper; Cooling 1
                 Pipes; Copper; Plastic; Cooling 8
    •
    •
    •
```

We leave it to the reader to analyze searching and data base creation and maintenance.

The KWIC index shown as data base 9a on the next page is just the same as the subject index 9.4, except that it uses another type of subject descriptors, content bearing words in the title. Using title words creates problems of terminology. For example, the searcher must recognize *Tubes* as signifying *Pipes*.

Data base 9a. *File 1.0 as main file and KWIC index as subject index*

A KWIC (Key-Word-In-Context) index based on titles shows each title under every content-bearing word. For example, the title *Vinyl hoses in appliances* is shown under *Vinyl, Hoses,* and *Appliances.*

Searching

Query 1: Copper AND Pipes

Looking under *Copper* and examining each entry listed under *Copper* for terms signifying *Pipes* leads to the relevant titles. Examination is possible in the KWIC index itself, since each entry consists of the full title. The searcher could even examine the entry for a third term, or for a concept implied by the title as a whole.

Query 1a: Production AND Pipes

One might be tempted to use two-step look-up, first for *Production* and then, in the alphabetical sequence of terms following *of,* for *Pipes;* one would find document 10. As is obvious in the sample index (but often not so obvious in real-life indexes), documents 4 and 6 would be missed because *Steel* or *Copper,* respectively, intervenes between *Production* and *Pipes.* In a KWIC index, entries are made only under *single* descriptors and not, as in file 7.4, under descriptor pairs. Therefore, look-up must be only by single descriptors, not by descriptor pairs. In a search for an AND combination of descriptors—for example, *Production* AND *Pipes*—one can look up *Production* and limit the search to the entries found there, but one must examine every single entry in its entirety for the presence of *Pipes.* An index by descriptor pairs would need a lot more space.

Creating and Maintaining the Data Base

As with all indexes, initial sorting of entries and later interfiling of entries for new documents are needed. *Requires* more *space* than a single entry index giving only document numbers and less than a card catalog (to be discussed next).

Data base 9a. *File 1.0 as main file and KWIC index as subject index*

File 9a.4. *KWIC index*

	↓
Copper tubes for	air conditioning equipment. 1
Vinyl hoses in	appliances. 7
Artificial	arteries: Plastic helps surgeons. 3
	Artificial arteries: Plastic helps surgeons. 3
The production of PVC	capillaries. 12
Copper tubes for air	conditioning equipment. 1
Spiral copper tubes as	cooling elements. 8
All about	copper. 11
The production of	copper pipes. 6
The production of	copper rods. 5
Spiral	copper tubes as cooling elements. 8
	Copper tubes for air conditioning equipment. 1
How to draw	copper wire. 2
How to	draw copper wire. 2
Precision methods in wire	drawing. 9
Spiral copper tubes as cooling	elements. 8
Copper tubes for air conditioning	equipment. 1
Artificial arteries: Plastic	helps surgeons. 3
Vinyl	hoses in appliances. 7
Precision	methods in wire drawing. 9
The production of copper	pipes. 6
The production of	pipes. 10
The production of steel	pipes. 4
Artificial arteries:	Plastic helps surgeons. 3
	Polyvinylchloride reactions. 13
	Precision methods in wire drawing. 9
The	production of copper pipes. 6
The	production of copper rods. 5
The	production of pipes. 10
The	production of PVC capillaries. 12
The	production of steel pipes. 4
The production of	PVC capillaries. 12
Polyvinylchloride	reactions. 13
The production of copper	rods. 5
	Spiral copper tubes as cooling elements. 8
The production of	steel pipes. 4
Artificial arteries: Plastic helps	surgeons. 3
Spiral copper	tubes as cooling elements. 8
Copper	tubes for air conditioning equipment. 1
	Vinyl hoses in appliances. 7
Precision methods in	wire drawing. 9
How to draw copper	wire. 2
	↑
	(words in this column are in alphabetical order)

Data base 10. *Data base 4 with full entries in lieu of document numbers*

This is the data structure of the *card catalog*. We show only the subject descriptor index; within subject descriptor we have sorted the entries by date, which is most helpful (sorting by first author is conventional). The document numbers in a real card catalog would be call numbers referring to shelf location. File 10.0 (main file) is not needed, files 10.1–10.3 (author, date, and title index) are not shown.

Searching

For queries with one descriptor, simple look-up works fine. For queries with two descriptors ANDed, one can look under one descriptor and then examine entries for the other *in the file itself*. There is no need to access another file.

Query 4: Pipes AND Date 1971 or later

The sorting sequence allows for two-step look-up: First look under *Pipes,* then within *Pipes* under *1971*. This is supported by two-level sorting: The file is first sorted by subject descriptor, then within subject descriptor by date. This structure can also be seen as an index by subject descriptor–date combination (as in data base 7 for subject descriptors). Since there is only one date per document, no additional entries are needed.

Creating and Maintaining the Data Base

When creating the indexes, the entire document record is carried along with the document number. In the following, we compare *space requirements* for two data structures, assuming 10,000 documents with two authors, one title, and three subject descriptors per document.

Main file; indexes by author, title, and subject	700 pages

Main file, 10,000 entries, 2-column format, 25 entries/page	400 pages
Indexes, 60,000 entries, 4 column format, 200 entries/page	300 pages

Book catalog, 60,000 entries, 2 col., 25 entries/page	2,400 pages

If more information is included in the full entries, the difference becomes larger. The same is true if the average number of entries per document is increased; just picture the descriptor-pair index with full entries.

Data base 10. *Data base 4 with full entries in lieu of document numbers*

File 10.4. *Subject descriptor index with full entries*

Appliances
   7 Hut, D. D. 1972:
          Vinyl hoses in appliances.
          Pipes; Plastic; Appliances.

Artificial
   3 Dunn, A. K. 1970; Elm, B. C.; Hut, D. D.:
          Artificial arteries: Plastic helps surgeons.
          Pipes; Plastic; Artificial; Medicine.

Cooling
   1 Adam, S. J. 1973:
          Copper tubes for air conditioning equipment.
          Pipes; Copper; Cooling

   8 Irk, H. R. 1973; Simon, L. A.:
          Spiral copper tubes as cooling elements.
          Pipes; Copper; Plastic; Cooling.

•••

Pipes
   6 Gill, M. C. 1965:
          The production of copper pipes.
          Pipes; Copper; Production.

   3 Dunn, A. K. 1970; Elm, B. C.; Hut, D. D.:
          Artificial arteries: Plastic helps surgeons.
          Pipes; Plastic; Artificial; Medicine.

   4 Kerr, J. L. 1970:
          The production of steel pipes.
          Pipes; Steel; Production.

 10 Mann, M. M. 1971; Jackson, T. R.:
          The production of pipes.
          Pipes; Production.

   7 Hut, D. D. 1972:
          Vinyl hoses in appliances.
          Pipes; Plastic; Appliances.

   1 Adam, S. J. 1973:
          Copper tubes for air conditioning equipment.
          Pipes; Copper; Cooling.

   8 Irk, H. R. 1973; Simon, L. A.:
          Spiral copper tubes as cooling elements.
          Pipes; Copper; Plastic; Cooling.

 12 Simon, L. A. 1973:
          The production of PVC capillaries.
          Pipes; Plastic; Production.

Data base 11. *Meaningful identifiers in data base 6*

Meaningful identifiers carry some information about an entity. For example, a document can be identified as *Elm 1970* or *HE337.35–1975,371* (*HE337.35* is the call number or shelf location of *Traffic Quarterly,* 1975 is the year, and 371 is the first page of the article). Meaningful identifiers not only give more information in the index entries, they also create order in the main file so that it can be used for look-up—for example, by first author in file 11.0; this eliminates the need for an author index. (There should be cross-references for second authors—for example, Simon 1973 see Irk 1973.) The effort of creating the author sequence is shifted from the author index to the main file. Space is saved. However, meaningful identifiers need between 10 and 25 characters, whereas simple numbers require only 6 or 7.

In the choice of identifiers one can emphasize maintaining a useful order in the main file or giving useful information about the document identified. For example, the author-date identifier leads to a quite useful arrangement in the main file, but in the index entries the author is not terribly useful. Conversely, the journal in which an article appears does not produce as useful an arrangement in the main file, but as information in the index entries it is very useful. In many data bases identifiers are chosen to achieve an arrangement of the full records in the main file by broad subject categories or to achieve a meaningful shelf arrangement (e.g., call numbers based on subject classification, or part numbers).

File 11.0. *Main file arranged by first author*

File 11.4. *Subject descriptor index*

Adam, S. J. 1973:
Copper tubes for air conditioning equipment.
Pipes; Copper; Cooling.

Berry, W. K. 1970:
Polyvinylchloride reactions.
Plastic; Reactions.

Dunn, A. K. 1970; Elm, B. C.; Hut, D. D.:
Artificial arteries: Plastic helps surgeons.
Pipes; Plastic; Artificial; Medicine.

Elm, B. C. 1971; Timm, S. T.:
Precision methods in wire drawing.
Wire; Copper; Steel; Production; Precision.

Ford, H. X. 1965; Simon, L. A.:
All about copper.
Copper

•••

Appliances
    Hut   1972

Artificial
    Dunn   1970

Cooling
    Adam   1973
    Irk   1973

Copper
    Adam   1973
    Elm   1971
    Ford   1965
    Gill   1965
    Irk   1973
    Ruth   1969
    Timm   1968

•••

11.2 FUNCTIONS AND CHARACTERISTICS OF DATA STRUCTURES

A data structure and associated processes serve the following purposes:

Searching

Data structures serve to retrieve (identify, select, find) all entities in the store that fulfill the conditions specified in the query formulation. There are two *search modes:*

- *Examination:* In this mode, the searcher or the search program examines data about an entity to see whether the entity meets the query specifications. The focus is on the entity. One looks at the requisite data about the entity to determine whether it meets the query specifications.
- *Look-up:* In this mode, the structure of the data base is used to identify entities worthy of further examination. In other words, relying solely on the structure of the data base, the searcher or search program selects a subset of entities such that further searching can be restricted to the subset.

Look-up may lead directly to the final set of entities that meet the query specifications. If not, it must be followed by examination or by a second look-up step.

Output of Data about an Entity

For each entity retrieved, the searcher or computer program must assemble the data required by the output format.

Data structures and associated processes considered as a whole, as well as individual relations or files, differ in the degree to which they support these functions.

Examination and output are both dependent on the ease with which data about an entity can be assembled. For a single file, this depends simply on the *amount of information given in each entry*—more precisely, the correspondence between the information required and the information given. The entries in subject index 4.4 give only the document number; the amount of information is close to zero. Subject index 8.4 gives document number and date, subject index 11.4 gives author and date, the KWIC index 9a.4 gives all subject descriptors, and the one file 1.0 and the one file 10.4 give full data about each document. For a data base as a whole, ease of assembling data on an entity depends on the number of files to be accessed and the ease of access. The less information in the entries of the individual files, the more files must be accessed. *Ease of access* is dependent on the *manipulative power* of the search system and many other factors that are beyond this discussion. We give one simple example: If a printed data base gives the main file and the indexes in two separate physical volumes, accessing the main file under entity numbers found in the index is much easier than if both are in the same physical volume.

Look-up is dependent on the *degree of order* established and maintained in the data base. Some effort for creating the order is needed to make searching by look-up possible. Examining the sample data bases sharpens one's intuitive understanding of order and degree of order. Section 11.4 elaborates further on these concepts. Look-up is also dependent on the *manipulative power* available, as the comparison of the three implementations of data base 4 (computer, peek-a-boo, printing on paper with human processing) readily shows.

Amount of information in each entry, degree of order, and *manipulative power* emerge as important *parameters for characterizing individual files and data structures as a whole.*

Before discussing some more abstract concepts in Sections 11.4–11.6, we analyze a data structure of particular importance for bibliographic and similar ISAR systems. This analysis also illustrates the principles just summarized.

11.3 MAIN FILE AND INDEX FILE(S) AS A DATA STRUCTURE

Data base 6 combines a main file giving full records on the main entities with one or more index files providing different avenues for access; this structure is frequently used, particularly in bibliographic and similar retrieval systems. It is the prevalent structure in data bases implemented by writing, typing, or printing on paper and human searching, since the amount of processing needed to search a data structure that disperses the data on the entity of interest is not practical for the human searcher. Also, giving full records under every access point, as in data base 10, requires much space. The main file may also consist of the entities themselves.

11.3.1 NOTES ON TERMINOLOGY

The main file is sorted by the identifier of the main entity, called the *primary key* (e.g., call number for books on shelves). An index file provides access by one or more types of descriptors, called *secondary keys;* the index files are called *secondary indexes.* A *primary index* (e.g., a stack directory) facilitates access to a file by its primary key. This latter problem is not considered in this chapter.

A main file that is created simply by adding new input records at the end without further processing is often called a *direct file.* A typical example is a bibliographic file on magnetic tape in which document records are arranged by accession number (a unique number assigned to each document in order of accession). Meaningful identifiers make the main file more useful for searching. However, updating is more difficult: New records must be inserted in their proper place.

Simple indexes like the one in data base 6, which give for each descriptor a list of entity identifiers, are often called *inverted files* because a process of sorting, or inverting the order, is involved in their creation. Typical implementations of an inverted file are peek-a-boo cards or a computer-stored index.

Direct files and inverted files are extremes: A direct file has a very low degree of order but lots of information in each entry (a full record); an inverted file has a high degree of order but hardly any information in the entries (except that meaningful entity identifiers do convey some information). Amount of information and degree of order in a file can be varied independently; the distinction between direct file and inverted file, while useful, is of limited scope and too simplistic to analyze and/or design adequately the many types of file organization occurring in practical situations (see elaboration in Section 11.5). An illustration of the inadequacy of this oversimplification for describing files is the treatment of the card catalog in the literature: Some authors classify the card catalog as a direct file, basing their classification on the fact that the catalog cards give full information; others classify the card catalog as an inverted file, basing their classification on the fact that the card catalog contains a good degree of order and can be used for searching by look-up.

11.3.2 SOME USAGE AND DESIGN CONSIDERATIONS

Since each secondary index requires extra processing and extra storage space, the system designer may decide to omit secondary indexes that are not very important in searching (e.g., a secondary index by date). Searching by date is still possible through examination of entries as discussed for data base 6.

Instead of having separate indexes for different types of descriptors, one could interfile all types of descriptors in one big index. Examples are the dictionary catalog (interfiling personal authors, corporate entries, titles, and subject descriptors) and the computer-stored MEDLINE index file. (In MEDLINE all descriptor types form one alphabetical sequence in which each descriptor is marked by its type; if the same character string designates two types of descriptors—for example, a title word and a medical subject heading—two records are made in the index file.)

In a manual index file one might include more information in the entries so that some examination can take place in the index file itself without the cumbersome access to the main file.

11.3.3 A MAIN FILE OF ENTITIES AS PART OF THE DATA STRUCTURE

Often one needs not just the information in entity records but the entities themselves, either for their own value (grocery products, documents, museum objects, parts) or as sources of data (documents, records). A structure of three files is standard for this purpose:

1. Index files furnishing entity identifiers.
2. Main file of entity records. This file supports examination without obtaining the entities themselves, which might require a long walk, the use of the mail, or special equipment, such as a movie projector; take lots of time, such as previewing a movie; or otherwise be cumbersome. This file also gives the location of an entity, which might be different from the entity identifier (for example, grocery products are identified by their Universal Product Code, and the entity records give the shelf location).
3. Main file of the entities themselves (shelves with grocery products, museum objects, parts, books, or file cabinets with records) arranged by location number.

In this data structure the user needs three steps to obtain entities. The number of steps can be reduced by modifying some files and eliminating others, but only at a price. For example:

- The index file could give not just the entity ID but the full entity representation in each entry, thus eliminating the main file of entity records, as in a card catalog or in Index Medicus. But space is a problem.
- The index file could use the location number as ID so that the searcher can go directly to the file of entities without looking at the entity representations in the main file. (However, this may be cumbersome as noted in the description of the main file of entity records in the preceding list.)
- The main file of entities could be arranged by meaningful identifiers (e.g., by subject) so that look-up is possible in the file of entities itself. No file of entity representations is needed in this case, but the degree of order, and therefore searchability, is lower than in an index file. The records of an organization, newspaper clippings, and reprints in a personal file are often kept in this fashion. Often such an arrangement is augmented by an index file (e.g., shelves on which books are arranged in subject order, augmented by a catalog).

11.4 THE CONCEPT OF ORDER

Searching by look-up depends on the degree of order and on the manipulative power of the search mechanism. There is no easy measure for the degree of order in a file or relation; this section gives some examples to facilitate an intuitive understanding of the concept.

When comparing two files, one can often see clearly that one has more order than the other. For example, file 1, sorted by subject descriptor and within subject descriptor by date, has more order than file 2, sorted only by subject descriptor. File 3, sorted by subject descriptor and, within each subject descriptor, by a second subject descriptor (that is, sorted by subject descriptor pairs) has more order than file 4, which is simply sorted by subject descriptor. Due to the higher order in file 3, look-up under descriptor pairs is possible. On the other hand, file 5, sorted by author and title, has neither more nor less order than file 6, sorted by author and date; the two files have different orders.

A file in which entities are sorted into very specific classes has a higher degree of order than a file in which entities are sorted into broad classes. For example, file 7, an author index in which authors' names are sorted in the usual manner, has more order than file 8, in which author names are sorted by first letter only. Note that for author searching the latter file is still far superior to a completely unordered file. While file 8 is less searchable than file 7, it is also much easier to maintain. It is much easier to stick a new entry with the author name *McArthur* in the *M* section than to file it in its correct place in the sequence of all authors starting with *M*. This is an example of the general rule: less order—less work for file creation and maintenance. While this example is a bit extreme, the principle it illustrates may often be used to advantage to simplify or eliminate fine points of filing rules.

Index file 9—providing access by subject descriptor, date of creation, and country of origin—has a higher degree of order than file 10, providing access only by subject descriptor. If we assume they use the same index language, index file 11, which is based on an average of 20 subject descriptors assigned to an entity, has more order than index file 12, which is based on an average of 5 subject descriptors per entity. In file 11 one can locate through look-up all documents dealing with a given topic, even if the topic is minor, or all persons with a given skill, even if the skill is minor.

Three ingredients of the degree of order emerge: the number of criteria used in sorting (sortkeys), the specificity of the descriptors (broadly defined) used for sorting, and the number of access points per entity. The last criterion should be applied to a data base as a whole, since access from different points of view might be provided through different index files. The descriptors used for sorting may be less specific than the descriptors used for indexing; in one of the preceding examples, the indexing descriptor was *McArthur,* but the sorting descriptor was *M.*

Often it is not meaningful to compare two files with respect to degree of order; the files may simply be ordered on a different principle. For example, there is no point in saying that an author index contains more or less order than a subject index to the same collection. Which of these orders is useful depends entirely on the query. In that sense order is a relative concept; order for what purpose? Order by author is of very little use for a subject search.

In data-processing terminology, descriptors by which a file is ordered are called *sortkeys.* (Likewise, descriptors used in searching are called *search keys.*) A library catalog may be arranged by sortkey 1: author, and sortkey 2: title. This arrangement means that entries are first sorted by author, then *within author* by title. A personnel file could be sorted by sortkey 1: social security number. Or, it might be sorted by sortkey 1: salary level, sortkey 2: department where employed, and sortkey 3: name. Or, it might be sorted by sortkey 1: salary level and sortkey 2: name. One might even print out several files, each in a different order, for ease of human searching. This problem of detailed sorting sequence is much less important for files that are searched by computers.

Faceted classification as a method of file organization is concerned with just that problem of sorting sequence for human searching. Consider a collection of instructional materials that is indexed from the three aspects (facets): subject matter, grade level, and medium used (see Fig. 11.2).

The arrangements differ in the order in which the three facets are used for sorting; in classification terminology this problem is referred to as *citation order.*

The precise order in which the entries in a file are arranged is determined by the *filing rules.* The filing rules specify, first, what sortkeys to use in what order. Second, the filing rules determine the sequence of values within one sortkey. Some filing situations appear deceptively simple. For example, sorting the names of persons and organizations in alphabetical sequence seems to present few problems. However, even a look at the phone book reveals the complications. How should abbreviations be handled? Should diacritical marks be considered in the order? What about foreign names? In a library catalog, particularly a dictionary catalog, things get even more complex. The same word or group of words may appear as a name of a corporate body, a title, and a subject descriptor. How should they be filed? One option is to ignore the difference, which increases the work of the knowledgeable searcher. (The searcher who does not know the filing rules must look through all entries filed under that particular word anyway, since he or she does not know the difference.) Another problem is whether to file names starting with *Mc*

```
Sortkey 1: Subject matter          Sortkey 1: Grade level
Sortkey 2: Grade level             Sortkey 2: Medium
Sortkey 3: Medium                  Sortkey 3: Subject matter

Mathematics                        Grades 1-4
    Math. Grades 1-4                   1-4. Slides
        Math. 1-4. Slides                  1-4. Slides. Mathematics
        Math. 1-4. Movie                   1-4. Slides. Language
    Math. Grades 5-6                       1-4. Slides. Art
        Math. 5-6. Slides              1-4. Movie
        Math. 5-6. Movie                   1-4. Movie. Mathematics
Language                                   1-4. Movie. Language
    Lang. Grades 1-4                       1-4. Movie. Art
        Lang. 1-4. Slides          Grades 5-6
        Lang. 1-4. Movie               5-6. Slides
    Lang. Grades 5-6                       5-6. Slides. Mathematics
        Lang. 5-6. Slides                  5-6. Slides. Language
        Lang. 5-6. Movie                   5-6. Slides. Art
Art                                    5-6. Movie
    Art. Grades 1-4                        5-6. Movie. Mathematics
        Art. 1-4. Slides                   5-6. Movie. Language
        Art. 1-4. Movie                    5-6. Movie. Art
    Art. Grades 5-6
        Art. 5-6. Slides
        Art. 5-6. Movie
```

Fig. 11.2   Two subject arrangements with different sortkey order.

together with the names starting with *Mac* or whether to file them strictly in their place in the alphabet. There are good reasons for either choice. (Computers, even microcomputers, can be programmed to search for exact alphabetical match or for phonetic match.)

Both the file-building mechanism and the searching mechanism must know the filing rules. A user searching a printed catalog needs to know the filing rules. A user of an on-line search system does not need to know the filing rules; once he or she keys in the correct form of a name or a subject descriptor, the computer does the searching. Small indexes can get by without elaborate filing rules. For larger indexes, such as library catalogs, elaborate filing rules are necessary, at least for human searching. The filing rules need not specify the place of an entry in the file completely as long as a user can find an entry (or verify its absence) by examining a small number, perhaps 5 or 10, entries. Some rule systems aspire to the unnecessary ideal of a completely specified place for each and every entry, which makes them rather complex. Simplification would lead to considerable decrease in file-building cost and moderate, if any, increase in file use cost.

11.5 THE TWO-DIMENSIONAL CONTINUUM OF FILE TYPES

Many data structures combine files of several types to exploit their strengths and avoid their weaknesses. Here we consider two parameters that influence the searchability of an individual file, namely, *amount of information per entry* and *degree of order*.

The degree of order that can be achieved in a file depends on the information available in the total data base; creating a subject index requires that subject descriptors be first assigned. But for an individual file the two parameters can be varied independently from each other (as long as one disregards cost), giving rise to the two-dimensional continuum of file types shown in Fig. 11.3. Both parameters influence the searchability of a file.

A *partitioned file* is a file that is divided into a few major sections so that a search can be limited to one or perhaps two sections. A data base of full text news that is searched sequentially by a special purpose high-speed scanning unit at one million characters (500 pages) per second can be partitioned into domestic and foreign issues to shorten search time whenever the search can

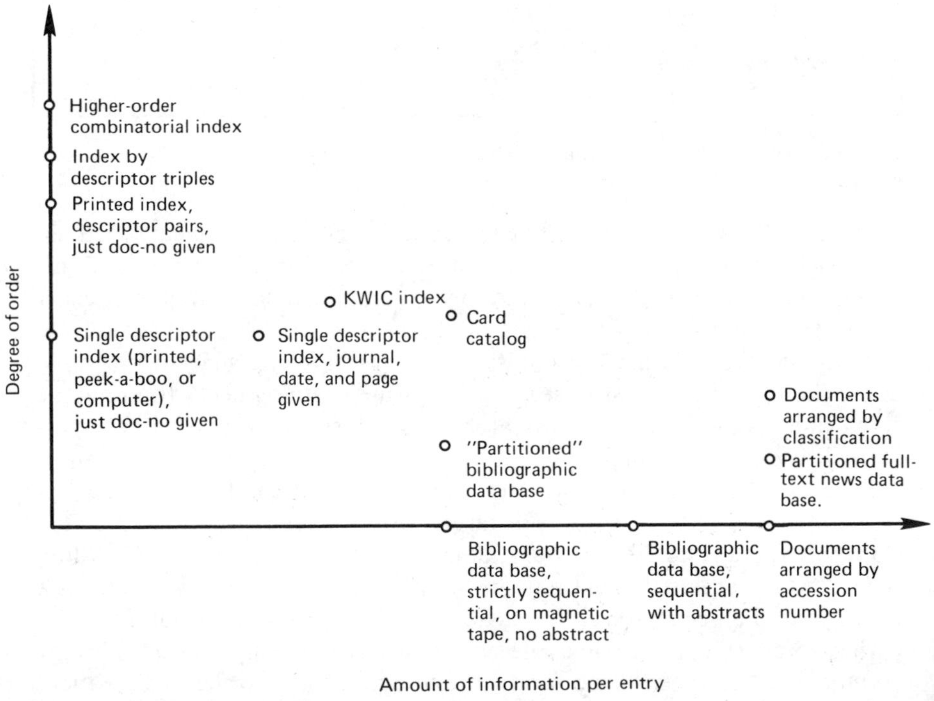

Fig. 11.3 The two-dimensional continuum of file types.

be restricted to one of these sections. The data base has a minimum of order, which allows a minimum of look-up searching—narrowing the records to be examined to one half of the total records in the file. The price for this convenience in searching is more effort in file building; incoming records must be sorted into domestic and foreign. The choice of sections is very important. It should be possible to restrict most searches to one section; on the other hand, sections should be nonoverlapping—that is, an entity should go into one and only one section. These two requirements often conflict with each other. The conflict may be resolved by fiat: Entities may be assigned to one and only one section even if they pertain to several. To the extent that sections do overlap, the partitioned file needs more storage space than the nonpartitioned file.

I I.6 TRADE-OFFS BETWEEN DATA BASE COSTS AND SEARCHING COSTS

The trade-offs discussed here are very important for data base design. In general, as amount of information and/or order in the data base increase, costs for data base building, maintenance, and storage increase, and costs for searching decrease. Most of the discussion in this section refers to individual files and relations that make up a data base. Total data base cost is the sum of the cost for all the files.

11.6.1 AMOUNT OF INFORMATION

As the total amount of information in the data base increases, input costs increase. An individual file usually gives only part of the information available in the data base; for example, a machine-readable file may include very complete bibliographic records, but the records in a printed catalog produced from the machine-readable file may be very brief. The more information is given in the entries in the individual file, the higher the storage cost and the lower the cost for searching; the quality of searching may be higher. These effects on searching depend on the ease with which a second file giving more information can be accessed.

The file medium influences the relationships between amount of information and storage cost. For example, in a card catalog more information per entry does not increase storage cost as long as all information is on one card. On the other hand, in a printed catalog storage cost varies directly with the amount of information per entry. The cost per character stored is much lower for microfilm than for hard copy. On the other hand, the desire to put an entire medium-sized catalog on one microfilm cassette may put a premium on storage space.

11.6.2 DEGREE OF ORDER

As the degree of order increases, costs for file building and maintenance increase, costs for storage may increase, and costs for searching decrease.

Higher order can be achieved in several ways, each requiring more work in sorting. Using more sortkeys requires more sorting passes. Using more specific sorting descriptors requires more sorting time. (Sorting by full author takes longer than sorting merely by the first letter.) Assigning more descriptors to each entity or sorting by descriptor pairs requires sorting of more elements and storing more entries, therefore more storage space (all the more so if the entries give much information). Using an additional sortkey requires more entries if the data element used is repeating.

Since the degree of order combines with the manipulative power of the search mechanism to produce look-up searchability, costs for the search mechanism should be considered as well.

The relationship between the degree of order and storage requirements depends on the file medium. For example, in peek-a-boo cards the storage space needed is independent of the number of descriptors per entity but very dependent on the total number of different descriptors in the index language. In a card catalog it is just the other way around: Storage requirements vary directly with the average number of descriptors per entity and are almost independent of the total number of different descriptors.

11.6.3 DESIGN CONSIDERATIONS

If cost is no object, one can build a file with both a high degree of order and a large amount of information (e.g., place full abstracts under 20 subject descriptors). But for a file to be maintained at constant cost, the designer can emphasize either degree of order or amount of information or select a medium course. Figure 11.4 shows (fictitious) lines of constant cost in the two-dimensional continuum of file types. Detailed cost studies would be needed to determine the precise shapes of these curves. The choice of the design depends entirely on the purpose of the file. For example, if browsing is an important technique for successful searches, then the amount of information given in each entry must be enough to support browsing. This means fewer entries per entity and thus less order.

How much should be spent on data base building and maintenance (including storage) obviously depends on the amount of searching. If many

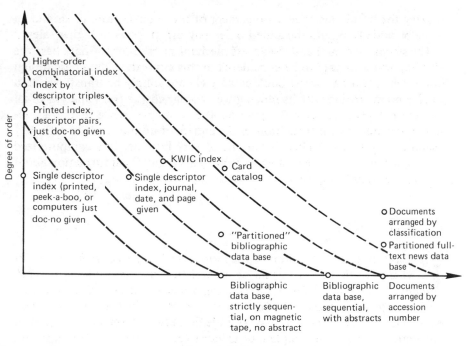

Fig. 11.4   Lines of constant cost in the two-dimensional continuum of file types (illustrative only).

searches are done, high costs for building the data base are more than offset by lower costs for searching. However, if there is only a moderate amount of searching, then costs for building the data base should be held down. While each individual search is more expensive, there are not enough searches to justify a big investment in building the data base.

A more satisfying response, made possible through computer network technology, is the pooling of search requests from many different places. The investment for building the data base is made once, and the data base is made available in a central place where everybody can search it cheaply. Search services such as SDC, Lockheed/Dialog, and BRS operate on this principle.

Other factors to be considered in deciding on the size of the investment in building the data base are the response speed required (speedy response requires an elaborate data base even if there are only a few requests) and quality of searching and resulting benefits. For example, should the user of a mail-order catalog be expected to find the piece of merchandise he or she is looking for in the classified arrangement of the main section, or should an index be added? Would the added index pay off in terms of higher sales?

The storage medium and the access mechanism used for the data base are also important factors to be considered in this context. A data base design that is best for a hard copy book catalog cannot simply be transferred to a catalog on microfilm with its much lower storage cost; a fresh analysis of all the alternatives is needed. To give another example, while giving a considerable amount of information in the entries of an index file is definitely useful to a human searcher, it may be of very little use in a computerized system; a computer system can very rapidly access all the information about an entity available anywhere in the data base.

11.7 DEFINITIONS

This section gives definitions of the terms *relation, file, data base,* and *index,* which are based on formal characteristics, and definitions of *bibliography, bibliographic data base, catalog, directory, substantive data base, numeric data base,* and *nonbibliographic data base,* which are based on content characteristics. The typology and the definitions given are meant to be illustrative rather than complete or exhaustive. This section also illustrates the broad spectrum of systems to which the principles of ISAR can be applied, and thus the need to discuss these principles on a general level.

A *relation* is a set of ordered pairs (or triplets and so on) of entities (the general term is tuples) as illustrated in the University Data Base (Chapter 3). Examples would be the relation *Has student* (with pairs *Course offering, Person*) and the relation *Text used* (with pairs *Course offering, Document*).

File is a more general term. A file is a set of records or a set of actual entities; the records could be just pairs (triplets and so on), in which case the file is a dyadic (triadic and so on) relation. Relations, particularly dyadic (pairwise) relations, are very simple, disciplined structures. But records can also have a more complex structure, consisting of many data elements arranged in groupings on several levels, any one of which may be repeating (hierarchical record structure). Such a file would not be a relation as just defined. A file may be a complex, undisciplined structure, which may be difficult to handle.

Examples of files include a patient file, an employee file, the circulation file of a library, a newspaper clipping file, books on shelves, grocery items on the shelf of a store, and a group of museum objects (the last three fall under the broad definition of file given here, even though they would not commonly be called files). More examples for specific types of files are found throughout this section.

A *data base* is a system of one or more relations or files. The term *data base* is generally used with the connotation that the relation(s) are stored in machine-readable form, but we shall use it in a more general sense, independent of the storage medium. A file of correspondence is a data base, a traditional library with its shelves and catalog is a data base, and the data stored in somebody's brain form a data base. The term *data base* may be construed very broadly as being synonymous with information system or more narrowly to refer to the entity store of an ISAR system (Fig. 5.6). Search services offering access to on-line data bases often call these data bases files. For example, DIALOG File 82 is the data base Predicasts US Time Series Online, which in the Lockheed DIALOG system consists of a main file and several index files. Examples of data bases are given under the specific types that are discussed in the following definitions.

An *index* is any file that facilitates access to the records or entities in a second or main file. Thus, a catalog is a type of index. A stack directory showing which call number ranges are to be found on each floor of a library is a *primary index;* it makes it easier to find a book based on call number, the primary key by which the books are arranged in the main file, namely, the shelves. Author and subject catalogs are *secondary indexes;* they provide quick access by additional types of descriptors. A bibliography can also be used as an index if one considers all existing documents as the main file. The term *index* is often used with the connotation that the records or entities referred to are represented very briefly (often just by a number) in the index file.

Examples of Secondary Indexes

Index	Index refers to
Library catalog	Documents
Subject index to *Chemical Abstracts*	Documents as represented by abstracts in the main section
Back-of-the-book index	Pages or sections of the book
Index to a store catalog	Page number or page ranges
Index to Dewey Decimal Classification	Class numbers

A *bibliographic data base* is a data base that focuses on the main entity type *document.* A *bibliography* is a bibliographic data base that lists documents falling into its scope, regardless of the physical location of these documents. A bibliography usually consists of a main file containing full document records, perhaps arranged in broad subject groupings, and index files arranged by author, subject, and perhaps other data elements. Searching a bibliographic data base produces document records, not the documents themselves.

Examples of bibliographies are the *Bibliography of Agriculture, Index Medicus, Chemical Abstracts* (all recurrent bibliographies that appear regularly, the indexes being cumulated annually and perhaps for longer periods), *Report Bibliography on Exceptional Children,* and a bibliography of reference sources (e.g., the one compiled by Sheehy, LC call number Z1035.1.S43.1976 with supplement 1981).

A *catalog* is a data base with one main entity type in which the main entities are members of a circumscribed collection. The catalog provides access to these entities from various data elements; it gives the call number, an order number, or a similar identification for each object.

Examples of catalogs are a museum catalog; an exhibit catalog; a store catalog (such as Sears); a catalog of stamps for sale; a library catalog (a bibliographic data base listing only documents in one library's collection) or a union catalog, such as the *National Union Catalog,* which provides access to the items in several collections.

Many users and reference librarians use a catalog when a more comprehensive listing should be consulted. If all books on *bibliotherapy* (therapy of mental problems through reading suitable books) are wanted, the catalog of a medium-size library is not a sufficient source; a comprehensive bibliography is needed. A store catalog is not a good place to get an overview of 12-inch color television sets available; a more comprehensive listing (e.g., *Consumer Reports*) is needed. All Greek vases showing the goddess Athena cannot be found in the catalog of one museum. A catalog based on a very comprehensive collection can serve as a comprehensive listing as well; for example, the published catalog of the Library of Congress, now enlarged to form the *National Union Catalog,* is a very complete bibliography of books.

A *directory* in the narrow sense is a data base that focuses on persons, organizations, academic programs, and so on (entities with an address).

Examples of directories are a telephone directory, the membership directory of the American Society for Information Science, a directory of human service agencies in a metropolitan area, a directory of colleges and universities and their academic programs, and the information directory of an organization.

In a wider sense the term *directory* is also used for data bases in which the main entities are large information sources—for example, a *directory* of machine-readable bibliographic data bases. (However, *bibliography* would be the better term here.)

A *substantive data base* (our term) is a data base that delivers tailor-made packages of substantive data for most search requests; a substantive data base can deal with any type of entity imaginable.

Examples of substantive data bases are the Registry of Toxic Effects of Chemical Substances (RTECS), which summarizes for each substance data on toxicity experiments; econometric data bases offered through firms such as Data Resources Inc. (DRI) and containing numerical data; or the Predicasts US Time Series data base, which gives data such as the U.S. copper production from 1960 to date, by year; an encyclopedia; and a cookbook.

A *numeric data base* is a substantive data base containing numbers about entities and entity relationships.

A *nonbibliographic data base* is any data base in which documents are not the main entity. This includes substantive data bases but also, for example, a data base of research projects, which may be used to find pointer data (where can I go to find a certain piece of information?) and to find substantive data (e.g., how much money is spent for cancer research?).

PART IV

Index Language Functions and Structure

CHAPTER 12

Terminological Control

OBJECTIVES

The objectives of this chapter are to explain the problems of terminological control as applied in indexing and searching and to define *thesaurus* with its synonym-homonym structure (all terms), *classificatory structure* (concepts expressed by preferred terms), *index language* (subject descriptors), and also *lead-in vocabulary* (lead-in terms).

INTRODUCTION: THE PROBLEM OF TERMINOLOGICAL CONTROL

Controlling entity identifiers is essential for retrieval success. This chapter deals with subject retrieval and thus is concerned with control over subject descriptors, that is, identifiers for subjects or concepts. The principles discussed apply to controlling identifiers in general. In free-text entity representations—such as names of organizations or titles, abstracts, or full text of documents—concepts are identified by terms. But free terms used as concept identifiers present many problems. Consider searching in a machine-readable bibliographic data base using terms in titles, abstracts, or full text (*free-text searching* or searching with an *uncontrolled vocabulary*.) The topic is *Harbors,* which may seem like a very simple query. Since any term is searchable, why not try the query formulation *Harbors*. It will find some relevant documents but by no means all (low recall). A look at the sample list of terms occurring in the data base in Fig. 12.1a shows *Harbor* (singular), *Harbour,* and *Port*. To achieve high recall one must look for all these terms. Thus the query formulation should be

Harbor OR Harbors OR Harbour OR Harbours OR Port OR Ports.

Academic achievement	3	Mechanisation	2
Aeroplane	5	Mechanised	2
Aeroplanes	5	Mechanization	2
Aesthetics	1	Mechanized	2
Ailment	4	Natrium	9
Airplane	5	Plastic	10
Airplanes	5	Plastics	10
Airport	6	Pneumonia	4.1
Airports	6	Polyethylene	10.1
Automated	2	Polyp	4.2.1
Automatic	2	Polyvinylchloride	10.2
Automation	2	Port	7
Chloroethylene		Ports	7
homopolymer	10.2	PVC	10.2
Disease	4	Scholastic achievement	3
Diseases	4	School success	3
Docking facilities	7	Ship	8
Docking facility	7	Ships	8
Educational achievement	3	Sick	4
Esthetics	1	Sickness	4
Harbor	7	Sodium	9
Harbors	7	Tumor	4.2
Harbour	7	Tumors	4.2
Harbours	7	Tumour	4.2
Ill	4	Tumours	4.2
Illness	4	Vessel	8
Illnesses	4	Vinyl	10.2

Fig. 12.1   Terminological control and its uses: (a) Terms from an uncontrolled vocabulary Also index to Fig. 12.1b (53 terms).

The very richness and variety of the terminology used in natural language causes problems in retrieval. Overcoming these problems requires *terminological control* either in indexing or in searching. A data base using an *uncontrolled vocabulary* requires *terminological control in searching* through query term expansion; a query term is replaced by an OR-combination of the query term itself with any morphological and spelling variants, synonyms, and quasi-synonyms. This is a challenge for the searcher: When searching for *Aesthetics,* would you always remember to include "OR *Esthetics*"? When searching for *Illness,* would you always remember to include

Illness OR Disease OR Sickness OR Ailment?

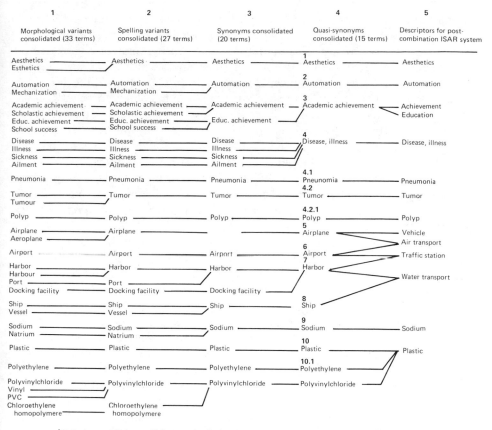

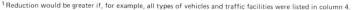

Fig. 12.1b   Stepwise reduction of a set of terms.

Applying terminological control effectively requires a search aid (Fig. 12.1). An alphabetical index (Fig. 12.1a) leads from *Illness* to *Disease, illness* (column 4 of Fig. 12.1b). (*Disease, illness* is one term to designate a concept that includes anything that might be called *Disease, Illness, Sickness,* or *Ailment*.) Following the lines from right to left, the searcher finds in column 1 all the terms and spelling variants to use.

Terminological control in searching is feasible in a computerized search system, particularly if query term expansion is done through the search program, thus taking the burden off the searcher. (Whether free-text searching is desirable is quite another matter; see Chapter 13). In a manual search system, such as a card catalog or printed index, looking under many synonyms and quasi-synonyms is time consuming. Entities or references to entities related to one concept should be collocated in one place in the file, not scattered in many places. Thus they must be filed under *one* term or other concept identifier. This unique concept identifier may be created from scratch or selected from the spelling variants, synonyms, and quasi-synonyms referring to the concept. This is *terminological control in indexing* by using a *controlled vocabulary*. From any term in column 1 the indexer is led to the corresponding descriptor in column 4. The same is true for the searcher. Thus the structure of Fig. 12.1b ensures that indexers always use the same terms for a given concept and that searchers use that same term.

To sum up: with terminological control in searching, the structure of Fig. 12.1b is used from right to left for query term expansion. With terminological control in indexing, the structure is used from left to right for index term consolidation; the one query term found is sufficient to retrieve all entities relevant to a given concept.

Homonyms present a further—and less tractable—problem. The term *Port* used in free-text searching may return also documents on *Telecommunication ports* and on *Port wine*. The following example made the news: Somebody was searching a newspaper data base for reports on *Bats in Texas*. Using the query formulation *Bat** AND *Texas* (the * signifies any term starting with the three-letter sequence *Bat*), he found articles on the *Batting averages of Texas baseball teams*. In a system with an uncontrolled vocabulary a search program with access to a sophisticated search thesaurus can use context to determine the applicable meaning of a homonym. A controlled vocabulary contains a unique term for each meaning of a homonym.

Finally, hierarchy is very important for high recall; hierarchical relationships between concepts are shown in Fig. 12.1b, columns 4 and 5. When looking for *Plastic,* a searcher should also consider the narrower terms *Polyethylene* and *Polyvinylchloride,* including, if the vocabulary is uncontrolled, also its spelling variants *Vinyl* and *PVC* and its synonym *Chloroethylene homopolymer.*

As a last example consider a search for *Disease* AND *Employment* in an ISAR system with an uncontrolled vocabulary. The *Disease* component must be expressed broadly by combining the following terms with OR:

> *Disease* and its plural *Diseases,* its equivalent terms *Illness, Sickness, Ailment* (each with its plural), and *Sick* (a morphological variant of *Sickness*), and all the narrower terms of *Disease,* such as *Pneumonia* and *Tumor* (with *Tumour*) and, under that, *Polyp* (including plurals).

The *Employment* component should be expressed as

> *Employment* OR *Employed* OR *Employee* OR *Occupation* OR
> *Occupational* OR *Job* OR *Work,*

including plurals and such forms as *Job-related.*

A computerized ISAR system using a controlled vocabulary requires only elemental descriptors because it can search for descriptor combinations; for example, to search for documents on *Harbor,* one would use the query formulation

> Traffic station AND Water transport.

Sometimes it is useful to avoid very specific concepts—such as *Polyethylene*—as descriptors and use a broader concept—such as *Plastic*—instead in order to keep the index language simple.

So far this discussion has concentrated on the use of a vocabulary structure in searching and indexing. But such a structure must be created before it can be used. Such an effort starts from a set of terms collected from query statements; document titles, abstracts, or full texts; position descriptions; and similar free-text entity representations; such a set is shown in Fig. 12.1a. The initial set of terms—5,000 for a small-to-medium size thesaurus, 50,000 for a large one—is rather unwieldy and does not allow for the kind of easy overview that is essential for developing a logical conceptual structure. Fortunately, the large set of terms can be reduced to a much smaller and more manageable set of concepts without loss of content through the following steps:

- Consolidate singular/plural and other morphological and spelling variants (Fig. 12.1a to 12.1b, column 1 and then column 2);
- Consolidate synonyms (column 2 to column 3);
- Consolidate quasi-synonyms (column 3 to column 4).

Once the vagaries of terminology are dealt with, the designer can concentrate on the conceptual structure and, for a controlled vocabulary system, descriptor selection.

12.1 CONCEPTS VERSUS TERMS:
THE SYNONYM–HOMONYM STRUCTURE

One must carefully distinguish between the plane of concepts and the plane of terms (or other concept identifiers), lest confusion reign. The relationships between concepts and terms (or other concept identifiers, such as class numbers and mathematical or pictorial symbols) are muddy at best; there is no one-to-one relationship. Often several terms designate the same concept; such terms are called *synonyms*. Some examples are *Natrium* and *Sodium, Lawyer* and *Attorney, Fixed in concentration* and *In exchange capacity* (both designating the same state of an ion in chemistry), and *Placed under government ownership* and *Nationalization*. Morphological and spelling variants add to the multiple term forms all designating the same concept. On the other hand, often one term has several meanings; such a term is called a *homonym*. Some examples are *Port-1 (harbor), Port-2 (telecommunication)*, and *Port-3 (wine)* or *Socialization-1 (economics)* and *Socialization-2 (social psychology)*.

To ensure retrieval of all (or most) entities relevant to a concept requires *terminological control*. For this purpose, the synonym-homonym structure establishes a one-to-one correspondence between concepts and terms. The designer develops this structure by selecting or creating a preferred term or other concept designation from a group of synonyms (and quasi-synonyms) and disambiguating homonyms by a number and/or a parenthetical qualifier. (If there is only one term for a concept, that is the preferred term.)

The preferred term serves as the focal point where all information about a concept is collected, providing a basis for intelligent decisions in thesaurus development. For example, the entry under *Harbor* (preferred term with *Port* as nonpreferred synonym) gives the information that the concept can be expressed as a combination (*Traffic station* AND *Water transport*), or that it occurred in 43 queries (term *Harbor* 25, term *Port* 18). This information is not repeated under *Port*. The result is a file that is both smaller (perhaps 2000 concepts versus 5000 original terms) and draws all information about a concept together in one place. In a system with an uncontrolled vocabulary the preferred term for a concept serves as a focal point from which the searcher is led to other terms designating the concept and to broader, narrower, and related concepts. In a system with a controlled vocabulary the thesaurus developer must decide which concepts should be used as descriptors. This decision should be made only once for each concept (not first for *Harbor* and then again for *Port*), and it should use all available information about the concept. If frequency of occurrence is used as a criterion in descriptor selection, one should establish the *concept* frequency (as opposed to *term* frequency; see the preceding example). This discussion illustrates that selecting preferred terms is important for any type of system, not just for systems using a controlled vocabulary. Also, with a controlled vocabulary a preferred term is not always a descriptor, but rather a descriptor candidate.

12.2 GROUPING CLOSELY RELATED CONCEPTS: THE EQUIVALENCE STRUCTURE

There are some true synonyms. These are terms completely equal in meaning, such as different terms for the same concrete object or process, or different names for the same chemical substance. But usually differences in language indicate subtle differences in meaning, connotation, or affective value—for example, *Developing countries* and *Underdeveloped countries*. These terms designate closely related or widely overlapping concepts; such concepts can be grouped in a class of *equivalent concepts*. The corresponding terms are called *equivalent terms* or *quasi-synonyms*. For example,

Disease, Illness, Sickness, and Ailment

For developing the conceptual structure and for indexing and retrieval, it is useful to form a new broader concept that contains all of the original concepts. The thesaurus builder must choose a term or notation to identify the new concept, perhaps creating a new term, such as *Disease, illness* (one term).

Equivalency occupies a middle ground between synonymy and hierarchy. For purposes of thesaurus development, particularly for constructing the overall hierarchy, it may be convenient to disregard small differences in meaning and consider only the newly formed concept, such as *Disease, illness,* thus further reducing the number of concepts to be considered. In an individual thesaurus it is often sufficient to treat equivalent terms as synonyms. For example, *Disease, Illness, Sickness,* and *Ailment* may be treated as synonyms of the new term *Disease, illness.* The four individual concepts lose their conceptual identity and are completely absorbed in the new concept. A thesaurus entry might be

Sickness USE ST Disease, illness (ST = Synonymous Term) or
Sickness USE ET Disease, illness (ET = Equivalent Term)

In a specialized thesaurus one may want to preserve the individual concepts, perhaps even use them as descriptors:

Sickness   BT Disease, illness (BT = Broader Term)
(*Sickness* is a separate descriptor)

In a thesaurus data base, one should introduce a special relationship BT-EQ; for example

Sickness BT-EQ Disease, illness

The builder of an individual thesaurus using the data base can then decide in each case how to treat this relationship.

Figure 12.2 shows examples of synonyms, quasi-synonyms, and homonyms.

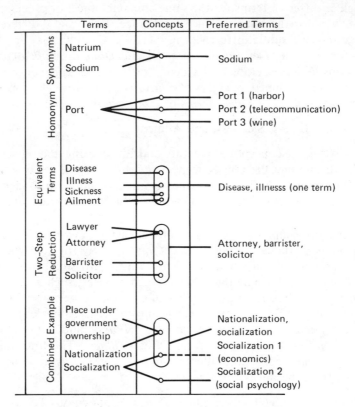

Fig. 12.2   Synonyms, quasi-synonyms, and homographs.

12.3 CLASSIFICATORY STRUCTURE

The set of all concepts as represented by the preferred terms, together with the relationships among these concepts, is called the *classificatory structure* (our term). The main relationships in the classificatory structure are

BT   Broader Term (really Broader Concept)
NT   Narrower Term
RT   Related Term

12.4 INDEX LANGUAGE

An index language is the set of subject descriptors used in an ISAR system. A *descriptor* (*broadly defined*) is any entity identifier, such as a person identifier, which is used for recording relationships to other entities and thus can be used for retrieval. A *subject descriptor* is an identifier for a subject or concept that can be used in retrieval. Following common usage, we will use the term *descriptor* with the meaning of subject descriptor unless stated otherwise.

In a system with an uncontrolled vocabulary, a descriptor can be any term. (Any term is admissible in the index language.) However, in the remainder of the book we shall assume a controlled vocabulary (terminological control in indexing) unless specified otherwise. A subject descriptor then designates unequivocally a concept used for indexing and retrieval; subject descriptors are selected from the pool of preferred terms (every subject descriptor is a preferred term but not vice versa). Most commonly the term *descriptor* is used with these connotations.

Likewise, the term *index language* in the broad definition given here includes natural language as used in an uncontrolled vocabulary. However, index language is commonly understood to imply a controlled vocabulary; we adhere to this common usage unless stated otherwise. The same is true for the terms *system vocabulary* and *classification* (*classification scheme*), which are quasi-synonyms of index language.

Examples of descriptors are *Pipe; Form of government; Theory; France; Graduate-level text;* 635.652 *Kidney beans* (as agricultural product), DDC; HD9235.B4 *Beans* (as agricultural product), LCC; NQCL.MACH.003 *Reactor,* a descriptor produced by combining two components and a serial number in the Semantic Code system; and A57B34C10D45 *Kidney bean Kernels Whole Canned,* a descriptor produced by combining four components, each from a different facet.

In the last four examples the concept is identified both by a notation and by a term. Which is used to record relationships with other entities depends on the system using the index language. The essential point is that the concept is available for retrieval, no matter how it is identified. Sometimes one distinguishes *descriptor text* (e.g., Kidney beans) and *descriptor notation* (e.g. 635.652).

Some index languages list all descriptors that can be used. Others allow for the building of compound descriptors from building blocks as in the preceding canned beans example. Sometimes a special type of descriptors, called role indicators, is used to produce compound descriptors:

Insulin—*Therapeutic use;* Diabetes—*Drug therapy*
Noise—*Effect;* Children—*Cause*

In some index languages these may be further combined to form still more compound structures to be used as descriptors, for example,

(Noise—*Effect*): (Children—*Cause*) (one descriptor)
{[(Noise—*Effect*): (Aircraft—*Cause*)]—*Agent*}:
    (Children—*Affected*)   (one descriptor)

Relators serve the same function but have a different format:

Noise *Caused by* Children
(Noise *Caused by* Aircraft) *Acting on* Children

Role indicators and relators are syntactical elements. Not all index languages have a developed syntax.

12.5 THESAURUS

A thesaurus is an aid for searching and—in a controlled vocabulary system—for indexing. It gives relationships among concepts, between concepts and terms, and among terms.

In an ISAR system using a *controlled vocabulary,* the index language consists of descriptors selected from the pool of preferred terms. For the benefit of indexers and searchers a thesaurus also includes the remaining preferred terms and the nonpreferred terms as *lead-in terms,* which form the *lead-in vocabulary.* Thus the indexer or searcher need not guess the term used as descriptor; looking under any term that comes to mind leads to the descriptor(s) to be used (Fig. 12.1, using the index 12.1a and then going from left to right in 12.1b). *Natrium* (nonpreferred lead-in term) leads to the synonymous descriptor *Sodium; Polyethylene* (preferred lead-in term) leads to the broader descriptor *Plastic.* The following table illustrates a more complex case:

Thesaurus builder's working file			User version		
Port	SEE ST	Harbor	Port	SEE ST	Harbor
				USE BT	:Traffic station
					:Water transport
Harbor	ST	Port	Harbor	ST	Port
	USE BT	:Traffic station		USE BT	:Traffic station
		:Water transport			:Water transport

In summary, a thesaurus for an ISAR system using a controlled vocabulary consists of an index language and a lead-in vocabulary. The index language consists of all the descriptors and the relationships among descriptors. The lead-in vocabulary consists of all lead-in terms and the relationships among them, and it leads from each lead-in term to the appropriate descriptor(s) to be used, possibly specifying the nature of the relationship between lead-in term and descriptor(s). This specific definition of thesaurus is illustrated in Fig. 12.3. Figure 12.4 further clarifies the distinction between nonpreferred terms, preferred lead-in terms, and descriptors.

A simple thesaurus for an ISAR system using an *uncontrolled vocabulary*

Synonym-homonym structure	Relates terms to concepts; preferred terms for 1-1 correspondence.
Equivalence structure (quasi-synonyms or equivalent terms)	Groups together closely related concepts resulting in new broader concepts.
Classificatory structure	Concepts as expressed by preferred terms, and their interrelationships.
Index language (system vocabulary, classification scheme)	Descriptors; selected preferred terms actually used in entity representations and query formulations.

Thesaurus (Controlled vocabulary system)
All terms

Lead-in vocabulary Lead-in terms		Index language Descriptors
Nonpreferred lead-in terms	Preferred lead-in terms	
Natrium ——USE ST———		→ Sodium
Illness ——USE ET———		→ Disease, illness
	Polyethylene ——USE BT——	→ Plastic
Port ——SEE ST———	→ Harbor ——USE BT——	→ : Traffic station : Water transport
	Preferred lead-in terms	Descriptors
Nonpreferred terms	Preferred terms Classificatory structure	

Fig. 12.3   Index language and thesaurus: definitions.

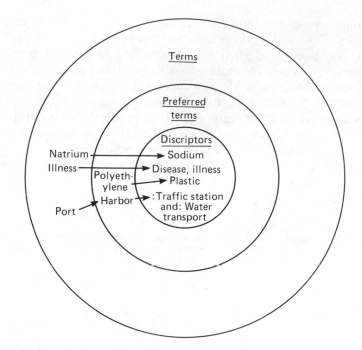

Fig. 12.4   All terms, preferred terms, descriptors.

consists of a classificatory structure and a set of further search terms. The concepts (preferred terms) in the classificatory structure lead to further search terms. Essentially, the structure of a thesaurus is the same whether it is used for a controlled vocabulary or an uncontrolled vocabulary ISAR system, except that with an uncontrolled vocabulary there is no need to select descriptors from the preferred terms. But the *use* of the thesaurus is different (see Fig. 12.1b). With a controlled vocabulary, the thesaurus structure is used from left to right for index term consolidation; with an uncontrolled vocabulary, the thesaurus structure is used from right to left for query term expansion. More complex thesaurus structures do not select preferred terms but link terms directly to each other, specifying the type and/or the strength of the relationship.

A computer can be programmed to look up terms from query statements, organization descriptions, documents, and the like, and convert them to the corresponding descriptors or expand a query term. A computer program needs a very complete thesaurus, since unlike humans it cannot find other terms under which to look if a term is not found. Even minor morphological and spelling variants must be included unless the program can recognize their relationship to the base form.

CHAPTER 13

Index Language Functions

OBJECTIVE

The objective of this chapter is to enable the reader to make intelligent decisions about the type of index language, indexing, and query formulation to be used in a given information system, considering costs and benefits of each alternative. This requires thorough understanding of the role of the index language in the ISAR system, particularly its role as a communication device between user and indexer, and of the concept of request-oriented indexing.

13.1 REVIEW: THE INFORMATION RETRIEVAL PROBLEM

The retrieval problem is to find entities relevant to a query statement. We begin this chapter by summarizing the solutions discussed in Section 5.2. (We assume an ISAR system with one main entity type, for example *Document,* and we emphasize subject searching in the discussion.)

The most *direct solution* is to *search the whole* (*unorganized*) *collection.* During the search process, the query statement—the problem for which information or entities are needed—is foremost in the searcher's mind and provides a frame of reference for analyzing entities. The process is request- or problem-oriented. The searcher examines entities from the user's point of view, thus serving as the user's agent. This process is truly user-oriented, but it needs to be organized more efficiently.

A *first economy measure* is to *cut perusal time by preparing entity representations.* But this creates a problem: What information should be included in the entity representations so that they form a sufficient basis for judging relevance?

A *second economy measure* is to *batch queries* and search the entire collection from the point of view of several queries simultaneously. This causes

225

another problem: The searcher must keep in mind many query statements at once and analyze each entity from the point of view of each of those query statements.

A *third economy measure* combines the previous two by *collecting anticipated queries and analyzing entities in advance.* For example, a reference librarian in a small library may keep an interest profile for each member of the clientele to be served, analyze incoming entities with respect to these interest profiles, and route them to users accordingly. This is a logical development of the method of batching queries. It is also a logical development of the method of preparing representations; the problem of which viewpoints to consider in preparing the representations is now solved: The anticipated queries provide the necessary guidance.

Some query statements are descriptors unto themselves, for example,

I need to know about anything that endangers our business.

However, as a rule, a query statement combines several components, each of which is a separate descriptor. For example,

New technological developments that endanger our business.
Components: *Technology* AND *New developments* AND *Danger to our business*
I need material on the corrosion of steel pipes.
Components: *Corrosion* AND *Steel* AND *Pipes*

Entities are analyzed with respect to these components.

Lastly, *retrieval can be aided by providing a retrieval mechanism,* such as a computer search system, a printed index, or shelf arrangement by subject.

All methods discussed serve to provide more efficient organization for the basic retrieval process, which consists of looking at an entity and deciding whether or not it is relevant for a given query. In this process the query (the problem of the user) is the primary concern, and the entities are examined in light of this query. This might be obscured in the method of anticipated queries, where, for every incoming entity, the indexer looks at a list of queries. The indexer must be very careful to retain the basic purpose of the process in this case, too. He or she must internalize the conceptual framework derived from the anticipated queries, examine each entity (e.g., read and understand a document, find out about a course, analyze an organization) from the point of view of this framework (that is, examine the entity from the point of view of each of the queries listed), and for each make a judgment as to whether the entity is relevant.

Indexing must be request-oriented if is to be a full substitute for the elementary process of judging relevance from the point of view of a query. The indexer must judge relevance with respect to anticipated queries. The following section discusses in detail the method of request-oriented indexing and how it can be implemented through the checklist technique of indexing.

13.2 THE ROLE OF THE INDEX LANGUAGE IN INDEXING

Request-oriented indexing (problem-oriented indexing) is a logical development of the method of anticipated queries. It contrasts with entity-oriented indexing, where the focus is on the entity and its faithful description. Entity-oriented indexing is the approach most commonly used; many writers do not even consider alternatives. However, the preceding examination of the retrieval problem shows that request-oriented indexing promises improved performance, possibly at higher cost. The ISAR system designer should consider both approaches.

This section expounds request-oriented indexing so that the reader can (1) consider the full range of alternatives in ISAR system design and (2) appreciate the shortcomings that arise in existing systems using entity-oriented indexing and adjust search strategy accordingly.

13.2.1 DISADVANTAGES OF ENTITY-ORIENTED INDEXING

The shortcomings of entity-oriented indexing can be seen most clearly in a system using *shelf arrangement as the retrieval mechanism*. The original idea behind shelf arrangement is to collocate entities relevant to the same anticipated query in one place to produce a request-oriented arrangement. Unfortunately, while many entities are relevant for several anticipated queries, an entity can be shelved in one and only one place. The indexer confronted with this problem easily falls into the trap of considering the arrangement of entities on the shelves as an end in itself, forgetting the ultimate purpose, retrieval. He or she concentrates on the entities and forgets about the queries. This entity-oriented approach has negative consequences for the design of the index language and for the process of indexing.

Design of the Index Language for Shelf Arrangement

The requirements of shelf arrangement determine the selection of descriptors, their arrangement, and the indication of relationships between them. Shelf arrangement requires suitable headings for groups of entities in the collection, pigeon holes into which entities will fit neatly. When several viewpoints can be used for the subdivision of a group of entities into narrower groups, the designer of the index language must choose one. For example, consider a group of documents on *Physics;* it could be subdivided by the following criteria:

- *by Quality:* Good, Medium, Bad
- *by Level of treatment:* Elementary school, High school, Undergraduate, Graduate
- *by Type of document:* Textbook, Journal article, Research report, and so on
- *by Subtopics of physics:* Mechanics, Acoustics, Electromagnetism, Optics, and so on.

If the subdivision by *Subtopic of physics* is chosen and if this leads to reasonably sized groups in the collection at hand, the other viewpoints are not considered in the index language; one cannot then search by *Type of document, Level of treatment,* or *Quality.* The designer could decide to further subdivide the documents within one area of Physics (e.g., *Optics*) by *Type of document.* The point is that this decision is not based on the importance of the aspect *Type of document* for searching but rather on its usefulness for defining the arrangement of the documents on the shelves. Very general concepts, such as *Threshold* or *Effects,* and very specific concepts that are not helpful for arrangement are omitted from the index language, although they are very useful for the formulation of queries. Furthermore, a large number of hierarchical relationships is needed for complete searching, but only some of these are selected for shelf arrangement, resulting in an artificial monohierarchical structure.

The Process of Indexing for Shelf Arrangement

In a system for shelf arrangement, indexing an entity by a descriptor is tantamount to assigning the entity to a group or class of entities. Only one descriptor must be used for an entity. This one descriptor is the entity representation, albeit a very incomplete one. It leaves out many aspects for which the entity is relevant.

In reality there are often three or four classes for which the entity is relevant and which, therefore, should be considered. The indexer must choose the optimal alternative, the one that would result in the highest benefit derived from retrieval and use of the entity. However, the indexer is usually under time pressure when looking for the proper class for an entity; as soon as he or she has found a class into which the entity fits reasonably well, the indexer is satisfied and does not look for other alternatives. Thus, the indexer often uses satisficing (stopping as soon as a satisfactory alternative is found) rather than optimizing (finding all alternatives, then selecting the best one). The indexer considers finding a place for an entity on the shelf as an end in itself, rather than as a means for later retrieval. This approach is heavily entity-oriented rather than request-oriented.

The entity-oriented attitude induced by the requirements of shelf arrangement often carries over to systems with much more flexible search devices, even those using computer searching, in which the technical constraints of shelf arrangement no longer exist. For example, indexing in ERIC (Educational Resources Information Center) is based on the premise that the document is primary and that one must faithfully express the contents of the document by an appropriate combination of descriptors. The negative consequences are much the same as those discussed for shelf arrangement.

The Design of the Index Language with Entity Orientation

Concepts that might be very important for searching but do not suggest themselves from the entities are not included in the index language. For example, in a bibliographic index language developed from words in titles, one would hardly expect to find descriptors such as

> Important for long range transportation planning
> Danger to our business
> Read immediately

The Process of Indexing with Entity Orientation

Entity-oriented indexing is carried out in two steps:

1. Identification of indexable matter: Examine the entity (read a document or abstract, look carefully at a painting, or analyze a food sample) and note subjects (For a document: What is it about?).
2. Translation into the index language: Using the terms noted in step 1, consult an alphabetically arranged thesaurus to find the descriptor(s) to be used.

As soon as the indexer has found a descriptor for every subject he has identified—that is, as soon as the indexer is satisfied that the entity is well represented through the descriptors assigned—the indexing task is considered finished, no matter how many other descriptors there might be under which the entity should be found.

An extreme form of entity-oriented indexing applied to documents is the *extraction-and-translation method of indexing,* in which the indexer simply underlines important terms in the text of the document or in an abstract and then translates these terms into the index language. The translation step can easily be automated. To a lesser extent this is true of the extraction step as well. In this method only concepts that are represented by a term in the text

1.   A document or data item dealing with the
Percentage of children of blue-collar workers attending college.

Document-oriented indexing:
Blue-collar workers (social class); College attendance
Request-oriented indexing would add
Intergenerational social mobility.

For a sociologist this may be the most important descriptor under which this document should be found. The indexer acts as the sociologist's agent in reading the document or abstract and should, as would the sociologist, recognize that the document is relevant for *Intergenerational social mobility* ("scientific prethinking"). This requires that the indexer know the concepts of interest to the user and that the indexer know the field well so that he or she can recognize relevance even if it is not obvious.

2.   Consider the topic
Treaty on Nonproliferation of Nuclear Weapons.
A thorny issue in negotiating this treaty was the inspection problem. Participants had to agree to inspection of their nuclear power plants by citizens from other countries, which is an infringement on sovereignty and furthermore provides an opportunity for industrial espionage. An indexer comes across a document that deals with the U.S. threat to Swiss pharmaceutical companies to ban their products from the U.S. market unless they allow inspections of their plants by Food and Drug Administration personnel. Document-oriented indexing would assign the descriptors *Switzerland, United States, International trade, Drugs (pharmaceutical)*, and, perhaps, *Inspection.* But since this document deals with the problem of inspection by foreign nationals, it is highly relevant for somebody working on the *Nonproliferation Treaty* and should be indexed by that descriptor. Even better, introduce a descriptor *Inspection by foreign nationals* (inspired by the analysis of information needs) so that the concept can be expressed directly in indexing and searching.

Fig. 13.1   Entity- vs. request-oriented indexing. Examples.

are considered; other concepts suggested by the overall context of the document are neglected, although they might be clearly needed for a representation of the content. The method discussed first, while focused on the document and the representation of its content, at least allows the indexer to note such concepts.

13.2.2   REQUEST-ORIENTED INDEXING: GENERAL APPROACH

Request-oriented indexing has a different focus. The indexer asks: Under which descriptors should this entity be found? The examples in Fig. 13.1 show the difference. In request-oriented indexing the queries are primary and the entities are analyzed with a view to queries (see the examples in Fig. 13.2). Ideally, the indexer would think of all the possible queries and decide for which ones the entity at hand is relevant. A systematic procedure for both

---

1. In the *ISAR system of a company* the following descriptors are very useful:

Danger to our business
Technological developments that could improve our products
Market gaps for our products.

If competent indexers analyze entities from the point of view of these descriptors and make good relevance judgments, then management personnel responsible for planning and research and development can be provided with information important for their task. For example, an article on integrated circuit technology published 15 years ago should have been indexed under the first descriptor by an indexer working for a slide rule company because it foreshadowed cheap pocket calculators, which make slide rules obsolete. Management, made aware of these developments, could take proper planning steps (get out of the business of manufacturing slide rules and perhaps start developing pocket calculators). If management was not made aware of these developments, the company might well have gone out of business.

2. The purpose of an *ISAR system for curriculum development* is the retrieval of topics and instructional materials that contribute to specified educational objectives. (As an example, consider the argument that the study of Latin develops a sharpened sense of language and logical thinking.) Thus the entities sought are topics and instructional materials, and each of these must be indexed by the educational objectives it serves. But how could this be done without drawing up a list of all educational objectives in the first place? Such a list will be hierarchically structured because there are objectives, subobjectives, sub-subobjectives, and so on.

3. A *curator in the Department of Anthropology* of the Smithsonian Institution is very much interested in any pictorial representation of Indians, however minor a part of a painting, drawing, or print it might be. Introducing the descriptor *Contains picture of Indians* communicates this interest to all staff members indexing pictures and thus instructs them to watch out for pictures of Indians. The curator can save a lot of work by simply using the new descriptor for retrieval.

Fig. 13.2   Request-oriented indexing. Examples.

the design of the index language and the process of indexing makes this feasible.

The Design of the Index Language with Request Orientation

Development of the index language starts from a list of anticipated queries, that is, statements of need, which in turn are derived from an analysis of the problem situation of the users. As a result, the index language contains a descriptor for any concept (viewpoint, aspect) occurring in anticipated queries, such that any anticipated query can be expressed by a combination of descriptors. Usefulness for searching is the primary criterion in descriptor selection. The descriptors are arranged in a meaningful hierarchy that communicates the user's conceptual framework to the indexer.

The Process of Indexing with Request Orientation

The index language thus derived from anticipated queries communicates to the indexer the user's needs; it establishes the framework for the analysis of entities. Request-oriented indexing proceeds primarily from the index language, not from the entities. The indexer assimilates the conceptual framework provided by the index language and examines the entity at hand with that framework in mind. He or she then considers each descriptor in the index language and makes a relevance judgment: Should the entity be retrieved under the descriptor? Through this procedure all aspects for which the entity is relevant are elicited. The index language serves as a checklist in indexing.

It could be argued that request-oriented indexing is not possible because one cannot anticipate *all* future needs or *all* descriptors that will be needed for expressing future queries. Nonetheless one *can* anticipate many future needs by considering all possible sources of data, including technological forecasts, and analyzing these data; this is better than nothing. Additional entity-oriented indexing can add descriptors that might prove useful later although a need for them was not anticipated (see Section 13.2.4). Ingenious searching can sometimes compensate at least partially for the omission of a descriptor from the index language (see Section 13.3). In other cases it may just not be possible to respond to an unforeseen request because it would involve examining a large number of entities.

Truly request-oriented indexing requires that the index language be adapted to the specific needs of the clientele to be served. While the index language designer need not know the interests or needs of any specific user, he must know the total "pool" of all interests or needs. Moreover, he must arrange them in a framework that is manageable by indexers. This is difficult in information systems that are geared to a very broad audience, such as *Chemical Abstracts* or the *Reader's Guide*. The number of interests may simply be too large. But request-oriented indexing can still be useful: Viewpoints such as reading level may be useful for the entire audience. Furthermore, the audience may consist of a number of distinct groups; in that case a separate indexer could be assigned to deal with documents of interest for one group using an index "sublanguage" adapted to the specific needs of that group. All of this requires a thorough study of user needs, using a representative sample of the clientele to be served.

The set of descriptors assigned to an entity through request-oriented indexing using a well-structured index language is biased by the anticipated queries represented in the index language. Many authorities interpret this as a bias imposed on the user by the system designer and conclude that hierarchically structured index languages and request-oriented indexing using the checklist technique should not be applied at all; instead they recommend relying solely on a faithful description of the entity at hand (e.g., the contents of a document), preferably in the language of the document itself. However, this conclusion is not warranted: Request-oriented indexing identifies important retrieval clues that would not be assigned in the usual entity-oriented approach to indexing. Indeed, the retrieval clues derived through request-oriented indexing are the more important clues. The indexing bias is imposed not by the system designer but by user interests uncovered in a study of needs; this is a desirable bias. Moreover, descriptors can be added through supplementary entity-oriented indexing as discussed in Section 13.2.4.

13.2.3 REQUEST-ORIENTED INDEXING: IMPLEMENTATION

This discussion leads to a procedure for request-oriented indexing: First learn and comprehend the conceptual framework provided in the index language. Then index each entity in two steps:

Step 1: Examine the entity, paying particular attention to the aspects covered in the index language.

Step 2: Decide for each descriptor in turn whether or not the entity is relevant—whether or not the entity should be retrieved under this descriptor (remember that each descriptor is a component of an anticipated query).

The descriptors should be printed on an indexing form. Ideally, the indexer should check "yes" or "no" for every descriptor in the index language; in reality, one makes do with checking only "yes" explicitly, assuming that no check means "no" (but it could be an oversight). The list of descriptors serves as a checklist for the indexer. We call this method *checklist technique* of indexing.

The checklist technique reduces the task of judging relevance with respect to all possible anticipated queries to the task of judging relevance with respect to a much smaller number of descriptors. Unfortunately, looking at 1000 or 5000 or even more descriptors for every entity to be indexed is still not a feasible task. However, request-oriented indexing can be made feasible by combining three techniques.

Selection of Checklist Descriptors

Select a limited number of descriptors that are particularly important to the organization setting up the ISAR system; these *checklist descriptors* receive special attention in indexing. The regular indexer must learn them and have them in mind so that he or she goes through them more or less subconsciously while indexing; an indexer can do this for up to 1000 descriptors. Proper display of the index language (or of the subset of checklist descriptors) aids in this task, as discussed in the following section. The not-so-regular indexer must rely on a well-structured display and more explicit checking of descriptors.

Display of the Index Language

The index language should be presented in a classified structure that is both conceptually and graphically well designed. Many index languages can be displayed on a few pages in such a way that the overall structure and the relationships between the descriptors become clear at a glance. It is known from learning theory that a meaningfully structured body of text can be learned and remembered more easily than a nonstructured body of text. A list of words can be remembered more easily than a list of nonsense syllables; a list of words arranged in a meaningful sequence (using a principle that is easily recognized by the learner) can be learned more easily than a list of words arranged in random order. Since the indexer should internalize the user's framework represented in the index language, classified structure is very important. A good classified display also refreshes the indexer's memory and leads him or her to the appropriate descriptors, thus making sure that no important aspects of the entity are overlooked. This is likely to enhance indexing consistency. The classified structure also assists a searcher in formulating the query (see Section 13.3).

Stepwise Refinement

The number of descriptor–entity comparisons can be reduced drastically by employing a top-down approach: The set of descriptors is subdivided into (usually overlapping) subject fields in such a way that the indexer looking at the heading of a subject field can immediately decide whether there is an expectation that the entity is relevant to any of the descriptors contained in the subject field. Each subject field is divided into subfields, and so on.

As an example, let us consider indexing a document on the problem of *Prayers in Public schools*. Scanning a list of top level subject fields, the indexer marks, among others, *Education* and *Politics* for further scanning:

X Education
   Communication and language
   Society
X Politics
   International politics
   Law

Economics
Technology
Problems of developing nations
Sociocultural change
-
-
-

In this way she discards many of the subject fields and reduces the number of descriptors to be considered to a fraction of the index language. Within each subject field the indexer, using the same procedure again, scans the subfields, and so on.

Politics
    System of government
X State and organs of the state
-
-
-

X Constitution
    -
    -
    -

Political process
Internal politics
Public administration

This process ensures that the indexer does not overlook the descriptor *Constitution,* which is important for indexing the document. Another indexer may have checked *Law* rather than *Politics.* That, too, would have led to *Constitution* through the chain

Law
    Public law
        Constitution

Thus *Constitution* has two broader concepts. An index language that explicitly provides for this situation is called *polyhierarchical* (an index language for shelf classification restricts each narrow topic to one broader topic and is therefore called *monohierarchical*). The hierarchy developed for the purpose of the checklist technique of indexing has several levels of subdivision. It is complemented by cross-references among descriptors associated in other ways. The resulting structure, a network of descriptors, leads the indexer to the descriptors for which the entity at hand is relevant.

The interests of the users determine the selection of checklist descriptors and also the division of the descriptors into fields and subfields (note the field *Sociocultural change* in the preceding example).

In a very crude form, request-oriented indexing can be reduced to a few indexing instructions such as:

> Index each chemical compound, its effects and applications
> OR
> Index each topic by the educational objectives to which it might contribute

This is better than nothing, but hardly sufficient.

The request-oriented approach applies also to preparing abstracts and similar entity representations. The same article is abstracted differently for *Chemical Abstracts* and for *Biological Abstracts.* The abstracting rules of RINGDOC (a pharmaceutical abstracting/indexing service) reflect the problems of the pharmaceutical industry; they instruct the abstractor to emphasize the chemical structure, the manufacture, and the effects of drugs, giving a detailed list of points to watch out for. The major part of the abstract may thus summarize perhaps one-fourth of the document; the other three-fourths are of minor interest for RINGDOC users and are mentioned only very briefly.

Figure 13.3 shows an excerpt from the indexing form of the *Chemical Kinetics Index,* which illustrates the principles discussed. The most important descriptors are preprinted; the indexer need only check the applicable ones. There is room for entering other applicable descriptors. The MEDLARS indexing form displays for check-off a small number of descriptors of general application, called check tags, such as *Animal experiments, Human, Male,* and *Female.* (These descriptors are also displayed on the MEDLARS search form shown in Fig. 13.4.)

13.2.4 SUPPLEMENTARY ENTITY-ORIENTED INDEXING

The bias introduced through pure request-oriented indexing may result in the loss of parts of the information that might be important for unexpected queries coming up in the future. For example, if objects have been indexed by material and geometrical form, a user with the unexpected query *Very large objects* is out of luck. The size of an object is an aspect that might suggest itself to an indexer working in an entity-oriented mode; it could have been added easily to the representation of the object. For another example, consider an ISAR system on transportation technology. Assume a study of needs shows that only the technical aspects of transportation systems are of

WHAT TYPE OF REACTION MECHANISM?

Addition: $AB + CD \rightarrow E$

    Insertion

Charge-Transfer: $A^+ + B \rightarrow A + B^+$

                $A^- + B \rightarrow A + B^-$

Collisional-Fragmentation:

                $A + B \rightarrow C + D + E$

(re) Combination: $A + B \rightarrow A-B$

    (Bond formation)

Cyclization

Decyclization

Dissociation: $A-B \rightarrow A + B$

    (Bond fission)

Elimination: $E \rightarrow AB + CD$

Energy-Transfer: $A^* + B \rightarrow A + B$

    (Collisional)

Fluorescence

Four-Center-Exchange:

             $AB + CD \rightarrow AC + BD$

Substitution: $A + BC \rightarrow AB + C$

    (Atom-trans, abstract, disproport, metathesis)

GAS PHASE ION OR ELECTRON REACTION? (Combine with mechanism types at will)

Collisional-Ionization (neutrals or ions)

Electron-Attachment (to neutral)

Electron-Detachment (from negative ions)

Electron-Impact-Ionization:

             $A + e \rightarrow A^+ + ne$

Electron-Impact-Excitation

Ion-Electron Combination

Ion-Molecule (reaction, chemical change)

Ion-Pair-Formation

Ion-Pair-Neutralization

THEORETICAL DEVELOPMENTS OR FIELD?

Absolute-Rate-Theory

Anharmonic-Oscillator

Calculation (num. results)

    Exact (treatment of model)

Collision-Dynamics

Detailed-Rates (master eq.)

Force-Constant

Harmonic-Oscillator

Hartree-Fock

Irreversible-Stat.-Mech.

Irreversible-Thermodynam.

Molecular-Orbital

Monte-Carlo

Perturbation-Treatment

    Time-Dependent

    Stationary

Phenomenological (macroscopic)

Rate Theory (miscellaneous)

Scattering

    Classical

    Semiclassical (WKB)

    Quantum-Mechanical

        Born-Approx.

        Born-Oppenheimer

        Distorted-Wave

        Resonance

Statistical-Mechanics (eq.)

Statistical-Rate-Theory (phase space)

Stochastic (fluctuations)

Trajectories

Unimolecular (rate theory)

Debye

Fermi

WAS A TECHNIQUE DEVELOPED, INTERPRETED, OR VERY IMPORTANT?

Acoustics (ultrasonic)

Actinometry

Analysis (chemical)

Calorimetry

Computer (simulation or instrumentation)

Cryogenics

Electric-Discharge

Field-Emission

Flash-Filament

Flash-Photolysis

Flow-Reactor

Interferometry

Laser

Mass-Spectrometer

Mass-Spectrometry

Molecular-Beam

Optics

Polarography

Pressure

Shock-Wave

Spectrometer

Spectrometry (frequency)

Time-of-Flight (mass. spec.)

Vacuum-Technique

Gas-Chromatography

Field-Ionization

Microscopy

Mössbauer

Diffraction

Crystal-Growth

Fig. 13.3 Indexing form for use with the checklist technique. (Chemical Kinetics Index)

interest; hence the place where these transportation systems operate is not indexed. If a query involving place comes up unexpectedly, it cannot be answered. Or assume that the needs of National Science Foundation staff are well met by broad indexing of research projects and proposals. A user who, at a later time, wanted to use the NSF data base to search for research projects on specific topics would have to make do with low precision.

One can take out insurance against the contingency that a concept will be needed for searching later, even though such use is not anticipated now. This is achieved by indexing with additional descriptors suggested by the entity at hand. The premium is increased cost for indexing and for updating and maintaining the files. As with any insurance, one must weigh the risk (the likelihood that a concept will be needed in searching) against the premium (the cost for indexing with the concept). Supplementary entity-oriented indexing does not ensure that every request put to a system can be treated satisfactorily. If the concepts in the request were neither anticipated (and therefore not used in request-oriented indexing) nor suggested by the entities (and therefore not used in supplementary entity-oriented indexing), then search performance for that request will be low. For example, when indexing objects, one would not normally consider the aspects *Weight, Price, Place where made,* or *Is decorated* unless specifically instructed to do so. Entity-oriented indexing does not absolve the system designer from the task of anticipating queries by thoroughly studying needs.

In document retrieval the author's vocabulary—terms found in title, abstract, or text—provide useful retrieval clues in addition to the standardized descriptors. This is true particularly if the index language is not capable of expressing very specific concepts or shades of meaning and if some users are interested in the usage history of a *term* rather than in documents on a *concept.* Using author's terms in retrieval also serves as a hedge against misinterpretations or omissions on the part of the indexer. Similarly, when indexing a person, we can use terms from a description of skills in his or her resume in addition to standardized descriptors.

While looking for descriptors expressing concepts suggested by the entity, the indexer will often use the alphabetical index to the index language (which is rarely used in request-oriented indexing as implemented by the checklist technique). However, the indexer should not rely on the alphabetical index in the entity-oriented indexing mode either; having found a descriptor through the alphabetical index, she should look it up in a well-structured display to make sure the descriptor is really appropriate. The alphabetical index should be used only as an entry to a classified display unless cost considerations dictate otherwise. One could even use the checklist technique in entity-oriented indexing; this would promote consistent use of descriptors.

13.3 THE ROLE OF THE INDEX LANGUAGE IN SEARCHING

13.3.1 THE CHECKLIST TECHNIQUE APPLIED TO QUERY FORMULATION

To arrive at an optimal query formulation, one must identify descriptors under which relevant entities might be found (to ensure appropriate recall) and descriptors that could be used to increase discrimination. The searcher should go through the list of descriptors and ask herself for every descriptor: Are entities indexed by that descriptor likely to be relevant to my (or the client's) problem? Could this descriptor be used to narrow the query formulation? Thus the searcher goes through the descriptor list, using the top-down approach discussed in Section 13.2.3. If this is too much effort, she should at least follow cross-references. For example, a searcher looking for documents on *Relation to own culture* should consider other descriptors as well and use the formulation

> Relation to own culture OR Socialization of
> the individual OR Culture and personality

to ensure reasonably high recall. On the other hand, the query formulation should include all limiting selection criteria explicitly. A fourth-grade teacher might submit a written search request for *Audiovisual materials on science,* which might be simply formulated as

> Audiovisual materials AND Science.

Much to his surprise, the teacher will get not only material suitable for fourth-grade level, but also material on junior high school and senior high school level (or even college level, depending on the scope of the collection of instructional materials). The query formulation should have been

> Audiovisual materials AND Science AND Fourth-grade level.

By browsing through an index language that is displayed in a well-designed classified structure, a user can clarify and focus on her own image or concept of her need. The structure of the index language serves as a catalyst to crystallize the need. This results in a better query formulation and better retrieval results. However, there is the danger that the user will slant his or her real needs toward what can be easily formulated in the index language at hand. This danger can be minimized by first exploring the need without the assistance of the index language structure. Preferably, the user formulates a written statement of the need before interacting with the structure of the index language.

Figure 13.4 shows a query form that illustrates some of the principles discussed.

13.3.2 COMPENSATING FOR THE LACK OF REQUEST-ORIENTED INDEXING

If the index language does not provide the descriptors needed for an adequate expression of the need stated, the searcher must use ingenuity and think about various approaches to track down relevant entities as illustrated through the examples in Fig. 13.5.

The searcher must think of *all* possible approaches; otherwise recall will suffer. It is one thing for an indexer who knows that *Long range transportation planning* is a topic of interest to recognize the relevance of the document being analyzed for this topic. It is quite another thing for the searcher to think of all the possible topics, such as *Shopping habits,* that might have implications for long-range transportation planning.

Another difficulty is that some documents on *Shopping habits* or *Flexible work time* are very important for *Long range transportation planning,* but others may have no or only very marginal relevance. The indexer who sees the document can make the judgment, but the searcher has no choice but to retrieve all documents on these topics; as a result, discrimination will suffer.

The examples suggest that *requests for specific empirical data* or facts or concretely described entities are usually *supported through entity-oriented indexing,* whereas *requests based on general, abstract, or theoretical concepts* usually *require request-oriented indexing.* For some general requests the searcher may be able to generate a number of concrete queries that among them will retrieve much of the material needed for the abstract request; to some extent low indexing effort can thus be compensated by increased search effort. This is an example of the familiar trade-off between effort expended in data base building and effort expended in data base use.

13.4 THE ROLE OF THE INDEX LANGUAGE IN DATA BASE ORGANIZATION

A data base or individual file provides the link between a query formulation and the entities indexed. The index language is of major importance for the file organization:

• The more specific the descriptors available for look-up in a file, the higher the degree of order in that file. For example, in a search for documents on *Job performance of firefighters,* looking under the specific descriptor *Job*

SEARCH REQUEST FORM	DATE

1. Individual who will actually use the bibliography	Title

Organization

Address

2. Request submitted by (if different from above)

3. Detailed statement of requirements (Please be as specific as possible as to purpose, scope, definitions, limitations, etc.)

4. Title of project for which search is requested (Omit if not applicable)

5. Medical terms pertinent to request (optional)

6. Check criteria that can be used to limit the search

☐ Human	☐ Animal	☐ In Vitro
☐ Male ☐ Female ☐ Pregnancy		
☐ Infant, newborn (to 1 mo) ☐ Infant (1–23 mos) ☐ Child preschool (2–5) ☐ Child (6–12) ☐ Adolescence (13–18) ☐ Adult (19–44) ☐ Middle age (45–64) ☐ Aged (65)	☐ Cats ☐ Cattle ☐ Chick Embryo ☐ Dogs ☐ Frogs ☐ Guinea pigs ☐ Hamsters ☐ Mice ☐ Monkeys ☐ Rabbits	☐ Case report ☐ Clinical research ☐ Comparative study ☐ Review

7. Limit languages to	☐ Accept all ☐ English ☐ Foreign (Specify)	☐ 8. Limit publication date to	9. Print specifications: ☐ 3 × 5″ cards ☐ Paper

Fig. 13.4　Search request form. (Modified from MEDLARS form PHS-4667-1, rev 5-66)

---

1. Intergenerational social mobility

One subsearch: all entities that report on a situation where parents are in one social stratum and the child or children attend a school that prepares for a job in another social stratum. We would need to think about many other subsearches to achieve reasonable recall.

2. Nonproliferation treaty

Assume there is no descriptor *Inspections by foreign nationals*. We could formulate one subsearch thus: all entities indexed by *Inspection* and a country and by at least one other country or international organization.

3. Long-range transportation planning

Some topics to be used in subsearches are:
Development of residential patterns
Where do firms locate
Forecasts of gasoline availability and pricing
Alternate fuels for individual cars
Shopping habits
Flexible work time
Carpooling
Attitudes to mass transit

Fig. 13.5   Compensating for the lack of request-oriented indexing. Sample searches for documents or survey/statistical data.

performance returns a much smaller set of documents than looking under the broad descriptor *Applied psychology*.

• The more specific the descriptors used in indexing, the more information they convey about the document (assuming that the indexing descriptors are included in the entry). To a searcher examining a document record, the specific descriptor *Job Performance* conveys more information about the document than the broad descriptor *Applied psychology*.

In many files, entities or entity representations should be physically collocated for browsing and examination in a logical sequence. The index language is at the heart of achieving such a useful arrangement. Examples are a mail-order catalog, a department store, a handbook of statistical data, a file of newspaper clippings, and a stockroom for parts.

The groups of entities or entity representations must be defined with the browsing needs in mind, and the specific groups must be arranged in broader groups again from the browsing point of view. In many applications the lowest level groups should be fairly broad; an example is the main section of an abstracting/indexing service in which collocation of entries serves primarily the purpose of current awareness. A group with the heading *Applied psychology* (possibly subdivided by type of document or another formal criterion) is appropriate for this purpose; a group with the specific heading *Job performance* would not be. From the point of view of building the file, it would be sufficient to index documents by the broad descriptor *Applied psychology*. However, using only such broad descriptors would be shortsighted; it reflects preoccupation with building the file. Assigning the descriptor *Applied psychology* would indeed be sufficient to file the abstract in its proper place. However, the user browsing the file would profit much from more specific indexing by descriptors such as *Job performance,* because it would provide more information about the document. The document should be indexed with the specific *indexing descriptor, Job performance,* and filed under the broader *filing descriptor, Applied psychology.* Likewise, for a file of organizations, one might use the broad filing descriptor

Information centers   in the   *Social sciences*

but index specifically by such combinations as

Special libraries   in   *Economics*
Data archives   in   *Sociology*
Clearinghouses   in   *Urban planning*

These specific indexing descriptors provide useful information to the searcher. Specific indexing also gives flexibility in file organization. If experience shows that narrower descriptors, such as *Job performance,* would be useful for filing after all, or that all *Data archives* should be collocated no matter what their subject field, it is an easy matter to rearrange the file cards accordingly. On the other hand, if we do not look ahead—if we index merely for the purpose of proper filing in the present arrangement, using the descriptor *Information centers in the social sciences*—then later reorganization of the file will require reindexing. Furthermore, a specific descriptor can do double duty; *Job performance* is appropriate for the subject index and also causes the abstract to be placed under *Applied psychology* in the main file. In a system that provides both a printed index and a computer search capability (for example, Index Medicus and MEDLINE), very specific descriptors are used for computer searching and mapped to descriptors of medium specificity appropriate for the printed index. Specific indexing, even if not needed to create files presently used, keeps future options open. To conclude, the specificity of indexing descriptors and the specificity of filing descriptors should be determined separately, each for its own purpose.

This principle is important also for cooperation in cataloging. For example, the Library of Congress (LC) assigns the most specific Dewey Decimal class that any library might need, but a library using LC's cataloging might well determine that a broader class would be more appropriate for filing arrangement on its shelves. For instance:

Class assigned by LC:	331.127	*Labor force mobility*
Class used by Library:	331.1	*Industrial relations*
or even	331	*Labor economics*

13.5 CHOOSING THE BEST INDEXING APPROACH

There is no one "correct" approach to indexing. In some situations entity-oriented indexing is appropriate; in others, request-oriented indexing; and in still others, a combination. In deciding on the approach to be used in a particular situation, one must consider the costs for indexing and the costs for searching weighed against the expected ultimate benefits (or at least against the expected ISAR system performance). Since hardly any experimental data comparing request- and entity-oriented indexing are available, the following discussion draws on the logical analysis of the two approaches presented in the previous sections.

In the case of descriptors of general application like the MEDLARS *check tags* (see Fig. 13.4), the checklist technique of indexing has only advantages; it can be used by indexers on all levels of sophistication, it is faster than writing these descriptors on the form, and it promotes consistently correct use of these descriptors. Thus the searcher can rely more on these descriptors. The following considerations apply to request-oriented indexing on a higher conceptual level.

13.5.1 COST OF INDEXING

Request-oriented indexing costs more than entity-oriented indexing. The construction of an index language for request-oriented indexing requires a study of needs and much thought and expertise. Indexing must be done thoroughly; intelligent relevance judgments take time. Reliable request-oriented indexing requires subject experts capable of judging the relevance of an entity for a given concept. (One might speculate that even nonsubject specialists would do better indexing in the request-oriented mode than in the entity-oriented mode, but the results of their judging relevance would not be as reliable.) Entity-oriented indexing, particularly of the extraction-and-translation variety, can be done by indexers who are not subject experts or even through a computer program. (Many bibliographic data bases do not even do their own indexing but use titles and/or abstracts or other existing representations for searching, in effect using the author or abstractor as indexer.) On the other hand, it would be extremely difficult to approximate the kind of relevance judgments needed for request-oriented indexing through a mechanized procedure. If request-oriented indexing is the main approach, then additional entity-oriented indexing increases the cost of indexing.

13.5.2 QUALITY OF INDEXING

An increase in indexing quality brings lower search cost and better search results. The checklist technique of indexing promotes correct and consistent use of descriptors, whether the overall approach to indexing is request- or entity-oriented. Request-oriented indexing provides a richer set of retrieval clues for an entity. Request-oriented indexing increases the likelihood that an entity (such as a document or a time series of statistical data) that is *Important for long-range transportation planning* is indeed indexed by that descriptor. However, some descriptors representing aspects for which an entity is relevant may not be assigned with the same reliability as descriptors that merely express obvious characteristics of the entity. Consider the following intuitive estimates for indexing a document entitled *Attitudes of the residents of the Washington, D.C. Metropolitan Area toward METRO.*

	Probability of assignment	
Descriptor	with entity-oriented indexing (%)	with request-oriented indexing (%)
Survey research	60	80
Attitudes	95	95
Washington, D.C. Metropolitan Area	95	95
Local rail transit	95	95
Mass transportation	70	90
Important for long-range transportation planning	10[a]	50

[a] if that descriptor is in the index language for entity-oriented indexing

One might argue that indexers should be discouraged from indexing implications of a document, since indexing consistency would suffer. But that is a bit like rejecting half a loaf because one cannot have a whole one. It would certainly be better to find 50% or even 30% of the relevant entities in a search for

Important for long-range transportation planning

than only 10% or none at all. Furthermore, the entities that are retrieved because an ingenious indexer has seen their implications for long-range transportation planning might suggest topic areas under which to search further. In the *long-range transportation* search, for instance, other topic areas might be *Attitudes* AND *Mass transportation, Shopping habits,* and *Flexible worktime.* A first-round search retrieves at least some relevant entities because an indexer working in the request-oriented mode recognized implications. The entities retrieved then help in the formulation of several second-round searches, which compensate for the indexer's failure to recognize implications in the case of other entities. While consistently good indexing is desirable, indexing consistency that results from reducing well-indexed entities to the level of badly indexed entities is detrimental to retrieval performance.

13.5.3 Cost and Quality of Searching

Whether request-oriented indexing is worth the price depends on the number and types of requests and on the importance of search quality. If most requests are specific and concrete, request-oriented indexing may not be needed. For requests that can be answered with entity-oriented indexing, albeit with greater search effort, the matter can be settled based on cost alone. If many requests need request-oriented indexing for a high-quality answer, and if these requests are important, then the ISAR system designer must determine whether the ultimate benefits derived from these requests justify the increased cost of request-oriented indexing.

This discussion is based on the assumption that the requests fully reflect needs. However, this is not always the case. For example, an ISAR system may be used only to search for specific empirical data, because it is not suitable for general searches due to its entity-oriented indexing, thus compelling the users to submit only searches for specific empirical data. In this case entity-oriented indexing is not sufficient, because it does not support potential use.

13.6 THE FUNCTIONS OF HIERARCHY: A SUMMARY

This section summarizes the functions of hierarchy and classified arrangement in indexing and query formulation, searching and processing, data base organization, and cooperation.

Functions in Indexing and Query Formulation

1. Facilitate the *checklist technique for indexing and for query formulation* (especially browsing through the descriptors available).

2. *Assist the indexer and the searcher in the choice of the appropriate level of generality.* A general rule for searching is: Use the most specific descriptor

that still includes the topic requested. A general rule for indexing is: Use the most specific descriptors that still cover the aspects or concepts for which the entity is relevant. Since the classified display shows at a glance descriptors both broader and narrower than the descriptor being considered, it assists the indexer and searcher in the application of this rule.

Functions in Searching and Processing

3. Facilitate *inclusive searches.* For example, a search for *Meat, inclusive* would retrieve entities indexed by the narrower descriptors *Beef, Pork, Lamb,* and *Venison* as well; this would be particularly useful for searches combining two broad descriptors, such as *Food additives* in *Meat.* In mechanized ISAR systems inclusive searching is implemented through a search program that utilizes hierarchical relationships stored in the computer; in manual systems inclusive searching is facilitated through classified arrangement. Inclusive searching is particularly important for SDI, where broad queries are common.

4. Facilitate the formation of *aggregates in statistical analysis.* For example, one may want to know the per capita consumption of *Meat* (including *Beef, Pork, Lamb,* and *Venison*) or of *Meat, Poultry,* and *Seafood* combined.

Functions in Data Base Organization

5. Facilitate *specific indexing and more general filing arrangement* where appropriate.

6. Facilitate the *collocation of related entities* in files. Collocation in turn facilitates inclusive searching; for example, a search for *Meat, inclusive* can be conducted much more easily in a classified subject catalog (in which *Beef, Lamb, Pork,* and *Venison* follow immediately after *Meat*) than in the more customary alphabetic subject catalog. Helpful collocation also brings related entities to the attention of the searcher; it facilitates browsing.

Functions in Cooperation between Systems

7. Facilitate *shared subject indexing.*

Hierarchy also plays a very important role in the construction of index languages and thesauri.

13.7 A PHILOSOPHY OF INDEXING AND CLASSIFICATION

This section summarizes the rationale for request-oriented indexing using a logically structured index language.

Two opposing principles for building an index language and thesaurus can be found in the literature:

1. Follow the vocabulary of the user as closely as possible; omit terms not contained explicitly in the user's vocabulary, even if they are necessary for logical coherence.

2. Follow, insofar as possible or even exclusively, the vocabulary of the entity creator (e.g., document author) so as not to distort the meaning of the entity creator. Accordingly, include in the index language only terms appearing in author-prepared entity representations such as the text or title of documents, food names given by manufacturers, or self-descriptions of persons or organizations; omit terms not appearing explicitly in such sources, even if they are necessary for logical coherence. (Principle of literary warrant.)

Each of these principles has merit; but the exclusive use of one or the other fails to solve the problems of communication that have been outlined in the previous sections. It is the task of a thesaurus to support optimal service to the user by providing the foundation for indexing and retrieval operations. This task requires more than following the user's or the author's vocabulary as closely as possible. There is no such thing as "the user"; there are many users, and their viewpoints often contradict each other. There is no such thing as "the author" either; there are many authors, and they often use different terminology. Authors and users often have different purposes: The use a user makes of an entity is often quite different from what the author thought the entity would be useful for. The indexer serves as the user's agent by indicating possible uses of each incoming entity. The indexer must analyze the entity at hand and then make a sound relevance judgment that is as useful as (or perhaps even more useful than) the user's own relevance judgment would be. At his best the indexer does "scientific prethinking." By analyzing entities as the user's agent, the indexer saves the user time. Ideally, the indexer evaluates each entity critically, something the user may not be able to do for lack of time or lack of expertise or both.

In order that the indexer can fulfill this demanding role, he or she must have a clear picture of the problems or tasks of the user and the information or entities needed to solve these problems. If there were only very few users, they could communicate their interests directly to "their" indexer. However, the normal situation is quite different: There are many users, most of whom the indexer does not know. Hence the mental frameworks of many users must be combined into one logical coherent structure that can be understood and internalized by the indexer. Careful analysis of needs and critical examination of the conceptual structure of the subject field at hand are needed to develop such a framework. The index language thus constructed serves as a communication device from the users to the indexers; it provides the framework that allows for a meeting of minds to take place.

The index language, once constructed based on the analysis of the needs of all users, also serves as a communication device from the information system to the individual user. It gives the user a mental framework, a knowledge map, a guide through the collection of information or entities available in the information system. (In a library where materials are arranged in a meaningful order or in a grocery store the user literally has a map of where to find what.) If the structure of such a knowledge map can be made congenial to the user's own mental framework, so much the better. But the user's framework may be less suitable, less powerful for organizing the subject matter at hand than an index language (or classification) constructed through careful consideration of the foundations of the subject. The index language then ceases to be a mere tool for retrieval and becomes a powerful agent for education, enriching the user's mind. The conceptual framework developed for the external information system can be used to improve organization of the user's own internal information system. This takes on particular significance with an information system for children or students, since young minds are apt to absorb the organizing principles used in such a system and use them to build their own view of the world. Hence, an index language should use structural principles derived from modern classification theory—such as the principle of facet analysis to be discussed in Chapter 14—and a semantic organization based on the newest insights and paradigms of the subject fields covered.

To conclude, the maker of an index language and thesaurus is confronted with the challenge of clarifying the muddled terminological and conceptual systems of a field (or perhaps several fields combined) and detecting its underlying logical structure, thus laying a foundation for successful communication.

CHAPTER 14

Index Language Structure 1: Conceptual

OBJECTIVES

The objectives of this chapter are to discuss the principles of conceptual structure—hierarchy, concept combination, and their interaction—and the application of these principles to searching; and to enable the reader to use facet analysis to uncover the conceptual structure of a field for improved indexing, searching, and index language construction.

INTRODUCTION

The entity type *Concept* (*Subject, Topic*) plays an important role in the retrieval of entities, either directly, as in a search for all *Documents* on *Nongraded grouping* (of students), or indirectly, as in a search for all *Students* attending *Schools* that are on the *Elementary level* and use *Nongraded grouping*. Retrieval based on concepts is called *subject retrieval*. There are many relationships among concepts; these make up the index language structure. This structure serves essential functions in indexing, data base organization, and searching. Many of the considerations in this chapter, especially the discussion of hierarchy, apply to the relationships among entities of other types as well.

Index language structure has two intertwined aspects: conceptual and data base organizational. We first give some examples of conceptual analysis. A concept, such as *Frozen beans,* can be generated by combination:

Food product [< has source> *Bean* AND < is in state> *Frozen*];

Or we can analyze a compound concept, such as *Ship:*

Object [< is a> *Vehicle* AND < serves for> *Water transport*]

Or, shortened,

> *Ship* = *Vehicle* : *Water transport.*

Or we can establish hierarchical relationships between concepts:

> *Beans* <is a> *Vegetable* or, less precisely,
> *Beans* <has Broader Term> *Vegetable.*

The question of data base organization arises in the decision whether to use *Frozen beans* as a descriptor, thus grouping all *Frozen bean* products together, or whether to use just the elements *Beans* and *Frozen* as descriptors, which must then be combined in retrieval. Hierarchical relationships, too, serve for data base organization—such as putting all *Vegetables* (*Beans, Peas, Spinach,* etc.) together on grocery shelves. This chapter emphasizes the conceptual aspects of index language structure; in the next chapter emphasis shifts to data base organization.

14.1 HIERARCHY

Consider the following examples. In a search for *Frozen vegetable* products, all *Frozen bean* products should be found; *Frozen vegetable* is broader than *Frozen beans.* The *Food and Drug Administration* includes the *Bureau of Foods.* In some universities, the *Psychology* Department covers *Social psychology.* An indexer having determined that a document is relevant for the concept *Method of instruction* should check further whether the document is relevant for *Individualized instruction.*

These are examples of hierarchy. Hierarchy serves many functions: It facilitates the checklist technique of indexing and query formulation, assists in the choice of the appropriate level of generality, facilitates aggregation in statistical analysis, allows for specific indexing and more general filing arrangement, facilitates the collocation of related entities, and facilitates shared subject indexing. A hierarchical relationship should be introduced whenever it serves one of these functions. With respect to the retrieval function there is a pragmatic *hierarchy test,* stated here for retrieval of documents:

> Should a search for documents dealing with *A* find all (or most) documents dealing with *B?* If yes, *A* is broader than *B* (and conversely, *B* is narrower than *A*). (This formulation can easily be generalized to other types of entities and relationships used in retrieval.)

Even though hierarchical relationships exist between *concepts,* the usual expressions are *Broader Term* (BT) and *Narrower Term* (NT); we follow this widespread usage.

The *traditional approach to hierarchy building* (exemplified in such systems as the Library of Congress Classification and the Dewey Decimal Classification) derives from the attempt to create a neat and meaningful arrangement for a set of entities in which every entity has its unique place; this is a problem in data base organization, not primarily a problem of conceptual structure (compare Section 13.1.2). Such an arrangement can be brought about by first grouping the entities so that each group corresponds to a concept and then constructing a neat and meaningful arrangement of these concepts. This can be done from the top down, subdividing the set of concepts into mutually exclusive groups, subdividing each group in turn into mutually exclusive subgroups, and so on. Or the arrangement can be developed from the bottom up, assembling the concepts into larger and larger groups. If a concept does not fit naturally anywhere into the arrangement, it is forced somewhere. If a concept would fit into different places, it is more or less arbitrarily assigned to one of them; no concept is allowed to have more than one broader concept. This is the principle of *monohierarchy;* it is artificial and imposes many constraints.

In contrast, the *modern approach to hierarchy building* establishes all hierarchical relationships that are useful for searching and the other functions just listed. Each pair of concepts (A, B) is analyzed to see whether it meets the hierarchy test. If so, a hierarchical relationship is established.

Examples:

BT = Broader Term (really Broader Concept)

Beans	BT	Vegetable
Zoology	BT	Biology
Biology	BT	Science
Constitution	BT	The state (BT Govt. and politics)
	BT	Public law (BT Law)
Social psychology	BT	Sociology
	BT	Psychology

In the example many concepts have two broader concepts; this situation is called *polyhierarchy*. Other concepts end up having just one broader concept, but with polyhierarchy this is not a restriction imposed by the system. Still other concepts may be left without any broader concept at all. These concepts form the top of the hierarchy; they may be broad subject fields such as *Science,* but they may also be specific concepts that happen to have no broader concepts such as *Packaging* (in the Dewey Decimal Classification there is no class number for this concept as a whole, only class numbers for the compound concepts *Economic aspects of packaging* and *Technical aspects of packaging*) or *Weights and measures* (in DDC this is wrongly placed under 380 *Commerce,* even though *Weights and measures* may occur in a purely scientific-technical context). Figure 14.1a shows a polyhierarchical structure.

The principle of polyhierarchy is very important. If the rigid principle of monohierarchy is used, many arguments result from the question of which of several broader concepts is the "true" broader concept, since only one is allowed. But there is no point in arguing whether *Social psychology* should be placed under *Sociology* or under *Psychology.* Either solution would be inadequate; it belongs under both. Polyhierarchy avoids such futile arguments. This illustrates one of the most important insights of modern classification research: A polyhierarchical scheme allows for a better representation of the conceptual structure of any field; many problems encountered in the construction of rigid monohierarchical schemes are revealed as fictitious. In this book *hierarchy* means *polyhierarchy.*

These ideas are also useful in designing organizational structures where rigid monohierarchy does not do justice to the complex interrelationships between parts of an organization that are due to the intrinsic interrelatedness of the real-world problems they are dealing with. For example, the responsibility of the *Bureau of Foods* has strong linkages with the *Food and Drug Administration* (in the *Public Health Service*), particularly with respect to food safety, but equally strong linkages with the *Department of Agriculture,* particularly with respect to the nutritional value of food. These linkages should be reflected in the organizational structure, which could show the *Bureau of Foods* as subordinate to and dealing with both the *FDA* and the *Department of Agriculture.* Likewise, it makes little sense if the Sociology Department and the Psychology Department argue over who should cover *Social psychology.* They should cooperate and develop a joint plan of courses.

The hierarchical relationships detected must be displayed clearly in order to communicate to a reader the conceptual structure of a field, in particular to facilitate the checklist technique of indexing and query formulation. A graphical display as shown in Figure 14.1a is useful for small sets of concepts (e.g., in an on-line display), but for a large printed display all concepts must be arranged in a linear sequence with headings and subheadings for easy scanning. The arrangement should express as many of the hierarchical relationships as possible and should collocate related concepts. *Any hierarchical relationships that are left over are expressed through cross-references* as shown in Figure 14.1b. The problem of choosing one place for a concept that

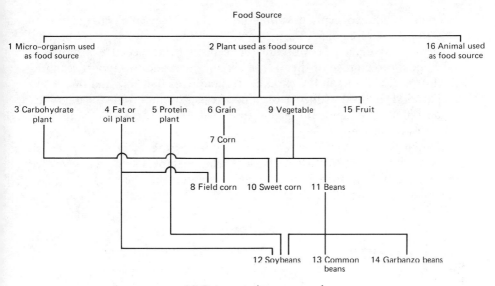

(a) Representation as a graph.

Food Source

1   **Microorganisms used as food source**

2   **Plant used as food source**

    3   Carbohydrate plant NT 8

    4   Fat or oil plant NT 8, 12

    5   Protein plant NT 12

    6   Grain

        7   Corn NT 10

            8   Field corn BT 3, 4

    9   Vegetable

       10   Sweet corn BT 7

       11   Beans

          12   Soybeans BT 4, 5

          13   Common beans

          14   Garbanzo beans

   15   Fruit

16   **Animal used as food source**

(b) Representation as a linear sequence with cross-references.

Fig. 14.1   Polyhierarchy. Excerpt from Food source facet.

has two broader concepts now *does* arise, since listing the concept in both places is often impractical. Furthermore, concepts that do not have broader concepts need a place. New broader concepts may be needed as headings to facilitate a rapid grasp of the overall arrangement and to support scanning the list of descriptors in the checklist technique of indexing and query formulation. The linear sequence of concepts is also important for data base organization, especially the arrangement of entities (e.g., documents or groceries on shelves).

Complementing the hierarchical relationships are *associative relationships,* usually called *Related Term* (RT) relationships. Concept A is related to concept B if an indexer or searcher weighing the use of A should be reminded of the existence of B.

Examples:

Political ideas	RT	Social philosophy
Nongraded grouping	RT	Montessori method
	RT	Individualized instruction
Copyright	RT	Reprography

To sum up: hierarchy must never be a straightjacket in which the universe of knowledge has to fit somehow or other. On the contrary, a properly designed hierarchy shows the manifold relationships between concepts and thus assists in indexing and searching. Whenever a hierarchy sets constraints, it is faulty; whenever it helps the indexer or searcher, it serves its purpose.

14.2 CONCEPT COMBINATION AND SEMANTIC FACTORING. FACET ANALYSIS

Concepts can be combined to form new concepts, such as *Beans* : *Frozen* or *Meat* : *Canned.* Conversely, a compound concept, such as *Frozen beans,* can be analyzed to determine its components, *Beans* and *Frozen.* Earlier we gave a less trivial example:

Ship   = Vehicle : Water transport.

Likewise,

Automobile = Vehicle : Road transport
Aircraft   = Vehicle : Air transport

The components are called *semantic factors,* and the process of analyzing a compound concept into its components is called *semantic factoring.*

Semantic factoring can be carried further; for example:

Vehicle   = Means : Transportation : Mobile   or
Water transport = Water : Transportation

Carrying this process to the end leads to *elemental concepts* that cannot be factored further. In terms of elemental concepts, *Ship* can be expressed as

Ship   = Means : Transportation : Mobile : Water

Semantic factoring establishes conceptual relationships between a compound concept and less compound concepts; for example:

Ship   < has semantic factor >   *Vehicle*
Vehicle < is semantic factor of > *Ship*

This gives the index language builder two options with respect to treating *Ship*. Option 1 is to use *Ship* as a subject descriptor; the relationships to the concepts that are its semantic factors should then be shown in the index language for the benefit of the searchers. Option 2 is to omit *Ship* from the index language and instruct the indexer to use instead the combination *Vehicle : Water transport,* if these are descriptors, or *Means : Transportation : Mobile : Water.* The choice between these two options is a matter of data base organization to be discussed in Chapter 15. Depending on the option chosen, a searcher can use *Ship* as the query formulation, or he must use the appropriate combination (e.g., *Vehicle* AND *Water transport*). Either way, a search for *Vehicle* will find documents dealing with *Ship* or objects that are *Ships* (in general, entities that are in a relationship with *Ship*).

A compound concept used as descriptor is called a *precombined descriptor;* an elemental concept used as descriptor is called an *elemental descriptor.* An ISAR system that uses primarily precombined descriptors, so that concepts are combined prior to indexing, is called a *precombination system.* An ISAR system that uses primarily elemental descriptors, which then are combined in query formulations (after the indexing is completed), is called a *postcombination* system. (The terms *precoordinate* and *postcoordinate* are also used, but they do not express the idea as well.) (See Chapter 15 for elaboration.)

Semantic factoring, the *conceptual* decomposition of compound concepts according to their meaning, should not be confused with the linguistic decomposition of multiword (composite) terms. For example, *Rare earth metals* is a multiword term designating an elemental concept (a class of chemical elements); semantic factoring is not useful in this case. On the other hand, the single-word term *Ship* designates a compound concept. The single words in a multiword term that designates a compound concept are not always the appropriate terms for the semantic factors. A striking example is *White House* (in the sense "the White House announces" or "a White House aide"):

White House = Administrative agency : Chief executive
officer : United States

This meaning of *White House* has nothing to do with *White* and *House;* *White House* is related much more closely to *10 Downing Street* than to the *White rabbit* from *Alice in Wonderland.* On the other hand, the linguistic structure often *does* reflect the conceptual structure, as in the *Frozen beans* example.

The following examples illustrate semantic factoring further.

Bus   = Vehicle : Road transport : Passengers : Large capacity
Truck = Vehicle : Road transport : Freight   : Large capacity
Trade negotiations = International negotiations : Foreign trade
Lego standard   = Rectangular block : Thick : 2 rows wide :
    block   4 rows long
Bean curd   = Cheese-product analog : Soybean :
                         Protein concentrate : Semisolid

(Bean curd, or tofu, is made by preparing a liquid from soybean flour and water, curdling, draining, and pressing into molds.)

Semantic factoring is best understood by doing it. The task of expressing a compound concept through components occurs also in formulating a query and in indexing an entity, but then the compound concept to be expressed may not have a name. Usually one can readily discern the semantic factors of a concept.

Facet analysis is helpful for finding all semantic factors and for solving difficult cases. Facets are aspects or viewpoints from which entities—such as food products or subjects (topics, themes) in an area such as education—can be analyzed. Fig. 14.2 gives the outline of a faceted classification for *Food products.* If the system rules specify indexing only by main ingredient, this scheme comes close to the ideal type of a faceted scheme: Every food product has exactly one descriptor from each facet. (Indexing by all ingredients results in many combinations of a *Food source* term with a *Part* term.)

It is best to use a list of facets that is adapted to the subject field at hand. The list of questions in Fig. 14.3a are helpful in eliciting the semantic factors of a concept. This leads to elemental concepts. Figure 14.3b shows sample facet headings to be used for the arrangement of elemental concepts. It can serve as a starting point for developing a subject-specific list. Fig. 14.4 shows the outline of a faceted classification for *Education.*

Product type
Ingredients
    Food source (Species or variety of plant or animal)
    Part of plant or animal
Physical state and form
    Physical state
    Physical form
Processing
    Degree of cooking
    Treatment applied
    Preservation method used
Packaging
    Packing medium
    Container type
    Food contact surface
User group

Fig. 14.2   Facets for the analysis of food products.

Of which class is it (the concept) a member or a subclass?
What is it made of?
What are its distinctive properties? Is it in a specific state, condition, or circumstance?
Does it participate in a process? What is it capable of?
Does it determine, cause, influence, produce, or act upon something else? Is it determined, caused, influenced, produced, or acted upon by something else?
Has it a specific purpose, is it a means or instrument to achieve something else? Is it a goal or end achieved or to be achieved by something else?
Is it a theory of something or an aspect of looking at something? Is it looked at under a specific aspect or viewpoint?
Is it a part of something?
Is it or is it not accompanied by something else or accompanying something else? Is it in a specific environment?
    (a)   Questions to elicit the semantic factors of a concept.

Things, objects, ideas
Materials
Properties, states, conditions, characteristics
Processes
Goals, objectives, purposes
    (b)   Facet headings to arrange elemental concepts.

Fig. 14.3   General facets.

Persons

> Subdivided by role
>> Students, educands
>> Teachers, educators
>
> Subdivided by . . .
>> (A faceted classification of personal attributes)

Educational objectives and content

> Subdivided by general objectives
>
> Subdivided by subject taught
>
> 1   Science
>> 1.1 Physics
>>> 1.1.1 Mechanics
>>>
>>> 1.1.2 Optics
>>
>> 1.2 Chemistry
>>
>> 1.3 Biology
>>> 1.3.1 Botany
>>>
>>> 1.3.2 Zoology
>
> 2   Social studies
>
> 3   Language arts
>
> Curriculum (the structure of a subject)
>> (RT Learning–teaching processes)

Learning–teaching processes and activities

> Methods of instruction

Learning–teaching materials

Learning–teaching environment

> For example, School, Other formal group, Home
>
> One subfacet: Sponsorship

Grade level

> 1   Elementary school (ES)
>> 1.1 First grade
>>> •
>>>
>>> •
>>>
>>> •
>>
>> 1.6 Sixth grade
>
> 2   Junior high school (JH)
>
> 3   Senior high school (SH)
>> 3.1 10th grade
>>> •
>>>
>>> •
>>>
>>> •

Fig. 14.4   Outline of a faceted classification for education
(some detail filled in for illustration).

A list of facets, once established, serves as a checklist for analyzing compound concepts: Each facet can be construed as a question (e.g., What is the product type? What is the food source?) and the proper semantic factor for the food product (compound concept) at hand is the answer to that question. A list of facets thus serves as a framework for the analysis of compound concepts or topics; it is a *facet frame*. Some facets may not be applicable, or the concept may be too broad to have a value specified. Take, for example, the food product *Cut green beans;* the indexer cannot specify values for the facets *Preservation method used* (it could be frozen or canned), or *Container*. On the other hand, one facet may take several values, as in a bread made from wheat and rye.

14.3 INTERACTION BETWEEN CONCEPT COMBINATION AND HIERARCHY

We have discussed two principles of index language structure: hierarchy and semantic factoring or concept combination. These two principles do not exist in isolation from each other; Section 14.2 already gave examples of their interaction. *Beans* is broader than *Frozen beans:* A search for all bean products (search term: *Beans*) certainly should find all frozen bean products. *Frozen* is also broader than *Frozen beans*. *Frozen* and *Beans* are also the semantic factors of *Frozen beans*. Likewise, the two semantic factors of *Ship—Vehicles* and *Water transport*—are also broader terms of *Ship*. See Section 14.2 for many more examples.

Hierarchical structures can be generated using this interaction principle. A simple example is shown in Fig. 14.5; the structure is simple because there are no hierarchical relationships within the facets. Starting from four *generating concepts* (in bold frames), arranged in two facets, one proceeds through the following steps:

1. Form all possible between-facet combinations; there are $2 \times 2 = 4$ combinations and four original concepts, for a total of eight concepts (four generating, four produced by combination). (Within-facet combination are omitted to keep matters simple.)
2. Using the hierarchy test, determine all hierarchical relationships in the set of eight concepts; there are eight:

Fresh plant product   Frozen plant product
    BT   Fresh   BT   Frozen
    BT   Plant product   BT   Plant product
Fresh animal product   Frozen animal product
    BT   Fresh   BT   Frozen
    BT   Animal product   BT   Animal product

3. Represent the polyhierarchical structure in a graph as in Fig. 14.5a.
4. Represent the polyhierarchical structure as a linear sequence with cross-references as in Fig. 14.5b. This figure shows two out of many possible arrangements.

Note how the pattern of facet A is repeated under each element of facet B (solid lines) and how the pattern of facet B is repeated under each element of facet A (broken lines). Thus, one partial view of this structure is that the pattern given in facet A is used to subdivide each element of facet B (linear arrangement 1); another partial view is that the pattern of facet B is used to subdivide each element of facet A (linear arrangement 2). Projecting these two partial views into one results in the total view of the structure as represented in the graph. In each of the linear arrangements representing a partial view, we introduce cross-references to make the representation complete. (A1B2 and B2A1 designate the same combination of concepts; the sequence of the notational elements is adapted to arrangement 1 and arrangement 2, respectively.)

When dealing with the conceptual aspects of index language structure, the designer is concerned with introducing *all* useful hierarchial relationships: Both viewpoints are equally important and should have equal weight, as in the graph. But the designer must also deal with the data base organizational aspects of index language structure. A linear sequence representing the hierarchical structure can be used as a guide in arranging entities, such as groceries or documents, or entity representations, such as abstracts. In such an arrangement, collocation is used for retrieval, and it does make a difference whether one collocates all *Fresh* products and all *Frozen* products while distributing *Plant products* and *Animal products* across the file, as in arrangement 1, or whether one collocates all *Plant products* and all *Animal products* while distributing *Fresh* products and *Frozen* products across the file, as in arrangement 2; see Section 15.5.2.

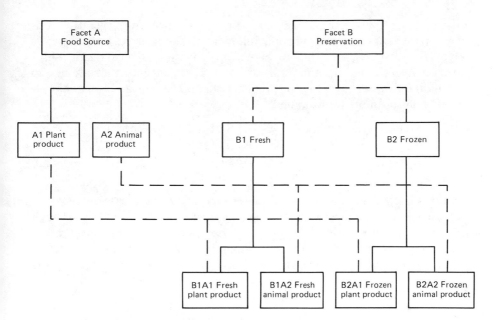

(a)   Graphical presentation.

Arrangement 1	Arrangement 2

Arrangement 1

Preservation more important
(bold and solid lines)

A   Facet A.   Food Source
   A1 Plant product NT B1A1, B2A1

   A2 Animal product NT B1A2, B2A2

B   Facet B. Preservation
   B1 Fresh
      B1A1 Fresh plant product BT A1
      B1A2 Fresh animal product BT A2
   B2 Frozen
      B2A1 Frozen plant product BTA1
      B2A2 Frozen animal product BT A2

Arrangement 2

Food source more important
(bold and broken lines)

A   Facet A.   Food source
   A1 Plant product
      A1B1 Fresh plant product BT B1
      A1B2 Frozen plant product BT B2
   A2 Animal product
      A2B1 Fresh animal product BT B1
      A2B2 Frozen animal product BT B2

B   Facet B. Preservation
   B1 Fresh NT A1B1, A2B1

   B2 Frozen NT A1B2, A2B2

(b) Representation as a linear sequence with cross-references.

Fig. 14.5 Hierarchical structure generated by two facets. No hierarchy within facets.

A more complex example is given in Fig. 14.6, where two generating concepts are added to facet A, introducing hierarchy in facet A. Now there are eight combinations, for a total of 14 concepts. The hierarchical relationships in facet A are given, not the result of combining concepts; they are due to *autonomous subdivision* (our term). There are now many additional hierarchical relationships, for example,

A1.1B2 Frozen vegetable BT   A1B2 Frozen plant product
                                 BT   A1.1 Vegetable
                                 BT   B2 Frozen
                                 BT   A1 Plant product

The first broader concept has itself two components; in this case the first step of broadening is achieved not through omitting a component but through substituting the broader concept *Plant product* for the original concept *Vegetable;* the hierarchical relationship is due to *substitution* (our term) rather than combination. The last two broader concepts are implied by the first one:

                                         BT Frozen
Frozen vegetable BT Frozen plant product
                                         BT Plant product

The graphical representation shows both chains; this obviates the need for a direct line from *Frozen vegetable* to *Frozen* or from *Frozen vegetable* to *Plant product,* which would only be confusing. In arrangement 1, the chain to *Frozen* is shown through the arrangement itself; in arrangement 2, it is shown through the cross-references:

A1.1B2 Frozen vegetable   BT   A1B2 Frozen plant product
A1B2 Frozen plant product   BT   B2 Frozen

Showing cross-references only to the immediately superordinate or subordinate hierarchical level cuts down on the number of cross-references; furthermore, the user following such a chain sees each broader concept in its total environment within the index language structure and thus is better able to grasp the parts of that structure relevant to the task at hand.

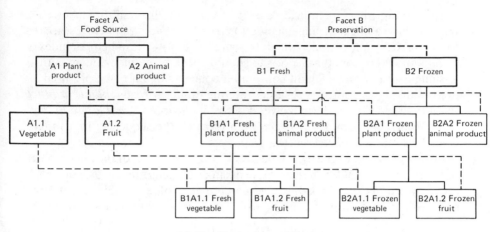

(a) Graphical representation.

Arrangement 1
Preservation more important

A   Facet A   Food Source

    A1   Plant product NT B1A1, B2A1
        A1.1 Vegetable NT B1A1.1, B2A1.1
        A1.2 Fruit NT B1A1.2, B2A1.2
    A2   Animal product NT B1A2, B2A2

B   Facet B   Preservation

    B1 Fresh
        B1A1 Fresh plant product BT A1
            B1A1.1 Fresh vegetable BT A1.1
            B1A1.2 Fresh fruit BT A1.2
        B1A2 Fresh animal product BT A2
    B2 Frozen
        B2A1 Frozen plant product BT A1
            B2A1.1 Frozen vegetable BT A1.1
            B2A1.2 Frozen fruit BT A1.2
        B2A2 Frozen animal product BT A2

(b) Representation as a linear sequence with cross-references. Arrangement 1.

Fig. 14.6 Hierarchical structure generated by two facets.

This example is more indicative of the complexity in a real-life hierarchy. It shows how a linear arrangement with cross-references can help a searcher to find all descriptors under which to search and how it can help an indexer to find all descriptors that he or she should check when indexing an entity. Assume a system in which all compound concepts of Fig. 14.6 are used as precombined descriptors. A user entering under *Frozen plant product* should be reminded of the narrower descriptors *Frozen vegetable* and *Frozen fruit*. In arrangement 1 this is achieved through the sequence; in arrangement 2, through crossreferences.

Proper guidance of the user depends on correct analysis of the hierarchical relationships. Consider the common mistake of determining broader concepts by simply choosing the two components of a combined concept, neglecting substitution as a mechanism for forming broader concepts:

A1.1B2 Frozen vegetable   BT   A1.1   Vegetable (1 level up)
                           BT   B2   Frozen (*2* levels up,
        omitting the intervening concept A1B2 Frozen plant product)

This mistake causes omission of the reciprocal cross-reference:

A1B2   Frozen plant product   NT A1.1B2   Frozen vegetable

and thus the user searching for *Frozen plant product* is not reminded to search also under *Frozen vegetable*.

The same problem occurs in query formulation with elemental descriptors. Assume a search for B2 *Frozen* AND A1.1 *Vegetable* did not turn up enough material; hence the query formulation must be broadened. Not considering substitution of A1 *Plant product* for A1.1 *Vegetable,* the searcher might use the broadened formulation B2 *Frozen*. This is a drastic move, and the query formulation is probably too broad. The searcher should consider B2 *Frozen* AND A1 *Plant product*.

Note again how the elements of facet B, *Fresh* and *Frozen,* are subdivided by the pattern of facet A, and vice versa; using the same pattern of subdivision for both *Fresh* and *Frozen* makes for consistency in the structure. Schemes such as LCC and DDC show many inconsistencies that could have been avoided through proper facet analysis.

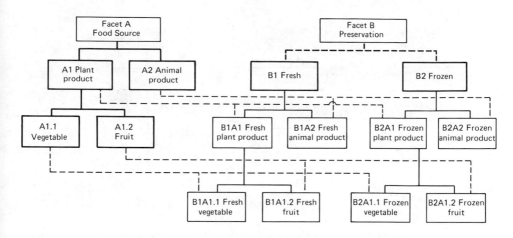

Arrangement 2
Food source more important

A   Facet A   Food Source

   A1   Plant product
      A1B1   Fresh plant product NT A1.1B1, A1.2B1; BT B1
      A1B2   Frozen plant product NT A1.1B2, A1.2B2; BT B2
      A1.1   Vegetable
         A1.1B1   Fresh vegetable BT A1B1
         A1.1B2   Frozen vegetable BT A1B2
      A1.2   Fruit
         A1.2 B1   Fresh fruit BT A1B1
         A1.2 B2   Frozen fruit BT A1B2

   A2   Animal product
      A2B1   Fresh animal product BT B1
      A2B2   Frozen animal product BT B2

B   Facet B   Preservation

   B1   Fresh NT A1B1, A2B1
   B2   Frozen NT A1B2, A2B2

(b)   Representation as a linear sequence with cross-references. Arrangement 2.

Fig. 14.6   Hierarchical structure generated by two facets (repeated).

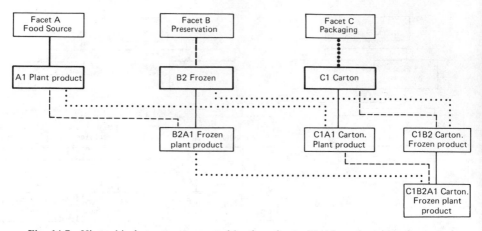

Fig. 14.7 Hierarchical structure generated by three facets. No hierarchy within facets (only one concept in each facet).

Most subjects have more than two facets. Figure 14.7 shows a hierarchical structure generated by three facets, with just one concept in each facet for simplicity. One can now subdivide A1 *Plant product* by adding B2 *Frozen* (broken line) or by adding C1 (Packed in) *Carton* (dotted line). There is a third combination on the same level, C1B2 (Packed in) *Carton. Frozen.* Finally, one can combine all three concepts.

Figure 14.8 derives from Fig. 14.7 by adding A1.1 *Vegetable* and A1.2 *Fruit* under A1 *Plant product.* Each of the three combinations in Fig. 14.7 that contain the component A1 *Plant product* is now subdivided into narrower concepts by substituting A1.1 *Vegetable* and A1.2 *Fruit,* respectively. A different way of looking at this structure is as follows: Starting with the structure generated by facets B and C, consisting of B2 *Frozen,* C1 *Carton,* and their one combination, C1B2, one subdivides each of these three concepts by the pattern of facet A. One could also start with the structure generated by facets A and B and subdivide each of its seven elements by the pattern of facet C.

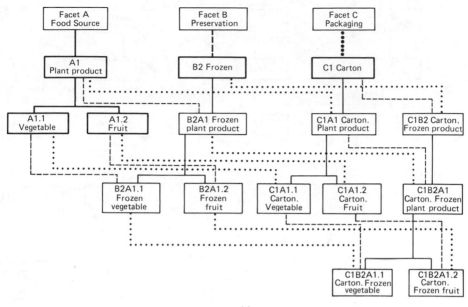

(a)

(a) Graphical representation.

Linear Arrangement (one of many possible)

A Facet A. Food source

    A1 Plant product NT B2A1, C1A1

        A1.1 Vegetable NT B2A1.1, C1A1.1

        A1.2 Fruit NT B2A1.2, C1A1.2

B Facet B. Preservation

    B2 Frozen NT C1B2

        B2A1 Frozen plant product NT C1B2A1; BT A1

            B2A1.1 Frozen Vegetable NT C1B2A1.1; BT A1.1

            B2A1.2 Frozen fruit NT C1B2.A1.2; BT A1.2

C Facet C. Packaging

    C1 Carton

        C1A1 Carton. Plant product NT C1B2A1; BT A1

            C1A1.1 Carton. Vegetable NT C1B2A1.1; BT A1.1

            C1A1.2 Carton. Fruit NT C1B2A1.2; BT A1.2

        C1B2 Carton. Frozen BT B2

            C1B2A1 Carton. Frozen. Plant product BT B2A1, C1A1

                C1B2A1.1 Carton. Frozen vegetable BT B2A1.1, C1A1.1

                C1B2A1.2 Carton. Frozen fruit BT B2A1.2, C1A1.2

(b) Representation as a linear sequence with cross-references.

Fig. 14.8 Hierarchical structure generated by three facets. Hierarchy in Facet A. (Fig. 15.5 shows the same structure in a different format.)

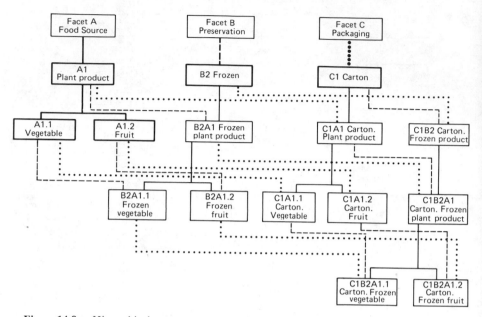

Figure 14.8a Hierarchical structure generated by three facets. Graphical representation (repeated).

In this structure one can follow the three kinds of hierarchical relationships (going from the top down). Starting from A1 *Plant product,* one finds A1.1 *Vegetable* and A1.2 *Fruit,* which are *narrower by autonomous subdivision;* and B2A1 *Frozen plant product* and C1A1 *Carton. Plant product,* which are both *narrower by combination* (adding the component B2 and C1, respectively). Continuing from B2A1 *Frozen plant product,* one finds B2A1.1 *Frozen vegetable* and B2A1.2 *Frozen fruit,* which are both *narrower by substitution,* and C1B2A1 *Carton. Frozen plant product,* which is narrower by combination (adding the component C1). This last concept can be further subdivided by substitution. To find broader concepts, one goes from the bottom up. Again, one can broaden a component to arrive at a concept broader by substitution, or drop a component to arrive at a concept broader by combination.

The following example shows a whole hierarchical chain generated by substitution:

	B2A	Frozen any food source	↑	
	B2A1	Frozen plant product		
narrower	B2A1.1	Frozen vegetable		broader
	B2A1.1.2	Frozen beans		
↓	B2A1.1.2.3	Frozen garbanzo beans		

The bottom concept, *Frozen garbanzo beans* combines all *Frozen* products with a very narrow restriction with respect to facet A *Food source:* Only *Garbanzo beans* will do. A search with this query formulation finds only a tiny portion of all frozen products. The next level loosens the restriction somewhat: any type of *Beans* is satisfactory. The next level loosens the restriction still more, to *Vegetable* and—even broader—*Plant product*. A search now finds a sizeable portion, maybe more than half, of all frozen products. It is not such a big step, then, to be satisfied with *any* food source so that a search would find all frozen products. In short, starting from the very specific *Garbanzo beans,* the food source restriction is relaxed more and more until it fades away entirely. B2A *Frozen any food source* is the same as B2 *Frozen*. Broadening a concept by dropping a component turns out to be the last step in a series of substituting ever broader concepts in that component. Figure 14.9 illustrates this chain through nested Venn diagrams.

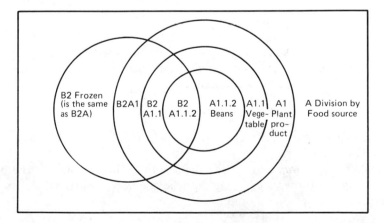

Fig. 14.9   Hierarchical chain generated through substitution.

The principles discussed in Sections 14.1–14.3 are basic to the understanding of index language structure and query formulation. The sample search discussed in the next section illustrates and clarifies these principles further.

14.4 APPLICATION AND ILLUSTRATION: SEARCHING

This section explores the effects of broadening and narrowing a query formulation and thus illustrates the application of hierarchy and concept combination to searching. It also introduces formally the idea of inclusive searching, which is closely wedded to hierarchy. This illustration uses a sample search in a small bibliographic ISAR system in the area of transportation. The index language used is shown in Fig. 14.10, a list of documents retrieved by various query formulations in Figs. 14.11 and 14.12. The query statement for the search is

Vehicles for rail transport.

The query formulation for this topic is straightforward:

E6 Vehicles AND B2 Rail transport.

Assume an ISAR system in which each document is shown in the index file only under the descriptors assigned to it. (Documents are not also shown under broader descriptors.) A search with this formulation finds the four documents indexed by B2 (see Fig. 14.12, the box labeled B2 Rail transport, general references). There are clearly other relevant documents in the collection; they are indexed by B2.3 *Intercity railroads* or B2.7 *Local rail transit*. To find these relevant documents, one should use the formulation:

E6 AND (B2 OR B2.3 OR B2.7).

This formulation asks for B2 OR any of its narrower terms. This type of query occurs often. The ISAR system should make the searcher's life easier by allowing for the query formulation:

E6 AND B2 Rail transport, *inclusive*

B2 *inclusive* means B2 OR any of its narrower terms. It is shorthand for (B2 OR B2.3 OR B2.7).

Sometimes one *wants* to restrict the search to documents indexed by B2 itself to find documents covering the whole area of rail transport, such as document 24. Then one should use

B2 Rail transport, *general references*.

B/D   Division by mode of transportation
    B1   Ground transport
        B2   Rail transport
            B2.3   Intercity railroad BT R4
            B2.7   Local rail transit BT R2
        B4   Road transport
        •
        •
        •

E   Division by facilities vs. vehicles
    E5   Methods to move persons or freight
        E6   Vehicles
            F   Vehicles subdivided by power supply
            G   Vehicles subdivided by type of propulsion
H   Materials to build facilities or vehicles
J   Passenger vs. freight transport
K   Traffic operations
L   Transportation providers
M   Creation and maintenance of systems and components
N   Organization and administration
Q   General and other concepts
R   Geographic range
S   Geographic location

Fig. 14.10   A faceted classification for transportation.

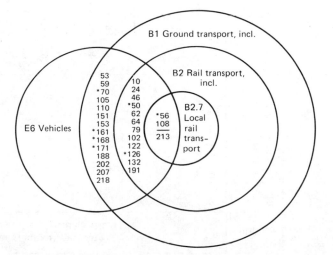

Fig. 14.11   Search results shown in Venn diagrams. (Documents marked by * are also relevant for B2.7 *Local rail transit*.)

Query Formulation E6 Vehicles AND	Document	Indexed by E6, other descriptors, and by
B1 Ground transport, gen ref.	* 70 Electric vehicles, a bibliography	B1
	*161 High-speed ground transportation tube vehicle concept	B1
B2 Rail transport, gen ref.	* 24 The concise encyclopedia of world railway locomotives (includes local rail transit locomotives)	B2
	* 50 Technical description of the Stockholm underground railway (should be indexed B2.7)	B2
	*126 Rolling stock for London Transports Victoria line (should be indexed B2.3)	B2
	191 Turbotrain (should be indexed B2.3)	B2
B2.3 Intercity railroad	10 Turbo train appraisal	B2.3
	46 Prediction of domestic air traffic passengers	B2.3
	Abstract: Examines passenger preference between super express train and air travel	
	62 Progress in railway mechanical engineering	B2.3
	64 Le turbo train des Chemins de Fer Nationaux du Canada	B2.3
	79 Aerodynamics of high speed train	B2.3
	102 Diesel–electric locomotive handbook	B2.3
	108 The Alaska Railroad	B2.3 (also B2.7)

B1 Ground transp., gen ref

B2 Rail transport, inclusive = B2 gen ref. OR B2.3 OR B2.7

B1 Ground transport, inclusive = B1 gen ref, OR B2 inclusive OR B4	**B4 Road transport**		122 The official railway equipment register (only intercity railroads)	B2.3
			132 Advanced passenger train	B2.3
		B2.7 Local rail transit	* 56 Teito Rapid Transit Authority's automatic train operation	B2.7
			108 The Alaska Railroad (B2.7 erroneous descriptor)	B2.7 (also B2.3)
			*213 The rapid tramway	B2.7
		B4 Road transport	53 National tank truck carriers directory	B4
			59 Russel's official national motor coach guide	B4
			105 An origin-destination study of truck traffic in Michigan	B4
			110 Where buses face air competition	B4
			151 Operation team valley	B4
			Abstract: Bus service to new development	
			153 Truck equivalency	B4
			168 National electric automobile symposium	B4
			171 A system for rapid transit on urban freeways	B4
			188 Satellite airport systems and community	B4
			202 Specialized motor carriage	B4
			207 The downtown parking system	B4
			218 Official motor carrier directory	B4

Fig. 14.12 Inclusive mode versus general reference mode. (Documents marked by * are also relevant for B2.7 *Local rail transit*.)

To give another example, a query for *Psychology of marketing* should be formulated as *Psychology, inclusive* AND *Marketing* to find documents on people's attitudes, information-gathering habits, readability of advertisements, and decision making processes—all narrower terms of *Psychology*. On the other hand, when looking for an introductory psychology text, one should use *Psychology, general references*. The user is not interested in any document that deals with just one or a few narrower terms of *Psychology;* he wants only documents that deal with the whole of *Psychology*. Having just one mode to search for a broad descriptor like *Psychology* would never do: If the one mode is defined as *Psychology, general references,* the psychology of marketing search would require a very large OR-combination of *Psychology* and all its narrower terms. If the one mode is defined as *Psychology, inclusive,* the textbook search would have very low discrimination (there are many textbooks on subfields of psychology).

In summary, a descriptor that has narrower descriptors under it can be used in two modes in searching. The descriptor in the *general references* mode finds just the entities indexed by the descriptor itself. The descriptor in the *inclusive* mode finds all entities that are indexed by the descriptor itself *or any of its narrower descriptors.*

Inclusive searching can be implemented in two ways. One way is *expanding the query term* (e.g., B2 *Rail transport, inclusive*), resulting in the OR-combination of the appropriate narrower descriptors. The other way is *generic posting* in building the index file: Posting refers to the operation of showing a document (e.g., document 56) under one of its descriptors (e.g., B2.7 *Local rail transit*) in the index (e.g., punching hole number 56 in the peek-a-boo card for B2.7, or listing document 56 with B2.7 in a printed index). Generic posting is posting a document to a descriptor broader than one of its assigned descriptors—for example, posting document 56 to B2 *Rail transport* (broader than B2.7) and to B1 *Ground transport* (still broader). Generic posting in a peek-a-boo file results in a peek-a-boo card for a broad descriptor in the inclusive mode, for example, B2 *Rail transport, inclusive.* But the original peek-a-boo card showing just the documents indexed by B2 itself—B2 *Rail transport, general references*—should also be preserved. The following table illustrates this.

Index term	Entries in the index file		
	First entry	Entries due to generic posting	
B2.7	B2.7	B2 inclusive	B1 inclusive
B2	B2 general references	B2 inclusive	B1 inclusive

We now return to the query on Vehicles for rail transport. Assume it requires very high recall. The query formulation should be broadened, for example, by substituting B1 *Ground transport, inclusive* for B2 *Rail transport, inclusive:*

E6 Vehicles AND B1 Ground transport, inclusive.

Figures 14.11 and 14.12 show the additional documents retrieved. Some of them are

53 National tank truck carriers directory,
    indexed by B4 Road transport
59 Russell's official national motor coach guide, indexed by B4
70 Electric vehicles, a bibliography
    indexed by B1 Ground transport
105, 110, 151, 153: some more documents on trucks and busses.
161 High speed ground transportation tube vehicle concept
    indexed by B1 Ground transport
168, etc., some more documents on trucks, busses, and cars
    indexed by B4 Road transport

Document 70 appears relevant because it covers vehicles for all kinds of ground transportation; document 161 appears relevant because it covers vehicles for a specific type of ground transportation that is closely related to rail transportation (*Tube transport* is not in the index language). The other documents found are not relevant. With this particular query formulation, a slight increase in recall is paid for with a large decrease in discrimination; B1 *Ground transport, inclusive* brought in not only the two additional relevant documents indexed by B1 but also the many, many irrelevant documents indexed by B4 *Road transport*. However, we can do much better; the following query formulation will add only the two additional relevant documents:

E6 AND B2 inclusive OR B1 Ground transport, general references

Now assume that you are to search for the topic

Vehicles for local rail transit.

In Figs. 14.11 and 14.12 the relevant documents are marked with an asterisk. A good query formulation for this topic should follow the principles discussed.

14.5 CONCEPTUAL ANALYSIS, FACET ANALYSIS: ELABORATION

14.5.1 Developing a Scheme of Facets

A scheme of facets is very helpful for semantic factoring and for organizing elemental concepts into a coherent structure. But deriving such a scheme—or facet frame—is a difficult task. It is the task of discerning the structure of a field from an unwieldy set of 10,000 concepts compiled from patient histories, document titles and abstracts, query statements, or any other source.

This task can be accomplished with the *bottom-up approach:* The designer first factors each concept in the list as far as possible, resulting in a list of elemental concepts, and then arranges the elemental concepts into facets with hierarchical structure within each facet.

The task can also be accomplished with the *top-down approach:* The designer first examines the phenomena in a subject field, resulting in a facet frame. For example, medicine deals with the *Organisms affected*—which in turn can be characterized by *Species* (including humans), *Age,* and *Sex;* the *Organ, organ system, or body region* affected; the *Type of disease; Disease causes,* including disease causing agents; and *Therapeutic measures,* including drugs. Next the designer develops for each facet a hierarchically structured list of elemental concepts, starting from major subdivisions and working downward.

A *combination approach* is best. Problem analysis leads to a preliminary facet frame. A number of obvious concepts suggest themselves for each facet. The designer uses this preliminary classification as a guide in factoring the concepts of the original list, adding new elemental concepts, and even new facets, as needed.

A universal scheme of facets emerges from the comparison and integration of several schemes developed for individual subject fields. For example, the food scheme has a facet *Food source,* which covers the organisms used in the production of food. The same list of organisms can be used in medicine for the facet *Organism affected. Anatomical part* is another facet that medicine and food have in common. The food facets *Physical state* and *Physical form* are clearly very general, and so on.

14.5.2 Recognizing General Concepts

Semantic factoring leads to general concepts that are not explicitly recognized in a field but that may be quite useful, not only for retrieval but also for general discourse in the field. For example, *Railroad station, Harbor,* and *Airport* all contain a common aspect (what is left after extracting the semantic factors *Rail transport, Water transport,* and *Air transport,* respectively). Since there is no name for this general concept, the designer invents one: *Traffic station.* In a search for passenger handling in an airport, documents on passenger handling in railroad stations might be quite useful; thus the topic may be more appropriately stated as passenger handling in traffic stations.

Another example comes from the area of alcoholic beverages—more specifically, distilled spirits. Applicable government regulations define *Neutral distilled spirits,* which are distilled to such a degree that no distinctive flavor or aroma is left. Then they define a long list of other distilled spirits, such as *Whiskey, Rum, Brandy,* and *Tequila.* These are all compound concepts: The semantic factors corresponding to the food source (*Grain, Sugar cane, Plant producing fruit or berry,* and *Agave,* respectively) can be extracted easily. A general concept is needed to be used as the other semantic factor; since the subject field does not provide such a concept, the designer creates *Distinctive distilled spirits.*

Sometimes a general concept—perhaps not new but rather so obvious as to be easily overlooked—is detected "through contrast" in a new facet. For example, consider the original concept *Reading instruction for deaf children.* One semantic factor is *Deaf,* an elemental concept new to the scheme. It does not fit into any of the existing facets, so the designer introduces

> Person by presence or absence of handicap
>   Deaf

Immediately she sees that this needs to be fleshed out:

> Person by presence or absence of handicap
>   Handicapped
>   Physically handicapped
>   Hard of hearing, deaf
>   Visually handicapped, blind
>   Mental handicapped
>   Not handicapped

Handicapped does not cover the universe of persons. The designer must introduce *Not handicapped* to make the facet complete. *Not handicapped* is easily overlooked both in index language construction and in indexing and searching. A teacher just looking for *Reading instruction* may have no use for material on reading instruction for the handicapped since it does not apply to his or her situation; the teacher should be able to search for

> Reading instruction AND NOT handicapped

14.5.3 SUBFACETS

Individual concepts in a facet may in turn be subdivided by several *subfacets*. For example, consider the facet *Part of plant or animal* in the food classification. In the subdivision *Part of animal* and, under that, *Meat part of animal,* there are two viewpoints for further subdivision, giving rise to two subfacets:

> Meat part of animal by type of cut
> > Leg
> > Rib
> > etc.

> Meat part of animal by presence of bone
> > Meat with bone
> > Meat without bone, boneless

14.5.4 FACET ANALYSIS AND RELATIONSHIPS
AMONG PRECOMBINED DESCRIPTORS

The elemental concepts arranged in the facet structure capture the essence of a field. But often compound concepts are used as descriptors or included as lead-in terms and hierarchical and associative relationships between them must be established. This can be done easily (even automatically) using the model from Section 14.3. But there may be a few residual relationships that cannot be so derived; for example *Prayer in schools in the U.S.* is related to *Relation between church and state in the U.S.* and *Constitution—U.S.; State-controlled planned economy* is related to *Economy of Eastern European countries after World War 2.* These relationships cannot be derived by logical inference as in Section 14.3; rather, they are based on relationships in the real world and must be determined empirically.

14.5.5 ADVANTAGES OF SEMANTIC FACTORING AND FACET ANALYSIS

1. Semantic factoring renders explicit all essential aspects of a concept. This explicitness allows for a thorough analysis of the relationships between concepts in an index language or thesaurus. This is of special importance for establishing links between disciplines. Semantic factoring is an excellent tool for the analysis of traditional classification schemes, such as LCC, which arrange a large number of compound concepts in a monohierarchy; it helps detect the many hierarchical relationships that are missing.

2. Semantic factoring reveals general concepts that are not explicitly

recognized in a field but that may be quite useful, not only for retrieval but also for general discourse in the field.

3. Semantic factoring leads to *a (comparatively) small set of elemental concepts* by means of which all compound concepts can be expressed through combination. This creates the option of reducing the index language to a (comparatively) small number of elemental descriptors, provided that the data base structure and retrieval mechanism allow for combination searching. For example, an index language for education need not include a descriptor for every combination of a grade level with a curriculum subject. An index language for transportation need not include the individual descriptors *Railroad station, Bus terminal, Parking garage, Harbor,* and *Airport;* the one descriptor *Traffic station* will do. One can search for any specific type of traffic station by combining with the appropriate mode of transportation. Likewise, the food classification need not include *Whiskey, Rum, Brandy, Tequila,* etc., in the *Product type* facet; the one descriptor *Distinctive distilled spirits* will do.

14.6 HIERARCHY: ELABORATION

14.6.1 HIERARCHICAL VERSUS ASSOCIATIVE RELATIONSHIPS

Hierarchical relationships are used in inclusive searching. For example, if the thesaurus includes the hierarchical relationship

Grain NT Wheat,

a search for *Grain, inclusive* retrieves, among others, all entities that are in a relationship to *Wheat.* In the example this is fine because it is hard to imagine that anybody searching for *Grain, inclusive* would not want to find entities related to *Wheat* also.

But take the hierarchical relationship

Grain   NT   Corn

Some people (the expansive group) might agree with that relationship, whereas others (the restrictive group) might not want to find entities related to *Corn,* especially *Sweet corn,* when searching for *Grain, inclusive.* The index language designer has two options. Option 1 is to introduce the hierarchical relationship and thus please the expansive group of users; the restrictive group will either have to be satisfied with retrieving entities they do not consider relevant or formulate their query as

Grain, general references OR   Wheat OR Rye OR
Barley OR   Rice   OR . . .   (Corn is not included.)

Option 2 is to omit the hierarchical relationship and please the restrictive group. In that case, the designer should at least introduce the associative relationship

> Grain   RT   Corn

A user with an expansive definition of *Grain* could then use the query formulation

> Grain, inclusive   OR   Corn

The associative relationship reminds this user to add *OR Corn*. Another example of the same problem is what relationship should be established between *Fruit* and *Tomato*. The index language designer should choose the relationship that minimizes total user effort.

14.6.2 TYPES OF HIERARCHICAL RELATIONSHIPS

The pragmatic definition of hierarchical relationships given in Section 14.1 is not concerned with the details of the "meaning" of a relationship. However, an examination of the meaning of relationships leads to a better understanding of their nature and is useful for the development of the hierarchical structure. The most important types of hierarchical relationships are the following.

Class Inclusion

A relationship of the form class/subclass or class/member of a class (hierarchy in the logical sense). For example,

> Vegetable   NT   Leafy vegetable
> Leafy vegetable   NT   Spinach

A logically narrower concept has all the characteristics of the broader concept and, in addition, at least one further characteristic. Thus, we can always say, "*B* (the narrower concept) is an *A* (the broader concept) that has the characteristic *C*." For example: *B Leafy Vegetable* is an *A Vegetable* with the characteristic *C The leaves are eaten*.

Topic Inclusion

A relationship between two areas of knowledge, one including the other. For example,

> Psychology   NT   Personality
> Science   NT   Physics   NT   Optics

Whole—part

A relationship between two physical objects, one including the other. For example,

Automobile   NT   Automobile engine

(Note that we do not say *Automobile*   NT   *Engine,* because there are many engines that are not part of an automobile.)

Possible use

A relationship based on the possible use of a substance or idea. For example,

Solvent   NT   Alcohol
(*Solvent* is a possible use of *Alcohol*)

Other types of relationships

A relationship between two concepts that does not fall under any of the previous types but is nevertheless useful as hierarchical relationship. For example,

Electron tubes   NT   Characteristic curve of electron tubes

Some rules for the construction of index languages use a strict logical definition of hierarchy, admitting only class inclusion relationships, and excluding, for example, whole–part and use relationships. However, hierarchy serves a purpose and hierarchical relationships should be introduced whenever they serve this purpose, that is, whenever they serve any of the functions listed in Section 13.6.

14.6.3 INTRODUCING NEW BROADER CONCEPTS

Building a hierarchy often leads to an awareness of gaps that should be filled by the introduction of a new, broader concept, particularly for searching. For example, a classification of *Government and politics* may have arrayed the following concepts:

The state
Constitution
Legislative body
Administration, executive branch

The designer feels that searches for the OR-combination of these four concepts may be frequent and therefore introduces a new, broader concept—*The state, broadly defined*—to include them all. This concept, once introduced, is also useful for indexing comprehensive documents. (The Medical Subject Headings Tree Structures include a number of such broader concepts; but these are available only for searching, not for indexing, as indicated by the label *Non-MeSH*. But a separate type of descriptors that are available only for searching is confusing and should be created only if the number of descriptors in a system is severely limited, which is not the case for MEDLINE.)

In the next example the individual concepts to be included under a new, broader concept are part of different subject areas, where they remain as narrower terms also.

> Relation to culture, broadly defined
> > Relation to own culture (Culture)
> > Relation to other culture (Culture)
> > Informal education (Education)
> > Socialization of the individual (Sociology)
> > Adaptation—readaptation (Sociology)
> > Culture and personality (Social psychology)
> > Attitudes, opinions (Social psychology)

Again the designer expects many searches in which all of these concepts would be ORed; introducing the broader concept makes the searcher's life much easier. Instead of entering seven descriptors connected by OR, he or she enters just one descriptor. Moreover, the searcher working without the benefit of this new, broader concept may well forget one or the other of the narrower concepts included. The new, broader concept is also useful to the indexer who considers, for example, using the descriptor *Informal education*. Following the BT cross-reference to *Relation to culture, broadly defined,* he or she finds a list of candidate descriptors to be used in addition to or instead of *Informal education*.

This example illustrates very clearly that hierarchy building must go beyond arranging a set of concepts in a neat structure; the designer must identify all concepts and all relationships that can help the indexer or searcher.

Sometimes a broad concept can replace several narrower concepts in the index language. If the number of descriptors in the index language is to be kept to a minimum, this may provide an impetus for finding new broad concepts. For example, consider the newly formed concept

> Stonework, glass, ceramics
> > Stonework
> > Glass
> > Ceramics

It can replace the three narrower concepts:

Stonework USE BT Stonework, glass, ceramics

and likewise for *Glass* and *Ceramics*.

Broad concepts also serve as headings to clarify the arrangement of the descriptors in the display of an index language. This is very important, particularly for the checklist technique of indexing and query formulation. Sometimes the impetus for introducing a new, broader concept comes from the need for such a heading. For example,

Employment of specific groups
  Employment of children
  Employment of women
  Employment of handicapped persons
  Employment of jail inmates

Meat part by presence of bone
  With bone
  Boneless

Broad concepts introduced originally for their value as headings are also useful for indexing comprehensive documents. Some systems, such as LCC and Thesaurofacet, introduce broader concepts as headings but do not include them in the index language as descriptors; this is confusing.

14.7 CONCEPT FORMATION IN THESAURUS BUILDING

The major concern in building an index language or thesaurus is the development of a conceptual framework that mediates between the searcher and how he expresses his interest on the one hand and the information provided by the author and how she expresses her findings on the other. This must be accomplished within the limitations of the ISAR system at hand, especially within constraints on the size of the index language. This task requires thorough conceptual analysis and the formation of new concepts; it challenges the creativity of the thesaurus builder.

New concepts are formed in consolidating quasi-synonyms (Section 12.2), in semantic factoring or facet analysis (Section 14.5.2), and in building the hierarchy (Section 14.6.3).

Careful facet analysis reveals *cross-disciplinary concepts;* such concepts should be "pitched at the level of abstraction permitting them to embrace concepts that are substantially identical and whose differences are largely a consequence of the idiosyncrasies of the fields in which they are used." Such concepts would contribute both to the efficiency of ISAR systems—by making it possible to reduce the number of descriptors in the index language—and to the "transferability of knowledge across disciplines."

Other problems of concept formation occur in ISAR systems that deal with socioeconomic information from different countries, for example, an ISAR system that deals with information on education in the *United States, France,* and *Germany.* Each country has its own structure of educational institutions. The challenge is to develop a common structure that is applicable to all countries. This would allow for a reduction in the number of descriptors. But even if we retain each country's terms in the index language, the newly developed common structure facilitates searching for general concepts, such as *Elementary schools,* in all countries. Such a common structure is also essential for the gathering of comparative educational statistics. A lot of careful work on definitions is needed to establish the entries in the common structure, as anybody having worked in or with comparative statistics can testify. The thesaurus builder should rely on work done by experts in comparative education in this instance.

A last example of concept formation in thesaurus building is the typology of international organizations given in Fig. 14.13. This typology was the result of the joint efforts of a classificationist (who contributed the approach of facet analysis) and a subject expert. Once this analysis is completed, it becomes clear that the facets derived, except for facet 4, are useful in a much wider context.

A further aspect of concept formation in thesaurus building and particularly in thesaurus updating is the broadening of the meaning of descriptors that occurs as they are used.

This finishes the discussion of the conceptual aspects of index language structure. The next chapter examines index language structure with emphasis on its functions in data base organization.

Facet 1:   International organizations by level
            Private international organizations
            Quasi-governmental international organizations
            Governmental international organizations
Facet 2:   International organizations by membership
            Universal membership
              SN (Scope Note)
                No restrictions as to geographical location, political system, main religion, or
                other characteristics of membership countries
            Limited membership
              SN Members only from one region or, for example, from Islamic countries or
              industrial countries
Facet 3:   International organizations by scope and orientation
            Covers entire range of politics
              SN For example, United Nations; International Federation of Socialist Parties
            Covers only specific function
              SN For example, World Health Organization; International Federation of
              Documentation
Facet 4:   International organizations by internal cohesion
            SN Basic tendency, not momentary developments
            Loose groupings
            Cohesive organizations
Facet 5:   International organizations by organizational structure
            Centralized structure
            Decentralized structure

Fig. 14.13   Facet analysis: Typology of international organizations.

CHAPTER 15

Index Language Structure 2: Data Base Organization

OBJECTIVES

The objectives of this chapter are to explain the relationship between the conceptual structure of the index language on the one hand and data base organization on the other with a view to indexing and searching as well as to system design; to elucidate the structure of traditional classification schemes, such as DDC and LCC, thus enabling the reader to put them to best use and to prepare user aids; and to set forth design characteristics for index languages/classification schemes and their implications for index language use.

INTRODUCTION

While the distinction between conceptual structure and data base organization is important, in practice they both work together in the task of storage and retrieval; they are closely intertwined and one cannot be treated without reference to the other. While Chapter 14 emphasized conceptual aspects of index language structure, it referred to implications for data base organization. This chapter applies the principles of conceptual structure to the analysis of data base organization and the closely related problem of presenting an index language, particularly an index language that includes many precombined descriptors.

Sections 15.1–15.3 deal with general principles: a statement of the problem to be solved by data base organization, the principle of grouping entities for ease of retrieval, and the relationship of grouping of entities to their description. Sections 15.4–15.6 deal with practical applications: selection of precombined descriptors considering the search mechanism available, organization of the index language so indexers and searchers can find the descriptors needed (descriptor-find index and designation and arrangement of descriptors), and use of a unified index language for different search mechanisms.

15.1 THE PROBLEM

A data base contains many entities linked through relationships. The data base organization must support retrieval of entities based on their relationships to other entities (see Chapters 3 and 11). This chapter concentrates on a specific case: the retrieval of focal entities, such as documents or food products, based on their relationships to just one other type of entity, namely, concepts (subjects). Each focal entity can be seen as linked to one very compound concept, made up of many components and called entity representation, to be matched against the search concept, usually a less compound concept called query formulation.

Example 1

Document concepts

1. Methods of reading instruction in first grade, good document
2. Needs for funding for the use of microcomputers in first grade reading instruction for visually handicapped children in New York City in 1984, good document

Document representations in terms of elemental concepts

1. Method of instruction; Reading; First grade; Good
2. Method of instruction; Reading; First grade; Good; Handicapped; Eyesight; Microcomputers; Funding; Needs assessment; New York City; 1984

Query formulation	Documents to be retrieved
Method of instruction AND Reading AND First grade AND Good AND Handicapped	2
Method of instruction AND Reading AND First grade AND Good (coextensive with document 1)	1, 2
Method of instruction AND Reading AND First grade	1, 2
Method of instruction AND Reading	1, 2
Method of instruction AND Language	1, 2
Method of instruction AND Language AND Elementary school	1, 2
Method of instruction AND Handicapped	2
Equipment AND Elementary school	2
Funding AND Education AND NY City AND 1984	2

Example 2

- *Query formulation* (broad, asks for an aggregate number)
  Retail value AND Sales AND Large electrical appliances AND Florida
  AND 1980
- *Money number concept* (specific, to be included in aggregate)
  Retail value of refrigerators sold in Miami in July, 1980
- *Money number representation*
  Retail value; Sales; Refrigerators; Miami; July, 1980

To compute this number, the system must retrieve all money numbers with a representation narrower than the query formulation and then add them.

In each case the system must retrieve all entities that have a representation equal to or narrower than the query formulation. To visualize this process, picture a wall-size hierarchy graph with concepts representing entities and/or queries. Locate the query concept and from it follow all hierarchical lines all the way down, assembling a subset of concepts. Find all entities linked to (represented by) any concept in the subset. The organization of the data base must support quick identification of all such entities at a reasonable cost and within the constraints set by the technical device used (e.g., the printed page, a card catalog, or computers).

15.2 GROUPING ENTITIES. SEARCHING IN GROUPED FILES

15.2.1 THE IDEA OF GROUPING AND PRECOMBINED DESCRIPTORS

This section explores the idea of grouping entities to aid in retrieval and its implication for the nature of the index language. The simplest ISAR system is one without grouping, in which entities are indexed by (directly linked to) elemental concepts. Compound concepts do not occur explicitly in the data base; they do not belong to the domain of the entity type *Concept.* However, the linkage of entities to compound concepts is present in the data base implicitly; all documents related to a compound concept, such as *Reading instruction,* can be found with the query formulation

Method of instruction AND Reading

Likewise, all food products related to the compound concept *Frozen cut beans,* can be found with the query formulation

Beans AND Cut into medium-sized pieces AND Frozen.

The retrieval mechanism (e.g., computer or peek-a-boo cards) then quickly identifies all entities indexed by the requisite elemental descriptors.

In such a system compound concepts are not used in indexing but are formed later in query formulation; hence the system is called a *postcombination system*. A sample system (main entity type: document) is shown in Fig. 15.1. Figure 15.1a is the main file (a list of documents); Fig. 15.1b is a subject index (a peek-a-boo file here shown as a printed index); and Fig. 15.1c shows some query formulations and the documents retrieved by them.

A postcombination system permits searching for any and all combinations of elemental descriptors. The searcher can specify just the topic she is looking for and thus attain high discrimination. The principles of conceptual structure can be used directly in formulating the query in a straightforward manner. But postcombination is not possible in a card catalog, in a printed index, or in the retrieval of entities from shelves. Furthermore, a postcombination system requires many entries per entity in the index file, making for large index files. Each entity retrieved in the index by its accession number must be found separately in the main file, and with very large collections this may lead to excessive effort even in a computer system. Hence we are looking for ways to organize retrieval more efficiently.

One hint comes from the analysis of the sample peek-a-boo system shown in Fig. 15.1. Assume it accommodates 5000 documents (5000 hole positions, one document per position). What if the collection grows beyond that limit? Could the system somehow accommodate more than 5000 documents within the limits of 5000 hole positions per card without losing retrieval power? Examine the document representations in Fig. 15.1a. Pay close attention to the descriptors assigned. What about documents 1 and 5? 6 and 7? The descriptors assigned to documents 1 and 5 are identical. Consequently, the two documents exhibit identical retrieval behavior: Whenever document 1 is retrieved, document 5 is retrieved also; whenever document 1 is not retrieved, document 5 is not retrieved either. Using two different peek-a-boo card holes for these two documents is a waste of capacity; using number 1 for *both* documents frees hole number 5.

Accommodating more than 5000 documents is made possible by grouping—putting all documents having exactly the same descriptors into one group—and letting each peek-a-boo hole position correspond to a whole group rather than to an individual document. This is illustrated in Fig. 15.2; Figure 15.2a gives a list of the documents arranged according to the groups formed (the main file), and Fig. 15.2b shows the corresponding index (given here in lieu of a peek-a-boo file). The sample searches given in Fig. 15.2c show how the system works: A query formulated in terms of elemental descriptors serves to find group numbers in the index (Fig. 15.2b); the group numbers serve to find individual documents in the main file (Fig. 15.2a).

Since only documents having exactly the same elemental descriptors and thus exhibiting identical retrieval behavior are allowed in a group, a search via the groups retrieves exactly the same documents as a search in the original system shown in Fig. 15.1. Due to the very strict criterion, groups are small; in a real-life collection in which only the most important descriptors are assigned to a document, one might expect groups of 2–5 documents on the average. (If more and/or more specific descriptors are assigned, indexing reflects minor differences between documents and thus group size decreases and the number of groups increases.)

Both data base organizations can be viewed as essentially the same: The searcher consults an index file, finds numbers, looks under those numbers in the main file, and finds documents. The only difference is that in the data base organization in Fig. 15.1 the searcher finds just one document under each number, whereas in Fig. 15.2 he finds one or more documents since *now a number refers to a document group.* For example, in search c2 the searcher must locate four documents in the main file in Fig. 15.1a but only two groups in the main file in Fig. 15.2a. This could be viewed simply as a technical convenience: The index file is smaller by a factor of two or three, and as a bonus, each access to the main file nets two or three documents instead of just one. The system in Fig. 15.2 is still viewed as a pure postcombination system in which documents are indexed by (linked directly to) elemental descriptors, which are combined in searching to retrieve suitable documents.

However, the same physical data base can be viewed as a quite different system in which the nature of the main file has changed radically from the simple list of documents arranged by accession number given in Fig. 15.1a to the grouped list of documents given in Fig. 15.2a. The simple list of documents has no order with respect to subject. The grouped list brings together documents that deal with or are relevant for a given topic. This topic is expressed as a combination of elemental concepts, which is the same for all documents in the group; this combination of elemental concepts is the *group representation.* Put differently: For purposes of retrieval, each document is linked directly to a highly compound concept, such as concept #7:

#7 Curriculum; Biology; First grade; Good document.

It is linked to elemental concepts, such as *Biology,* indirectly via a chain such as

Document 10 ----------------> #7 ---------------> Biology
              < deals with >   < has component >
Document 10 < --------------- #7 < --------------- Biology
              < is treated in >   < is component of >

Doc. no.	Descriptors
1	Method of instruction; Reading; First Grade; Good
2	Traffic station; Inland water transport; Medium
3	Method of instruction; Reading; First grade; Bad
4	Curriculum; Science; Fourth grade; Medium
5	Method of instruction; Reading; First grade; Good
6	Traffic station; Ocean transport; Freight; Bad
7	Traffic station; Ocean transport; Freight; Bad
8	Traffic station; Inland water transport; Freight; Medium
9	Curriculum; Biology; First grade; Good
10	Method of instruction; Reading; Elementary School; Bad
11	Curriculum; Biology; First grade; Bad
12	Curriculum; Biology; First grade; Medium
13	Curriculum; Biology; Elementary school; Medium
14	Method of instruction; Reading; Ninth grade; Good
15	Method of instruction; Physics; Fifth grade; Bad
16	Method of instruction; Biology; Sixth grade; Medium
17	Method of instruction; Reading; Elementary school; Bad
18	Method of instruction; Reading; First grade; Bad
19	Curriculum; Reading; Second grade; Bad
20	Curriculum; Biology; First grade; Good
21	Curriculum; Science; Fourth grade; Medium

(a) List of documents (main file)

Education
General concepts
   Curriculum   4,9,11,12,13,19,
     20,21
   Method of instruction   1,3,
     5,10,14,15,16,17,18
Subject
   Reading   1,3,5,10,14,17,18,19
   Science, incl.   4,9,11,12,13,
     15,16,20,21
   Science, gen. ref.   4,21
   Physics   15
   Biology   9,11,12,13,16,20
Grade level
   El. school, incl.   1,3,4,5,
     9,10,11,12,13,15,16,17,18,
     19,20,21
   El. school, gen. ref.   10,
     13,17
   First grade   1,3,5,9,11,
     12,18,20
   Second grade   19

Fourth grade   4,21
Fifth grade   15
Sixth grade   16
Junior high, incl.   14
   Junior high, gen. ref.
   Ninth grade   14
Transportation
Traffic facil. vs. vehicles
   Traffic station   2,6,7,8
Mode of transportation
   Water transport, incl.   2,6,
     7,8
     Water transport, gen. ref.
     Ocean transport   6,7
     Inland water transp.   2,8
Passenger vs. freight transp.
   Freight   6,7,8
Document quality
Good   1,5,9,14,20
Medium   2,4,8,12,13,16,21
Bad   3,6,7,10,11,15,17,18,19

(b) Index to documents

c1   Method of instruction AND Reading AND First grade AND Good
    Doc. no. 1,5

c2   Method of instruction AND Reading AND First grade
    Doc. no. 1,3,5,18

c3   Method of instruction AND Reading AND El. School, incl.
    Doc. no. 1,3,5,10,17,18

c4   Method of instruction AND Reading
    Doc. no. 1,3,5,10,14,17,18

c5   Biology AND First grade AND (Good OR Medium)
    Doc. no. 9,12,20

c6   Elementary school, incl. AND Good
    Doc. no. 1,5,9,20

(c) Sample searches.

Fig. 15.1   No grouping. Extreme postcombination

Group #1   Method of instruction; Reading; First grade; Good
            #1.1 Doc. 1 Method ; Reading; First grade; Good
            #1.2 Doc. 5 Method ; Reading; First grade; Good

Group #2   Traffic station; Inland water transport; Medium
            #2.1 Doc. 2 Tr. station; Inland water transp.; Medium

Group #3   Method of instruction; Reading; First grade; Bad
            #3.1 Doc. 3 Method ; Reading; First grade; Bad
            #3.2 Doc. 18 Method ; Reading; First grade; Bad

Group #4   Curriculum; Science; Fourth grade; Medium
            #4.1 Doc. 4 Curriculum; Science; Fourth grade; Medium
            #4.2 Doc. 21 Curriculum; Science; Fourth grade; Medium

Group #5   Traffic station; Ocean transport; Freight; Bad
            #5.1 Doc. 6 Tr. station; Ocean transport; Freight; Bad
            #5.2 Doc. 7 Tr. station; Ocean transport; Freight; Bad

Group #6   Traffic station; Inland water transp.; Freight; Medium
            #6.1 Doc. 8 Tr. station; Inl. w. transp.; Freight; Med.

Group #7   Curriculum; Biology; First grade; Good
            #7.1 Doc. 9 Curriculum; Biology; First grade; Good
            #7.2 Doc. 20 Curriculum; Biology; First grade; good

Group #8   Method of instruction; Reading; El. school; Bad
            #8.1 Doc. 10 Method; Reading; El. school; Bad
            #8.2 Doc. 17 Method; Reading; El. school; Bad

Group #9   Curriculum; Biology; First grade; Bad
            #9.1 Doc. 11 Curriculum; Biology; First grade; Bad

Group #10   Curriculum; Biology; First grade; Medium
            #10.1 Doc. 12 Curriculum; Biology; First grade; Medium

Group #11   Curriculum; Biology; Elementary school; Medium
            #11.1 Doc. 13 Curriculum; Biology; El. school; Medium

Group #12   Method of instruction; Reading; Ninth grade; Good
            #12.1 Doc. 14 Method; Reading; Ninth grade; Good

Group #13   Method of instruction; Physics; Fifth grade; Bad
            #13.1 Doc. 15 Method; Physics; Fifth grade; Bad

Group #14   Method of instruction; Biology; Sixth grade; Medium
            #14.1 Doc. 16 Method ; Biology; Sixth grade; Medium

Group #15   Curriculum; Reading; Second grade; Bad
            #15.1 Doc. 19 Curriculum; Reading; Second grade; Bad

(a) List of narrow groups with documents.

Education
General concepts
  Curriculum   #4,#7,#9,
    #10,#11,#15
  Method of instruction   #1,
    #3,#8,#12,#13,#14
Subject
  Reading   #1,#3,#8,#12,#15
  Science, incl.   #4,#7,#9,#10,
    #11,#13,#14
  Science, gen.ref.   #4
  Physics   #13
  Biology   #7,#9,#10,#11,#14
Grade level
  El. school, incl.   #1,#3,#4,
    #7,#8,#9,#10,#11,#13,#14,
    #15
  El. school, gen. ref.   #8,#11
  First grade   #1,#3,#7,#9,#10
  Second grade   #15

Fourth grade   #4
Fifth grade   #13
Sixth grade   #14
Junior high, incl.   #12
  Junior high, gen.ref.
  Ninth grade   #12
Transportation
Traffic facil. vs. vehicles
  Traffic station   #2,#5,#6
Mode of transportation
  Water transport, incl.   #2,#5,#6
  Water transport, gen.ref.
  Ocean transport   #5
  Inland water transp.   #2,#6
Passenger vs. freight transp.
  Freight   #5,#6
Document quality
Good   #1,#7,#12
Medium   #2,#4,#6,#10,#11,#14
Bad   #3,#5,#8,#9,#13,#15

(b) Index to narrow groups (descriptor-find index).

c1 Method of instruction AND Reading AND First grade AND Good
      Group no.   #1
      Doc. no.   1,5

c2 Method of instruction AND Reading AND First grade
      Group no.   #1,   #3
      Doc. no.   1,5,   3,18

c3 Method of instruction AND Reading AND El. School, incl.
      Group no.   #1,   #3,   #8
      Doc. no.   1,5,   3,18,   10,17

c4 Method of instruction AND Reading
      Group no.   #1,   #3,   #8,   #12
      Doc. no.   1,5,   3,18,   10,17,   14

c5 Curriculum AND Biology AND First grade AND (Good OR Medium)
      Group no.   #7,   #10
      Doc. no.   9,20,   12

c6 Elementary school, incl. AND Good
      Group no.   #1,   #7
      Doc. no.   1,5,   9,20

(c) Sample searches.

Fig. 15.2 Narrow groups. Extremely high precombination.
      All documents within one group have exactly the same representation

The searcher profits from the order in the main file; he or she needs to access the main file in fewer places (in search c2, this means two group numbers instead of four document numbers). This is particularly important if a file access involves not just looking in a list but inserting a different microfiche in a reader or walking to a place in the stacks.

The order in the grouped main file does not come without a price. Whenever a new entity comes in and has been indexed, its representation in terms of elemental descriptors must be compared with all the group representations established so far. If an exact match is found, the entity is assigned to the existing group; otherwise, a new group is established.

Saying that an entity belongs to group #7 gives exactly the same information as indexing it by the four elemental concepts that make up #7. So the elemental concepts might as well be omitted once they have led to the group. Going one step further, the indexer could skip the step of indexing a new entity by elemental descriptors and instead compare it directly with the group representations. *If he finds a group topic that matches exactly,* he indexes the entity with that group number—that is, he links it to the specific topic that is expressed by the group representation. The group number serves as a precombined descriptor in indexing. If no exact match is found, the indexer creates a new group. However, in practice there would be a tendency to make do with a near match, which has detrimental effects on retrieval (see Section 15.2.2).

In searching, the main task is to identify the groups containing relevant entities; once that is done, the relevant entities can be found easily in the main file by means of the group numbers (in the sample system the searcher looks in the file in Fig. 15.2a to find the relevant documents). Group numbers are used as precombined descriptors in the file in Fig. 15.2a. Thus when searching the file in Fig. 15.2a, there is no need for combining descriptors in searching; combination searching has been shifted to the step of finding the appropriate group numbers (precombined descriptors) in the index file in Fig. 15.2b (See Section 15.5 for elaboration).

The change in viewpoint calls for a change in terminology; instead of *group* we now say *class*. The term *class* refers to three things:

- The *class representation,* a compound concept (e.g., Biology; Curriculum; First grade; Good)
- The *class number* (e.g., #7)
- The *set of entities* in the class (e.g., documents 9 and 20)

We use the term *class* to refer to all of these simultaneously, often with emphasis on the class representation.

The new terminology permits a concise description of the data base in Fig. 15.2 as seen from the new viewpoint: The classes serve as descriptors; the set of all classes forms the index language. Documents can be indexed by the appropriate class. The main file in Fig. 15.2a is ordered by classes and thus makes it easy to find all entities belonging to a class. Put differently, in the data base in Fig. 15.2 compound concepts are included explicitly; they do belong to the domain of the entity type *Concept*. Entities are linked explicitly to compound concepts, and their relationships to elemental concepts are indirect, via linkages among concepts. A system that uses compound concepts in indexing (i.e., that uses precombined descriptors) is called a *precombination system*. The original set of elemental descriptors is the *core classification* (our term), and the set of all descriptors, including the precombined descriptors, is the *extended classification* (our term). The index file in Fig. 15.2b lets the searcher find classes (precombined descriptors) in terms of their conceptual components; it is a *descriptor-find index*.

A class representation is a combination of many elemental concepts; it is a highly precombined descriptor. In the system in Fig. 15.2 precombination is carried to the extreme because a class includes just the entities whose representation in terms of elemental concepts is coextensive with the class representation. Put differently, the class representations have as many components as the entity representations constructed from elemental descriptors in the postcombination system in Fig. 15.1. With extreme precombination one class—one highly precombined descriptor—is sufficient to express all aspects for which an entity is relevant. This capability is maintained by adding new classes (new precombined descriptors) whenever the need arises. The classes are mutually exclusive; there is never a need to assign an entity to two classes. Working with classes rather than with individual entities does not diminish retrieval power in any way; for every conceivable query formulation exactly the same subset of entities is retrieved. In other words, *extreme precombination* (using very highly precombined descriptors) and *extreme postcombination* (using elemental descriptors that can be combined in searching) *lead to the same retrieval results*. As we shall see in the following section, retrieval power suffers when the degree of precombination is lowered.

15.2.2 FROM IDEAL TO REALITY: LIMITED PRECOMBINATION

The advantages of grouping entities can be enhanced by forming broader classes. Class representations can be broadened by dropping a component or by substituting a broader component concept (Section 14.3). Both methods were used to arrive at the broad classes shown in Fig. 15.3a. But there is a price. Indexing an entity by one of these broad classes tells less about the entity than indexing it by the original elemental descriptors. Indexing is both less exhaustive (e.g., the quality aspect *Good, Medium, Bad* is lost in most

Class #1   Method of instruction; Reading; El. school, incl.
#1.1 Doc. 1 Method; Reading; First grade; Good
#1.2 Doc. 3 Method; Reading; First grade; Bad
#1.3 Doc. 5 Method; Reading; First grade; Good
#1.4 Doc. 10 Method; Reading; El. School; Bad
#1.5 Doc. 17 Method; Reading; El. School; Bad
#1.6 Doc. 18 Method; Reading; First grade; Bad

Class #2   Traffic station; Inland water transport; Medium
#2.1 Doc. 2 Tr. station; Inland water transp.; Medium

Class #3   Curriculum; Science, incl.; El. school, incl.
#3.1 Doc. 4 Curriculum; Science; Fourth grade; Medium
#3.2 Doc. 9 Curriculum; Biology; First grade; Good
#3.3 Doc. 11 Curriculum; Biology; First grade; Bad
#3.4 Doc. 12 Curriculum; Biology; First grade; Medium
#3.5 Doc. 13 Curriculum; Biology; El. school; Medium
#3.6 Doc. 20 Curriculum; Biology; First grade; Good
#3.7 Doc. 21 Curriculum; Science; Fourth grade; Medium

Class #4   Traffic station; Water transport, incl.; Freight
#4.1 Doc. 6 Tr. station; Ocean transport; Freight; Bad
#4.2 Doc. 7 Tr. station; Ocean transport; Freight; Bad
#4.3 Doc. 8 Tr. station; Inland water tr.; Freight; Med.

Class #5   Method of instruction; Reading; Junior high school
#5.1 Doc. 14 Method; Reading; Ninth grade; Good

Class #6   Method of instruction; Science, incl.; El. school, incl.
#6.1 Doc. 15 Method; Physics; Fifth grade; Bad
#6.2 Doc. 16 Method; Biology; Sixth grade; Medium

Class #7   Curriculum; Reading; El. school, incl.
#7.1 Doc. 19 Curriculum; Reading; Second grade; Bad

(a) List of classes with documents (main file).

classes) and less specific (e.g., the class may refer to *Elementary school* when the original elemental descriptor was *First grade*). Thus it may be useful to retain the original elemental descriptors even if retrieval access is based on classes. Note the alternate document numbers, such as #4.2.

Figure 15.3b shows the descriptor-find index to the broad classes, and Fig. 15.3c presents some sample searches. A specific query must first be broadened so that it combines only concepts used in the broad class representations; thus discrimination is lost when searching on the class level. If the entries contain the original specific elemental descriptors, discrimination can be restored in a second search step by examining document entries.

Thus, indexing by broad classes leads to a loss both in retrieval performance and in information given by an entity representation (which is the class by which the entity is indexed). With narrow classes there is no such loss.

Education
General concepts
  Curriculum   #3,#7
  Method of instruction   #1,#5,#6
Subject
  Reading, incl.   #1,#5,#7
  Science, incl.   #3,#6
Grade level
  El. school, incl.   #1,#3,#6,#7

Junior high, incl.   #5
Transportation
Traffic facil. vs. vehicles
  Traffic station   #2,#4
Mode of transportation
  Water transp., incl.   #2,#4
    Inland water transp.   #2
Passenger vs. Freight transp.
  Freight   #2,#4
Quality of document
Medium   #2

(b) Index to broad groups (descriptor-find index).

c0 Broad query   Method AND Reading AND El. school, incl.
   formulation   Class no.   #1
   for c1,c2,c3   Doc. no.   1,3,5,10,17,18

c1 Original qf   Method AND Reading AND First grade AND Good
               Must broaden to c0, find Class #1, examine document records, narrow
               results to doc. 1, 5

c2 Original qf   Method AND Reading AND First Grade
               Must broaden to c0; find Class #1; examine document records, narrow
               to doc. 1, 3, 5, 18

c3 Original qf   Method AND Reading AND El. school
               Broad to start with, co-extensive with c0, all documents in class #1 are
               relevant

c4 Original qf   Method of instruction AND Reading
               Broad to start with, find
               Class no.   #1,   #5
               Doc. no.   1,3,5,10,17,18,   14

c5 Broadened qf   Science, incl. AND Elementary school, incl.
               Class no.   #3
               Doc. no.   4,9,11,12,20,21

c5 Original qf   Biology AND First grade AND (Good OR Medium)
               Must broaden to c5 broad; find Class #3; examine, narrow results to
               doc. 9,12,20

c6 Original qf   Elementary school, incl. AND Good
               Must broaden by omitting *Good;* find classes #1,#3,#6,#7. Examine,
               narrow to doc. 1,5,9,20

(c) Sample searches (qf = query formulation).

Fig. 15.3   Broad classes or groups, high precombination.
        A class (group) may be broader than a document representation in the class
        (broadened by omitting quality descriptors and/or broadening other descriptors).

The listing of entities in broad classes is quite successful in collocating related entities. This is useful for browsing. It also reduces even more the number of points in which this file must be accessed to gather all entities about a topic. A broad search that corresponds precisely to a class (such as sample search c3 in Fig. 15.3c) has very good retrieval results, and all the relevant entities are very conveniently assembled in one place. On the other hand, a specific search (sample search c5) or a broad search that does not correspond to a ready-made class (sample search c6) requires examination of many entries. If the file does not allow for detailed examination because only the class numbers have been used for indexing, then discrimination is low. Searches for abstract concepts, such as *Structure,* are not possible at all, unless that concept was considered in the definition of classes.

An entity may belong to two or more broad classes. For example,

> Document 8 Traffic station; Inland water transp.; Freight; Med.

belongs to both of the following:

> Class #2 Traffic station; Inland water transport; Medium
> Class #4 Traffic station; Water transport, inclusive; Freight

A document on *Ports in the Great Lakes* belongs to both of the following:

> DDC Class 386.5 Lake transport
> DDC Class 386.8 Inland water transportation ports

Lunch meat made from *Turkey Liver* belongs to both of the following:

> Lunch meat made from organ meat
> Poultry-based lunch meat

If the system allows only one class for each entity, as is the case in shelf arrangement, then a more or less arbitrary decision must be made among several possible broader classes. For example, DDC instructs the cataloger to index a document on *Ports in the Great Lakes* by 386.8 *Inland water transportation ports.* As a consequence, this document will not be found under 386.5 *Lake transport.* In a thorough search for *Lake transport,* the searcher should look not only under 386.5, but also under 386.8.

15.2.3 ACCESS ADVANTAGES OF GROUPED FILES

Even in a postcombination system a grouped main file has advantages. A system that uses elemental descriptors in indexing and provides a postcombination index as in the data base in Fig. 15.1, but arranges the main file as in Fig. 15.3a, using the alternate document numbers in the index, permits specific and flexible retrieval *and* increases the likelihood that documents retrieved through the index are collocated in the main file. A traditional library uses this setup. The subject catalog treats each book as an individual entity; yet due to the shelving by subjects, it is quite likely that the books found in a subject catalog search are all shelved on the same floor rather than scattered over several floors. This leads to a significant savings in working time. Grouping is also useful to decrease access time in large computer files.

One of two principles can be applied in forming groups:

1. *Request-oriented grouping brings together entities that are likely to be asked for together,* minimizing the average number of groups to be consulted in a search.
2. *Entity-oriented grouping brings together entities as they go together,* minimizing the average number of groups in which an entity must be included.

Under the first principle the groups overlap more than under the second principle; on the other hand, search costs are lower under the first principle.

The advantages of grouping are much enhanced if the groups themselves are arranged in a meaningful sequence; see Section 15.5.2 for elaboration.

15.3 GROUPING VERSUS DESCRIPTION OF ENTITIES

There are two approaches to organizing an unordered collection of entities (documents, parts, biological specimens, or whatever):

1. put like entities together and thus form classes, or
2. develop a list of descriptive characteristics and prepare for each entity a description (or representation) using these characteristics.

At first these two approaches seem quite different; they might even be perceived as diametrically opposed. The first tries to establish a global order within a set of entities, and thus concentrates on overall structure. The second concentrates on the individual entity and its description without regard to the overall structure. However, on closer examination, it becomes clear that the two approaches are intricately related and dependent on each other.

The formation of classes requires at least an implicit list of entity characteristics whereby the similarity of entities is judged. Explicit implementation involves developing descriptions of the entities and then forming classes based on these descriptions. This approach was used in Section 15.2.1. It is an approach now frequently used in biology, anthropology, and other sciences; it is known as numeric taxonomy. The methods used for class formation there (as well as in some document retrieval systems) are more complex than the very simple method used in Section 15.2.1 and usually require computer programs. In Section 15.2.1 the criterion to decide whether two entities should go in the same class was simple: Do they completely agree in their description in terms of elemental descriptors (i.e., in their descriptive characteristics)? In a more sophisticated procedure one computes a quantitative measure of nearness between two entities based on the number of matches or near matches in their individual descriptive characteristics and then applies a more or less complex *clustering* program, which subdivides (partitions) the collection of all entities into clusters such that the entities within each cluster are nearer to each other than to entities in other clusters. The more exhaustively and the more specifically the individual features of each entity are described, the smaller the initial (narrow) classes. These initial classes, can be broadened as shown in Section 15.2.2.

This discussion has shown how description of entities can be used to arrive at a subdivision of the total collection into classes, that is, to derive an overall structure. Conversely, the assignment of an entity to a class constitutes a description of that entity. How good the description is depends on the nature of the classes. For example, in Section 15.2.1 assigning a document to class #7 (indexing the document by the precombined descriptor #7) provides as good a description as indexing by the four elemental descriptors

Curriculum; Biology; First grade; Good.

But in Section 15.2.2 assigning a document to class #3 provides only a more general description.

So far the discussion has assumed implicitly that the classes of entities would be mutually exclusive. In the context of traditional classification schemes the term *class* is often used with that connotation. However, in mathematics such a connotation does not exist at all; a class is simply a set of entities with some common characteristic. Thus, the set of all entities dealing with *Curriculum* is a class, and so is the set of all entities dealing with *Biology*. Thus, if an entity is described by five characteristics, it belongs to five classes, one for each characteristic. These classes are, of course, not mutually exclusive, but overlapping; there are entities that belong both to the class *Curriculum* and to the class *Biology*. In fact, the method of postcombination indexing is based on retrieving all entities that belong to two or more classes. In an ISAR system in which many elemental descriptors are used to index an entity, there is a high degree of overlap between the entity classes corresponding to the descriptors. Conversely, in a system with extreme precombination, such as the system described in Section 15.2.1, there is no overlap between classes at all; each entity belongs to one and only one class. The more the descriptors are precombined, the less the classes overlap. (see the examples in Section 15.2.2). Degree of precombination of descriptors and degree of overlap between classes measure essentially the same system characteristic (high precombination corresponding to low overlap). This underscores again the close interdependence between forming classes and describing individual entities.

15.4 POSTCOMBINATION AND PRECOMBINATION

15.4.1 POSTCOMBINATION VERSUS PRECOMBINATION AS A MATTER OF DEGREE

Figure 15.4 illustrates that precombination is a matter of degree. The designer should choose the degree of precombination best suited to the types of queries expected and the retrieval mechanism used. The degree of precom-

Title

Needs for funding for the use of microcomputers in first grade reading instruction for the visually handicapped in New York City, 1984.

1. *Postcombination.*   Each entity is indexed by many elemental descriptors (data base 15.1); many entries for each entity; small index language.

    Method of instruction; Reading; First grade; Good; Handicapped; Eyesight; Microcomputers; Funding; Needs assessment; New York City; 1984

2. *Moderate precombination.*   Each entity is indexed by a few moderately precombined descriptors, as in a card catalog; a few entries for each entity; medium index language.

    Method of reading instruction; Instruction—Elementary school; Visually handicapped; Funding for educational equipment—New York City—1984; Funding for the handicapped—New York City—1984

    (Note the overlap among precombined descriptors. Note also the omission of the elemental concept *Needs assessment;* it is not contained in any precombined descriptor.)

3. *High precombination.* Each entity is indexed by only one highly precombined descriptor, as in a shelving system (data base 15.2); only one entry for each entity; large index language.

    Equipment for reading instruction for the handicapped. New York City.
    (Closest precombined descriptor available)

Fig. 15.4 Document representation in ISAR systems with different degrees of precombination.

bination is an important attribute in the analysis of an existing index language. Degree of precombination is an issue in data base organization, not an issue in the conceptual structure of the index language. The same basic conceptual structure can be used with any degree of precombination (see Section 15.6).

Postcombination should be used if the search mechanism permits easy retrieval by descriptor combinations. The lead-in vocabulary may retain compound concepts and show the combination of elemental descriptors to be used.

Moderate precombination is used, for example, in a regular library subject catalog that employs subject headings. Moderately precombined descriptors make it possible to search for compound concepts even if the search mechanism does not permit retrieval by combining descriptors, and they reduce the number of descriptors per entity (20 cards for each document in a card catalog would be impractical). The index language should include all concepts from the core classification so that the indexer can assign the elemental concepts that are not covered by any precombined descriptor assigned to the entity. In a computerized system precombined descriptors can be combined to form a still more compound query concept; for example,

Methods of reading instruction AND Visually handicapped

In a manual system the searcher looks under one descriptor and then examines the entities found to see whether the other required descriptors are present.

High precombination is needed in single–entry systems, such as arrangement of documents or groceries on shelves by subject, so that one descriptor assigned to an entity adequately reflects the topics for which an entity is relevant and makes them available as access points. The formation of classes of entities based on their relationships to elemental concepts introduces highly precombined descriptors, whether or not these are expressly named.

In a postcombination system the analysis of concepts into their semantic factors serves to detect compound concepts, which are then excluded from the index language; this keeps the number of descriptors down. In a precombination system the analysis of compound concepts into their semantic factors serves to establish relationships among the descriptors (precombined or elemental). These relationships can then be used for establishing a descriptor-find index, for creating a linear arrangement with cross-references, and, most importantly, for increasing the convenience and power of retrieval with a data base management system. For example, a document indexed by *Ship* and *Engine* can be retrieved in a search for *Vehicle* AND *Engine* due to the relationship *Vehicle* < is semantic factor of> *Ship*. A data base management system can use the relationships among concepts to find all entities related to a concept either directly (the concept is among the index terms for the entity) or indirectly (the concept is a component of or otherwise broader than an index term assigned to the entity).

Extreme postcombination may lead to *false drops*. The document

>   Cars used in subway link to airport

is indexed by

>   Vehicles; Local rail transit; Traffic stations; Air transport.

It is found in a search for *Aircraft,* since the query formulation is

>   Vehicles AND Air transport.

Elemental descriptors belonging to different compound concepts are mixed up. Role indicators and links or relators (see Section 12.4) prevent such false combinations; they make for a powerful and very flexible index language at the price of somewhat complex rules. To eschew the complexity of syntax while at the same time avoiding false drops, the designer can introduce precombined descriptors, such as *Subway car* or *Aircraft.*

15.4.2 Deciding on the Overall Degree of Precombination

The following points are important in making a decision.

Mechanical Devices Available in the ISAR System

If the search mechanism does not allow for combining descriptors in searching (e.g., shelf arrangement, card catalog, printed index), precombined descriptors are required, since most searches are for compound concepts. If combination searching is possible, such as in a computerized system, elemental descriptors suffice (unless ease of indexing, saving storage space, or avoidance of false drops dictate otherwise); in addition, fairly broad precombined descriptors may be useful for grouping of entities.

Number of Descriptors To Be Used for Indexing an Entity

If the descriptors are elemental, many are needed to index any one entity. This requires much effort unless at least the frequently used descriptors are printed on the indexing form so that the indexer can just check them. It also requires storage space. If the descriptors are precombined, a few will generally suffice to index an entity. The same considerations hold for queries.

*Number of Descriptors Included in the Index Language
and Difficulty of Indexing and Query Formulation*

In a long list of precombined descriptors it is hard to find the appropriate descriptors for indexing or query formulation. A descriptor-find index is needed, and indexers and searchers must be trained. It may be easier to combine elemental or quasi-elemental descriptors (unless roles and links are used). However, this may not be true if the elemental descriptors are very abstract; it is easier for an indexer or searcher to use the descriptor *Ship* than to form the combination *Means : Transportation : Mobile : Water* (The combination *Vehicles : Water transport* is much easier). From the point of view of ease of understanding, a low degree of precombination is probably best, using as precombined descriptors those compound concepts that the user would expect to see as a unit. A facet frame can provide guidance in finding the proper combination of elemental concepts in indexing and query formulation.

*Matching Descriptor Combinations Used by Searchers
with Those Used by Indexers.*

This problem arises when most descriptors are elemental. A good lead-in structure in the thesaurus promotes consistency.

15.4.3 DECIDING ON INDIVIDUAL PRECOMBINED DESCRIPTORS

Unless the system at hand uses extreme postcombination, the index language builder must decide which of the myriad possible compound concepts should be included in the index language, that is, selected as precombined descriptors. This section discusses the criteria used in these decisions; it also discusses the decision process.

With single entry, such as in shelf arrangement, the index language should provide for every entity a precombined descriptor that describes it reasonably well. In some systems new precombined descriptors are introduced as they are needed for new entities (see faceted classification later in this section). In other systems one makes do with the nearest precombined descriptor available, even if it does not cover all the elemental concepts for which the entity is relevant. In a system of moderate precombination with multiple entry, the following *rules* are helpful:

Use a compound concept as precombined descriptor *if it is used frequently in indexing or searching;* this *reduces the number of descriptors needed to index an entity* or to formulate a query.

Use a compound concept as precombined descriptor *if its components oc-cur frequently in different syntactic relationships;* this *prevents false com-binations.* For example, retain *Library schools* (schools teaching about libraries) and *School libraries* (libraries serving schools) or *Administrative personnel* and *Personnel administration.* (But often the lack of syntactic relationships does not result in ambiguity, such as *Household : Tools.*)

Use a compound concept as precombined descriptor *if it is needed for logical completeness in the hierarchy or for the checklist technique of index-ing.* For example, since *Agrarian reform* can be expressed easily as a com-bination of *Agriculture* and *Reform,* it may not seem required as a descrip-tor. However, an indexer using the checklist technique to index a document that is relevant to *Agrarian reform* will scan the descriptors listed under *Agriculture* to see whether the document is relevant. If the indexer finds *Agrarian reform* listed, he will surely use it. If the indexer does not find *Agrarian reform,* he might well overlook the descriptor *Reform.* The docu-ment would then be missed by searches for *Agrarian reform* as well as any other searches that include the component *Reform.* This example suggests a related rule: If a concept of general application is important for searching, the most important combinations containing that concept should be in-cluded as precombined descriptors to make sure that the general concept is not overlooked in indexing.

Use a compound concept as precombined descriptor *if any of its narrower concepts are descriptors;* for example, introduce the precombined descriptor *Aircraft* if its narrower concepts, such as *Airplane* or *Helicopter,* are descriptors.

Use a compound concept as precombined descriptor *if there is doubt.* A precombined descriptor can easily be replaced by a combination of elemental descriptors. The reverse is much more difficult; introducing a precombined descriptor after many documents are indexed requires that every entity in-dexed by the corresponding combination of elemental descriptors be ex-amined to see whether it warrants indexing by the new precombined de-scriptor.

In each individual case, the benefits derived from the use of a precom-bined descriptor should be weighed against the cost, especially the increase in the number of descriptors in the index language and the concomitant com-plication of indexing. Statistics of descriptor use and retrieval performance are useful to monitor the effects of the decisions made.

As to the decision process, one option is to give the indexer complete freedom to introduce new precombined descriptors on the spot. An example is the use of a faceted classification with high precombination. While only elemental concepts (core descriptors, called "foci" in faceted classification) are listed explicitly, the indexer creates a combination of core descriptors that is just right for the entity at hand. The compound concept created is added to the data base—if it does not exist already—and the entity is linked to it. For example, a catalog card is filed under the compound concept. The new compound concept is a precombined descriptor. Since the list of precombined descriptors is continually growing without any control, a descriptor-find index is very important. Another example is the free formation of subject headings consisting of a main heading and a standard subheading. The other option is to require approval for precombined descriptors. This is usually done by permitting only precombined descriptors that are *enumerated* in a pre-made list, which may be updated from time to time, considering suggestions from indexers and—in good systems— searchers.

15.4.4 PRECOMBINED DESCRIPTORS IN INDEXING AND SEARCHING

A precombined descriptor available in the index language takes priority over a combination of two less compound descriptors. If the index language contains the precombined descriptor *Frozen beans,* the indexer should use it rather than the combination *Beans: Frozen.* Likewise, the indexer should use the descriptor *Visually handicapped* rather than the combination *Handicapped: Eyesight.* The searcher looking under *Visually handicapped* has a right to expect all relevant entities under this descriptor; this is why the precombined descriptor was introduced in the first place. The searcher should not have to look under a combination of elemental descriptors, too.

An entity should be indexed by all applicable precombined descriptors. If the index language contains a large number of precombined descriptors, thorough indexing can get a bit tricky. Assume the index language includes the precombined descriptors

    A1.1 Vegetables : B2 Frozen AND
    A1 Plant : B2 Frozen : C1 Carton

but not

    A1.1 Vegetables : B2 Frozen : C1 Carton

(Locate these concepts in the hierarchy displayed in Fig. 15.5; this is the same hierarchy as in Fig. 14.8; descriptors are underlined.) Assume an indexer must index the food product

    Frozen vegetable packed in carton (A1.1B2C1)

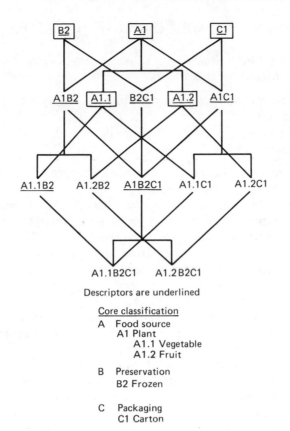

Fig. 15.5   Finding precombined descriptors in a hierarchical structure.

How does he find the precombined descriptors he should use? The general rule of request-oriented indexing says to use all descriptors under which the entity is to be found. (A specific descriptor implies all its broader descriptors; for example, if the food is indexed by A1.1B2 *Vegetables. Frozen,* it need not also be indexed by A1.1 *Vegetable.*) The food product at hand should be found under any descriptor that is broader than the product representation A1.1B2C1; locate this concept in the hierarchy and follow each hierarchical chain upward until you come to a descriptor. The descriptors thus found are A1.1B2, A1B2C1, and A1.1 (via A1.1C1); A1.1 is implied by A1.1B2, so it is not needed.

15.5 ORGANIZING AN INDEX LANGUAGE FOR ACCESS

Searching by subject or any other criterion requires two steps, the first of which is also needed for indexing:

Step 1: Find the descriptors needed for formulating a query or indexing an entity.

Step 2: Find the focal entities that are in the proper relationship to the descriptors.

Both steps involve retrieval operations in an integrated data base, and the ISAR system should support them.

With postcombination, step 1 is easy. There is a fairly small number of elemental descriptors. The relationships between descriptors are not overly complex; only a few have more than one broader term. The index language can be shown easily in a classified arrangement of descriptors (preferably divided into facets) with some cross-references added, supplemented by an alphabetical index. Even an alphabetical arrangement alone with all relationships expressed through cross-references might do.

The difficulty with a postcombination system comes in step 2. Since most searches are for compound concepts, the search mechanism must allow searches for *a combination of descriptors.*

With high precombination it is just the other way around: There is a large number of precombined descriptors. With extreme precombination—as in the data base in Fig. 15.2—the number of precombined descriptors is of the same order of magnitude as the number of main entities (in the example documents). The Library of Congress Classification fills 30 volumes. There is a complex web of hierarchical and associative relationships (see Chapter 14, especially Section 14.3). The searcher must find in this huge web all the precombined descriptors that are equal to or narrower than the search topic.

In other words, the searcher must find all precombined descriptors that contain among their components the elemental concepts that make up the search topic. That is a big job, and it requires the capability of *searching for precombined descriptors with a combination of elemental concepts.* Step 2 is easy with high precombination. The searcher simply looks under the precombined descriptors to find the focal entities.

In a postcombination system, combination searching is needed in step 2, retrieving focal entities; in a precombination system, combination searching is needed in step 1, retrieving precombined descriptors. With moderate precombination some combination searching is needed in step 1 and some combination searching in step 2.

The remainder of this section deals with the problem of finding precombined descriptors. With modern technology, the most natural solution is the one illustrated in the data bases in Figs. 15.2 and 15.3, namely, a *descriptor-find index*—preferably for on-line searching—in which the searcher can formulate a query as a combination of elemental concepts and find all precombined descriptors that contain these concepts. Such a descriptor-find index is part of an integrated data base that permits searching through a chain. The descriptor-find index leads from elemental concepts to compound concepts. Other parts of the data base structure—for example, a document-find index or a main file arranged by precombined descriptors—lead from compound concepts to documents or other entities. Descriptor-find indexes are discussed in Section 15.5.1.

Another, more limited way of providing access to precombined descriptors, which was developed before combination search mechanisms were available, is to arrange them in a meaningful sequence that collocates related descriptors. Arrangement of descriptors is discussed in Section 15.5.2.

15.5.1 DESCRIPTOR-FIND INDEXES

Two examples will illustrate this concept further.

Example 1: A Descriptor-Find Index for the LC Classification

In the data base in Fig. 15.2, a core classification of elemental concepts was given and the descriptor-find index developed naturally through the procedure by which precombined descriptors were formed. In the Library of Congress Classification the precombined descriptors were not formed in the same systematic procedure. There is no core classification (many core concepts may not even be included per se as descriptors), only a large unwieldy list of precombined descriptors. Facet analysis (see Sections 14.3 and 14.5) results in a core classification of elemental concepts and a representation for each class in terms of core concepts (Figs. 15.6a and b). These can be used to construct a descriptor-find index, preferably as an on-line file. For example, the query formulation

L20 Traffic facility AND L37 Water transport

retrieves a list of LC class numbers, such as

HE550-560 Ports, harbors, docks, wharves, etc.
NA6330 Dock buildings, ferry houses, etc.
VA67-79 Naval ports, bases, reservations, docks, etc.

L00 Transportation and traffic	R00 Engineering
L10 Vehicles	R30 Acoustics
L20 Traffic facilities	R37 Soundproofing
L25 Traffic stations	
L33 Air transport	T70 Military vs. civilian
L37 Water transport	T73 Military
	T77 Civilian
P00 Buildings, construction	
P23 Buildings	U00 America
P27 Architecture	U15 US
P43 Construction	

(a) Core classification.

HE550–560   Ports, harbors, docks, wharves, etc.
              = L25 Traffic stations : L37 Water transport :
                T77 Civilian

NA2800   Architectural acoustics
              = P27 Architecture : R30 Acoustics

NA6300–6307   Airport buildings
              = L25 Traffic stations : L33 Air transport :
                P23 Buildings : T77 Civilian

NA6330   Dock buildings, ferry houses, etc.
              = L25 Traffic stations : L37 Water transport :
                P23 Buildings : T77 Civilian

TC350–374   Harbor works
              = L25 Traffic stations : L37 Water transport :
                R00 Engineering

TH1725   Soundproof construction
              = P23 Buildings : P43 Construction : R37 Soundproofing.

TL681.S6   Airplanes. Soundproofing
              = L10 Vehicles : L33 Air transport : R37 Soundproofing.

TL725–726   Airways (Routes). Airports and landing fields. Aerodromes
              = L20 Traffic facilities : L33 Air transport

VA67–79   Naval ports, bases, reservations, docks, etc.
              = L25 Traffic stations : L37 Water transport :
                T73 Military : U15 US

VM367.S6   Submarines. Soundproofing
              = L10 Vehicles : L37 Water trans. : R37 Soundproofing.

(b) LC classes with decomposition into semantic factors.

L10	L10:L33:R37	TL681.S6 Airplanes. Soundproofing
	L10:L37:R37	VM367.S6 Submarines. Soundproofing
L20	L20:L33	TL725-726 Airways, airports, etc.
L25	L25:L33:P23:T77	NA6300-6307 Airport buildings
	L25:L37:P23:T77	NA6330 Dock buildings, ferry houses, etc.
	L25:L37:R00	TC350-374 Harbor works
	L25:L37:T73:U15	VA67-79 Naval ports, bases, etc.
	L25:L37:T77	HE550-560 Ports, harbors, docks, etc.
L33	L10:L33:R37	TL681.S6 Airplanes. Soundproofing
	L20:L33	TL725-726 Airways, airports, etc.
	L25:L33:P23:T77	NA6300-6307 Airport buildings
L37	L10:L37:R37	VM367.S6 Submarines. Soundproofing
	L25:L37:R00	TC350-374 Harbor works
	L25:L37:R23:T77	NA6330 Dock buildings, ferry houses, etc.
	L25:L37:T73:U15	VA67-79 Naval ports, bases, etc.
	L25:L37:T77	HE550-560 Ports, harbors, docks, etc.
P23	L25:L33:P23:T77	NA6300-6307 Airport buildings
	L25:L37:P23:T77	NA6330 Dock buildings, ferry houses, etc.
	P23:P43:R37	TH1725 Soundproof construction
P27	P27:R30	NA2800 Architectural acoustics
P43	P23:P43:R37	TH1725 Soundproof construction
R00	L25:L37:R00	TC350-374 Harbor works
R30	P27:R30	NA2800 Architectural acoustics
R37	L10:L33:R37	TL681.S6 Airplanes. Soundproofing
	L10:L37:R37	VM367.S6 Submarines. Soundproofing
	P23:P43:R37	TH1725 Soundproof construction
T73	L25:L37:T73:U15	VA67-69 Naval ports, bases, etc.
T77	L25:L33:P23:T77	NA6300-6307 Airport buildings
	L25:L37:P23:T77	NA6330 Dock buildings, ferry houses, etc.
	L25:L37:T77	HE550-560 Ports, harbors, docks, etc.
U15	L25:L37:T73:U15	VA67-69 Naval ports, bases, etc.

(c) Descriptor-find index (KWOC format using notation).

Fig. 15.6   A descriptor-find index for LC classification

L10 Vehicles AND R30 Acoustics, inclusive

retrieves

TL681.S6 Airplanes. Soundproofing
VM367.S6 Submarines. Soundproofing

Fig. 15.6c shows a KWIC-type descriptor-find index. Two examples of descriptor-find indexes actually implemented as printed indexes are the *Relative Index* to DDC (with many limitations) and a *chain index* to a set of precombined descriptors generated from a faceted classification. All of these bring together distributed relatives—precombined descriptors that share an elemental concept but are scattered in the arrangement—and thus complement the access provided by a meaningful arrangement.

Example 2: A Newspaper Clipping File

A large newspaper clipping file contains from one million to ten million documents. Each document (each clipping) is very small compared to average journal articles or books. Usually many of these documents, perhaps 20 or more, are needed to answer a request. Dealing with each document as an individual unit would require an index of tremendous size. It would also be very cumbersome to access the file of the documents themselves in so many different places. Just picture accessing 20 articles appearing over three years in five different newspapers on microfilm. The situation cries out for forming classes. For each class (precombined descriptor) there is a folder containing the relevant clippings. The folder heading is the name of the class. Each folder has assigned to it a combination of elemental concepts (core descriptors), which is the folder representation. There may be 50,000–500,000 folders. Sample folders are:

> *Bilateral relations* between *France* and the *US*
> *Soviet Reactions* to *Bilateral relations* between *France* and the *US*
> *Bilateral relations* between *Great Britain* and the *US*

In this file a user can find conveniently all clippings relevant to a topic, provided she knows in which folders to look. To find these folders, the user consults an index of folders (precombined descriptors), that is a descriptor-find index. A user interested in the topic

> *Bilateral relations* between *France* and the *US*

would AND the three core descriptors and find the first two sample folders, among others. A user interested in

> *Bilateral relations* of the *US* (with any other country)

would retrieve all three sample folders, among others.

Retrieving precombined descriptors based on their relationships to elemental concepts is the same type of operation as finding documents or other entities based on their relationships to concepts. Just using a different view to describe the system of newspaper clippings illustrates this point. We redefine documents and call each *folder* a document. (Some libraries do indeed periodically take all the clippings in an important folder, bind them into book form, and treat the result like any other book in their book collection.) The folder heading is seen as the title of this new document, and the folder representation is seen as the representation of this document. In this view, retrieving folders is seen as retrieving documents. Thus the same index can be viewed as a descriptor-find index (consider the folder headings as precombined descriptors assigned to all clippings in their folder) or as a document-find index (consider the folder headings as document titles).

These examples illustrate that *combination searching is needed in any system*. The only difference between postcombination and precombination systems is how the workload of combination searching is distributed between the two search steps. In most postcombination systems the user receives excellent assistance in combination searching as a matter of course through the data base organization and search mechanism (such as an on-line retrieval system for documents or other entities). In precombination systems the user is presented with an extensive list of precombined descriptors (with LCC this includes 30 volumes), but is left on her own in searching for the right descriptors, since there is usually no descriptor-find index. The only assistance the user has for combination searching is the more or less meaningful arrangement. It is high time for the construction of on-line descriptor-find indexes to assist the users of existing precombination systems that cover large collections and that will be with us for quite some time to come.

15.5.2 ARRANGEMENT AND DESIGNATION OF DESCRIPTORS

Arrangement and designation of descriptors play an important role in organizing an index language for access. Any system—regardless of degree of precombination—requires the helpful arrangement of core descriptors (the elemental concepts used as descriptors in a postcombination system or used to produce precombined descriptors in a precombination system). A helpful arrangement of precombined descriptors may serve as a limited substitute for a descriptor-find index or as a supplement to it.

Descriptors can be arranged in classified (subject) order or in alphabetical order. A meaningful classified arrangement serves the following interrelated functions (see Section 13.6 and 13.7 for a more complete discussion):

Orientation of the user in an index language.

Communication of a useful conceptual framework that helps users organize information or entities (e.g., in memory).

Organization of a collection of entities so that the user has a framework for orientation in the collection. Materials that are needed together or should be examined together should be collocated. Section 15.2 has shown that grouping entities into classes—each corresponding to a precombined descriptor—can be helpful for the user; grouping related classes together—arranging the precombined descriptors in a meaningful classified sequence—takes this principle a step further. This use of arrangement is also important when presenting to the user the mini-data base that answers his request. Computer output has the advantage that the arrangement can be tailored to the purpose at hand; many lessons for this task can be learned from writers on library classification.

Organization of a set of precombined descriptors so that precombined descriptors can be found in terms of their components. With this function, the classified arrangement serves as a substitute for a descriptor-find index. However, a linear arrangement can express only a fraction of the many hierarchical and associative relationships that exist between the precombined descriptors. Collocating all the precombined descriptors in the area of *Law* disperses the descriptors for many other subjects, such as *Food, Transportation,* or *Education,* creating *distributed relatives.* Deciding on a particular arrangement means deciding which hierarchical relationships to show through the arrangement and which to show through crossreferences or not at all. The arrangement should be based on the hierarchical relationships most important to the user. To some extent a systematically developed network of cross-references can guide the user to relevant precombined descriptors not collocated in the arrangement; with a high degree of precombination the number of cross-references becomes unwieldy, and a descriptor-find index should take their place.

Arrangement of descriptors is closely intertwined with their designation—the choice of descriptor identifiers. The designation system must be chosen so that it leads to the desired arrangement. For example, a classified arrangement requires notations as descriptor identifiers.

In the arrangement of core descriptors the choices are limited. One can arrange them either in a meaningful classified order with notations as descriptor identifiers (of course accompanied by terms) or alphabetically with terms as descriptor identifiers. With precombined descriptors there are many more options that differ in the degree to which the components of a precombined descriptor determine its place in the sequence. These options are discussed in the remainder of this section. They apply whether the components (core descriptors) are identified by notations or by terms. While arrangement is more fundamental, and decisions on arrangement should logically precede decisions on designation, designation rules are easier to understand and therefore discussed first.

The following core classification is used in all examples.

Facet A Food source		Facet B Preservation		Facet C Packaging	
A1	Plant product	B1	Fresh	C1	Carton
	A1.1 Vegetable	B2	Frozen	C2	Bag
A2	Animal product	B3	Sterilized		

Designation of Precombined Descriptors

Option 1 is to create the identifier of a precombined descriptor by *combining the identifiers of its components in fixed citation order* (in the example: Facet A, Facet B, Facet C):

A1.1B3C2   Vegetable : Sterilized : Bag
A2B1   Animal product : Fresh
A2B1C1   Animal product : Fresh : Carton

This rule for designation completely determines the arrangement of precombined descriptors. Examples are faceted classification used in a precombination system and the LC Subject Headings (with the citation order main heading—subheading). This rule should be used in a system that allows the indexer to freely introduce new precombined descriptors, because otherwise the same descriptor might end up with two or more designations, filed at two or more different places.

Option 2 is to create the identifier of a precombined descriptor by combining the identifiers of its components *in a free citation order,* determined ad hoc in each individual case. For example:

A2B1   Animal product : Fresh
B1A2C1   Fresh : Animal product : Carton
C2B3A1.1   Bag : Sterilized : Vegetable

This designation rule still determines the arrangement of precombined descriptors to a considerable degree, but not completely.

Option 3 is to *choose the identifier of a precombined descriptor without being bound by the descriptor components* (the identifier is an *independent symbol*). Examples are LCC (the independent symbols being class numbers) and the main headings in a subject heading list, the independent symbols being terms. For example:

A1.5   Sterilized vegetables packed in a bag
A2.3   Fresh meat
A2.5   Fresh meat packed in cartons

This designation rule gives the designer complete freedom in the arrangement of precombined descriptors (including an arrangement following a fixed set of rules).

Arrangement of Precombined Descriptors

Option 1 is to arrange precombined descriptors in a *sequence that is mandated by their components in a fixed citation order.* This arrangement option allows designation option 1 or 3 (designation option 1 is shown in the example). The example includes only part of all possible combinations of core concepts.

A1   Plant product
    A1B1   Plant product : Fresh
        A1B1C1   Plant product : Fresh : Carton
        A1B1C2   Plant product : Fresh : Bag
    A1B3   Plant product : Sterilized
        A1B3C1   Plant product : Sterilized : Carton
        A1B3C2   Plant product : Sterilized : Bag
        A1.1B3   Vegetable : Sterilized
    A1C1   Plant product : Carton
    A1C2   Plant product : Bag
A2   Animal product
    A2B1   Animal product : Fresh
    A2B2   Animal product : Frozen
    A2B3   Animal product : Sterilized
B1   Fresh
    B1C1   Fresh : Carton

In the citation order chosen, subdivision by preservation is always second and follows the standard order B1 *Fresh,* B2 *Frozen,* B3 *Sterilized.* Subdivision by packaging is always third and follows the standard order C1 *Carton,* C2 *Bag.* The facet of highest importance to the user should be put first so that, for example, all *Plant product* descriptors are together. The precombined descriptors containing *Fresh,* an element of the second-placed facet, are scattered throughout the arrangement (*distributed relatives*). The citation order is independent of the order in which the facets are listed; for example, it could be BCA or CBA.

Option 2 is to arrange precombined descriptors in a *sequence that is mandated by their components but with free citation order.* Arrangement option 2 allows designation option 2 or 3 (designation option 2 is shown in the example). Descriptors that are out of order as compared to option 1, fixed citation order, are marked by *.

A1   Plant product
    A1B1   Plant product : Fresh
    A1B3   Plant product : Sterilized
        A1B3C1   Plant product : Sterilized : Carton
        A1B3C2   Plant product : Sterilized : Bag
        A1.1B3   Vegetable : Sterilized
    A1C1   Plant product : Carton
       *A1C1B1   Plant product : Carton : Fresh[1]
    A1C2   Plant product : Bag
       *A1C2B1   Plant product : Bag : Fresh[1]
A2   Animal product
    A2B2   Animal product : Frozen
    A2B3   Animal product : Sterilized
B1   Fresh
   *B1A2   Fresh : Animal product[1]
    B1C1   Fresh : Carton

In this method, subdivision by method of preservation, for example, may be first, second, or third. But wherever subdivision by preservation is used, the standard sequence B1 *Fresh,* B2 *Frozen,* B3 *Sterilized* applies.

Option 3 is to arrange precombined descriptors in a freely chosen sequence that is not mandated by the descriptor components. Arrangement option 3 requires designation option 3.

A1   Plant product
    A1.1   Fresh plant product
    A1.2   Sterilized plant product
       *A1.3   Sterilized plant product packed in bag[2]
       *A1.4   Sterilized plant product in carton[2]
       A1.5   Sterilized vegetable
    A1.6   Plant product packed in carton
       *A1.7   Fresh plant product packed in carton[1]
    A1.8   Plant product packed in bag
       *A1.9   Fresh plant product packed in bag[1]
A2   Animal product
   *A2.1   Sterilized animal product[3]
   *A2.2   Fresh animal product[3]
   *A2.3   Frozen animal product[3]
B1   Fresh
    B1.1   Fresh product packed in carton

[1] Nonstandard citation order
[2] Nonstandard sequence *Bag–Carton*
[3] Nonstandard sequence *Sterilized–Fresh–Frozen*

In this option the designer subdividing a topic—e.g., *Judaism* or *Reformation*—by geographic area can choose a sequence of countries most appropriate in the context of the topic. She would start with Israel and other Middle East countries for *Judaism* and with Germany and Switzerland for *Reformation*. Still another sequence of countries may be appropriate to subdivide *Economic development*. The designer should use this freedom judiciously. If a topic does not suggest a particular point of view for sequencing countries, a standard sequence is most helpful. Perhaps there should be two or three standard sequences, each appropriate for a range of topics.

The meaningful geographic subdivision of some concepts requires more than just varying the sequence of countries; countries may not be the most appropriate geographic areas. For example, the geographic subdivision of *Vegetation* should use such concepts as *Tropics, Subtropics,* etc. Arrangement option 3 leaves the designer free to create for each concept a tailor-made scheme of geographic areas. Again, in order to preserve the clarity of the index language, such schemes should not proliferate beyond what is necessary. In this discussion, geographic subdivision is just an example. The considerations apply also to subdivisions by historical periods or by any other concept.

The principles of designation and arrangement are further illustrated by their application to subject headings. The main headings and the subheadings are independent elements designated by terms and arranged alphabetically. Many subject headings are created by combining a main heading with a subheading, and for those headings the place in the arrangement is determined by the components. The citation order is fixed: main heading–subheading. A closer look reveals a more complex situation. Often the linguistic structure of the main heading reflects the conceptual structure, as in *Radio engineering* or *Aircraft*. Should the citation order be *Radio engineering* (direct form) or *Engineering, radio* (inverted form); *Aircraft* or *Craft, air?* The problem of direct versus inverted headings reveals itself as a problem of citation order.

15.6 A UNIFIED INDEX LANGUAGE FOR DIFFERENT SEARCH MECHANISMS

The degree of precombination in an index language must be adapted to the search mechanism; an on-line system and a printed index are best used with different degrees of precombination. Sometimes access to the same collection of documents or other entities is provided through several search mechanisms, for example, the on-line system *MEDLINE* and the printed *Index Medicus*. In such a case it is desirable to adapt the index language used to the search mechanism while maintaining a common conceptual base. More generally, if information systems overlap in their subject scopes or their collections, it is desirable, both from the point of view of their users and from the point of view of sharing indexing effort, to have index languages that share their conceptual base. A solution for this problem evolves from the concepts developed in this chapter.

At the beginning is a *core classification* consisting of elemental or quasi-elemental *core descriptors* as defined in Section 15.2. This is the index language for a postcombination system. In a precombination system (e.g., a card catalog or a printed index), precombined descriptors are introduced as needed, extending the core classification to result in the *extended classification* with a descriptor-find index. The core classification stays the same, across systems of different types (e.g., on-line system and printed index) and across systems of the same type (e.g., the card catalogs of three libraries using the same core classification). The extended classification may vary from one precombination system to another, depending on local needs. Indexing can be done once and for all using the core classification. The precombined descriptors to be used in each system can then be derived automatically. One indexing step thus provides descriptors for on-line searching, subject headings, DDC classes, LC classes, and precombined descriptors in any other scheme. (Such an approach is used in the PRECIS system as applied in the British Library.) The core classification must be very specific, and indexing must consider the interests of all organizations involved. A properly designed core classification could thus take the role of the old dream, a universal classification. This is made possible by concentrating on the basic principles of conceptual structure and leaving aside details of arrangement and data base organization on which agreement cannot be reached and is not even always desirable.

PART V

ISAR Systems Operation and Design

CHAPTER 16

Indexing Specificity and Exhaustivity

OBJECTIVES

The objectives of this chapter are to enable the reader to assess or develop indexing criteria and procedures and to use knowledge of indexing criteria for writing query formulations that exploit all the possibilities offered by the indexing and also compensate, to the extent possible, for any weaknesses in indexing.

16.1 IMPORTANCE OF INDEXING FOR SYSTEM PERFORMANCE

The quality of retrieval depends on indexing, query formulation, and comparison/match (see the ISAR system diagram, Fig. 5.6). All of these functions depend, in turn, on the index language. Indexing is the basis for the other two functions and thus sets an upper limit for retrieval performance; actual performance depends on the sophistication of query formulation and of the search procedure. An ISAR system that retrieves documents based on words in their titles can achieve—through extensive terminological control in searching and a sophisticated search procedure—peformance results comparable to an ISAR system that uses trained indexers but lacks sophistication in query formulation and search procedure. An ISAR system using request-oriented indexing in which the query formulators make full use of the possibilities is likely to be best.

Chapter 13 set forth two approaches to indexing—request-oriented indexing and entity-oriented indexing—and analyzed their effect on retrieval performance. Section 16.2 examines additional characteristics of indexing that are useful in explaining retrieval performance, namely, exhaustivity and specificity. Section 16.3 examines the effects of these parameters on retrieval performance. It is extremely important for the searcher to know both the general approach to indexing and the levels of exhaustivity and specificity in order to formulate queries properly. Section 16.4 discusses the design of indexing rules and procedures.

16.2 DEFINITION OF EXHAUSTIVITY AND SPECIFICITY OF INDEXING

The example in Fig. 16.1 gives an intuitive understanding of exhaustivity and specificity for the case of indexing documents. Moving down a column of the table adds more and more aspects for which the document is relevant—exhaustivity increases. Moving across a line makes the descriptor expressing an aspect more and more specific—specificity increases. For instance

Airports—Small airports—Aquadromes

16.2.1 DEFINITION OF EXHAUSTIVITY

Intended exhaustivity is defined as the importance threshold to be used by the indexer when deciding about descriptors. The following are sample instructions conveying the intended exhaustivity to indexers:

High importance threshold—low exhaustivity (few descriptors)

Request-oriented rule	Use a descriptor only for entities that are highly relevant in a search for the descriptor
Entity-oriented rule	Index only the main topics of a document. Index only the first ingredient of a food.

Low importance threshold—high exhaustivity (more descriptors)

Request-oriented rule	Use a descriptor also for entities that are just marginally relevant.
Entity-oriented rule	Index also minor topics of a document. Index all ingredients of a food product.

Document:

Floating Airport: key to inter-city traffic

Rutgers University proposes anchoring fleet of Rutgers Aquadromes around Manhattan Island as landing space for STOL and VTOL aircraft; concept is based on construction of floating platforms, 1,000 feet in diameter, made of *concrete* and circular in shape; Aquadromes practicability studies using *models* are being planned now; these involve use of fully instrumented unconcrete models which will be *tested for failure: sequential tests* will be used to assess *reliability of operation.*

The access to the Aquadromes by *helicopter* and by connection to the *subway system* is also considered. Further aspects of the study involve flight operations and inter-urban *mass-air-transportation,* especially the airbus concept in the *Tri-State Region of Connecticut, New Jersey, and New York.*

Descriptors:

Exhaustivity \ Specificity	Low	Medium	High
Low	Inter-city traffic[1] Airports US Aircraft New technological developments[1,2]	Intercity traffic Small airports New York State New generation aircraft New technological developments	Inter-city traffic Aquadromes New York City STOL aircraft VTOL aircraft New technological developments
High	Building materials Models Reliability Statistics Aircraft Ground transport Mass transportation US Traffic planning[2] Feasibility Study[1,2] Good[1,2] To be read immediately[1,2]	Concrete Models Reliability Statistical tests Helicopters Rail transport Mass transportation Connecticut New Jersey New York State Traffic planning[2] Feasibility Study[1,2] Good[1,2] To be read immediately[1,2]	Concrete Models Reliability Sequential tests Helicopters Local rail transit Mass transportation Connecticut New Jersey New York State Traffic planning[2] Feasibility Study[1,2] Good[1,2] To be read immediately[1,2]

[1] Concept must be available in index language, otherwise, it cannot be used in indexing or searching

[2] Descriptors assigned only by checklist technique

Fig. 16.1   Exhaustivity and specificity of indexing.

If an indexer assigns all descriptors required by the importance threshold, whether 3 descriptors (threshold high) or 25 descriptors (threshold low), indexing is very complete. On the other hand, if the indexer assigns only half the descriptors required, indexing is incomplete. This defines *completeness of indexing*. Intended exhaustivity and completeness combine to produce *actual exhaustivity*. It is actual exhaustivity that matters in the discussion of retrieval system performance. Therefore, we use the term *exhaustivity* to mean *actual exhaustivity*.

Measuring exhaustivity can be tricky. The number of descriptors assigned to an entity is often correlated with exhaustivity, but it must be qualified. At the same level of exhaustivity a simple part needs far fewer descriptors than a complete automobile. A long document often needs more descriptors than a short one. However, a 20-page journal article may need 15 descriptors at a medium level of exhaustivity, whereas an economics textbook needs just one: *Economics, general references* (i.e., all subjects of economics covered). Incorrect descriptors increase the count without contributing to exhaustivity. Some systems do generic posting in indexing; with this method, an indexer using, for example, *Garbanzo beans,* must add the broader descriptors *Beans, Pod vegetables, Vegetable, Plant*—four additional descriptors that do not add to exhaustivity. One precombined descriptor may contribute as much to exhaustivity as several elemental descriptors; for example, the one LC class

LA361.A1 History of education. S.Carolina. Official document

is as exhaustive as the four elemental descriptors

History, Education, South Carolina, and Official document.

Therefore, measuring exhaustivity requires that all descriptors be reduced to elemental concepts, particularly when comparing two systems. Thus, as a rule, the higher the degree of precombination, the fewer descriptors are required at a given level of exhaustivity. (But if the index language contains many overlapping precombined descriptors, the number of descriptors required in indexing increases, see Section 15.3.4.)

16.2.2 DEFINITION OF SPECIFICITY

Specificity is the generic level at which the concepts assigned to the entity are expressed. Indexing by *Aquadromes* is more specific than indexing by *Airports;* indexing by *Helicopters* is more specific than indexing by *Aircraft.*

ISAR system A may be consistently more specific than system B; however, often one system is more specific in one aspect, and the other system more specific in another aspect. For example, A may use *Aquadromes* and *Aircraft,* while B uses *Airports* and *Helicopter.*

As with exhaustivity, descriptors must be reduced to elemental components before specificity can be assessed:

Methods of instruction for reading in elementary schools

is a very specific descriptor due to its being precombined. Yet the set of directly assigned elemental descriptors

Methods of instruction; Reading; Second grade

provides more specific indexing with respect to the grade level aspect. This is true even though the components, when taken as individual descriptors, are less specific than the precombined descriptor.

Intended specificity is the standard defined by the descriptors in a system's index language and/or other instructions. Comparing two index languages with respect to the level of intended specificity involves reducing each index language to the set of elemental concepts needed to generate all its descriptors and establishing correspondence between the elemental concepts.

Actual specificity may fall short of the standard set by intended specificity, due to the indexer's inability to differentiate between specific concepts or due to insufficient information used in indexing.

16.3 EFFECTS OF EXHAUSTIVITY AND SPECIFICITY OF INDEXING ON RETRIEVAL PERFORMANCE

The effects of exhaustivity and specificity depend on the specific search situation at hand; general statements about them are misleading. Exhaustivity is beneficial in some searches and detrimental in others. Furthermore, the query formulation must be adapted to the level of exhaustivity: One query formulation may be best for a low exhaustivity system and another formulation for a high exhaustivity system. In each case we must compare the retrieval results with the query statement as originally put. In many experiments investigating the effects of exhaustivity, the same query formulation is used with ISAR systems using different levels of exhaustivity. This is bad search practice, and the results of such experiments are useless as guides for practice.

	Search situation	
No.	Query statement	Document relevant?
1	All documents that deal in any way with the building and use of models	Yes
2	Documents on the design and construction of models	No
3	Models of airports	Yes

16.3.1 EFFECTS OF EXHAUSTIVITY

Figure 16.2 illustrates the effects of exhaustivity in three search situations as defined by the query statement and the relevance judgments for the sample document on *Aquadromes,* which mentions the use of models (columns on left page). The next two pairs of columns give, for each level of exhaustivity, the query formulation *to be used with that level of exhaustivity* and the retrieval performance, which is extrapolated from the observation of whether or not the sample document on *Aquadromes,* and thus others like it, is retrieved or rejected.

We shall now discuss each line in Fig. 16.2. In the first line the topic is very broad: Any document mentioning models in any way is wanted. There is only one concept in the query statement, and thus the query formulation is *Models* regardless of the level of exhaustivity. High exhaustivity is clearly better in this situation. The importance threshold of the user and the importance threshold used in high exhaustivity indexing agree. Recall and discrimination are not perfect because of disagreements between indexer and

Low exhaustivity ISAR system		High exhaustivity ISAR system	
Query formulation	Retrieval performance	Query formulation	Retrieval performance
Models	Document incorrectly rejected Recall very low Discr. very high	Models	Document correctly retrieved Recall high Discr. high
Models	Document correctly rejected Recall high Discr. high	Models	Document incorrectly retrieved Recall very high Discr. very low
Airports	Document correctly retrieved; many other documents dealing with airports but not with models incorrectly retrieved Recall very high Discr. low	Airports AND Models	Document correctly retrieved; other documents dealing with airports but not with models correctly rejected Recall high Discr. high

Fig. 16.2   Effects of exhaustivity on retrieval performance. Sample document on aquadromes.

searcher in judging relevance: The indexer assigns the descriptor to some documents that the user thinks not quite important enough and vice versa. Low exhaustivity is clearly bad in this search situation. The indexer's importance threshold is much higher than the user's, leading to very low recall. The gain in discrimination (a document judged important enough to be indexed by *Models* with low exhaustivity is surely relevant to the query) cannot make up for the loss in recall.

The second line gives a quite different query statement. This user wants only documents specifically on models—how to build them, what materials to use, what tools to use to work on those materials, how to design the model, how to execute the design, and how to use models (e.g., a book on the use of models in different contexts, with emphasis on model use rather than the substantive area). The query formulation must again be *Models* with both levels of exhaustivity; there is no other choice. However, now low exhaustivity is better. The importance threshold applied by the indexer and the importance threshold envisioned by the user agree. High exhaustivity is bad

	Search situation	
No.	Query statement	Document relevant?
1	All documents that deal in any way with the building and use of models	Yes
2	Documents on the design and construction of models	No
3	Models of airports	Yes

Fig. 16.2   Effects of exhaustivity on retrieval performance (repeated).

in this second search situation because now—as distinct from the first search situation—it leads to low discrimination. Of course, exactly the same documents are retrieved, but many of the documents judged relevant for query statement 1 are not relevant for query statement 2. In other words, while the searcher is forced to use the same query formulation, the documents relevant for query 2 form a small subset of the documents relevant for query 1. The small gain in recall (a document relevant for query statement 2 would surely have been indexed by *Models* with high exhaustivity) cannot make up for the loss in discrimination.

Line 3 gives a specific query statement combining two concepts; the query formulation that comes first to mind is

(3.1)   Airports AND Models

This formulation works fine for high exhaustivity: The sample document (and others like it) is indexed by *Models* and is retrieved; recall is good. But with low exhaustivity the sample document is *not* indexed by *Models;* its

Low exhaustivity ISAR system		High exhaustivity ISAR system	
Query formulation	Retrieval performance	Query formulation	Retrieval performance
Models	Document incorrectly rejected Recall very low Discr. very high	Models	Document correctly retrieved Recall high Discr. high
Models	Document correctly rejected Recall high Discr. high	Models	Document incorrectly retrieved Recall very high Discr. very low
Airports	Document correctly retrieved; many other documents dealing with airports but not with models incorrectly retrieved Recall very high Discr. low	Airports AND Models	Document correctly retrieved; other documents dealing with airports but not with models correctly rejected Recall high Discr. high

mention of models is sufficient to make it relevant for the request but not sufficient to meet the high importance threshold used with low exhaustivity indexing. Thus, the query formulation (3.1) would miss the sample document and others like it, producing intolerably low recall; the formulation for the low exhaustivity system should be

(3.2)   Airports

The searcher cannot use *Models* as a criterion limiting the search because too many relevant documents would be missed. Thus, low exhaustivity gives good recall but very low discrimination. On the other hand, with high exhaustivity *Models can* be used as a descriptor limiting *Airports,* thus enhancing discrimination. To sum up, in a single-descriptor search for *Models,* high exhaustivity sometimes leads to low discrimination; but when *Models* is a second descriptor, qualifying the main concept *Airports,* high exhaustivity leads to high discrimination because it allows the searcher to introduce the qualification AND *Models* in the query formulation without fear of losing many relevant documents.

If only one level of exhaustivity is allowed, the designer can either choose low exhaustivity and please user 2 or high exhaustivity and please users 1 and 3. The obvious solution is to allow for two levels of exhaustivity in the same ISAR system by using *weights* in indexing—for instance, weight 2 for important descriptors (those that would be assigned with low exhaustivity) and weight 1 for the less important descriptors (those that would be added with high exhaustivity). Now the query formulation can be adapted much better to the query statement. Query formulation 1 becomes *Models* (weight 1 or 2); query formulation 2 becomes **Models* (weight 2). Moreover, descriptors of different weights can be mixed in one query formulation, for example, for query 3

   *Airports AND Models.

16.3.2 EFFECTS OF SPECIFICITY

This analysis is much simpler. Highly specific indexing gives the searcher the option of expressing the search concepts through very specific descriptors, thus enhancing discrimination. However, this option may miss relevant entities. For instance, a document relevant for *Local rail transit* may have been indexed, erroneously, by the broader term *Rail transport* or by the neighbor term *Railroad*. In other examples, a job seeker qualified for an open job of *Furnace operator* may have been indexed by the broader term *Foundry worker;* a data set relevant for a study on attitudes to *Power* may have been indexed by the neighbor term *Authority*. Thus, a search is more affected by indexing errors when using specific descriptors than when using broad descriptors.

Specific searching is an option, not a must. The searcher can always use a broader term in the inclusive mode. However, there are ISAR systems in which inclusive searching is difficult—for example, an alphabetical subject catalog or a computerized system that does not have a command for inclusive searching or a well-structured classified display of the descriptors where one could find all the narrower descriptors. The searcher may be forced to use the level of specificity used in indexing. As an example, consider a query on *Rutabaga* in a high specificity alphabetical subject catalog. Looking under *Rutabaga* will yield some material, perhaps 30% of all relevant material, which is not enough if high recall is required. Other relevant items are to be found under *Turnip* (due to incorrect indexing under this closely related vegetable), *Root vegetable* (either general documents or specific documents where the indexer did not find the specific descriptor), *Tuber vegetable* (documents indexed under an incorrect broader descriptor), and, finally, *Vegetable*. The searcher would find it hard to think of all these descriptors and look them up. On the other hand, in a low specificity catalog almost all relevant documents would be indexed under *Vegetable,* and the searcher would be forced to use that broad descriptor, resulting in very high recall and equally low discrimination. To complete the example, picture a search on the broad descriptor *Vegetable, inclusive* in the high specificity alphabetical subject catalog. In this situation recall is a function of the searcher's ability to identify the names of many specific vegetables; cross-references in the catalog help. High specificity is no help when searching with a broad query, and, as the example shows, in a poorly designed system it can actually be a hindrance. However, in a properly designed system that allows for inclusive searching, specificity of indexing is another device that gives the searcher flexibility, and it has no negative effects.

16.3.3 MISCONCEPTIONS ABOUT THE EFFECTS OF EXHAUSTIVITY AND SPECIFICITY

Beware of the oversimplification that exhaustivity of indexing always increases recall at the cost of discrimination and that specificity always increases discrimination at the cost of recall. With respect to exhaustivity this oversimplification is based on the following argument: If the same query formulation is put to two ISAR systems, the system with higher exhaustivity retrieves more entities, thus having a higher chance of retrieving relevant entities but also a higher chance of letting through irrelevant ones. This is, of course, true, but it is beside the point. The issue is not how two ISAR systems perform in response to the same query formulation, but how each of the systems performs in response to a query formulation optimally adapted to the system's capabilities. Performance depends on the interaction of query formulation with other components of the ISAR system, particularly indexing. Thus the searcher (tester) must derive, for each system, a query formulation adapted to the capabilities of that system so that each system gives the best results it can. These best results then form the basis for system evaluation and comparison.

This is brought out in search situation 3 in Fig. 16.2, where the best query formulation is different for low exhaustivity and high exhaustivity, respectively. Even if the query formulation is the same, the effect of increased exhaustivity on recall and discrimination depends entirely on the search situation; the query statement, and thus the relevance judgments, may be different. This is brought out by search situations 1 and 2 in Fig. 16.2: In 1, increased exhaustivity results in a very substantial increase in recall with a marginal decrease in discrimination. In 2, increased exhaustivity results in a marginal increase in recall with a very substantial decrease in discrimination. With respect to the effects of specificity, refer to the discussion in the previous section.

16.3.4 SUMMARY

This discussion can be summed up in three statements:

The effects of exhaustivity and specificity on retrieval performance depend on the search situation.
The query formulation must be adapted to the level of exhaustivity and specificity used in indexing.
The use of weights in indexing increases the flexibility of searching dramatically.

It is very important that the searcher know about exhaustivity and specificity of indexing in an ISAR system that he or she uses. Unfortunately, this information is usually contained in indexing manuals or given in indexer training, but not widely distributed to searchers. A searcher must make a special effort to obtain this information.

16.4 DESIGNING INDEXING RULES AND PROCEDURES

The designer should first determine the levels of exhaustivity and specificity needed to achieve the goals of the ISAR system and then should consider rules and procedures to achieve these levels, taking into account the following factors influencing exhaustivity and specificity.

16.4.1 FACTORS INFLUENCING EXHAUSTIVITY

Intended exhaustivity manifests itself in general rules as discussed in Section 16.2.1, but also in the general approach to indexing and in the index language. Request-oriented indexing may intentionally limit the descriptors assigned to those deemed important for searching, or it may increase exhaustivity by requiring the assignment of additional descriptors beyond those that merely describe an entity. The *index language* communicates the system designer's intent with respect to the concepts (aspects) to be considered in indexing. If the index language contains such concepts as *Intercity traffic, New technological developments,* and descriptors to indicate the evaluation and disposition of a document, such as *Good* or *Read immediately,* the indexer should use them whenever they apply. If the index language does not contain these descriptors, indexing cannot be (and presumably is not intended to be) as exhaustive. In other words, the more elemental concepts are covered in the index language, the higher the intended exhaustivity. An elemental concept can be covered explicitly—it is a descriptor—or implicitly—it is the component of a descriptor.

The *completeness of indexing* depends on the *amount of information* used in indexing and on the ability of the indexer. An indexer may read just the title of a document, or also an abstract, the outline, parts of the text, or the entire text. He may even consider additional information such as the ideological viewpoint of the author or the evaluation given in a review. When indexing a food sample, one may analyze it thoroughly or superficially. Indexing of a course may be based on the course title, a brief description found in the catalog of courses, the course outline and reading list, or attendance at class sessions. But the use of extensive information does not help if the indexer lacks the subject expertise to recognize the relevance of an entity for a given descriptor.

The amount of information used in indexing should be commensurate with the level of exhaustivity intended. For a fairly low level of exhaustivity in indexing, the abstract is usually quite sufficient. The full text of the document would reveal only a few concepts of requisite importance beyond those that could already be seen from the abstract. On the other hand, very exhaustive indexing requires the full text. Figure 16.3 gives two examples. However, a very important point is not shown in these examples: Reading the abstract or text may cause the indexer to modify or completely drop a descriptor assigned based on a misleading title.

16.4.2 FACTORS INFLUENCING SPECIFICITY

Intended specificity is simply the specificity of the descriptors in the index language. Actual specificity depends on the amount of information used in indexing and on indexer ability. Titles often use broad terminology, such as *Pesticides,* when in reality the document is relevant only for *DDT,* as can be seen from the abstract or the full text. Food product labels often use broad terms such as *Vegetable oil;* analysis is necessary to determine the specific type of oil. Again, the amount of information should be commensurate with the specificity intended. An indexer needs subject expertise to differentiate between specific concepts (e.g., between *Tropospheric propagation* (of radio waves) and *Ionospheric propagation*).

Information used / Intended exhaustivity	Descriptors assigned based on		
	Title	Abstract	Full text
Exhaustivity level 1	Aquadromes Intercity traffic (New technological developments)	Aquadromes Intercity traffic New York City STOL airplane VTOL airplane New technological developments	Aquadromes Intercity traffic New York City STOL airplane VTOL airplane New technological developments
Added in exhaustivity level 2	None	Concrete Models Reliability Sequential tests Local rail transit Mass transportation Connecticut New Jersey New York State Traffic planning Feasibility study	Same and, *in addition,* Ocean height variation Traffic volume Good To be read immediately
Added in exhaustivity level 3	None	Flight operations Airbus Flight control instrumentation	Same and, *in addition,* Runway length Vibration Noise effects Costs etc.

(a) Sample document: Floating airports: key to intercity traffic.

16.4.3 Cost Considerations

Everything else being equal, higher exhaustivity means more descriptors per entity. Higher specificity means more descriptors in the index language. Both increase file costs. The relationship of these two parameters to the cost for indexing is not so clear-cut.

Indexing is cheapest when the indexers are instructed to assign all descriptors that can be inferred easily from the title. With still lower exhaustivity (e.g., assigning the one best descriptor) the indexer must decide which one of several descriptors inferred from the title is best; this takes extra time. (On

Information used / Intended exhaustivity	Descriptors assigned based on		
	Title	Abstract	Full text
Exhaustivity level 1	Library automation Data base mgmt. Company Library	Library automation Data base management Company Library	Library automation Data base management Company Library File integration Total company information systems Reading for L737 Reading for L690
Added in exhaustivity level 2	None	Circulation control Periodical routing control Research accounting	Same, and, *in addition* Chemistry Laboratory notebook control Internal report distribution
Added in exhaustivity level 3	None	On-line systems In-house computers	On-line systems In-house computers Network access Key control Book reservation Circulation statistics Mailing labels

(b) Sample document: Applications of System 2000 data base management software at Rohm and Haas Research Libraries.

Fig. 16.3   Amount of information and exhaustivity of indexing.

the other hand, assigning the first descriptor that comes to mind when reading the title is cheapest of all. The indexer satisfices rather than optimizes when selecting the one descriptor to be assigned.) Increasing exhaustivity beyond what can be seen from the title requires more time since the indexer must now read more.

Increasing intended specificity may increase or decrease indexing costs. As a rule, the sheer increase in the number of descriptors in the index language makes the indexer's work more difficult. Deciding between several specific descriptors may require more expertise and/or more time:

Radio wave propagation   easy to assign
   Atmospheric propagation
   Scatter propagation   require expertise
      Ionospheric propagation
      Tropospheric propagation

But it may also be the other way around; for example, it is easier to index nuclear reactors by giving the specific name or type than by giving their general characteristics. Consider the following examples:

Reactor Beta   =   Graphite moderated reactor :
                           Carbon dioxide cooled reactor
Reactor Karlsruhe   =   Zirconium hydride moderated reactor :
                           Sodium cooled reactor

The specific name of the reactor may well appear prominently in the document; the indexer not intimately familiar with reactor technology would need to make considerable effort to determine the appropriate general descriptors. However, for users, the more general descriptors may be easier to understand and/or more useful.

CHAPTER 17

Searching

OBJECTIVE

The objective of this chapter is to explain the basic concepts and procedures that apply to both manual and computerized searching, thus enabling the reader to plan and execute a search strategy for any request using the appropriate sources, whether manual or computerized.

INTRODUCTION

Searching for information or for entities such as technical parts, merchandise, museum objects, or computer programs is a special case of problem solving; systems analysis provides a good framework for analyzing the task. The basic functions of the search process are shown in Fig. 17.1; note the parallel with the captions on the left side of Fig. 6.1.

		7.	8.
1.	Recognize and state the need (define objectives).	I	M
2.	Develop the search strategy (design):	N	O
	a. formulate the query conceptually;	T	N
	b. select and sequence sources;	E	I
	c. translate the conceptual query formulation into the language of each source.	R	T
		A	O
3.	Execute the search strategy (system operation).	C	R
		T	
4.	Review search results (evaluation 1).		
		during	
5.	Edit search results (system operation).	the	
		entire	
6.	Check helpfulness of the results (evaluation 2).	search.	

Fig. 17.1 Functions in the search process.

Searching, like most problem solving, is not a linear process that proceeds neatly from one step to the next. User and searcher must *state the need* for entities or information at the start of the search, but must also bear this function in mind during the entire search process. As the need is expressed in the language of a source, points requiring clarification may emerge. The real need may surface only after the user has received the search results, which help him to think more about the problem. The searcher reviews search results primarily at the end of the search, but also throughout the search to keep it on track. Interaction with sources, monitoring the progress of the search, and assessing options at decision points are conducted during the entire search process. Thus, several functions occur and flow together at every phase in the search. However, as the search progresses, the emphasis shifts from one function to the next; in that sense the sequence of functions is a sequence of steps.

The searcher's actions are governed by her *image* of the search. This image covers

- the entire process of search;
- the problem or working situation giving rise to the need, or the purpose for which the information or entities are needed;
- the user and her background;
- subject knowledge about the topic of the search;
- the availability of information or entities in general and individual sources, their coverage and searchability.

The image starts out as a frame of mind—a set of questions—and is constantly updated during the search process by gathering information pertaining to the elements listed and fitting it into the framework. Some functions (e.g., recognizing the need) serve primarily to update the image; other functions (e.g., executing the search strategy) serve primarily to produce output, but also update the image (for instance, the searcher learns more about a source and its suitability for the topic at hand). A search request form is useful for collecting and organizing the most important parts of this information; see Fig. 17.2.

There will always be wide variation among users and their backgrounds; topics and their complexity; and the backgrounds, skills, and styles of reference librarians, information specialists, and searchers. Thus, the following discussion can provide only general guidelines that must be adapted to the individual situation.

The elaboration of the search process should be commensurate with the complexity of the need. For simple needs (ready reference questions such as What is the population of Chicago? What is the telephone number of Apple

Name _____

Reference request worksheet

1. Topic—Query statement

   Where can I find the official text of the Republican Party's official position on women's rights?

2. User's background: Official of a women's organization.

3. User's purpose: Is preparing a discussion for a meeting.

4. Subject area: Politics/Government

5. Answer form: Substantive data ☐ References/documents ☑

6. Search requirements (recall, precision, accuracy, etc.)

7. Criteria for ending the search:

   When text or reference to text is found.

8. Conceptual query formulation (for information needed, usually substantive data)

   LIST: *Text*

   SELECT:

   Text < is official statement of > (*Organization* Republican party < has stand on > *Topic* Issue women's rights)

9. Conceptual query formulations to search for

   (1) Sources of sources, (2) Bibliographies,
   (3) Handbook-type sources, (4) "Ordinary" documents

   (2) Political news AND Very timely

           A   B   C
   (4) Republican party AND Women's rights AND Contains text of official statement
   (Note: Perhaps search under A AND B or under B AND C or under A AND C.)

10. Comments

Fig. 17.2 A search request form.

Computer Inc.?), the entire search process can be collapsed into one or two minutes, so that many functions are performed only perfunctorily. On the other hand, complex needs (What information is needed to assess the dangers of chlorinated biphenyls? What is the market for selling electronic equipment to the Soviet Union? What laws and regulations govern such transactions?) require a systematic and elaborate search process, in which each function receives explicit attention.

We have incorporated in this chapter the search tactics analyzed by Bates; they are given in parentheses—e.g., (S5. PINPOINT). Refer to Bates's discussion for elaboration.

17.1 RECOGNIZE AND STATE THE NEED. STATE SEARCH REQUIREMENTS

Summary

1. *Recognize the existence of a need.* Pursue the identification of needs as an active function of the information system.
2. Develop a *query statement* that expresses the need accurately in natural language, considering the problem giving rise to the search, the entities or information needed to solve that problem, and the background of the user. This function includes the *presearch* and the *reference interview.*
3. *State specific requirements for the search,* for example, recall and precision, deadline, and cost.

17.1.1 RECOGNIZE THE EXISTENCE OF A NEED

An information system should take the initiative in recognizing needs. But how? In a hospital, studying the records of each newly admitted patient indicates what information might be useful to the physician treating that patient; checking the records of old patients periodically for unusual developments uncovers additional information requirements. In a regulatory agency, keeping abreast of plans for new regulations or for modifying old ones shows information needs. In a company, keeping abreast of plans—such as the introduction of new products, the exploration of foreign markets, or the acquisition of another company—points to the information needed to arrive at good decisions.

Other needs are made known to the system by *users submitting search requests.* Short requests can be answered right away (some organizations have an express information desk). Sometimes a short or very short search request is only the tip of the iceberg, and a little probing will reveal a much larger need. The true information professional will spot this situation. Consider the following case: An elderly man calls an information and referral center. He says his faucet is dripping and asks for the name of a plumber who would come after hours to fix it. The information worker senses a tone of helplessness and despair in the voice of the caller and engages him in a conversation. It turns out that his wife is bedridden. He is looking after her, but he is no longer able to provide proper care, particularly since he has heart trouble. He really needs to know how he can find someone to help take care of his wife at a cost he can afford.

For long search requests, a search request form is helpful; it serves as a reminder to collect all essential items of information about the request from the user or other sources. Where appropriate, the user should submit or at least verify a written statement of the need; this forces the user to think through his problem and explicitly state what information or entities he needs.

If the user is either unable to articulate his need or is not in a state to talk about his real need before some rapport with the information specialist or reference librarian is established, a reference interview is in order at the start of the search.

Whatever the environment, it is not safe to assume that a user's demand for information or entities always corresponds to the true need. One of the searcher's foremost professional responsibilities is to contribute independent judgment and join with the user in an analysis of the problem and the needs arising from it.

The searcher cannot make this independent contribution without knowing about the problem at hand, the purpose for which the information or entities are sought. In a company or government agency the user should be prepared to reveal his purpose; it is, after all, not private business but the business of the organization. In a public library, asking the user for his purpose is a touchy issue; however, the user who does not reveal his purpose must be satisfied with less useful service.

17.1.2 DEVELOP THE QUERY STATEMENT

The basis for a good search is a clear statement of the need—the query statement—in the form of a phrase, sentence, or paragraph. To develop such a statement and for the further steps of the search, the searcher needs three kinds of knowledge:

- Knowledge of the purpose of the search, the problem, or working situation from which the need arises;
- Knowledge of the user's background: Does the user already have part of the information or entities needed? What is the general background of the user for assimilating new information or using new entities?
- Subject knowledge about the topic of the search.

With this knowledge the searcher can diagnose the need in a way that is independent of and complementary to the user's request. The searcher may have some of this knowledge already in her general background or from the search request form; she must acquire the rest either through the *reference interview* and/or, as a time saver to the user, from other sources through a *presearch*.

Information about the background of the user and the purpose of the search can be acquired from the organization's *information directory:* data about the user's education and career, a job description, a list of publications, a list of projects the user is working on, the user's interest profile for SDI, a list of previous searches done for this user, a description of the project or administrative function (if any) to which the request is related, and a description of the organizational unit of which the user is a member. Even if this information is not brought together in one place in an information directory, it can be collected from the records of the organization.

Printed sources are helpful for acquiring subject background: a brief article in a handbook such as a physician's desk reference or an encyclopedia, a review article in a journal, or references provided by the user. Background references can be obtained from the user when she submits the request or from a quick on-line or manual search.

The knowledge gained in the presearch leads to a much deeper understanding of the problem lying behind the need and, therefore, of the need itself. The searcher may detect areas of information or entities useful for solving the problem that escaped the user, who is not as familiar with the information or entities available. Thus, the statement of the need may be broadened. The knowledge gained through the presearch serves to

- prepare for the reference interview, if one is needed;
- find concepts and terms for the query formulation;
- judge the relevance of entities found, both during the search (thus improving the ability to adapt the search strategy) and in reviewing and editing search results.

A *reference interview* is often needed in order to

- further clarify the need and the role that the various items of information or entities requested play in the solution of the problem at hand;
- inform the user of sources, search possibilities and trade-offs, and related services important to the search.

At its best, the reference interview is a joint problem-solving session between the user and the information specialist. The user contributes knowledge of the problem and the information specialist contributes knowledge of sources, coupled with an understanding of the problem and general problem-solving methodology.

Well-directed questions can help the user clarify the definition of the problem and think of all types of information or entities that might be useful in solving the problem. (Section 17.2 suggests points to be addressed.) Make the user aware of useful information or entities that he did not mention or think of. The user may be unfamiliar with sources and thus not even aware of the possibility of getting this information or these entities at a reasonable cost. In this process a request for a specific entity (e.g., a specific document, a specific computer program) may be recognized as a request for substantive data "in disguise." It may well turn out that the entity requested is not the most useful one. In an information and referral center or a public library the information specialist must often establish a climate of mutual rapport and trust before the requester is able to talk about his or her real problem.

The reference interview may also deal with such matters as: What sources should be searched? What are the characteristics of each source, its pros and cons with respect to the search at hand? Should the search be limited to a specific collection (of a library, of a museum, of a catalog store)? What should the conceptual query formulation be? What terms should be used for free-text searching? Can the user really afford to restrict the search to English language material? Should he or she see English abstracts of materials in foreign languages to select those for which translations should be requested. (The user may not be aware of the possibility of obtaining translations.) Finally, the reference interview should address specific search requirements.

Holding the reference interview after the presearch has the advantage that the searcher can ask more pertinent questions, understand the user's answers better, and make more suggestions to the user.

Having done the presearch, the reference interview, or both, the searcher should have a clear image of the need; searcher and user must develop a common frame of reference by which to judge the relevance of the entities found. This common frame of reference should be succinctly expressed in the query statement.

Often the search can proceed to the next steps or even to the end without a reference interview. The reference interview may be fruitful at some later stage in the search—particularly when some initial search results are in hand. In complex searches, the searcher may need to consult with the user repeatedly during the search. Some users like to be present during the search; they can then evaluate search results immediately, and the search can be modified right away, if necessary.

17.1.3 DETERMINE SPECIFIC SEARCH REQUIREMENTS

User and searcher should agree on the requirements for the end product of the search. These include recall (based on all entities available anywhere), precision, uniqueness (avoidance of duplicate entities when searching multiple sources), avoidance of redundancy among documents found, novelty of retrieved entities for the user, validity, numerical precision (if applicable), and accuracy. (See Section 17.4 for a more detailed discussion.) User and searcher must also agree on a deadline and the cost.

The intended use of the search results and the value of the user's time are important in determining requirements. The searcher should consider the trade-offs between the elements listed and make the user aware of them: Low search effort (i.e., cost) or a close deadline (and especially a combination of the two) detract from search quality. If search costs and time frame are held constant, increase in recall must often be paid for by a more or less substantial decrease in precision.

17.2 DEVELOP THE SEARCH STRATEGY

Summary

The search strategy is a plan for the whole search. It consists of three components.

1. *Formulate the query conceptually.* The answer to a query is a mini data base whose structure is defined in the free-form query statement. The conceptual query formulation defines that structure explicitly in a rigorous format by giving the types of entities and relationships involved and the selection criteria for the entities and relationships to be included.
The conceptual query formulation serves two purposes:
a. selection of sources (a retrieval problem in itself);
b. search for information or entities in each source.

Often various types of information or entities are needed to solve the problem at hand, or the search is otherwise complex. This calls for breaking down the topic into subtopics and treating each subtopic separately. (F2. SELECT).

2. *Select sources and arrange them in a search sequence.*
3. *Translate the conceptual query formulation into the language of each source.* Sometimes the meaning of the query can only be approximated in the language of the source. While making the necessary compromises, it may be helpful to consult not only the conceptual query formulation but also the query statement.

In a systematic approach for each component the searcher generates possible solutions and then selects the best of these; in a word, he considers alternatives. (F3. SURVEY)

17.2.1 FORMULATE THE QUERY CONCEPTUALLY

The input to this operation is the query statement—a phrase, sentence, or paragraph that is a free-form description of the mini data base sought. The output of this operation is the conceptual query formulation, which describes the structure of the mini data base sought explicitly in a rigorous format. Often several conceptual query formulations are needed, corresponding to sections of the output or to subsearches.

Formulating the query conceptually is at the heart of searching and warrants extensive discussion. The discussion starts with the form of the conceptual query formulation—describing a general and a simplified format—and then proceeds to methods for structuring the search topic: facet analysis, sectioning search output, subsearches that piece together the answer, and chained subsearches where the information found in one step serves as the basis for selecting descriptors in the next step.

Searching for Substantive Data: General Format

The mini data base sought is defined by the entities and relationships included. These, in turn, are defined by their type (e.g., *Person, Library*) and by the criteria used to select from the type. Examples for query formulations in the general format are given in Figure 17.3; each query formulation consists of two components:

SELECT: Specification of *criteria for selecting* entities and relationships from the data base.

LIST: Specification of the *output format* for arranging the entities and relationships included in the answer.

Entity types are in italics; relationships are enclosed in < >.

Query Statement	Query formulation
Who is the instructor of course offering 3?	SELECT: *Course offering* COF3 < has instructor > *Person.* LIST: *Person.* Find all persons for which the SELECT statement becomes a true relationship (as stored in the data base). RESULT: Instructors of COF3: B. Simms, M. Zog
For FDST663 give title, subject, and prerequisite	SELECT: *Course* < is > FDST663; *Course* selected < has > *Title;* *Course* selected < deals with > *Subject;* *Course* selected < has prerequisite > *Course.* LIST: *Course; Title; Subject; Course.* RESULT:

Course no.	Title	Subject	Prerequisite
FDST 663	Seminar in meat canning	C6	FDST101

List libraries that have the 1968 volume of *Daedalus;* give their distance from Denver, CO.	SELECT: *Library* < has holdings of >
	    (*Journal* Daedalus < published in > *Date* 1968);
	Library selected < is located in > *Place-1;*
	Length-number < is distance of >
	    (*Place-1* selected, *Place-2* Denver, CO);
	Library selected < has > *Address.*
	
	LIST: *Library; Address; Length-number.*
	
	Comment: ( ) signifies a complex entity made up of elemental entities joined by a relationship.

I am interested in the production of copper. I need to know the countries producing more than 100,000 tons per year, and the trade balance of these countries.	SELECT: (*Country* < produces > *Material* Copper)
	    < amount is >
	    Weight-number which is greater than 100,000 tons;
	Money-number < is balance of trade of > *Country* selected.
	
	LIST: *Country; Weight-number; Money-number.*
	                                         (*continued*)

Query Statement	Query Formulation

List all students who received a grade of A in a course below the 600 level. For each student give the course number and the semester taken.

SELECT: *Course* < has course-no > between FDST000 and FDST599;
Course offering < is offering of > *Course* selected.
(*Course offering* selected < has student > *Person*) < assigned is > *Grade* A;
Semester < is time of > *Course offering* selected

LIST: *Person* (heading Student); *Course; Semester.*

RESULT: Students with grade A in course below 600 level

Student	Course	Semester
J. Doe	FDST257	1979Sp
R. Jones	FDST101	1979Sp
R. Jones	FDST257	1979F
A. Kim	FDST101	1979F
L. Tarr	FDST101	1979Sp

List all persons who are male and have a salary above $30,000. Give name, birth-date, residence, employer, and the building where he works.

(Compare Fig. 17.4, simplified format, first example.)

SELECT: *Person* [< has property > *Sex* Male AND < has salary > *Money-number* > 30,000];
Person selected < was born on > *Date;*
Person selected < lives in > *Building-1;*
Person selected < is employed by > *Organization;*
Person selected < works in > *Building-2.*

LIST: *Person; Date; Building-1; Organization; Building-2.*

Fig. 17.3   Query formulation for substantive data, general format.

Searching for Substantive Data: Simplified Format

Often the information sought has a simpler structure: The query asks for a list of focal entities (e.g., *Persons*) for which relationships to other entities are sought (e.g., *Person* selected < has property > *Rank, Person* selected < is instructor of > *Course offering, Person* selected < is author of > *Document*). Each combination of a relationship with an entity, such as < has property > *Rank,* constitutes an attribute (data element) of the focal entity, in the example *Person.* Criteria for the selection of focal entities can be expressed in terms of attributes of the focal entity combined through AND, OR, and (with caution) NOT; these criteria are specified in the SELECT clause. The information wanted for each focal entity can be expressed in terms of attributes (data elements) which, starting from a focal entity, select further entities from the data base; in the simplified format, specification of data elements is incorporated into the LIST clause. The resulting format is il-

FOR: *Person*

SELECT: < has property > *Sex* Male AND < has salary > *Money-number* > 30,000.

LIST: *Name;* < was born on > *Date;* < lives in > *Building;* < is employed by > *Organization;* < works in > *Building.*

           (Compare Figure 17.3, general format, last example)

FOR: *Technical component*

SELECT: < belongs to > *Product class* Silicone chip AND < use is > *Function* Memory AND < used in > *Technical product* Microcomputer AND < has property > *Error rate* Low.

LIST: *Technical data; Price; Production; Sales.*

FOR: *Chemical substance*

SELECT: < constituent is > *Chemical substance* Chlorine AND < use is > *Function* Food additive

LIST: *Chemical structure; Toxicity data; Economic data*

The last two examples use a less formal specification of the data elements, e.g., *Price* rather than < price is > *Money-number.*

Fig. 17.4   Query formulation for substantive data, simplified format.

lustrated through the query formulations in Fig. 17.4. In this case the term *query formulation* is often used to refer to the SELECT clause alone. In some experimental computerized ISAR systems, the query is expressed simply as a set of terms (no AND and OR), often extracted from the query statement, and the relevance of an entity is computed as a function of the number of terms in common between query formulation and entity representation, usually resulting in a value between 0 and 1; this *relevance coefficient* can be used to rank entities by expected relevance, listing the most relevant entities first.

Facet Analysis

Consider the query statement in Fig. 17.5. It deals with one focal entity type—*Food product.* The food products to be retrieved must meet the requirements stated. In this situation a *facet frame* is often useful. A facet frame is a series of questions, each asking the searcher to describe what is sought from a particular point of view. In answer to each question, the searcher fills in the appropriate descriptor(s)—that is, identifiers of entities (often concepts) related to the entity sought. When all the questions are answered, ANDing the concepts from all applicable facets yields the basic pattern of the SELECT clause. The next step is elaborating each component. The searcher looks for broader and narrower concepts (T1. SUPER and T2.

Query statement

　　Canned green beans with high salt content.

Facet frame

What type of product is it?	Vegetable product
What food source?	Beans
What part used?	Pod with immature seeds
In what form?	Any value acceptable
What degree of preparation?	Cooked
Any special treatments?	Salt added
What preservation method?	Sterilized by heat
What packing medium?	Water
What container?	Metal can OR Glass jar OR Plastic pouch
What food contact surface?	Any value acceptable
What user group?	Any value acceptable

Fig. 17.5　Query formulation using a facet frame.

SUB). The searcher also looks for related concepts to broaden the main concept by ORing it with related concepts, if necessary (S4. PARALLEL; the opposite is S5. PINPOINT).

Any well-structured vocabulary giving hierarchical relationships through arrangement or cross-references is useful in this step. Related concepts can be identified by looking for neighboring concepts in a hierarchy, following Related Term cross-references (T3. RELATE), or, as a last resort, looking for neighboring terms in an alphabetical list (T4. NEIGHBOR). Related concepts include logically opposite concepts, such as *Hot–Cold* (T9. CONTRARY). The basic query formulation can now be broadened by substitution (broaden one or more components) or by "decombination" (omit one or more components, S3. REDUCE); or the formulation can be narrowed by opposite moves (see Chapter 14). This approach can be incorporated into on-line assistance to the user (see Section 17.7).

The considerations on broadening by ORing related concepts (or narrowing by omitting them) apply equally to ORing synonyms and quasi-synonyms when developing the source-specific query formulation for free-text searching (see Section 17.2.4).

This exploration of the query formulation prepares for interaction with the system in an on-line or manual search.

Sectioning the Answer

Long answers (anything exceeding two pages) should be divided into sections by subject (e.g., *Canned green beans, baby food* vs. *Canned green beans, regular; Human* vs. *Animal studies*), by relevance (the section with the most relevant items first), by date, by language, or by any other useful criterion.

Subsearches

Often a search becomes more tractable when it is broken down into a number of subsearches, a technique well known from general problem solving. There are two types of subsearches: (1) The problem at hand requires information or entities of several kinds (e.g., text, pictures, numerical data) or on several topics (especially for drawing inferences). (2) One subsearch finds descriptors needed for the next subsearch (chaining subsearches).

It is helpful to treat subsearches separately but in parallel; there is interaction between the subsearches, and often the same source must be used for more than one subsearch.

Subsearches to Find Pieces

Often the information or entity needed is not available as one piece, but it is possible to find individual pieces that *in combination* solve the user's problem. For example, a technical part needed for a certain purpose may not be available, but a clever search uncovers several components that can be put together to make the part. Or when the answer to the user's question cannot be found directly, effort can be directed toward finding pieces of information from which the answer can be deduced by *inference*.

Consider a bibliographic search on the topic:

The effect of mercury in seawater on human health.

The most obvious query formulation is

Mercury AND Seawater AND Human health.

It may find some relevant references, but the user has no assurance that the references found give all the substantive data that can be gathered from available documents. A more thorough analysis shows that the following types of information *in combination* allow the user to make assessments with respect to the problem:

Mercury levels in seawater	—Mercury AND Seawater
Mercury absorption in seafood	—Mercury AND Seafood
Seafood consumption	—Consumption AND Seafood
The effect of mercury intake on human health	—Mercury AND Human health

An even more thorough approach would consider other sources of mercury in the diet as well, since the health risk is determined by the total mercury intake.

As another example consider this problem:

> The user has lots of chemical A and needs a cheap method to produce chemical F from it.

Produces

A————————▶F   Formulation: A AND F

Perhaps there is no direct method, or the direct method is expensive. The user should consider indirect methods:

A → C → F   Step 1:   A AND C
                         Step 2:   C AND F

C, D, and E may be other candidates for intermediate chemicals. D may lead to F via D1. Graphically it would look like this:

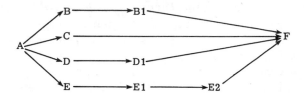

This example illustrates the context-dependence of relevance. If the system can provide a piece of information for each link in a chain from A to F, then all these pieces are relevant, because *in combination* they provide the information needed to convert chemical A to chemical F. If the user knows, say, E1→E2, and the system provides information on A→E, E→E1, and E2→F, then all these pieces are relevant as well because they complete the user's image so that he or she can solve the problem.

The principle illustrated in these examples is extremely important in the retrieval of information or entities for problem solving. The searcher should always analyze the query statement to detect pieces of information that can serve as premises from which the user can draw inferences and arrive at conclusions with respect to the problem. This approach can be very helpful in the reference interview; it can be a stimulus for the user to think more systematically about the problem and the types of information or entities needed for its solution.

Chaining Subsearches

The University Data Base allows for a query formulation that finds and lists all authors of textbooks used in FDST courses. The retrieval process for this query is a multistep chain: The system finds first all FDST courses, then their course offerings, next the textbooks used in these course offerings, and finally the authors of these textbooks. The entities found in one step serve as descriptors in the next step. In a data base developed from scratch, proper design of the conceptual schema assures that the steps in such a chain can be conveniently specified in the query formulation or, even better, derived by the system. But more often than not a search must do with existing data bases, and one data base may not have all the data needed for the chained search. For instance, a search for the *Sales of microcomputer companies* may need to employ one source to identify all *Microcomputer companies,* then use their names as access points in a second source to obtain the data. Or, a search for literature on the *Toxicity* of *Chlorinated biphenyls,* a class of industrial chemicals that pollute the environment, starts with an information system for chemical substances, such as the Chemical Abstract Service Registry, using a query formulation that specifies the chemical characteristics of *Chlorinated biphenyls.* The result is a list of chemical substances with their identifiers, CAS Registry numbers. Some CAS numbers in the list are:

001336363   OR   011104282   OR   011141165   OR   053469219

Since these numbers are also used in indexing documents, simply ORing the CAS numbers expresses the chemicals component of the query. There are search services that have both the CAS Registry system and bibliographic data bases, allowing for a direct transfer of the results of step one, searching for chemicals, into the query formulation for step two, searching for documents. A microcomputer used as an intelligent terminal to access search systems permits searching the CAS registry in one search system, storing the results (CAS numbers), and incorporating these results in the query formulation for a search in another data base—for example, Chemical Abstracts or the Registry of Toxic Effects—on another search system. Formulating the query conceptually and selecting sources are closely intertwined in this process.

These examples illustrate a general principle: All available information sources can be seen as one giant data base, even though they have been produced independently from each other. Each source provides (1) relationships between entities and (2) modes of access, which can be used in combination for chained searches (F6. SCAFFOLD).

17.2.2 Select Sources and Arrange Them
in a Search Sequence

If there were one giant integrated data base encompassing all entities and all information available anywhere, it would permit one-layer searches. A search would use a query formulation specifying the entities or information needed (the *primary query formulation*). But there is no such data base. Thus a secondary search must first locate a data base, a source likely to contain the entities or information needed: a handbook or a machine-readable data base containing substantive data, a specific document, a museum or a specific collection in a museum, or a store or a catalog store. Once such a source is found, the primary search uses the primary query formulation to search in that source for the entities or information needed. But finding such a source is a retrieval problem in itself; it requires a secondary search in a source of sources. This secondary search requires a secondary query formulation that specifies not the entities or information needed but rather a source in which the entities or information can be found. The search has two layers.

A source can be very general, such as an encyclopedia or handbook, requiring an explicit search to pick out just the information or entities needed, or it can be very specific, such as a journal article, and contain just the information needed and not much more, thus obviating the need for an elaborate primary search. A document may even be more specific than the query, giving only part of the information needed. To search for specific documents, one may consult a bibliography found in a source of sources—a three-layer search. Thus, a search often consists of two or more layers: a secondary search to find a source followed by the primary search in the source. The secondary search can be broad, finding a general source and leaving much work for the primary search. Or the secondary search can be very narrow, finding a very specific source and leaving little or no work for the primary search. The entire search process consists of a series of searches, each of which brings the searcher closer to the information or entities needed (Fig. 17.6). The process can be very short: from memory directly to the information or entities needed. Or it can be very long: from memory to a source of sources, to a more specific source of sources, to a bibliography, to a list of documents, and finally to the information or entities needed. The process may not be completely successful. The final sources arrived at may not have all the information or entities needed or a bibliography may not yield enough relevant documents. This would necessitate starting over at an earlier point.

Figure 17.6 shows many options. A searcher may have a preferred pattern (e.g., select a bibliographic source from memory and give the user a list of documents as answer) and, as a rule, may not consider other possibilities. If

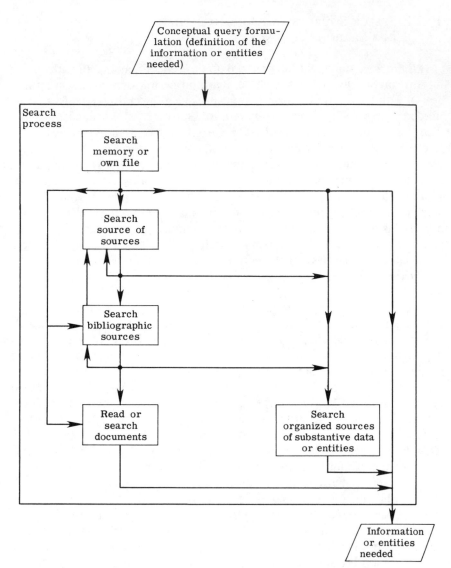

Fig. 17.6 Layers of the search process.

the pattern coincides with the requirements of the request, time is saved; but there is a danger of applying a pattern to searches for which it is not suitable.

A secondary search requires itself a (secondary) query formulation that derives from the primary query formulation (i.e., the conceptual query formulation for the information or entities needed as shown in Fig. 17.4). The source must cover the entities specified through SELECT and give the data specified by LIST for these entities. The following is an example of a specific secondary query formulation:

FOR: *Document*
SELECT: < deals with > *Concept* [Silicon chips AND Memory AND Microcomputer AND (Economic data OR Technical data)]
LIST: *Title;* < authored by> *Person;* <published in> *Journal*

This specific secondary query formulation looks for documents coextensive with the need. As can be seen, any entity or entity-relationship combination occurring in SELECT or LIST of the primary query formulation is a candidate for inclusion in the SELECT clause of the secondary query formulation. Since there may be no documents that give both *Economic data* and *Technical data,* we settle for one of these in selecting documents (OR) and piece the answer together from several documents. The documents found yield the substantive data needed with no or minimal search. A search for a handbook-type source (an organized source of substantive data) requires a much broader secondary query:

FOR: *Document*
SELECT: < belongs to> *Document class* Handbook-type AND < deals with> *Concept* [Electronic component AND (Economic data OR Technical data)] AND
           < provides access by> *Concept* (Memory AND Microcomputer)
LIST: *Title; Call number.*

A search in the handbook-type source with the primary query formulation yields the specific substantive data needed.

A tertiary search for a source of sources requires a still broader query formulation:

FOR: *Document*
SELECT: < belongs to> *Document class* Source of sources AND
           < deals with> *Concept* Technology AND
           < covers> *Document class* Handbook-type
LIST: *Title; Call number.*

A secondary search in the source of sources found then yields a handbook-type source, and a primary search in the handbook-type source yields the substantive data needed.

Another example of a query formulation for a specific document is:

FOR: *Document*
SELECT: < deals with > *Concept* [(Chlorinated OR CASNO
           001336363 OR CASNO 011104282 OR etc.) AND
           Food additive AND (Structure OR Toxicity OR
           Economic data)].
LIST: *Title;* < deals with > *Concept.*

17.2.3 TRANSLATE THE CONCEPTUAL QUERY FORMULATION INTO THE LANGUAGE OF EACH SOURCE

This process starts from the conceptual query formulation and expresses each of its components in the language of the source; the result is a source-specific query formulation for each source. This step is needed for every layer of the search—for example, for searching in a source of sources to find a handbook and then again for searching in the handbook.

The language of the source consists of identifiers of entities and relationships and a syntax that allows tying these identifiers together into a description of the mini data base defined in the conceptual query formulation. Such a query formulation can be quite complex (see the examples in Fig. 17.3). But the simplified format can be used whenever the search deals with a focal entity type (document, person, organization, food product) and the search requirements are given as data element values that a relevant entity must possess (see Fig. 17.4).

This section concentrates on simple query formulations. The general principles are the same for all types of descriptors, but subject searches are most difficult. Therefore, this section concentrates on finding appropriate subject descriptors. The subject descriptors used in a source make up its index language. The primary focus of this section, then, is translating the conceptual query formulation into the index language of the source.

In many respects this task is easiest in a source and search system that

- uses a controlled vocabulary in which all descriptors needed for the search are available;
- uses only elemental descriptors and allows searching for descriptor combinations;
- arranges the descriptors in a polyhierarchy showing all hierarchical relationships useful for searching;

- allows for inclusive searching such that *all* narrower descriptors are considered in the search;
- has sufficient exhaustivity of indexing so that most relevant documents have at least one descriptor for each conceptual component of the query formulation.

With such a source, translation of the conceptual query formulation is simple: Each search concept is translated into the appropriate descriptor. (S2. EXHAUST) (Sometimes an OR-combination of descriptors is needed, such as Dewey class 372 *Elementary education* OR 373 *Secondary education* when searching for *Schools* as opposed to *Universities and colleges*.)

Whenever one of these conditions is violated, complications arise. The following subsections deal with these complications.

The Source Does Not Use a Controlled Vocabulary

Searching without a controlled vocabulary is called free-text searching. It works fine for a quick and superficial search, where the only requirement is that a few relevant references be found. One can just use a few terms that come to mind without even consulting a thesaurus. This may be convenient for users doing their own searches, as long as they are aware that they run the danger of low recall. But for high recall searches, the searcher must look for many synonyms and is moreover confronted with all the difficulties discussed under the next three headings unless exceptional search assistance is provided. A full discussion is given in Section 17.2.4 when the reader can appreciate the issues better.

The Index Language Contains Precombined Descriptors

A precombined descriptor, such as *Eye neoplasms,* causes no problems as long as it appears as a narrower term under *both Eye* and *Neoplasms* and if these hierarchical relationships are used in inclusive searching. But for many sources the index language structure is not complete, causing problems in retrieval. For example, in MEDLINE *Eye neoplasms* appears as a narrower term under *Neoplasms* but not under *Eye.* Thus, a search for *Eye, inclusive* (alone or in combination with something else) retrieves documents on *Cornea, Retina, Eyelids,* etc., but it does not retrieve documents on the strength of their being indexed by *Eye neoplasms, Conjunctivitis, Glaucoma,* or many other precombined descriptors containing the component *Eye.* All these precombined descriptors must be ORed with *Eye, inclusive* to find everything having to do with *Eye.* The searcher not intimately familiar with MEDLINE might assume that the combination

Eye, inclusive AND Neoplasms, inclusive

retrieves all documents on *Eye neoplasms.* But this is not so: Due to the defect in the hierarchical structure, documents indexed by *Eye neoplasms* are missed by *Eye, inclusive,* and therefore by this query, unless they are also indexed by *Eye* or a narrower descriptor.

This point is so important that a further example is in order. Consider a search in the Predicasts data base for the topic *Use of plastic in motor vehicles.* The conceptual query formulation is

Plastic AND Motor vehicles.

Predicasts uses the Standard Industrial Classification Product Code as the index language. It contains two descriptors for the plastic component, namely,

2821 Plastic materials and 307 Plastic products

and one descriptor for *Motor vehicles,* namely,

371 Motor vehicles and parts.

Inclusive searching is provided: The code 2821 retrieves any items indexed by specific plastic materials, such as 28214 *Polyolefin resins,* 282141 *Polyethylene.* The same is true for 307 and 371. Thus, one might assume that the query formulation

(2821 OR 307) AND 371

finds all relevant items; indeed, if the system structure were completely logical, it would. However, there is also a precombined descriptor

307521 Plastic motor vehicle parts

This precombined descriptor is shown as a narrower term for 307 *Plastic products* but *not* as a narrower term for 371 *Motor vehicles and parts.* Nor are documents or statistical tables indexed by 307521 *Plastic motor vehicle parts* routinely indexed by 371 *Motor vehicle parts.* Due to these shortcomings in the index language, the query formulation developed so far would miss many important items. The following formulation compensates for the deficiencies in the index language

((2821 OR 307) AND 371) OR 307521.

Note that 307521 alone would not do since the data base contains many documents and statistical tables that deal with the amount of plastic used in automobile production but not with specific parts.

If there are many highly precombined descriptors, locating them in the index language listing and/or in an index or catalog to the collection becomes difficult, making the task of the searcher even harder, unless a descriptor-find index is provided.

Not All Useful Hierarchical Relationships Are Shown

The searcher must double her efforts to find all applicable descriptors. Hierarchical relationships that involve precombined descriptors are often missing, as we have just discussed.

Inclusive Searching Is Not Provided

In such a system an inclusive search for a broad term, such as *Vegetables,* requires an OR-combination of many descriptors, for example:

Vegetable OR Pod vegetable OR Beans OR Peas OR Head vegetable OR . . .

Indexing Exhaustivity Is Low

With low exhaustivity, entities are not indexed by descriptors that might be considered marginal; therefore, many relevant entities do not have a descriptor for each conceptual component and will thus be missed by the complete query formulation. The searcher should try partial combinations, omitting components that are less likely to appear in indexing (S3. REDUCE; the opposite is S2. EXHAUST). Consider the full formulation:

Students AND Attitudes AND Defense AND Expenditures AND Survey AND U.S.

The following partial combinations are worth trying:

Students AND Defense (AND Expenditures)
Attitudes AND Defense (AND Expenditures)

Sometimes concepts are implied by the source and can be omitted from the source-specific query formulation to increase recall without substantial loss in precision. For example, when searching *Engineering Index* for *Aircraft* AND *Wing,* the *Aircraft* component is implied since *Birds* are not covered. When searching ERIC for *Education* AND *Testing,* the *Education* component is implied. When searching *Electronics Abstracts* for *Electronic parts* AND *Testing,* the *Electronic parts* component is implied.

17.2.4 FREE-TEXT SEARCHING

Many machine-readable (and some printed) sources allow for free-text searching—that is, searching on words in titles and possibly abstracts (some even in full text). All words (except stop-words such as *and, or, of*) are used as descriptors. The terms *free vocabulary, uncontrolled vocabulary, free language,* and *natural language* are also used. Some sources rely exclusively on free-text searching; others offer a controlled vocabulary as well. In sources where the entities are not documents (e.g., a data base with patient data), free-text searching refers to searching descriptions written in unrestricted natural language, such as physician's notes, as opposed to searching with a controlled vocabulary of symptoms and diseases. Sometimes indexers assign free terms that can then be searched.

Free-text searching has both problems and opportunities. The problems were discussed in Chapter 13: There is no request-oriented indexing; topics that can be inferred from context but are not represented by a word or phrase in the text are not accessible. If recall is important, the searcher must think of all possible ways a concept may be expressed. The opportunities relate to the specificity of the descriptors, speed of updating the index language, and exhaustivity of indexing. We shall now discuss these problems and opportunities in detail.

To develop a good free-text query formulation for a moderate or high recall search, the searcher must do the following:

- Consider each concept in the conceptual query formulation and develop a list of all its narrower concepts.
- Consider each concept in this expanded concept list and find all the terms designating the concept. Furthermore, the searcher must find all terms designating concept combinations; these are, in effect, precombined descriptors in the uncontrolled vocabulary. Since there is no control, both the combination of elemental descriptors (e.g., *Medical* AND *Personnel*) and the precombined descriptors (e.g., *Physician*) are used side by side.
- Find morphological variants, which usually are closely related in meaning, for example, *Toxic, Toxicity, Toxicology,* and *Hypertoxic* (T7. FIX).
- Find all spelling variants of each term, including also such forms as *Online, On-line,* and *On line* and common misspellings. (With an unsophisticated retrieval program that recognizes only exact matches, misspellings in the data base may lead to substantial recall failures if they are not counteracted in searching!) (T10. RESPELL, T11. RESPACE)
- Find all possible word orders for phrases (e.g., *Information retrieval* and *Retrieval of information* or *Retrieval of legal information*) (T8. REARRANGE).

Truncation can save considerable work in enumerating individual terms. A root such as *:toxic:* finds records containing the term *Toxic, Toxicity, Toxicology,* or *Hypertoxic.* Thus, truncation allows for inclusive searching, but only insofar as conceptual structure is reflected in language structure. The root *:toxic:* does *not* find records that have the term *Poisonous* in them. Systems based on searching inverted files generally allow for right truncation but *not* left truncation. So *Hypertoxic* would not be retrieved by the stem *Toxic:*. All of the techniques described are cumbersome in manual systems; doing a high-recall search in a KWIC index based on titles is next to impossible.

On the other hand, free-text searching has advantages. As discussed earlier, quick and superficial searches are easier. Furthermore, when a controlled vocabulary does not contain a descriptor for a search concept, a free term may come in handy; for example, there may be no descriptor for *World model.* The absence of a suitable descriptor may have many reasons. It may simply be lack of anticipation by the index language designer; this sometimes happens with general concepts. The controlled vocabulary may have limited specificity so that it lacks appropriate descriptors for very specific searches. Many controlled vocabularies are not updated quickly enough to reflect new developments, making searches for new topics difficult. Terms for new concepts tend to appear more quickly in the literature than in a controlled vocabulary, but there is some delay also (a new concept is often discussed before a term for the concept gains currency). Also the indexing provided by abstracts, not to speak of full text, is often more exhaustive than controlled vocabulary indexing as practiced in many systems (even though concepts brought out only through request-oriented indexing are missing). Bringing controlled vocabulary indexing on a par with free-text in these areas may cost too much. Thus, free-text searching is often useful even if a controlled vocabulary is available. Combining both approaches is often the best way to search. But the searcher should keep in mind that the indexing provided by authors and abstractors is not request-oriented and may be highly inconsistent.

A good source relying on free-text searching should provide an extensive thesaurus to aid the searcher in finding all appropriate terms. Ironically, it is often claimed as a major advantage of using an uncontrolled vocabulary that a thesaurus is not needed, and such support for the searcher is the rare exception. Lacking such support, the searcher must look for his own sources of terms, such as thesauri from other systems, dictionaries, textbooks, and known relevant documents.

17.2.5 THE INTERPLAY BETWEEN CONCEPTUAL AND SOURCE-SPECIFIC QUERY FORMULATION

The conceptual query formulation should be developed without the encumbrance of any given index language and its limitations; otherwise, it may be skewed from what the user needs to what can be easily found in the source. This does not preclude using a well-done display of the conceptual structure of a field to assist in developing the conceptual formulation and even in arriving at a more precise statement of the need. (See Section 13.3.) Any good index language may provide such a structure.

Sometimes it is difficult to express the search topic accurately and straightforwardly in the index language. Particularly in free-text searching the subject might be expressed in a variety of ways. The searcher must think through these various ways and consider indirect approaches, compromises, and trade-offs between the complexity of the query formulation and search performance. For example, in a search for methods for detecting small amounts of chemical substances, the journal title *Mikrochimica Acta* might be a useful descriptor along with the subject descriptor *Trace*. A more complex formulation takes more time to develop and also requires more searcher and computer time in search execution. In the process of deriving a source-specific query formulation, ambiguities in the conceptual query formulation may come to light, so that the searcher must go back to the query statement. Often interaction is needed to arrive at a good source-specific query formulation.

17.3 EXECUTE THE SEARCH STRATEGY

This step requires knowledge of the data structure and search mechanisms of the sources to be searched. But this is not a merely mechanical task. Interaction with both the sources and the user may lead to modifications, not only in the query formulation but also in the statement of the need. All search steps and results should be well documented.

It is important to know when to stop part of the search, such as searching for sources or searching in a particular source, and when to stop the search as a whole. The following criteria are useful:

- *Success so far.* In a search for a specific piece of information or entity, the searcher asks if the needed piece of information or entity was found and if there is assurance that it is correct. In an open-ended search, the searcher determines if enough material was found. (See Section 17.4 for a fuller discussion of search evaluation.)

- *Avenues not yet pursued.* If there are none, the search ends even if it has not been successful.
- *Costs.* Are the returns of additional effort diminishing? Are the resources allocated to this search or this search run exhausted? (See Section 8.5.2 for a more detailed discussion.)
- *Deadline.*

17.4 REVIEW SEARCH RESULTS AND REVISE SEARCH

In this step the searcher interacts both with the sources and with the user. The statement of the need is often modified during that interaction.

The following criteria are useful in reviewing search results:

- *Precision.* Are the retrieved entities (organizations, documents, factual statements, numbers, etc.) really relevant to the subject of the inquiry? Or are there too many superfluous or only marginally relevant entities?
- *Recall.* Were enough of the relevant entities found? If any of the known relevant entities listed on the search request form were not found, the searcher should check why. (In some requests the absolute number of relevant entities found, rather than recall, may be the proper criterion.)
- *Avoidance of redundancy,* both with respect to duplicate documents and with respect to substantive data.
- *Novelty* of the results for the user.
- *Numerical precision.* Do numbers have enough significant digits?
- *Validity.* Are numbers valid, that is, are the definitions on which their collection is based the same as those required by the request?
- *Accuracy.*
- *Display.* Is the answer listing formatted for ease of comprehension? Are rows and columns in tables clearly labeled? Are graphs used where appropriate? Are large listings (more than 2 pages or more than 25–50 records) appropriately subdivided into sections, (e.g., by level of relevance or by subtopic)? Are the records sorted in the most useful order?

These criteria must be judged with reference to the user's requirements. Determining recall is difficult, since the base number of relevant entities is not known. However, the searcher may know the number of relevant entities expected by the user as stated on the search request form and may be able to estimate the number of relevant entities to be expected based on subject knowledge (number of organizations active, number of documents published, etc.).

If the search results are satisfactory or can easily be made so, the search proceeds to editing. Otherwise, the search strategy needs modification.

Selection of sources. Are all sources searched necessary? Or do some sources contribute mainly irrelevant material? Should other sources be searched? Should the time range be extended?

Query formulation. If too many superfluous entities were found (low precision), the formulation needs to be more specific. If not enough relevant entities were found, and if it may be assumed that this is due to low recall rather than the dearth of relevant entities in the collection, the formulation needs to be broader or more sources must be searched. If both precision and recall are low, the query formulation must be revised radically. Relevant records can suggest additional terms for narrowing or broadening the query formulation.

If the answer listing is not properly formatted, the searcher can *reformat* it manually or rerun a computer search.

17.5 EDIT SEARCH RESULTS AND SEND THEM TO THE USER

Editing transforms the search results into a more usable format or arrangement. In advanced systems editing can be done interactively with the computer.

Editing requires a number of steps: Arranging the results from all sources into a well-organized package, screening out irrelevant entities found in a computer search, highlighting the most important entities, adding more information for important entities (e.g., descriptions of important organizations, abstracts of important documents), and reformatting tables produced from a numeric data base. If appropriate, the searcher can analyze substantive data (found directly from substantive data bases or extracted from documents or both) and synthesize them into a report that is geared to the problem at hand. Preparing a cover sheet explaining the search completes the package to be given to the user.

The extent of editing depends on the usefulness of the "raw" search results, the preferences of the user, the expertise needed (the searcher may not be sufficiently familiar with the subject to do extensive editing), and on the tradeoff between information center costs and user savings.

17.6 CHECK WHETHER THE ANSWER WAS HELPFUL

The evaluation of search quality by the searcher should be supplemented by an evaluation through the user. Beyond evaluating search quality, the user and the information specialist can jointly assess the impact of the information or entities found on the solution of the problem at hand. This may lead to the recognition of a subsequent need that otherwise may go undetected. Impact assessment also furnishes important management information for decisions on how much should be spent for the information center and what the priorities should be within the information center.

Assessment of quality and impact requires user participation, either through a questionnaire returned to the head of the information service or through an interview with the searcher and/or the head of the information service (for quality control). Such a questionnaire or interview should cover the following points:

- Did the search results meet the user's expectations? If not, should the search be run again? The user may have suggestions for improving both the conceptual query formulation and the source-specific query formulations. How did the search results help the user in solving the problem at hand? Are there additional information or entities that would be helpful?
- Should a follow-up search be conducted? Should the topic of the search be included in the SDI profile of the user?
- What can be learned for future searches? User feedback contributes to the evaluation or appraisal of the search.

17.7 INTERACTION

Interaction is a mutual learning process: The retrieval system learns about the user's need so that it can retrieve material from a data base, and the user learns about ways to express his or her need to the retrieval system. Things get complicated by the fact that the retrieval system as seen by the end user may include an information specialist called *intermediary*. Thus, there is an interface between the end user and the intermediary and an interface between the intermediary and the retrieval system or data base. Most retrieval systems operational today can only accept a query formulation as put and use it to find material. Experimental systems have sophisticated ways to elicit information from the searcher—be it the end user or an intermediary—and construct their own image of the need, which then serves as the basis for retrieval. This section emphasizes learning by the searcher while interacting with a retrieval system or data base. The discussion applies equally to manual and to computer searching.

Learning—by the end user, the intermediary, or a machine search system—extends to two areas:

1. *Understanding the need itself:* The searcher may not know the need very well—the image of the need may be imprecise—either because the end user was not very clear about the need in his or her own mind or because the intermediary did not understand the end user's explanation of the need very well.

2. *Expressing the need:* Even if the searcher has a very good idea of the need, he or she may not know how to express this need in terms of the language of the source in order to meet search requirements, such as recall (or absolute number of entities found), discrimination, and novelty.

Each of the participants—the end user, the intermediary, and the retrieval system—interacts with the other two participants and with the data base, and constantly gathers the knowledge needed to do a successful search. Trying out different approaches and checking the results leads to clarification of the need and better ways to express the need. This requires constant evaluation of search results, in particular judging the relevance of the entities found. The end user's cooperation is helpful in this evaluation. Based on the information collected, the searcher and the system develop alternatives for and make decisions on the further course of the search. The reference interview is part of this interaction.

The relationships among subject descriptors (concepts) that are stored in the data base can be very helpful in preparing a subject search. A well-structured display of the index language may help the end user or the intermediary to get a better grasp of the problem at hand and thus to clarify the need. The end user or the intermediary can browse through the structured display and develop ideas while doing so. A display of the index language may also help the end user or intermediary to formulate the query conceptually and to select descriptors. The display suggests broader, narrower, and related concepts that should be considered. A display should show the hierarchical structure on several levels of detail; for an example, see the Dewey Decimal Classification. With an on-line thesaurus the top-level screen may show an overall outline; the searcher indentifies a broad topic, which is then expanded on a second-level screen, and so on. Relationships between concepts and other types of entities can also be used to identify additional avenues for searching. For example, in most archives records can be accessed only by the name of the organizational unit that generated them, and a subject search must make use of relationships that lead from the concepts searched to organizational units. Such relationships may be seen from finding aids, supplied from the searcher's own knowledge, or discovered during the search.

A computer search system can help the searcher to make good use of concept relations, for example, through an on-line descriptor-find index. It can also provide guidance in formulating the query, as in the following example of interaction with an end user. The system displays a series of questions, each corresponding to a facet of the query's subject domain, and the broad outline of this facet, asking the user to identify the relevant concept(s). Subsequent levels of detail are expanded as the user identifies the broad concepts in which her interest falls. The user is thus guided to analyze her need, divide it into facets, and find the correct descriptor(s) in each facet. Additional questions may deal with the user's background and purpose. Or the user types in the query statement, and the system derives a pattern for the query formulation and responds with an excerpt from the hierarchy for each of the concepts involved. This type of interaction may approach a reference interview conducted by the search system. The system forms its own image of the need.

Descriptor displays should give the number of entities indexed by that descriptor (the number of postings), so that the searcher can form at least a very rough image of the number of entities to be expected when a certain descriptor is used.

So far this discussion has centered on relationships that serve to find descriptors for a subject search—namely, relationships among concepts and relationships between concepts and other entities that might serve as descriptors in searching. Actual retrieval uses relationships between descriptors and the focal entities (e.g., documents or computer programs) sought. While looking at the material found (e.g., titles of laws or documents; names of organizations; abstracts of computer programs, documents, or research projects; sections of laws; economic or physics data; job descriptions), the user forms a more precise image of the need or he may recognize that the information or entities specified in the query statement are not helpful for solving the problem at hand after all and that the need must be restated. This interaction with information is a very important element of the problem-solving process. It is the essence of browsing.

From the relationships between focal entities (e.g., documents) and their descriptors, the searcher can also identify additional descriptors that lead to relevant entities as well as descriptors that lead to irrelevant entities and modify the query formulation accordingly (T5.TRACE); some retrieval systems do that automatically. In fact, the search might start with one or more known relevant entities; these lead to descriptors and perhaps even enable the retrieval system to derive a tentative query formulation. A computer search system can generate or modify its image of the need in response to relevance judgments. Thus, a searcher may never enter a query formulation per se, but start by giving some relevant entities; the system deduces relationships between entity characteristics and relevance and uses these relationships to predict relevance, that is, to retrieve a better set of entities likely to be relevant. These entities are displayed for the user who judges their relevance. Based on this feedback, the system refines its predictive relationships by changing the importance weight given to entity characteristics (some may disappear altogether, others may be added). The entity characteristics used can be any relationships to other entities such as subjects, persons (author, instructor), journal where published, date, etc.

We now return to the problem of the searcher's adjusting the query formulation in response to retrieval results. The less the searcher knows about the rules and conventions used by the indexers, the more important is the information derived from retrieval results. If the thesaurus contains a wealth of scope notes and if the indexers indeed follow these scope notes, then it should be possible to formulate the query correctly in the first place. If a controlled vocabulary is used but the searcher has no clear image of the definition of various descriptors important in the search, then he or she must derive such an image from preliminary retrieval results, which may show, for example, that *Authority* is used for the concept required by the search rather than the related descriptor *Power* originally employed in the query formulation. In free-text searching, interaction is particularly important, since there are no set rules followed by the "indexers"—the authors and abstracters— so that there are many ways in which the topic of the query can be expressed. Only through interaction can the searcher hope to uncover a reasonable fraction of these various ways of expression. It is harder to second-guess all authors and abstracters than it is to second-guess indexers working under stricter controls.

This approach is systematized in the following procedure for developing the query formulation for an on-line source: Choose a descriptor for the first conceptual component. Display some records of entities indexed by the descriptor to see whether its use in the source agrees with the concept needed in the search. If not, try a broader, narrower, or entirely different descriptor, or build an OR-combination with other descriptors. Continue the interaction until the expression for the first search concept is satisfactory. (It is often useful to establish a hierarchy of such expressions from broad to narrow.) Do the same for the other conceptual components. Find the combinations that collectively retrieve a reasonable number of relevant entities without pulling in too many irrelevant entities.

The following search illustrates interaction going through several iterations with emphasis on uncovering appropriate descriptors:

Query statement:

> For teaching purposes I need 200 abstracts of documents on transportation and traffic which conform to selection criteria such as representation of a variety of topics, the presence of both personal authors and corporate authors, and others. A variety of sources for abstracts is desirable.

Step 1: The searcher looks in the card catalog under *Transportation* and other subject headings. She notes documents that look interesting; their cards suggest additional subject headings under which to look; the searcher looks under those subject headings.

Step 2: The searcher goes to the shelves to find the books identified through the card catalog. On the spine of a book next to one of these she notes the name *American Transportation Association.* (This would not have happened in a collection arranged by accession number or some other principle unrelated to subject!) She checks that book. It is not relevant, but perhaps this association issues some publications containing abstracts.

Step 3: The searcher looks in the card catalog under *American Transportation Association* and finds an additional relevant document.

Step 4: The searcher gets this additional document from the shelves.

Interaction depends on the structure of the data base and the information output to the user. Interaction requires sufficient information on the entities found. For example, if only titles but not abstracts, job descriptions, or similar longer text can be displayed, judging the relevance of the entities found is difficult. If the descriptors assigned to an entity are not displayed, interaction cannot provide leads to additional descriptors. Interaction is also dependent on the relationships between entities that are available for searching. For example, if citation relationships between documents are available, a document can lead to other documents listed in its bibliography (going backwards) or citing it (going forward). The starting document may be one known beforehand or one retrieved during the search. If relationships between topically related entities are available, an entity can lead to topically

related entities. Topical relationships can be shown by physical collocation—for example, books on shelves or products in a grocery store (or even
records in a large machine-readable file). Or they can be shown through explicit pointers to other entities. Entities identified through such relationships
may in turn lead to additional descriptors, etc. The searcher (or a
sophisticated search system) should consider all sources of relationships.
Backward citation relationships are available in the documents themselves,
forward citation relationships from a citation index. Topical relationships
often exist among articles in the same journal, particularly in the same issue;
among books by the same author; or among products made by the same
manufacturer.

Interaction is navigation in a large interconnected data structure, following various paths led by relationships between all types of entities. For instance, a search may start from a book, find descriptors, find related
descriptors, find the course for which the book is used, find other books used
in the same course, find related courses, find books used in these, find the
descriptors assigned to these books, find more related descriptors, use all
these descriptors to find more books, etc.

17.8 MONITOR THE SEARCH PROCESS AND ASSESS RESULTS

Before the search starts and periodically during the search process, the
searcher should sit back, evaluate the results achieved so far, consider the
process that led to these results, and examine the plan for the remainder of
the search. He should consider the options, the effort needed, and resources
available. This promotes promising approaches, avoids spending much effort on dead ends, and, in general, "keeps the search on track and efficient."
The searcher should consider whether the problem or a subproblem is one
that he has seen before or is related to one he has seen before. If so, he can
use his previous experience for the conduct of the reference interview and the
planning of the search strategy, remembering points needing clarification
from the user, approaches that proved useful in eliciting such clarification,
sources that proved useful and those that did not, and descriptors used. It is
also a good idea to check whether somebody else did a similar search before
and use their experience. It may even be possible to use the results of a
previous search. But the searcher should also note differences between the
search at hand and previous searches and avoid using a previously developed
search pattern in a situation where it is not optimal. Also, new sources appear and existing sources change (especially sources searched on-line), making old patterns obsolete (M3. PATTERN).

During the reference interview the searcher should observe the reaction of the user and assess the contribution of user responses to the clarification of the need. Summarizing interview results so far, rephrasing a question, abandoning a line of questioning, or making a remark that puts the user at ease are among possible corrective actions.

Evaluating intermediate results during the search allows for corrective action such as reformulating the query or abandoning a source that turns out not to be promising even after the query formulation is modified. Rethinking the query formulation involves checking that it does indeed represent the original topic of the search (M1. CHECK) and that descriptors are spelled correctly (particularly important for highly technical terms, M4. CORRECT).

Upon completion of the search a *search appraisal* should be made using the criteria given in Section 17.4. A search appraisal includes the user's appraisal; an evaluation of the performance for the search as a whole, and for each data base searched, assessing the usefulness of the data base for the search topic; an assessment of the contribution of the individual search elements, especially the subject descriptors, to performance; an assessment of the search process as a whole; and suggestions for improvements in similar searches done in the future.

Good documentation of the search, including a description of search strategy, problems encountered in executing the search, and the search appraisal is helpful for future searches by the same or other searchers.

CHAPTER 18

Design and Evaluation of Information Systems

OBJECTIVE

The objective of this chapter is to develop an understanding of ISAR system design, testing, and evaluation as a summary and culmination of the book and to sharpen the facility of critically appraising reports of retrieval experiments.

INTRODUCTION

The task of information system design can be summarized as follows: Having determined the needs of the potential users and the performance requirements, use the knowledge of system components and their interaction to construct a system that meets these requirements. This chapter concentrates on ISAR system design.

Chapter 8 mentioned some design problems: Should a system providing information about a Pueblo village to children use a broad or a detailed classification? Should the library of an R and D laboratory use LCC or DDC? Should an ISAR system for technical reports use title searching or do careful request-oriented indexing? Should the yellow pages have a classified index? What classification of skills and job requirements is best for an employment service?

The following sample list gives a flavor of general ISAR system design issues, questions the designer must answer.

Developing the system rules, especially the conceptual schema. What entities and relationships should be included? What is the effect of each on retrieval performance? How should the list of entity values within each type be structured? In particular, how should the index language be structured?

What effect do a good facet structure and hierarchy have on the completeness of indexing and on the searcher's success in formulating the query and thereby on retrieval? What is the role of the lead-in vocabulary in achieving high quality indexing and query formulation? What search and data analysis capabilities should the system offer? How should the query command language be designed? How will the design influence error rate in query formulation and search quality? Is the power and complexity of the query language matched with the capabilities of the users?

Defining the indexing process, especially for subject indexing. Should the system rely just on terms chosen by the author in title, abstract, or full text, or on terms chosen by an abstractor? Or should there be a separate process for choosing index terms? If so, what should the general approach be, request-oriented or entity-oriented? How much information on an entity should be used in indexing? How will this affect completeness of indexing? Who should do the indexing, human indexers or a computer program? What is the process used by such a program? Does it just extract some terms, or does it use more sophisticated methods to predict the relevance of an entity for a subject descriptor? How qualified should the indexers be? How will their qualifications influence the quality of indexing? What should the level of exhaustivity and specificity be? How will these factors influence search quality, assuming that the search strategy will fully exploit the possibilities offered?

Defining the search and data analysis process. Who should formulate the queries, the user or an intermediary? What guidelines should be given to the searcher? How do the qualifications of the searcher influence the quality of query formulation, given the design of the query language? How much automation is there in query formulation? How much interaction should be possible in searching? How will interactive feedback, to the searcher or to the system or both, improve search quality or save search effort?

Designing the data structure. What physical form should be used: computer file, card catalog, or book catalog? In a computer, should the data be stored in dyadic relations or in internal records organized around a main entity? What order should the data base have, especially what indexes should it include? Should convenient inclusive searching be provided? Should it be implemented by creating index entries for broad descriptors or by expanding query terms at the time of search?

To make these decisions intelligently, the designer must know how individual design features influence the quality of system operations and data base content and ultimately system performance so that she can evaluate expected system performance against user requirements; the designer needs *engineering knowledge* of the ISAR system. There are two complementary sources for such engineering knowledge: (1) developing insight into the functioning of an ISAR system, both through logical reasoning—as we have done in this book—and through microanalysis of test results; (2) doing retrieval tests and using the resulting values of recall, discrimination, and other measures for prediction.

Testing an ISAR system involves designing, constructing, and operating it as one would a production system. This chapter reviews the process, with emphasis on testing, providing at the same time a review of and conclusion to the book.

Chapter 8 discussed problems of defining performance measures and relating them to system evaluation with respect to specific requirements. Performance measurement is needed not only for system design and maintenance but also for search strategy (Is performance satisfactory or should the strategy be changed? Do the retrieval results suggest changes?) It is also needed for postsearch action (For example, should another information system be searched? How reliable is the information found?). Thus, much of the discussion of testing methodology applies to conducting searches as well, and there are many parallels to Chapter 17.

An ISAR system consists of several components. The designer (and the searcher in developing a search strategy) should consider the contribution of each component to performance in each individual system ability. The problem is complicated by the fact that the components interact so that simple statements can only be misleading. For example, the influence of the index language on recall depends on the data base organization and the comparison/match method. For instance, the capability of inclusive searching enhances the usefulness of hierarchy in searching. (An inclusive search for *Vegetables* retrieves entities on all the narrower concepts, such as *Beans, Carrots,* and *Spinach* as well.) Furthermore, request and entity characteristics influence retrieval.

With some adaptation from Chapters 6 and 7, the steps of the design process can be summarized as follows:

Determine user requirements and abilities. Includes or is closely linked to:
  determine the scope of the information system;
  obtain search requests.
Develop the collection and obtain relevance judgments:
  develop the collection of entities;
  obtain presearch relevance judgments.
Design and construct the ISAR system.
Operate the ISAR system:
  index entities;
  formulate queries;
  retrieve entities and judge their relevance.

Evaluate ISAR system performance:
macroanalysis: compute performance measures;
microanalysis: analyze retrieval failures and successes
to gain insight into the functioning of the ISAR system.

Sections 18.1–18.5 discuss these steps and the methodological problems they present in retrieval testing, and Section 18.6 presents some conclusions on the use of test results in system design. Sections 18.7 and 18.8 discuss cost–benefit considerations and problem-orientation as design principles.

18.1 DETERMINE USER REQUIREMENTS AND ABILITIES

Chapter 7 discussed the use of data on needs and on user background, skills, and abilities in the design of ISAR systems. ISAR tests often deal with laboratory systems without an actual user group. But the tester should nevertheless keep in mind that ISAR systems do not operate in a vacuum; to the extent that the characteristics of the user environment affect performance in the areas to be tested, the test requires a scenario that simulates the user environment in which the ISAR system being tested will operate. Consider, for example, an ISAR system in which the translation from the query statement to the query formulation is automated. Its performance depends on the quality of the query statements, which in turn depends on the ability of the users to write such statements.

18.1.1 DETERMINE THE SCOPE OF THE INFORMATION SYSTEM

The scope of the information system is an element of the environment in which the ISAR system operates. The scope of a test system is usually limited to one subject field or subfield to avoid unmanageably large collections while making sure that the collection contains a reasonable number of relevant entities for the search requests to be used in the test. ISAR tests that use collections of limited scope hide problems that arise in multidisciplinary large collections. For example, if natural language is used as the index language, homonyms present a problem: *Mapping* in geography means preparing a map, whereas in mathematics it refers to the relationship between two sets. The query formulation

Map OR Maps OR Mapping

gives good discrimination in a collection restricted to geography but low discrimination in a multidisciplinary collection in which irrelevant mathematics documents will be found.

In a single-field collection the nature of the subject field may influence the results. Some fields have a very clear conceptual structure expressed in clear and relatively unambiguous terminology; others are in a state of conceptual and terminological confusion. In some fields people may be used to writing precise document titles; in others they may write catchy titles that bear little relationship to the document. In some fields searches may be mostly for specific individual topics; in others people may be interested in the relationships between broad concepts. Strictly speaking, the experimental results can be generalized only to the use of the ISAR techniques *in the specific subject field.* If one wants to generalize the results to another field, one must show that this other field is similar in the structure of its problems and terminology. Even more difficult is the generalization to situations where the collection spans several subject fields as discussed earlier.

18.1.2 OBTAIN SEARCH REQUESTS

The search requests must be representative of the search requests submitted in the situation to which the test results are to be generalized. Alternatively, retrieval results must be broken down by request characteristics. Depending on the purpose of the test, it is not sufficient just to collect query statements. It may also be necessary to obtain or simulate other data about the request—such as user's background or purpose, or specific requirements like recall, discrimination, or novelty—so that the responsiveness of the ISAR system to the specific requirements of each request can be tested.

Ideally, a test should use real-life requests from an operational environment. Requests generated in any other way may severely skew the test results. Retrieval results for individual requests may be heavily influenced by specific circumstances (as opposed to general effects). If descriptors to express the query are available in the index language, retrieval results are good. For example, if there is a subject heading corresponding precisely to the search topic, a search in a card catalog should be quite successful; otherwise, search results might be dismal. If somebody intimately familiar with the index language of the system generates artificial requests, it is quite likely that almost all requests can be expressed easily by descriptors; with real-life requests such good results can be obtained only if the index language was developed in a request-oriented mode based on a thorough assessment of user needs. If the queries are generated from entities in the test collection, as is done in some tests, retrieval results may be severely biased in favor of good performance, particularly for index languages whose vocabulary is close to terms used in entity titles or names. Generating queries from entities may be called entity-oriented query formulation; it is like standing the ISAR task on its head. If the collection contains many entities that are irrelevant for the query at hand but hard to distinguish from relevant entities, discrimination will be low. These few examples illustrate the influence that search requests can have on retrieval performance, independently from any design features of the ISAR system.

18.2 DEVELOP THE COLLECTION AND OBTAIN RELEVANCE JUDGMENTS

18.2.1 DEVELOP THE COLLECTION OF ENTITIES

Collection and ISAR system work together in producing retrieval results. Collection development is an important component of building an information system whether it is an operational or a laboratory system. Different types of collections need different ISAR systems for optimal results. The selection of the test collection is therefore critical lest the experimental results be severely biased. A test is conducted so that one can generalize to real-life situations, especially real-life collections. The test collection must be representative of the real-life collections of interest. Alternatively, the test must allow for a breakdown of retrieval results by entity characteristics so that its results can be extrapolated to collections of different composition.

The size of the test collection is critical. Experiments using real-life collections run into difficulties with respect to identifying all relevant entities. On the other hand, small collections compiled specifically for test purposes do not allow collection-independent selection of search requests because for most such requests there would be no relevant entities. Furthermore, small collections may vary in many ways from large, real-life collections. In particular, small collections must be restricted to a narrow subject scope in order to make meaningful test requests possible; the problems of narrow subject scope were discussed earlier.

18.2.2 OBTAIN PRESEARCH RELEVANCE JUDGMENTS

This is perhaps the most crucial design element of a retrieval test. If the judges miss a relevant entity that is subsequently retrieved by the ISAR system, the ISAR system is punished for finding an "irrelevant" entity rather than being rewarded for finding a relevant entity. Careful quality control by checking the judges' work is essential. (The same is true when using user relevance judgments for assessing the performance of an operational ISAR system, see Section 8.4.)

Ideally, every entity must be judged against every search request to establish a *recall base*. Even in small collections this task is so laborious that relevant entities are likely to be missed, particularly if relevance judgments are based primarily on titles or names (of documents, food products, positions, etc.).

In large collections examining all entities is not feasible. A broad search can identify a subcollection expected to contain most of the relevant entities; but checking through the subcollection is still laborious, and there is no guarantee that all relevant entities are indeed in the subcollection. The alternative of taking a random sample from the collection and checking through it for relevant entities holds very little promise; if a collection of one million entities contains fifty relevant entities, the chance of finding even one of these in a random sample of one thousand entities is only 5%. When testing an ISAR system that retrieves from an operational collection, one can identify relevant entities by other means—for example, asking the user to name relevant entities already known to him or her or searching other information systems. One then checks via simpler and more reliable access points (e.g., author and title for documents) which of these entities are in the collection, and considers these entities as a sample on which to base recall estimates. Assume the user names nine relevant entities, six of which are in the collection; if four of these six are retrieved, then the recall is estimated at .66. This method is also useful for measuring recall for an operational search. However, it has its problems: Can one really assume that the sample of known relevant entities is random? There might be two types of relevant entities, and all the ones the user names belong to only one type. Also, is such a sample large enough for a reliable recall estimate?

In a test of several ISAR systems retrieving from the same collection, a recall base can be formed by pooling the relevant entities retrieved by the different ISAR systems. There is no guarantee that this recall base is complete, and test results allow conclusions only on comparative performance of the ISAR systems, not on absolute performance. For a test of how well a given searcher (a reference librarian or a user) can search a given system, a recall base can be established by having a very experienced searcher do a very thorough search.

18.3 DESIGN AND CONSTRUCT THE ISAR SYSTEM

A test can focus on a given individual ISAR system or ISAR system component or on a type or class of ISAR systems or components. The following are examples of individual ISAR systems or components: the ISAR system of ERIC, the Library of Congress Classification (an index language), or person X as searcher (How well can he or she function within the limitations of the other components of the ISAR system at hand?). The following are examples of types of ISAR system components: computerized file and search mechanism, manual file and search mechanism, index languages using classified arrangement of descriptors, and index languages using alphabetical arrangement of descriptors. Testing a type of ISAR system or component requires construction of a representative implementation.

In the design of an ISAR system for testing, one should consider all the components: the conceptual schema, particularly the index language and the rules for indexing and query formulation, the indexing process, the searching process, and the organization of the data base and comparison mechanism. These components interact, making it very difficult to test one design feature independently from the others.

General design principles can be tested only through concrete implementation. Such an implementation may apply useful principles in an ineffective fashion, resulting in bad performance. This does not warrant conclusions on the principles. An ISAR system using a poorly structured hierarchical index language and therefore giving bad results does not warrant general conclusions on hierarchically structured index languages. One very important factor in the performance of a given index language is whether it contains descriptors appropriate for the formulation of queries used in the test. Differences on that score may overshadow differences resulting from index language structure. The way in which the hierarchy is displayed may also have considerable influence on the quality of indexing and query formulation. Both of these factors depend, in turn, on the mode in which the index language was constructed—request-oriented or entity-oriented. Likewise, role indicators and links used with inappropriate rules are bound to lead to inconsistencies among indexers and between indexers and searchers and thus to bad performance. Conclusions on the principle of using role indicators and links are not warranted.

It takes considerable effort to design and construct a new ISAR system. Often the resources available for an experiment do not permit full-blown execution of the tasks. This puts test results into question. A test on the effects of hierarchical structure in the index language does not produce reliable results if it uses a slipshod hierarchy and indexing and search procedures that do not take full advantage of the hierarchy.

This chapter concentrates on testing effects of the index language on system performance because it is a crucial ISAR system component. Any test of such effects must recognize the three functions of the index language in the operation of the ISAR system:

- To communicate the users' interests to each indexer so that the indexer can act as the users' agent in analyzing entities and making relevance judgments; this is perhaps the most important function of the index language.

- To assist the user (or a searcher who is acting for the user) in formulating a query that corresponds to the user's need. The manner in which the query is formulated depends a great deal on the capabilities of the ISAR system, particularly its index language and its exhaustivity and specificity of indexing.
- To enable the actual matching of the query formulation with entity representations. This function is ancillary to the first two and is often almost mechanical in nature.

An index language can be described by various characteristics, each of which can be considered an independent variable in its own right.

18.4 OPERATE THE ISAR SYSTEM

18.4.1 INDEX ENTITIES

The quality of indexing is influenced by the general approach (request-versus entity-oriented), the index language, the amount of information used, the amount of time spent, other indexing rules, and the indexers' background and capabilities. An investigation of request-oriented indexing must determine how well an index language does its job of communicating users' interests to the indexers. For this purpose, it must use many indexers, preferably in groups with similar backgrounds and capabilities, so that the interaction effect between index language and type of indexer can be observed. For a comparative test of several index languages, each entity must be indexed separately by a different indexer for each index language. Ideally, each entity should be indexed by many indexers within the same group to average out the effects of individual idiosyncrasies. To carry out an experiment with so many indexers is difficult. The alternative is to use a cut-and-dried process of indexing that creates a base list of terms extracted from titles and abstracts and then converts each term into the various index languages to be tested. But indexing, particularly request-oriented indexing, relies quite intentionally on human judgment; in a test of the request-oriented approach, human judgment cannot be eliminated for the sake of experimental control without rendering the whole experiment meaningless. In many experiments the resources available do not allow using so many indexers, and their conclusions are accordingly more tentative.

18.4.2 FORMULATE QUERIES

The effects of query formulation on retrieval performance are as important as the effects of indexing, perhaps even more so. In the general case, query formulation consists of selecting the entity and relationship types involved and combining them into a pattern, selecting the entity values to be used as search criteria, and communicating the query formulation to the system by means of the query language. In the simplified format (e.g., in a subject search for documents) query formulation consists of selecting subject descriptors and, if applicable, combining them with AND and OR. The quality of query formulation depends on the general approach to selection of entity values (e.g., subject descriptors). The approach might be the checklist method or translation of terms from the query statement. The quality of query formulation depends also on the structure of the lists of entity values within each type, especially the structure of the index language; the power and complexity of the query language; the information used; the amount of time spent; other rules and guidelines for query formulation; the searcher's background and capabilities; and the search mode (possibility of interaction and feedback).

Query formulation requires intelligent judgment; this is illustrated by the following observations, which are geared mainly to subject searching for documents or other entities. The data base structure can be of great help in query formulation. It can arrange the characteristics of the type of entity sought into a framework that guides the searcher's thinking. In particular, a faceted classification provides a facet frame, which is useful in analyzing the query topic and selecting subject descriptors. If there is a classified display, the searcher or the user can browse through it and thus clarify the image of the information or entities needed. The searcher can use the classified display for selecting descriptors at the proper level of generality and can use hierarchical relationships for automatically retrieving entities on the narrower descriptors as well (inclusive searching). Related Term cross-references suggest other descriptors to be used; the searcher must use intelligent judgment in deciding whether to follow, reject, or modify these suggestions. This is quite different from using *all* descriptors related to a query term for expansion of the query. The index language structure should support and not supplant intelligent judgment.

The proper logic of the query formulation in terms of AND and OR must also be derived by intelligent judgment or a very sophisticated computer program (just consider the ambiguity of natural language *and,* which may mean logical AND, as in *Pollution and wildlife,* or logical OR as in *The economic situation in the U.S. and Canada*). A good searcher utilizes all possibilities offered by the retrieval mechanism in developing the query logic. In order to derive a proper recall–discrimination graph for a search, one must start with the best narrow query formulation possible and then gradually broaden it each time in the optimal way. This again requires a good understanding of the query statement and intelligent judgment. Most ISAR systems and most types of index languages are designed for use by an intelligent searcher. Any attempt at eliminating human judgment in the name of experimental control will grossly distort test results.

Chapter 17 mentioned methods for assisting the user in deriving the query formulation and methods for searching that start from a query statement and/or known relevant entities. A test can compare these methods with the more traditional approach to query formulation. It is important that such a test use good query formulations that consider the points made here.

18.4.3 RETRIEVE ENTITIES AND JUDGE THEIR RELEVANCE

While actual retrieval is a mechanical task, the data structure and the retrieval mechanism are very important. They limit what can be done in query formulation; they also have a large effect on response time and costs.

All entities identified by the retrieval mechanism should be considered retrieved, for example, when the retrieval mechanism is look-up in a card catalog, *all* entities found under the descriptor should be considered retrieved; scanning the titles for relevance is postretrieval screening, not retrieval through the card catalog.

The entities retrieved should be judged for relevance even if all entities were judged against all queries beforehand. The second judgment serves as quality control.

18.5 EVALUATE ISAR SYSTEM PERFORMANCE

18.5.1 MACROANALYSIS: PERFORMANCE MEASURES

Once entities are retrieved and examined for relevance, adequacy, novelty, etc., performance measures can be computed. Figures are needed in sufficient detail to allow for evaluation of the test results in terms of a specific set of user requirements (see Section 8.3). Thus individual performance measures (recall, discrimination, novelty, etc.) should be reported, not just some total measure derived from them. Aggregate figures should be broken down by type of request. Entity-oriented data are also useful to determine relationships between the characteristics of entities (including who indexed them) and their retrieval behavior. If the experiment involves many searchers searching the same request, it is useful to know how many searchers found a given relevant entity and how many searchers found (erroneously) a given irrelevant entity. It is a shortcoming of many *testing* studies that they report only aggregate figures that do not allow for *evaluating* the ISAR system with respect to a specific purpose. Examples of measures reported are *average* recall or *average* discrimination, or, even worse, one measure combining the two.

Statistical analysis can uncover the effects of the various independent variables (characteristics of the ISAR system, the requests, and the entities) on retrieval performance; often interaction effects are important. To be noteworthy, effects must meet appropriate tests for statistical significance; small effects may well be due to chance alone, particularly if a small entity collection and/or a small sample of requests are used. Beware of studies that simply report results without the proper statistical analysis.

18.5.2 MICROANALYSIS: RETRIEVAL SUCCESSES AND FAILURES

A detailed study of experimental results can give insight into the workings of an ISAR system. Such a study involves examining the reasons for retrieval failure (erroneous retrieval and missed relevant entities) as well as the reasons for retrieval success (correct retrievals and correct rejections). It also involves studying queries for which performance was particularly poor or particularly good to find a reason that might explain the performance differential. Such detailed analysis provides insight into the effects of individual ISAR system components (which include the personnel operating the ISAR system) as well as the effects of characteristics of entities and queries.

18.6 RETRIEVAL TESTING AND SYSTEM DESIGN AND OPERATION

Retrieval tests must be interpreted with respect to the situation in which an ISAR system is to operate. A decision maker faced with the problem of selecting one of three ISAR systems may turn to a ranking of these ISAR systems based on a single figure of merit that is defined independently from the situation in which the ISAR system is to be used. Feeling secure, having based the decision on "quantitative scientific data," he may select an ISAR system that is quite unsuitable for the situation at hand. The data used were misapplied. ISAR systems can be evaluated only with respect to the requirements of a specific situation. General rankings are meaningless. Experimental data should be provided in sufficient detail to allow (1) extrapolation of the raw performance results obtained to results to be expected in a different situation and (2) evaluation of these expected performance results with respect to the requirements of the specific situation in which an ISAR system is to be used.

It is difficult to represent all factors important in a real-life situation in an artificial experimental setup. The results of an experiment that is conducted in a given situation are bound to that situation. Generalization requires careful comparative study of different experiments. For example, one might predict that a sophisticated ISAR system will work well if sophisticated indexers and/or sophisticated searchers are available for its operation but would produce poor results otherwise. Thus, if sufficiently qualified personnel are not available, one should choose a simpler ISAR system that is not capable of the same high quality performance but that will work better when operated by less qualified personnel.

Retrieval tests are fraught with methodological problems. Such tests must be scrutinized with great care before their results can be accepted as an ingredient for decision making. If an experiment was not designed and executed properly, then its results may be grossly misleading. Misinformation is worse than no information at all! As an example, consider the *Cranfield II* experiment, which was concerned with bibliographic retrieval. It was a monumental pioneering effort in retrieval testing and has advanced our understanding of testing methodology considerably. But the general validity of the results as a basis for system design is put into question by the experimental methodology used. The scope of the information system—high-speed aerodynamics—was very narrow. Query statements were generated after reviewing titles of documents in the collection; selection of documents for the collection was not a random process. While the total test collection consisted of 1400 documents and about 300 requests, the main test results reported are based on a subcollection of 220 documents and 42 requests. Relevance judgments were made hurriedly, primarily based on title, and there was little, if any, quality control. The judges demonstrably missed a large proportion of the relevant documents (perhaps as many as 80%). The index languages were not constructed with the care one would use in an operational system. Indexing was done strictly with the extraction-and-conversion method, that is, in an extremely entity-oriented mode that nullified the effect of the index language on eliciting relevant descriptors. (This was done to eliminate the indexer's judgment in the name of experimental control.)

Query formulation was also a mechanical process, extracting content terms from the query statements and translating them automatically into the various index languages used. To test the usefulness of Related Term relationships, each query descriptor was ORed with *all* its related terms. Broadening of query formulations was again mechanical, looking for four out of five, three out of five, etc., descriptors. Query statements developed after reviewing document titles tend to reflect the terminology of these titles. The *Cranfield* relevance judgments relied heavily on titles and show a demonstrated bias in favor of titles that agree in their terminology with the query statement. The result is a built-in bias; a retrieval process in which terms taken from query statements are matched with terms taken from document titles and abstracts is bound to show high agreement with the title-based relevance judgments and hence to produce highest *apparent* performance as measured in this test. *Real* performance is quite a different matter.

Finally, the major results are presented as a list of index languages tested ranked in order of normalized recall, a measure that combines recall and precision. Despite these shortcomings in the development of the test collection and the sample of requests, in relevance judgments, in indexing and retrieval procedures, and in the presentation of results, the *Cranfield* experiment has been and still is widely quoted as evidence that we should not spend much effort constructing controlled vocabularies and hierarchically structured index languages, since in the experiment free, title-based vocabularies performed as well or better. Many subsequent experiments have used the *Cranfield* test collection and thus suffer from its shortcomings.

A very important application of testing methodology is in-house testing for the purpose of continuous quality control. Failure analysis can indicate not only major changes needed, including personnel changes, but also small changes, such as the introduction of a new descriptor in the index language.

18.7 COST-BENEFIT ANALYSIS AS A DESIGN PRINCIPLE

An information system should provide a competitive return on investment in terms of saved user time or in terms of benefits due to better decisions or problem solutions. To make decisions in accordance with this principle, the designer must estimate for each design alternative the costs, the level of performance, and the contribution of that level of performance to saving user time or improving decisions. When assessing this contribution, the information system should be viewed as part of the overall information transfer network in which many other information systems operate (see Section 7.2.3, especially Fig. 7.1). The methods discussed in Sections 18.1–18.5 generate performance estimates. Cost data for the individual operations of an ISAR system can be collected from operational systems and from retrieval experiments.

The quality of the answers obtained from an ISAR system depends on the effort spent on building and maintaining the data base and the effort spent on searching and final screening of search results. Often low effort in data base building can be made up by high effort in searching while achieving the same answer quality, making the issue simply one of a trade-off between costs for data base building and costs for searching. But just as often deficiencies in the data base cannot be made up through search effort; for example, no search effort, however great, can extract quick answers from a large unordered data base.

Deciding on search effort for one individual request is a circumscribed problem; based on her knowledge of the data base and the functioning of the ISAR system, the searcher estimates the functional relationship between search effort and answer quality. Then she estimates the functional relationship between answer quality and benefits to be derived (preferably measured in dollars), computes a return on the search investment and selects the level of effort that maximizes the return.

There is also a trade-off within the search process itself, namely, between effort spent on the query formulation and the search proper and effort spent on postsearch screening. For example, in a search for the side effects of a chemical for which there are only 10 documents in a bibliographic data base, there is no point in spending any effort on elaborating the *Side effects* component of the query formulation; retrieving all documents dealing with the chemical and examining them individually requires less effort. On the other hand, if there are a thousand documents for a chemical in the data base, elaboration of the *Side effects* component pays off.

Decisions on searching effort are made on a pay-as-you-go basis. Decisions on effort in data base building are much more difficult to make. The designer must estimate the number and types of search requests to be expected and draw conclusions on the payoffs of each level of effort in terms of decreased search costs and increased search benefits. This requires good understanding of the improvements in performance to be expected from effort spent in the intellectual organization of the data base and in the implementation of the data structure and the retrieval mechanism. Sections 18.1–18.5 presented methods for achieving such understanding. This section gives a number of examples to illustrate the relations between effort (cost) and performance.

Building a bibliographic data base through request-oriented indexing costs much more than simply relying on titles for retrieval. The designer must study needs and spend a good deal of thought on the logical structure of the index language. The indexers must judge the relevance of the incoming entities for each of the descriptors in the index language. On the other hand, doing a high recall search in the title data base requires much effort, particularly if the search involves a concept like *Intergenerational social mobility*. The searcher must think of all the possible terms and term combinations that might signal the relevance of an entity for this topic. In some situations the only way to match the performance of request-oriented indexing would be to examine every entity in the collection. (See Section 13.3.)

A similar argument can be made for the use of a controlled vocabulary versus free-text searching (see Section 17.2.4), or for the use of hierarchy; it requires effort to construct but, through inclusive searching, facilitates searching with broad concepts, alone or in combination.

Indexing provides another example. Exhaustive indexing is more expensive both in terms of the indexing process itself and in terms of storage space needed but, when used with weights, allows the use of query formulations that correspond well to the search topic (see Section 16.3.1). To match search quality in a low exhaustivity system would be much more expensive, perhaps prohibitively so. Specific indexing is by and large more expensive (see Section 16.4.3), but it makes specific searches easier (see Section 16.3.2). The same is true for the use of role indicators and links in indexing. They add considerably to the cost of indexing and query formulation but allow for more discrimination in searching.

Similar considerations hold for the design of the data structure. For example, inclusive searching can be implemented either through generic posting (i.e., effort in building the data structure) or through query term expansion (i.e., effort in searching). Cheap (and rapid) access by a type of entity (e.g., subject) requires creation and maintenance of a relation sorted by subject identifiers (subject descriptors), such as a subject index; creating and maintaining this degree of order in the data base costs money (see Section 11.6). An increase in exhaustivity in indexing, coupled with providing access, is also an increase in order. Costs for storing a relation increase as the amount of information given for a type of entity increases; at the same time, costs for some searches decrease. As a practical example, consider the design of a subject index to a bibliography. In the document entries under each descriptor, what information should be included beyond the document number: the title, title and abstract, title and other descriptors assigned to the document, or other information? The more information, the more expensive the book. But searching becomes easier: The searcher looking under a descriptor can examine titles for relevance right then and there rather than having the laborious task of accessing each document under its number. One would expect not only less time for searching but also better quality searches, since page turning between the index and the main part of document entries is not exactly conducive to keeping one's mind on the topic. Getting the data needed for a true cost–benefit analysis in this case would be very difficult, because the user group is very open-ended (the patrons of all the libraries who buy the bibliography). When making a decision, the publisher will consider time-savings and benefits to the users only indirectly through the expected impact on the decisions of acquisitions librarians.

The last example points up a difficulty. Data base building and maintenance occur in a well-circumscribed context in which costs can be easily determined. Searching activity is often widely scattered, and its size, costs, and benefits are hard to measure. Moreover, the organizations that create data bases are often several steps removed from the searchers. This adds even more to the uncertainty of a cost–benefit analysis for information systems.

18.8 PROBLEM-ORIENTATION AS A DESIGN PRINCIPLE

From the outset this book has established an emphasis on information for problem solving and has used this emphasis as a guiding principle throughout. This concluding section traces the most important implications of this principle.

First, the design of an information system should be based on an analysis of the problems faced by the clientele to be served. The function of an information system is to match people who have problems with information or entities that can help solve these problems. It follows that an information system should actively identify people with problems and resulting needs. Many people are not aware of their needs or do not take the initiative to make their needs known; therefore, many problems will not be solved as well as they could be unless the information system takes an active role in identifying them. The match between needs and information or entities would be incomplete.

The users ultimately need substantive data or entities, not references to documents or sources of entities; references are just a means, not an end. The user should not have to read more than necessary to obtain the substantive data. Therefore, the goal of a bibliographic ISAR system is not to retrieve all relevant documents but rather to retrieve the smallest subset of documents that contain all the substantive data needed for the problem at hand. This leads to a third measure for ISAR system performance, in addition to recall and discrimination (or the more frequently used precision), namely *conciseness*. Conciseness is a measure of the extent to which the ISAR system can spare the user documents that merely repeat what is in other documents or in the user's knowledge already. This has important consequences for design: The ISAR system must have a model of the user's knowledge. Furthermore, the system should not only know what every document is about or relevant for, but it should also know enough about the contents of each document to detect if and how it overlaps with other documents or the user's knowledge. These considerations can be transferred to the retrieval of other types of entities. For example, the system should be able to retrieve the smallest subset of suppliers that among them can deliver all the technical parts the user needs (assuming that prices are equal).

Relevance cannot be judged for each entity individually or independently from the user's knowledge, as is often done in retrieval experiments and operational searches. If two documents *in combination* provide the substantive data needed, or two technical parts *in combination* provide a solution to the problem, they should be retrieved even if none of them individually is "relevant." The same is true for a document that complements the user's knowledge or a technical part that complements one that the user has already. The searcher must carefully analyze the problem at hand and perhaps do a number of subsearches, each directed to one subset of substantive data, as in the sample search on *The effects of mercury in seawater on human health.*

Judging relevance, therefore, means assessing the possible contribution of an entity or of the substantive data in a document to the solution of the problem at hand. If a user cannot do this alone, he should be assisted by an information specialist or by a machine dialog. Either could give to the user more information about an entity or show the user how an entity or the substantive data in a document can be used to solve the problem, perhaps by referring to a document that gives the prerequisite knowledge. The possibility that a user may not be able to recognize relevance calls into question retrieval experiments that rely solely on users to make relevance judgments. It also presents a problem in experimental retrieval systems that do not use query formulations but rely primarily on feedback provided through user relevance judgments to fashion and adapt the search.

The principle of problem-orientation is also important for the organization of the data structure. The data structure should facilitate access from the points of view important in searches. For example, in a grocery store ingredients of certain types of dishes are often arranged together in the shelves for convenience of access. We earlier discussed the example of a clipping service arranged by country and within country by subject if country is the major mode of search. Moreover, through its organization, the data structure should assist the user in the process of inquiry. Looking for a specific abstract and finding next to it another one that sparks a new idea for the solution of the problem at hand is an example.

Finally, problem-orientation should permeate the conceptual organization of the ISAR system. The conceptual schema, through the entity types and relationship types it provides, should guide indexers and searchers in structuring information in a problem-oriented way. We emphasized the problem- or request-oriented design of the index language. The index language should be seen as a communication device that conveys to the indexer the problems of the users and the mental framework of the users. Since there are many users, the task requires a master framework that envelops the mental frameworks of many users in a logical and coherent structure of a subject field and its problems. This requires a careful logical and conceptual analysis of the subject field using the twin principles of facet analysis and hierarchy. A properly designed facet frame captures the essential conceptual structure of a field and is instrumental in eliciting the concepts to be included in the index language, in assisting in the analysis of a search topic, and in the analysis of an entity in indexing. Semantic factoring, as aided by a facet frame, leads to the detection of general concepts that allow access from various points of view. The hierarchy of concepts within each facet should again show problem-orientation and lead the indexer or searcher to the appropriate subject descriptor. A hierarchical arrangement presents a point of view, but an index language with polyhierarchical structure can integrate many points of view. Furthermore, problems themselves can be introduced as subject descriptors so that it becomes possible to search for queries such as *New technological developments that endanger our business.* The index language thus constructed communicates to the indexer a framework of the users' problems and needs and thus enables the indexer to serve as the users' agent in analyzing entities through the checklist technique of indexing. This results in a truly problem- or user-oriented ISAR system.

Thus closes the circle that began in Chapter 2 with the maxim "Information is for problem-solving." It led us through the intellectual foundations and technical implementation of the various ISAR system components and functions—from designing the conceptual schema and constructing the index language to designing the data structure and to indexing and searching. The challenge is to match and integrate these components into a system that helps people.

Bibliography

Part 1 of the bibliography gives textbooks, readers, handbooks, and journals of interest. Part 2 is a highly select list of further readings that contribute important ideas to the field. A textbook of this scope naturally draws on the entire accumulated knowledge of the field, and it would be nigh impossible to trace the source of every idea covered.

Reviews known to this author are referenced in the textbook bibliography; Journal abbreviations are explained in the list of journals.

PART I: TEXTBOOKS, READERS, ETC.

INFORMATION STUDIES IN GENERAL

Annual Review of Information Science and Technology. White Plains, NY: Knowledge Industry Publications; 1966–   (First edited by Cuadra, Carlos, then by Williams, Martha. Various publishers through its history.)—A basic work for keeping up to date and for reference.

Encyclopedia of library and information science./Kent, Allen, ed.; Lancour, Harold, ed. New York: Marcel Dekker; 1968–

Machlup, Fritz 1980. *Knowledge: its creation, distribution, and economic significance.* 3 vols. Princeton, NJ: Princeton University Press; 1980–1984. v. 1. *Knowledge and knowledge production;* 1980. 264 pp.—v. 2. *The branches of learning;* 1982. 205 pp.—v. 3. *The economics of information and human capital;* 1984. 576 pp.

Machlup, Fritz, ed. 1983; Mansfield, Una, ed. *The study of information. Interdisciplinary messages.* New York: Wiley; 1983. 768 pp.

Saracevic, Tefko, ed. 1970. *Introduction to information science.* New York: Bowker; 1970. 751 pp.—A very good collection which includes many classics.

Information Systems in General

These textbooks deal with all components of an information system. They include, but are not limited to, a treatment of information storage and retrieval. They emphasize bibliographic information systems.

Batten, W. E., ed. 1975. *Handbook of special librarianship and information work*. London: Aslib; 1975. 430 pp.—Reviews: LQ 1976.10:485. SL 1976.11:550. JD 1976.3:80.

Kochen, Manfred, ed. 1967. *The growth of knowledge: readings on organization and retrieval of information*. New York: Wiley; 1967. 394 pp.—Reviews: LJ 1967.10:3651.—A classic; many of the papers are still worth reading.

Licklider, J. C. R. 1965. *Libraries of the future*. Cambridge, MA: MIT Press; 1965. 219 pp.

Loosjes, T. P. 1973. *On documentation of scientific literature*. London: Butterworths; 1973. 187 pp.—Reviews of 1967 edition: CH 1968.1:1212. LJ 1968.3:965.

Vickery, Brian C. 1973. *Information systems*. London: Butterworths; Hamden, CT: Shoestring Press; 1973. 350 pp.—Reviews: CH 1974.11:126. SL 1973.11: 537.

United States Commission on Federal Paperwork 1977.9; Horton, Woody, chairman. *Information resources management*. Washington, D.C.: U.S. Government Printing Office; 1977.9. 76 pp.

Synnott, William R. 1981; Gruber, William H. *Information resource management: opportunities for the 1980s*. New York: Wiley; 1981. 356 pp.—Reviews: CR 1983.2:#40,049.

Computerized Information Systems in Organizations

These books usually present an introduction to three interrelated topics: the function of an information system in an organization, computer technology, and the handling of data by computers. They usually do not cover the structure of index languages.

Ahituv, Niv 1982; Neumann, Seev. *Principles of information systems for management*. Dubuque, IA: Brown; 1982. 528 pp.—Reviews: CR 1982.8: #39,591.

Brookes, Cyril H. P. 1982; Grouse, Phillip J.; Jeffery, D. Ross; Lawrence, Michael J. *Information systems design*. Englewood Cliffs, NJ: Prentice-Hall; 1982. 477 pp.—Reviews: CR 1983.6:#40,374.

Davis, William S. 1981. *Information processing systems*. 2. ed. Reading, MA: Addison-Wesley; 1981. 504 pp.—Reviews: CR1981.7:#38,132.

Ein-Dor, P. 1978; Segev, E. *Managing management information systems*. Lexington, MA: Lexington Books; 1978. 191 pp.—Reviews: CR 1979.1:#33,928.

Kanter, Jerome 1984. *Management information systems*. 3. ed. Englewood Cliffs, NJ: Prentice-Hall; 1984. 448 pp.—Reviews: CR 1984.3:#8403-0151.

Murdick, Robert G. 1980. *MIS concepts and design*. Englewood Cliffs, NJ: Prentice-Hall; 1980. 610 pp.—Reviews: CR 1980.11: #36,994.

Taggart, William M. 1980. *Information systems*. Boston, MA: Allyn and Bacon; 1980. 602 pp.—Reviews: CR 1981.5:#37,824. CR 1981.7:#38,140.

Hayes, Robert M. 1974.; Becker, Joseph. *Handbook of data processing for libraries*. 2. ed. New York: Wiley; 1974. 688 pp.—Reviews: College and Research Libraries 1976.3: 170. J. Libr. Automation 1975.6: 162.—Still a very sound analysis of information systems, especially libraries, from the point of view of automation. The treatment of technology is, of course, outdated.

OFFICE INFORMATION SYSTEMS, OFFICE AUTOMATION, TEXT AND GRAPHICS INFORMATION SYSTEMS

Lieberman, Mark A. 1982; Selig, Gad J.; Walsh, John J. *Office automation: a manager's guide for improved productivity*. New York: Wiley; 1982. 331 pp.—Reviews: CR 1983.8:#40,551.

James, Geoffrey 1985. *Document databases*. New York: Van Nostrand Reinhold; 1985. 184 pp.—How to create and manipulate a database of text and graphics for printing and on-line viewing.

INFORMATION STORAGE AND RETRIEVAL—GENERAL

These books concentrate on information storage and retrieval, usually in the context of bibliographic systems. They often include substantial discussion of subject access, in particular the structure of index languages. Some of them concentrate on using computers for the more or less clerical functions of file building and maintenance and comparison/match.

Becker, Joseph 1963; Hayes, Robert M. *Information storage and retrieval: tools, elements, theories*. New York: Wiley; 1963. 448 pp.—Still quite a useful book, especially Section 3 on theory is recommended for more advanced studies.

Lancaster, F. Wilfrid 1979. *Information retrieval systems. Characteristics, testing, and evaluation*. 2. ed. New York: Wiley; 1979. 381 pp.—Reviews: IP 1980:57. JD 1982.3:47. LQ 1981.1:134.

Meadow, Charles T. 1973. *The analysis of information systems*. 2. ed. New York: Wiley; 1973. 420 pp.—Especially chapters 1, 7, 9, 10, 12, 13, 15, 16.

Needham, Christopher D. 1971. *Organizing knowledge in libraries. An introduction to information retrieval*. 2. ed. London: Deutsch; 1971. 448 pp.—Excellent modern approach to conventional library operations.

Vickery, Brian C. 1965. *On retrieval system theory*. 2. ed. London: Butterworths; 1965. 191 pp.—Reviews: Amer. Documentation 1967.1:50. LJ 1966.3:1205. SL 1971.3:122—Still a useful book; gives an overview.

ONLINE SEARCHING

These books treat information storage and retrieval with emphasis on concepts and techniques for searching online data bases (usually bibliographic data bases).

Gerrie, Brenda 1983. *Online information systems: use and operating characteristics, limitations, and design alternatives*. Arlington, VA: Information Resources Press; 1983. 189 pp.

Fenichel, Carol H. 1984; Hogan, Thomas. *Online searching: a primer.* Marlton, NJ: Learned Information; 1984. 184 pp.

Hoover, Ryan E., ed. 1980. *The library and information manager's guide to online services.* White Plains, NY: Knowledge Industry Publications; 1980. 270 pp.—Reviews: SL 1981.10:411.

Lancaster, F. W. 1973; Fayen, Emily G. *Information retrieval on-line.* New York: Wiley; 1973. 497 pp.—Reviews: JD 1974.9:362.

AUTOMATED INFORMATION STORAGE AND RETRIEVAL

These books, while often dealing also with other topics, emphasize automated methods for indexing and retrieval, drawing in particular on language analysis and probabilistic theories.

Maron, M. E., ed. 1978.4. *Theory and foundations of information retrieval.* Drexel Library Quarterly. 1978.4; 14(2). 107 pp.

Oddy, R. N., ed. 1981; Robertson, S. E., ed.; van Rijsbergen, C. J., ed.; Williams, P. W., ed. *Information retrieval research.* London: Butterworths; 1981. 260 pp.—Proceedings of a conference giving a good cross section of work in this area.—Reviews: IP 1983:399.

van Rijsbergen, C. J. 1979. *Information retrieval.* 2. ed. London: Butterworths; 1979. 208 pp.—Reviews: CH 1979.9:878. JA 1979.11:374. JD 1980.9:275.

Salton, Gerard 1975. *Dynamic information and library processing.* Englewood Cliffs, NJ: Prentice-Hall; 1975. 523 pp.—Reviews: CR 1976.1:#29,382. JD 1975.12:310. SL 1975.11:558.

Salton, Gerard 1983; McGill, Michael J. *Introduction to modern information retrieval.* New York: McGraw Hill; 1983. 448 pp.—Reviews: CR 1982.12:#39,910. IP 1983:402.

Sparck Jones, Karen 1974; Kay, Martin. *Linguistics and information science.* New York: Academic Press; 1973. 244 pp.—Reviews: CR 1974.12:#27,585. SL 1975.7:347.

ARTIFICIAL INTELLIGENCE AND EXPERT SYSTEMS

Schank, Roger C. 1984. With Childers, Peter G. *The cognitive computer: On language, learning, and artificial intelligence.* Reading, MA: Addison-Wesley; 1984. 268 pp.—An informal introduction with emphasis on knowledge representation.

Winston, Patrick Henry 1984. *Artificial intelligence.* 2. ed. Reading, MA: Addison-Wesley; 1984. 524 pp.—Comprehensive, somewhat formal treatment.

Nilsson, Nils J. 1980. *Principles of artificial intelligence.* Palo Alto, CA: Tioga; 1980. 476 pp.—Reviews: CR 1981.6:#37,973.—A fairly formal treatment of solution searching and deduction.

Charniak, Eugene, ed. 1976; Wilks, Yorick, ed. *Computational semantics: an introduction to artificial intelligence and natural language comprehension.* New York: North Holland; 1976. 294 pp. (Fundamental studies in computer science, v. 4).—Reviews: CR 1976.9:#30,259.

Barr, Aaron, ed. 1981; Cohen, Paul, ed.; Feigenbaum, Edward, ed. *The handbook of artificial intelligence.* Los Altos, CA: William Koffman; vol. 1, 1981. 388 pp.; vol. 2, 1982. 428 pp. ; vol. 3, 1982. 639 pp.—Reviews: CH 1983.1:131. CR 1983.9:#40,648. CR 1983.7: #40,463.—A classic reference work with clearly written articles.

Feigenbaum, Edward A. 1983; McCorduck, P. *The fifth generation*. Reading, MA: Addison-Wesley; 1983. 275 pp.—Reviews: LJ 1983.6.15:1247. NYT 1983.8.2:23.

Weiss, Sholom M. 1984; Kulikowski, Casimir A. *A practical guide to designing expert systems*. Totowa, NJ: Rowman and Allanheld; 1984. 174 pp.

Harmon, Paul 1985; King, David. *Expert systems: Artificial intelligence in business*. New York: Wiley; 1985. 256 pp.

Hayes-Roth, F., ed. 1983; Waterman, D., ed.; Lenat, D., ed. *Building expert systems*. Reading, MA: Addison-Wesley; 1983. 444 pp.

Michie, Donald 1982. *Introductory readings in expert systems*. New York: Gordon and Breach; 1982. 235 pp.—Reviews: CR 1983.10:#40,735.

Kowalski, Robert 1979. *Logic for problem solving*. New York: Elsevier North-Holland; 1979. 287 pp.

Winograd, Terry 1983. *Language as a cognitive process*. Reading, MA: Addison-Wesley; 1983. 640 pp.

Decision Support Systems

Bonczek, R. 1981; Holsapple, C.; Whinston, A. *Foundations of decision support systems*. New York: Academic Press; 1981. 393 pp.

Keen, Peter G. W. 1978; Scott Morton, Michael S. *Decision support systems: an organizational perspective*. Reading, MA: Addison-Wesley; 1978. 264 pp.—Reviews: CR 1979.2: #34,054.

Scott Morton, Michael S. 1971. *Management decision systems—computer-based support for decision making*. Boston, MA: Graduate School of Business Administration, Harvard University; 1971.216 pp.—Reviews: CR 1971.6: #21,367.

Sprague, Ralph M. 1982; Carlson, Eric D. *Building effective decision support systems*. Englewood Cliffs, NJ: Prentice-Hall; 1982. 351 pp.—Reviews: IP 1983:344.

Data Base Management Systems

These books concentrate on data schemas for formatted data and associated query languages. Many deal also with data structures and access methods that can be used to implement these schemata. Specific data base management software packages are also discussed. These books generally do not discuss the structure of index languages or rules for other entity types.

Atre, S. 1980. *Data base: structured techniques for design, performance, and management—with case studies*. New York: Wiley; 1980. 442 pp.—Reviews: CR 1981.6:#37,978.

Date, C. J. 1985. *An introduction to database systems. v. 1. 4. ed.* Reading, MA: Addison-Wesley; 1985. 574 pp.—Reviews: CR 1981.7:#38,392 (3. ed.).—An excellent introduction.

Date, C. J. 1983. *An introduction to database systems. v. 2.* Reading, MA: Addison-Wesley; 1983. 383 pp.—Reviews: CR 1983.8:#40,549.—A companion to the previous book, covering more advanced topics.

Date, C. J. 1983. *Database: a primer*. Reading, MA: Addison-Wesley; 1983. 265 pp.—An elementary introduction for users in business and home.

King, Judy M. 1981. *Evaluating data base management systems*. New York: Van Nostrand; 1981. 275 pp.—Reviews: CR 1982. 1: #38,878.—Broader than title, highly recommended.

Maier, David 1983. *The theory of relational data bases.* Potomac, MD: Computer Science Press; London: Pitman; 1983. 637 pp.—Reviews: CR 1984.3:#8403–0149.

Martin, James 1976. *Principles of data base management.* Englewood Cliffs, NJ: Prentice-Hall; 1976. 352 pp.—Reviews: CH 1976.9:856; CR 1976.8: #30,147.—Very introductory.

Martin, James 1977. *Computer data-base organization.* 2. ed. Englewood Cliffs, NJ: Prentice-Hall; 1977. 560 pp.

McNichols, Charles W. 1984. *Data base management with dBASE II* (hardback) - *dBASE II business applications: system design and software* (softcover). Reston, VA: Reston Publishing; 1984. 450 pp.—General introduction and system of dBASE II programs. dBASE III edition not before 1986.

Ullman, Jeffrey D. 1982. *Principles of data base systems.* 2. ed. Potomac, MD: Computer Science Press; London: Pitman; 1982. 484 pp.—Reviews: CR 1980.9:#36,742 (1. ed.)

Wiederhold, Gio 1983. *Data base design.* 2.ed. New York: McGraw Hill; 1983. 751 pp.—Reviews: CR 1983.8: #40, 550.

Horowitz, Ellis 1983; Sahni, Sartaj. *Fundamentals of data structures.* Rockville, MD: Computer Science Press; 1983. 564 pp.—Originally published 1976, reprinted often with corrections.—Reviews: CH 1977.5:412. CR 1978.4:32,817.

Maurer, Herman H. 1977. *Data structures and programming techniques.* Englewood Cliffs, NJ: Prentice-Hall; 1977. 228 pp.—Reviews: CH 1977.7:711. CR 1977.10:#32,230.

THE STRUCTURE OF INDEX LANGUAGES AND THESAURI

Bliss, Henry E. 1929. *The organization of knowledge and the system of the sciences.* New York: Holt; 1929. 433 pp.

Coates, Eric J. 1960. *Subject catalogues. Headings and structure.* London: The Library Association; 1960. 186 pp.—A classic.

Foskett, D. J. 1974. *Classification and indexing in the social sciences.* 2. ed. London: Butterworths; 1974. 202 pp.

Lancaster, Wilfrid 1972. *Vocabulary control for information retrieval.* Washington, DC: Information Resources Press; 1972. 233 pp.—Reviews: CR 1974.6: #26,818. International Classification 1975:49. JD 1973.6:240. LJ 1973.3.15:848. SL 1972.12:597.

Soergel, Dagobert 1974. *Indexing languages and thesauri: construction and maintenance.* New York: Wiley; 1974. 632 pp.—Reviews: International Classification 1975: 52. IP 1975.12:255. JD 1975.9: 229. LQ 1975.10: 435. SL 1976.3:175.

Vickery, Brian C. 1975. *Classification and indexing in science.* 3. ed. London: Butterworths; 1975. 228 pp.—Reviews: LQ 1976.7:340—Especially the preface to the first edition and chapters 1 through 3. In some respects the second edition (1959) is better.

JOURNALS

    ACM Transactions on Data Base Systems. 1976–
    ACM Transactions on Office Information Systems. 1983–
    Artificial Intelligence. 1970–
CH *Choice. 1963–*
    Communications of the ACM 1958–
CR *Computing Reviews. 1960–*
    Computing Surveys. The survey and tutorial journal of the ACM. 1969–
    Drexel Library Quarterly. 1965–

IP   *Information Processing and Management* (formerly *Information Storage and Retrieval*). *1963–*
JA   *Journal of the American Society for Information Science* (JASIS) (formerly *American Documentation*). *1950–*
JD   *Journal of Documentation* (J. Doc.). *1945–*
LJ   *Library Journal 1976–*
LQ   *Library Quarterly. 1931–*
       Online. 1977–
       On-Line Review. 1977–
SL   *Special Libraries. 1910–*

PART 2

CHAPTER 1   INFORMATION SYSTEMS FOR PROBLEM SOLVING

Kent, Allen 1975.12. *Generation, use, and transfer of information.* Information. 1975.12; 7(10): 306–310.
Mooers, Calvin N. 1959.3. *The next twenty years in information retrieval.—goals and predictions.* Western Joint Computer Conference. Proceedings (AFIPS Conference Proceedings). 1959.3; 15: 81–86.—Still a valid paper giving perspectives and new ideas.
Soergel, Dagobert 1977. *An automated encyclopedia—a solution of the information problem?* International Classification 1977; 4(1): 4–10. 1977; 4(2): 81–89.
Wiederhold, Gio 1981. *Data base technology in health care.* J. Med. Syst. 1981; 5(3): 175–195.
Keen, Peter G. W. 1980.3. *Decision support systems: translating analytic techniques into useful tools.* Sloan Management R. 1980.Spring; 21(3): 33–44.
Sprague, R., Jr. 1980.12. *A framework for the development of decision support systems.* Management Information Systems Quarterly. 1980.12; 4(4): 1–26.
Gevarter, William B. 1983.8. *Expert systems: limited but powerful.* IEEE Spectrum. 1983.8; 20(8): 39–45.
Kinnucan, Paul 1984.1. *Computers that think like experts.* High Technology. 1984.1; 4(1):30–42.

Notes

Bell Labs has programmed a computer to discover the shortest route from a house to a desired store and give directions on the terminal (ASIS Bulletin 1982.10: 10).

An example of a high-speed search device is the GESCAN 2. The machine can scan 2 Mbytes/second or 1,000 pages/second (1 page = 2,000 characters). It can search for four queries simultaneously (General Electric, Military and Data Systems Operations, Arlington, VA).

CHAPTER 2   THE NATURE OF INFORMATION

Ford, N. 1980.6. *Relating 'information needs' to learner characteristics in higher education.* J. Doc. 1980.6; 36(2): 99–114.—Also relevant for Chapters 7 and 17.

Parker, Edwin B. 1974. *Information and society*. Cuadra, C. ed. 1974. Library and information needs of the nation: Chapter 2, pp. 9–50.—(See references for Chapter 7.)

Taylor, Robert S. 1982.9 *Value-added processes in the information life cycle*. JASIS. 1982.9; 33(5): 341–346.—Also relevant for Chapters 4 and 7.

Belkin, Nicholas J. 1978.3. *Information concepts for information science*. J. Doc. 1978.3; 34(1): 55–85.

Whittemore, Bruce J. 1973.5; Yovits, M. C. *A generalized conceptual development for the analysis and flow of information*. JASIS. 1973.5; 24 (6): 221–231.

Rappaport, Anatol 1953.7. *What is information?* ETC: A review of general semantics 1953. Summer; 10(4): 247–260.—Reprinted in Saracevic, T. ed. 1970. Introduction to information science: paper 1, pp. 5–12.

CHAPTER 3   THE STRUCTURE OF INFORMATION

See also the textbooks on data base management and on artificial intelligence and the references given for Chapter 9. Also Jahoda 1980 listed for Chapter 17.

Simmons, Robert F. 1973. *Semantic networks: their computation and use for understanding English sentences*. Colby, Kenneth M., ed.; Schank, Roger, ed. Computer models of thought and language. San Francisco: Freeman; 1973: Chapter 2, pp. 63–113.

Lindsay, Peter H. 1972; Norman, Donald H. *Human information processing. Introduction to psychology*. New York: Academic Press; 1972. 737 pp.—Ch. 10. *The structure of memory*. pp. 374–401. ch. 11 *Memory processes*, p. 402–434.

Strong, Suzanne M. 1974.1. *An algorithm for generating structural surrogates of English text*. JASIS. 1974.1; 25(1): 10–24.

Sager, Naomi 1975.1. *Sublanguage grammars in science information processing*. JASIS. 1975.1; 26(1): 10–16.

CHAPTER 4   THE INFORMATION TRANSFER NETWORK

Murdock, John W. 1967.10; Liston, David M. *A general model of information transfer: Theme paper 1968 annual ASIS convention*. American Documentation. 1967.10; 18(4): 197–208.

Libaw, Frieda B. 1969.10. *A new, generalized model for information transfer: a system approach*. American Documentation. 1969.10; 20(4): 381–384.

Allen, Thomas J. 1969.3; Cohen, St. I. *Information flow in R & D laboratories*. Administrative Science Quarterly. 1969.3; 14(1): 12–19.—Introduces the idea of technological gatekeepers. An earlier version published as a report (Cambridge, MA: MIT. Sloan School of Management; 1966. 26 pp.) is a better introductory reading, particularly since it traces the origin of the idea to previous research on two-step information flow in mass communication.

Allen, Thomas J. 1977. *Managing the flow of technology*. Cambridge, MA: MIT Press; 1977. 320 pp.—Also relevant for Chapter 7.

Menzel, H. 1966.11. *Scientific communication: five themes from social science research*. American Psychologist. 1966.11; 21 (11): 999–1004.

CHAPTER 5   THE STRUCTURE OF INFORMATION SYSTEMS

Connor, Judith H. 1967.10. *Selective dissemination of information: a review of the literature and the issues.* Library Quarterly. 1967.10; 37(4): 373–391.

Chafetz, Morris E. 1976.5. *Toward increased quality consciousness for alcoholism literature.* JASIS. 1976.5; 27(3): 162–170.

Spaulding, F. H. 1976.9; Stanton, R. O. *Computer-aided selection in a library network.* JASIS. 1976.9; 27(5): 269–280.—A good example for the compilation of an information needs catalog and its use in collection development.

Weingand, Darlene E., ed. 1983. *Marketing for libraries and information agencies: a reader.* Norwood, NJ: Ablex; 1983. 176 pp.

Thomas, Robert J. 1982.9. *Marketing research in the scientific and technical information services industry: development and future directions.* JASIS. 1982.9; 33(5): 265–269.—This article contains many useful references.

CHAPTER 6   SYSTEMS ANALYSIS

The readings listed here may also contain relevant material for Chapters 7, 8, and 18. Conversely, the readings for Chapters 7, 8, and 18 deal with specific functions in systems analysis. See also the textbooks on information systems and on computerized information systems.

General Works on the Systems Approach and Systems Analysis

Weinberg, G. M. 1975. *An introduction to general systems thinking.* New York: Wiley; 1975. 279 pp.—Reviews: CR 1975.12:#29,225.

Churchman, Charles West 1972. *The design of inquiring systems: basic concepts in systems analysis.* New York: Basic Books; 1972. 288 pp.—Reviews: CH 1972.11:1147. CR 1973.5:#25,028. LJ 1972.3.1:878.

DeMarco, Tom 1979. *Structured analysis and systems specification.* Englewood Cliffs, NJ: Prentice-Hall; 1979. 325 pp.—Reviews: CR 1980.7:#36,501.

Bingham, John E. 1980; Davis, Garth W. *A handbook of systems analysis.* 2. ed. New York: Halstead (Wiley); 1980. 229 pp.—Reviews: CH 1973.10:1249 (first edition).

Lundeberg, Mats 1981; Goldkuhl, Goran; Nilsson, Anders. *Information systems development, a systematic approach.* Englewood Cliffs, NJ: Prentice-Hall; 1981. 336 pp.—Reviews: IP 1983:109.

Lucas, Henry C. 1974. *Towards creative systems design.* New York: Columbia University Press; 1974. 147 pp.—Reviews: CR 1975.3:#27,907.

Systems Analysis in Libraries

Dougherty, Richard M. 1982; Heinritz, Fred J. *Scientific management of library operations.* 2. ed. Metuchen, NJ: Scarecrow; 1982. 286 pp.

Warner, Edward S., ed. 1977.7; Palmour, Vernon E., ed. *Perspectives on library measurement.* Drexel Library Quarterly. 1977.7; 13 (3):1–103.

Methods for Collecting Data and Analyzing and Designing Procedures

Martyn, John 1981; Lancaster, F. Wilfrid. *Investigative methods in library and information science: an introduction.* Arlington, VA: Information Resources Press; 1981. 260 pp.

Aslib Research Department 1970.3. *The analysis of library processes.* J. Doc. 1970.3; 26(1): 30–45.—A very good treatment.

Gane, Christ 1979; Sarson, Trish. *Structured systems analysis: tools and techniques.* Englewood Cliffs, NJ: Prentice-Hall; 1979. 250 pp.—Reviews: CH 1979.2:1632. CH 1980.1: 1477. CR 1979.9:#35,033.

Ungson, G. R. 1982; Branstein, D. N. *Decision making: an interdisciplinary inquiry.* Boston, MA: Kent; 1982. 400 pp.—Reviews: CH 1982.12:614.

Cost-Effectiveness and Cost-Benefit Analysis

Lancaster, F. Wilfrid 1971.1. *The cost-effectiveness analysis of information retrieval and dissemination systems.* JASIS. 1971.1; 22 (1): 12–27.

Phyrr, Peter A. 1973. *Zero-base budgeting. A practical management tool for evaluating expenses.* New York: Wiley; 1973. 231 pp.—Reviews: CH 1973.11:1247. LJ 1974.3.1:629.

Hammond, Thomas H. 1980; Knott, Jack H. *A zero-based look at zero-base budgeting.* New Brunswick, NJ: Transaction Books; 1980. 145 pp.

Operations Research and Use of Models

Thompson, Gerald E. 1976. *Management science: an introduction to modern quantitative analysis and decision making.* New York: McGraw-Hill; 1976. 453 pp.—Reviews: CR 1977.3:#31,034.

Gass, Saul I. 1975; Sisson, Roger L. *A guide to models in governmental planning and operations.* Potomac, MD: Sauger; 1975. 415 pp.—Reviews: CR 1978.4:#32,844.

Lindquist, M. G. 1978.3. *Growth dynamics of information search services.* JASIS. 1978.3; 29(2): 67–76.—A good example of simulation as applied to information systems management, wherein the use of an online service is predicted as a function of public relations and quality of service.

Bommer, Michael 1975.5. *Operations research in libraries: a critical assessment.* JASIS. 1975.5; 26(3): 137–139.

CHAPTER 7   ASSESSMENT OF USERS' PROBLEMS AND NEEDS

The readings listed with Chapters 2, 4, and 6 may also contain relevant material.

General Readings

Faibisoff, Sylvia G. 1976.9; Ely, Donald P. *Information and information needs.* Information—Reports and bibliographies. 1976.9; 5(5): 2–16.

Parker, Edwin B. 1966.11; Paisley, William J. *Research for psychologists at the interface of the scientist and his information system.* American Psychologist. 1966.11; 21 (11): 1061–1071.—Reprinted in Saracevic, T., ed. 1970. Introduction to information science: paper 11, p. 85–94.—An excellent overview and introduction.

Wilson, Thomas D. 1981.3. *On user studies and information needs.* J. Doc. 1981.3; 37(1): 3–15.

Guides for Information Needs and Use Studies

Sieber, H. F. 1964.10. *The methodology of the DOD Scientific and Technical Information Use Study*. American Documentation Institute. 27th Annual Meeting. Proceedings. 1964.10;1: 235–242.

Kunz, Werner 1977; Rittel, Horst, W. J.; Schwuchow, Werner. *Methods of analysis and evaluation of information needs*. Hamden, CT: Shoestring; 1976. 84 pp.—Reviews: LJ 1978.3.1:525.

Lancaster, F. Wilfrid 1974. *Assessment of the technical information requirements of users*. Rees, Alan, ed. 1974. Contemporary problems in technical library and information center management: a state-of-the-art. Washington, DC: ASIS; 1974: 59–85.

Line, Maurice B. 1982. *Library surveys*. 2. ed. London: Clive Bingley; 155 pp.

Results of Information Needs and Use Studies

Bates, Marcia J. 1971.3. *User studies: a review for librarians and information scientists*. 1971.3. 60 pp. (ERIC: ED 047 738)—A good guide to the literature up to 1969.

Cuadra, Carlos A. ed. 1974; Bates, Marcia J., ed. United States National Commission on Library and Information Science. *Library and information service needs of the nation. Proceedings of a conference on the needs of occupational, ethnic, and other groups in the United States*. Washington, D.C.: GPO; 1974. 314 pp. (GPO no. 5203–00033).—Especially Chapters 2, 4–V, 4–XII, 6, and 7.

McCarn, Davis B. 1967. See Chapter 18.

Catalog Use Studies

Matthews, Joseph R., ed. 1983; Lawrence, Gary S. ed.; Ferguson, Douglas K., ed. *Using online catalogs: a nationwide survey*. New York: Neal-Schuman; 1983. 255 pp.

Bates, Marcia J. 1977.5. *Factors affecting subject catalog search success*. JASIS. 1977.5; 28(3): 161–169.

Lancaster, F. Wilfrid 1977. *The measurement and evaluation of library services*. Washington, DC: Information Resources Press; 1977: chapter 2, *Studies of catalog use*, p. 19–72.

Studies of Impact

Kegan, Daniel L. 1970.5. *Measures of the usefulness of written technical information to chemical researchers*. JASIS. 1970.5; 21 (3): 179–186.

Maizell, R. E. 1960.1. *Information gathering patterns and creativity: a study of research chemists in an industrial research laboratory*. American Documentation. 1960.1; 11(1): 9–17.

Johnston, Ron 1975.2; Gibbon, Michael. *Characteristics of information usage in technological innovation*. IEEE Transactions in Engineering Management. 1975.2; EM-22(1): 27–34.

Rothwell, R. 1973.10; Robertson, A. B. *The role of communication in technological innovation*. Research Policy. 1973.10; 2 (3): 204–225.—An excellent review.

Application of User Studies to System Design

Paisley, William 1971.11. *Improving on "ERIC-like" information systems*. JASIS. 1971.11; 22(6): 399–408.

Meadow, Charles T. 1983.7. *User adaptation in interactive information retrieval*. JASIS. 1983.7; 34(4): 289–291.

Chapter 8   Objectives and Performance Measures for ISAR Systems

Readings emphasizing the definition of objectives and performance measures are listed here. Readings that deal also with methods for measuring or testing are listed in Chapter 18. Further relevant readings can be found with Chapter 6.

Introduction

Joyce, Bruce R. 1970; Joyce, Elizabeth A. *The creation of information systems for children.* Interchange. 1970; 1(2): 1–12.—Source of the example cited.

Sections 8.1 and 8.2. Definition of Performance Measures

Cooper, William S. 1973.3. *On selecting a measure of retrieval effectiveness.* Part I. *Philosophy.* JASIS. 1973.3; 24(2): 87–100. Part II. *Implementation of the philosophy.* JASIS. 1973.11; 24(6): 413–424.

Soergel, Dagobert 1976.7. *Is user satisfaction a hobgoblin?* JASIS. 1976.7; 27(4): 256–259.—Presents a case against Cooper's philosophy. Coopers' response on pp. 263–264.

Orr, Richard H. 1973. *Progress in documentation: measuring the goodness of library services: a general framework for considering quantitative measures.* J. Doc. 1973.9; 29(3): 315–332.

Robertson, Stephen E. 1969.3. *The parametric description of retrieval tests.* Part I. *The basic parameters.* J. Doc. 1969.3; 25 (1): 1–27. Part II. *Overall measures.* J. Doc. 1969.6; 25 (2): 93–107.

Pollock, Stephen M. 1968.10. *Measures for the comparison of information retrieval systems.* American Documentation. 1968.10; 19(4): 387–397.—Reprinted in Saracevic, T., ed. 1970. Introduction to information science. New York: Bowker; 1970: paper 56, pp. 592–602.

Good, I. J. 1967.4. *The decision-theory approach to the evaluation of information retrieval systems.* Information Storage and Retrieval. 1967.4; 3 (2): 31–34.

Swets, J. A. 1963.7. *Information retrieval systems.* Science. 1963.7.19; 141(3577): 245–250. Reprinted in Kochen, M., ed. 1967. The growth of knowledge. New York: Wiley; 1967: p. 174–184. Reprinted in Saracevic, T., ed. 1970. Introduction to information science. New York: Bowker; 1970: paper 54, pp. 576–583.

Cooper, William S. 1968.1. *Expected search length: a single measure of retrieval effectiveness based on the weak ordering of retrieval systems.* American Documentation. 1968.1; 19 (1): 30–41.

Savage, T. R. 1967.10. *The interpretation of SDI data.* American Documentation. 1967.10; 18 (4): 242–261.

DeProspo, Ernest R. 1973.11; Altman, Ellen; Beasley, Kenneth E.; Clark, Ellen C. *Performance measures for public libraries.* Chicago: ALA. Public Library Association; 1973.11. 142 pp.—Reviews: LQ 1974.7:273.

Zweizig, Douglas 1982; Roger, Eleanor Jo. *Output measures for public libraries. A manual of standardized procedures.* Chicago: ALA. Public Library Association; 1982. 100 p.—Less sophisticated than the previous reference.

Section 8.3   Testing versus Evaluation

"To test is not to evaluate" is a quotation from

Fairthorne, Robert A. 1965.12. *Some basic comments on retrieval testing.* J. Doc. 1965.12; 21(4): 267–270.—Reprinted in Saracevic, T., ed. 1970. Introduction to information science. New York: Bowker; 1970: paper 57, pp. 603–606.

Section 8.4   Relevance and Relevance Judgments

The references given with Chapters 2, 7, and 17 may also contain relevant material.

General Review Articles

Saracevic, Tefko 1976. *Relevance: a review of the literature and a framework for thinking on the notion in information science.* Advances in Librarianship. 1976; 6: 79–138.—A slightly different version was published in JASIS. 1975.11; 26 (6): 321–343.

On the Definition of Relevance

Cooper, William S. 1971.6. *A definition of relevance for information retrieval.* Information Storage and Retrieval. 1971.6; 7(1):19–37.—Good background for the next article.
Wilson, Patrick 1973.8. *Situational relevance.* Information Storage and Retrieval. 1973.8; 9(8): 457–471.
Kemp, B. D. 1974.2. *Relevance, pertinence and information system development.* Information Storage and Retrieval. 1974.2; 10 (2): 37–47.—Reviews: CR 1975.3:#27,950.

Usefulness of Relevance as a Concept

Doyle, Lawrence B. 1963.10. *Is relevance an adequate criterion in retrieval system evaluation?* American Documentation Institute. 26th Annual Meeting. Proceedings. 1963.10: 199–200.
Cuadra, Carlos A. 1967.10; Katter, Robert V. *The relevance of relevance assessment.* American Documentation Institute. 30th Annual Meeting. Proceedings. 1967.10; 4: 95–99.

How People Judge Relevance

Rees, Alan M. 1967.10; Schultz, Douglas G.; et al. *A field experimental approach to the study of relevance assessments in relation to document searching.* 2 vols. Cleveland, OH: Case Western Reserve University; 1967.10. 287, 185 pp.
Rees, Alan M. 1966.11. *The relevance of relevance to the testing and evaluation of document retrieval systems.* Aslib Proceedings. 1966.11; 18(11): 316–324.
Cuadra, Carlos A. 1967; Katter, Robert V. *Opening the black box of 'relevance'.* J. Doc. 1967.12; 23(4): 291–303.—A very important paper.
O'Connor, John 1967.7. *Relevance disagreements and unclear request forms.* American Documentation. 1967.7; 18(3): 165–177.
Cook, Kenneth H. 1975. *A threshold model of relevance decisions.* Information Processing and Management. 1975.10; 11(5): 125–135.—A decision-theoretic model to explain users' relevance judgments.

CHAPTERS 9–11   DATA SCHEMAS AND DATA STRUCTURES

See also the textbooks on data base management.

Atkinson, Malcolm P. 1979.3. *Progress in documentation: data base systems.* J. Doc. 1979.3; 35(1): 49–91.

Kim, Won 1979.9. *Relational data base systems.* Computing Surveys. 1979.9; 11(3): 185–212.— Reviews: CR 1980.2:#35,813.

CHAPTER 9   DATA SCHEMAS AND FORMATS

Section 9.1   Designing a conceptual schema

Kent, William 1978. *Data and reality: basic assumptions in data processing reconsidered.* New York: Elsevier North-Holland; 1978. 211 pp.—Reviews: CR 1980.8:#36,591.

Shave, M. J. R. 1982. *Entities, functions, and binary relations: steps to a conceptual schema.* Computer Journal. 1981.2; 24 (1): 42–47.—Reviews: CR 1981.8:#38,330.

Leong-Hong, Belkis W. 1982; Plagman, Bernard K. *Data dictionary/directory systems: administration, implementation, and usage.* New York: Wiley; 1982. 328 pp.—Reviews: CR 1982.11:#39,846.

Allen, Frank W. 1982.6; Loomis, Mary E. S.; Mannino, Michael V. *The integrated dictionary/ directory system.* Computing Surveys. 1982.6; 14 (2): 245–286.—Reviews: CR 1982.8: #39,657.

Section 9.3   Criteria for the Design and Evaluation of Data Schemas

Marcus, R. S. 1978.1; Kugel, P.; Benenfeld, A. R. *Catalog information and text as indicators of relevance.* JASIS. 1978.1; 29(1): 15–30.

CHAPTER 11   DATA STRUCTURES AND ACCESS

Chapin, Ned 1969.11. *Common file organization techniques compared.* AFIPS 1969 Fall Joint Computer Conference. 1969.11; 35: 413–422.—Reviews: CR 1970.3:#18,580.

Shera, Jesse H. 1956; Egan, Margaret. *The classified catalog.* Chicago: American Library Association; 1956. 130 pp.

Bryant, Philip 1980.6. *Progress in documentation. The catalog.* J. Doc. 1980.6; 36(2): 133–163.

Ryans, Cynthia C., ed. 1981. *The card catalog: current issues. Readings and selected bibliography.* Metuchen, NJ: Scarecrow; 1981. 336 pp.—Reviews: LJ 1982.3.1:527. SL 1981.10:412.

Stevens, Norman D. 1980.6. *The catalogs of the future: a speculative essay.* J. of Library Automation. 1980.6; 13(2): 88–95.—Reviews: CR 1981.1:#37,311.

Fayen, Emily G. 1983. *The online catalog: improving public access to library materials.* White Plains, NY: Knowledge Industry Publications; 1983. 148 pp.

Matthews, Joseph R. 1982. *Public access to online catalogs.* Weston, CT: Online; 1982. 345 pp.

Section 11.1   Exploration of Data Structures

Articulated Indexes

Mills, J. 1955.4. *Chain indexing and the classified catalog.* Library Association Record. 1955.4;
57(4): 141–148.—See Needham 1971 (Textbooks ISAR), pp. 182–186 for a summary.
Sharp, John R. 1966.1. *The SLIC index.* American Documentation. 1966.1; 17 (1): 41–44.
Richmond, Phyllis A. 1981. *Introduction to PRECIS for North American usage.* Littleton, CO:
Libraries Unlimited; 1981. 321 pp.
Austin, Derek 1974. *PRECIS: A manual of concept analysis and subject indexing.* London:
Council of the British National Bibliography. 1974; 561 pp.—Reviews: JD 1976.3:85–96.
The review itself is a brief introduction to PRECIS.
Craven, Timothy C. 1977.3. *NEPHIS: A nested-phrase indexing system.* JASIS. 1977.3; 28(2):
107–114.

Section 11.4   The Concept of Order

The ALA filing rules. Chicago: American Library Association; 1980. 50 pp.
Wellisch, Hans H. 1983.9. *The ALA filing rules: flowcharts illustrating their application,
with a critique and suggestions for improvement.* JASIS. 1983.9; 34(5): 313–330.

Chapters 12–15   Index Language Functions and Structure

As is true for all parts of the book, much material can be found in the textbooks listed in Part 1. See also Chapter 7 references on studies of catalog
use, Chapters 16–18 and Chapter 18, especially Fugman 1985.3.

Fischer, Marguerite 1966.4. *The KWIC index concept: a retrospective view.* American Documentation. 1966.4; 17(2): 57–70.
Gebhardt, F. 1978.7; Stellmacher, I. *Design criteria for documentation retrieval languages.*
JASIS. 1978.7; 29(4): 191–199.
Landauer, T. K. 1983.7; Galotti, K. M.; Hartwell, S. *Natural command names and initial learning: A study of text-editing terms.* Communications of the ACM. 1983.7; 26(7):
495–503.—An important study with direct implications for the debate on natural language
versus controlled vocabulary in retrieval systems.
Pejtersen, A. M. 1983.12; Austin, J. *Fiction retrieval: experimental design and evaluation
of a search system based on users' value criteria.* Parts 1 and 2. J. Doc. 1983.12;
39(4):230–246./1984.3; 40(1): 25–35.—A very good experimental study of request-oriented
indexing.
Soergel, Dagobert 1974.5. *Automatic and semi-automatic methods as an aid in the construction of indexing languages and thesauri.* International Classification. 1974.5; 1(1): 35–39.
Lytle, Richard H. 1980.1. *Intellectual access to archives. I. Provenance and content indexing
methods of subject retrieval. II. Report of an experiment comparing provenance and content indexing methods of subject retrieval.* American Archivist. 1980.Winter; 43(1): 64–75
and 1980.Spring; 43(2): 191–206.

CHAPTER 13   INDEX LANGUAGE FUNCTIONS

Section 13.2   The Role of the Index Language in Indexing

Mooers, Calvin N. 1958; Brenner, C. W. *A case history of a Zatocoding IR system.* Casey, R. S., ed. 1958. Punched cards: their application to science and industry. 2. ed. New York: Reinhold; 1958: chapter 15, p. 340–356.—This is the seminal article on request-oriented indexing, called in the article "filtering technique"; the essential pages are 346–352.

Cooper, William S. 1978.5. *Indexing documents by Gedanken experimentation.* JASIS. 1978.5; 25 (3): 107–119.—See also the notes by Wilson and Cooper in JASIS. 1979.5; 30(3):169–172.

Feinman, R. D. 1973.1; Kwok, K. L. *The construction of journal-oriented classification schemes.* JASIS. 1973.1; 24(1): 71–72.

CHAPTER 14   INDEX LANGUAGE STRUCTURE 1: CONCEPTUAL

Fairthorne, Robert A. 1955.10. *Essentials for document retrieval.* Special Libraries. 1955.10; 46(10): 340–353.

Austin, Derek 1969.7. *Prospects for a new general classification.* J. of Librarianship. 1969.7; 1(3): 149–169.

Sokal, R. R. 1974.9. *Classification: purposes, principles, progress, prospects.* Science. 1974.9. 27; 185(4157): 1115–1123.

Niehoff, R. T. 1976.1. *Development of an integrated energy vocabulary and the possibilities for online subject switching.* JASIS. 1976.1; 27(1): 3–17.—Prefer to newer articles.

Reports on Systems

The Semantic Code and Syntol are examples of methods for the representation of knowledge. Today's systems could capitalize on the intellectual effort invested in them.

Perry, J. W., ed. 1958; Kent, Allen, ed. *Tools for machine literature searching. Semantic code dictionary, equipment, procedures.* New York: Wiley; 1958. 972 pp.

Gardin, Jean Claude 1965. *Syntol.* New Brunswick, NJ: Rutgers University. Graduate School of Library Service; 1965. 106 pp. (Rutgers Series on Systems for the Intellectual Organization of Information, v. 2.)—Reviews: LJ 1965.4.1:1694. SL 1965.12:136.—The following book is much better.

Cros, Rene C. 1968; Gardin, Jean Claude; Levy, Francis. *L'automatisation des recherches documentaires—Un modèle général, "le SYNTOL".* 2. ed. Paris: Gauthier-Villars; 1968. 260 pp.

Berthelot, A. 1979.11; Clague, S.; Schiminovich, S.; Zwirner, W. *The ICSU AB international classification system for physics: its history and future.* JASIS. 1979.11; 30(6): 343–352.

Section 14.5   Conceptual Analysis, Facet Analysis: Elaboration

Further relevant material is listed with Chapter 3.

Vickery, Brian C. 1960. *Faceted classification. A guide to construction and use of special schemes.* London: Aslib 1960. 70 pp. (reprinted with additional material 1968).

Grolier, Eric de 1962. *A study of general categories applicable to classification and coding in documentation.* Paris: UNESCO; 1962. 248 pp.

Katz, Jerrold J. 1964.12. *Semantic theory and the meaning of "good."* J. of Philosophy. 1964.12.10; 61(235): 739–766.

Sturtevant, William C. 1964.6. *Studies in ethnoscience.* American Anthropologist. 1964.6; 66(3,pt.2): 99–131.—A study of classification in other cultures with an approach very relevant for Section 14.5.

Section 14.7   Concept Formation in Thesaurus Building

The quotations on cross-disciplinary concepts are from

Singer, Joel David. 1971.6. *A general systems taxonomy for political science.* Morristown, NJ: General Learning; 1971: Section Transferability of knowledge.

CHAPTER 15   INDEX LANGUAGE STRUCTURE 2: DATA BASE ORGANIZATION

See also references for Section 11.1.

Jonker, F. 1959. *A descriptive continuum: A "generalized" theory of indexing.* Proceedings of the International Conference on Scientific Information. 1958.11. Washington, D.C.: National Academy of Sciences/National Research Council; 1959: v. 2, p. 1291–1311.

CHAPTERS 16–18   ISAR SYSTEM OPERATION AND DESIGN

References on Automated Methods of Information Storage and Retrieval

These references go well beyond the text.

Knowledge-based approaches and language analysis

See the textbooks on artificial intelligence and expert systems and references with Chapter 3.

Probabilistic approaches

Some of these references deal with indexing, some with searching, and some with both, but they all use the same underlying ideas and it is, therefore, useful to put them together. See also the section on automated ISAR in the textbook bibliography and Salton's work on SMART.

Salton, Gerard 1979.3. *Mathematics and information retrieval.* J. Doc. 1979.3; 35(1): 1–29.—A tight, well-written overview.

Maron, M. E. 1960.7; Kuhns, J. L. *On relevance, probabilistic indexing and information retrieval.* Journal of the ACM. 1960.7; 7(3): 216–244.—Reprinted in Saracevic, T., ed. 1970. Introduction to information science. New York: Bowker; 1970: paper 28, p. 295–311.—A seminal paper in the area.

Bookstein, Abraham 1975.1; Swanson, Don R. *A decision theoretic foundation for indexing.* JASIS. 1975.1; 26(1): 45–50.—Representative of a large number of similar papers by various authors.

Harter, Stephen P. 1975.7. *A probabilistic approach to automatic keyword indexing. Pt. I: On the distribution of specialty words in technical literature. Pt. II: An algorithm for probabilistic indexing.* JASIS. 1975.7; 26(4): 197–206 and 1975.9; 26(5): 280–289.—A very well-written exposition of the probabilistic, cost-based approach to indexing and searching.

The following references describe a particular method of indexing and searching: human experts provide indexing using a controlled vocabulary or relevance judgments with respect to a query, respectively, for a training set. Analysis of these data yields associations between document terms (or other easily ascertained entity characteristics) and descriptors from a controlled vocabulary or between entity characteristics and queries. A program then uses these associations to infer from entity characteristics the appropriate controlled vocabulary descriptors or relevance judgments with respect to queries.

Maron, M. E. 1961.7. *Automatic indexing: an experimental inquiry.* J. of the ACM. 1961.7; 8(3): 404–417.—The seminal paper on the subject.

Kar, Gautam 1978; White, Lee J. *A distance measure for automatic document classification by sequential analysis.* Information Processing and Management. 1978; 14(2): 57–69.

Hamill, Karen A. 1980.11; Zamora, Antonio. *The use of titles for automatic document classification.* JASIS. 1980.11; 31(6): 396–402.

Miller, William L. 1971.12. *A probabilistic search strategy for MEDLARS.* J. Doc. 1971.12; 27(4): 254–266.—Reviews: CR 1972.7:#23,497.

Robertson, Stephen E. 1976.5; Sparck Jones, K. *Relevance weighting of search terms.* JASIS. 1976.5; 27(3): 129–146.—A good summary of this area of research.

Robson, Allen 1976.7; Longman, Janet S. *Automatic aids to profile construction.* JASIS. 1976.7; 27(4): 213–223.

The SMART System

The SMART system is amply covered in books written or edited by Gerard Salton, some of them cited in the textbook bibliography. The following early references give a good idea of the conception and genesis of the system.

Salton, Gerard 1962. *The identification of document content: a problem in automatic information retrieval.* Proceedings of the Harvard Symposium on Computers. 1962: 273–304.

Salton, Gerard 1963.7. *Some hierarchical models for automatic document retrieval.* American Documentation. 1963.7; 14(3): 213–222.

Salton, Gerard 1964.1. *A flexible automatic system for the organization, storage and retrieval of language data (SMART).* Information Storage and Retrieval. Scientific Report to NSF No. ISR-5. Cambridge, MA: Harvard Univ.; 1964.1: I-1-I-42.

Salton, Gerard 1964.6. *The SMART system.—An introduction.* Information Storage and Retrieval. Scientific Report to NSF no. ISR-7. Cambridge, MA: Harvard Univ.; 1964.6: I-1-I-11.

CHAPTER 16   INDEXING AND SYSTEM PERFORMANCE

Maizell, R. E. 1971; Smith, J. F.; Singer, T. E. *Abstracting scientific and technical literature. An introductory guide and text for scientists, abstractors, and management.* New York: Wiley; 1971. 313 pp.

Borko, Harold 1978; Bernier, Charles L. *Indexing concepts and methods.* New York: Academic Press; 1978. 256 pp.—Reviews: JA 1980.3:126.

Rolling, L. 1981.3. *Indexing consistency, quality and efficiency.* Information Processing and Management. 1981.3; 17(2): 69–76.

Landau, Herbert B. 1969.10. *The cost analysis of document surrogation: a literature review.* American Documentation. 1969.10; 20(4): 302–310.—Very good.

Borko, Harold 1963.4; Chapman, Seymour. *Criteria for acceptable abstracts: survey of abstractor's instructions.* American Documentation. 1963.4; 14(2): 149–160.—Reprinted in Saracevic, T., ed. 1970. Introduction to information science. New York: Bowker; 1970: paper 33, p. 364–376.—A very good review.

Weil, Ben H. 1970.9. *Standards for writing abstracts.* JASIS. 1970.9; 21(5): 351–357.

Leonov, Valery P. 1974.10; Soergel, Dagobert. *Compressing and abstracting information for information utilities.* American Society for Information Science. 37th annual meeting. Proceedings. 1974.10; 11: 46–49.

Vernimb, C. 1969. *Indexing rules for the EURATOM Nuclear Documentation System (ENDS).* Luxembourg: EURATOM Center for Information and Documentation; 1969. 25 pp.—Just given as an example without quality judgment.

Schultz, Claire K. 1970.10. *Cost-effectiveness as a guide in developing indexing rules.* Information Storage and Retrieval. 1970.10; 6(4): 335–340.

Atherton, Pauline 1963.9. *Aid-to-indexing forms: a progress report.* New York: American Institute of Physics; 1963.9. (AIP/DRP 63-2)

Machine-Assisted Indexing

Hunt, Bernard L. 1975.7; Synderman, Martin; Payne, William. *Machine-assisted indexing of scientific research studies.* JASIS. 1975.7; 26(4): 230–236.

Automatic Abstracting

Edmundson, Harold P. 1961.5; Wyllys, R. E. *Automatic abstracting and indexing—survey and recommendations.* Communications of the ACM. 1961.5; 4(5): 226–234.

Edmundson, Harold P. 1969.4. *New methods in automatic extracting.* J. of the ACM. 1969.4; 16(2): 264–285.—Reprinted in Saracevic, T., ed. 1970. Introduction to information science. New York: Bowker; 1970: paper 34, p. 377–392.

Rush, James E. 1971.7; Salvadore, R.; Zamora, A. *Automatic abstracting and indexing II. Production of indicative abstracts by application of contextual inference and syntactic coherence criteria.* JASIS. 1971.7; 22(4): 260–274.

Mathis, Betty A. 1973.3; Rush, James E.; Young, Carol E. *Improvement of automatic abstracts by the use of structural analysis.* JASIS. 1973.3; 24(2): 101–109.

Borkowski, Casimir 1975.3; Martin, J. Sperling. *Structure, effectiveness, and benefits of LEXtractor, an operational computer program for automatic extraction of case summaries and dispositions from court decisions.* JASIS. 1975.3; 26(2): 94–102.

Automatic Indexing: Syntactic Approaches

See also references given under automated information storage and retrieval earlier.

Borkowski, Casimir 1967.7. *An experimental system for automatic identification of personal names and personal titles in newspaper text.* American Documentation. 1967.7; 18 (3): 131–138.

Borkowski, Casimir 1970.1; Cepanec, Louis; Martin, J. Sperling; Salko, Virginia; Treu, Siegfried. *Structure and effectiveness of the citation identifier, an operational computer program for automatic identification of case citations in legal literature.* JASIS. 1970.1; 21 (1): 8–15.

Dunham, G. S. 1978.3; Pacak, M. G.; Pratt, A. W. *Automatic indexing of pathology data.* JASIS. 1978.3; 29(2): 81–90.—Uses SNOP, a faceted classification of pathology, as the target index language.

CHAPTER 17   SEARCHING

Textbooks

Jahoda, Gerald 1980; Braunagel, Judith S. *The librarian and reference queries. A systematic approach.* New York: Academic Press; 1980. 192 pp.—Reviews: JD 1981.6: 93. LJ 1980.12.1: 2480.—Uses the entity–relationship model as a conceptual base.

Thomas, Diana M. 1981; Eisenbach, Elizabeth R.; Hinckley, Ann T. *The effective reference librarian.* New York: Academic Press; 1981. 224 pp.

Articles on the Entire Scope of Chapter 17

Bates, Marcia J. 1979.7. *Information search tactics.* JASIS. 1979.7; 30 (4): 205–214.

Bates, Marcia J. 1979.9. *Idea tactics.* JASIS. 1979.9; 30 (5): 280–289.—Bates' tactics, with the exception of F4. CUT, F7. CLEAVE, and M5. RECORD, are covered in Chapter 17 and individually referenced.

Fidel, Raya 1984.7. *Online searching styles: A case–study–based model of searching behavior.* JASIS. 1984.7; 35(4): 211–221.

Fidel, Raya 1983.5; Soergel, Dagobert. *Factors affecting online bibliographic retrieval: a conceptual framework for research.* JASIS. 1983.5; 34(3): 163–180.

Scheffler, F. 1972.1; March, Jacquelin; Bernados, John. *An experiment to study the use of Boolean NOT logic to improve the precision of selective dissemination of information.* JASIS. 1972.1; 23(1): 58–65.—Much broader than title indicates. Many good points on formulating queries for SDI.

Costs of Searching

Cooper, Michael D. 1976.9; DeWath, Nancy A. *The cost of on-line bibliographic searching.* J. of Library Automation. 1976.9; 9 (3): 195–208.

Elchesen, D. R. 1978.3. *Cost–effectiveness comparison of manual and on-line retrospective bibliographic searching.* JASIS. 1978.3; 29(2): 56–66.—A good study.

Section 17.1.2   Develop the Query Statement

The references listed here deal with the reference interview.

Basic Works on the Reference Interview

Taylor, Robert S. 1968.5. *Question negotiation and information-seeking in libraries*. College and Research Libraries. 1968.5; 29(3): 178–194.

White, Marilyn D. 1982. *The reference encounter model*. Dusha, C., ed. 1982. Theories in library and information science. New York: Bowker; 1982: 38–55.

Carmon, J. L. 1975.5. *Model the user interface for a multidisciplinary bibliographic information network*. Athens, GA: University of Georgia. Office of Computing Activities; 1975.5. 101 pp. + ca. 200 pp. appendices. (NTIS no. PB-242 964/56A)

Interviewing in General

Cannell, C. F. 1968; Kahn, R. L. *Interviewing*. In Lindzey, G., ed. 1968; Aronson, E., ed. *The handbook of social psychology*. 2. ed. Reading, MA: Addison-Wesley; 1968. vol.2: Chapter 15, pp. 526–595.

Stewart, Charles J. 1978; Cash, William B. *Interviewing: principles and practices*. 2. ed. Dubuque, IA: W. C. Brown; 1978. 286 pp.—Particularly chapter 2, The interviewing process and chapter 4, Questions and their use.

Brill, N. I. 1973. *Working with people: principles of the helping process*. Philadelphia, PA: Lippincott; 1973. 202 pp.

Additional References

Crouch, Wayne W. 1979. *The information interview: a comprehensive bibliography and an analysis of the literature*. Syracuse, NY: Syracuse University. ERIC Clearinghouse on Information Resources; 1979. 49 pp. (ERIC: ED 180 501).

White, Marilyn D. 1981.7. *The dimensions of the reference interview*. RQ. 1981.Summer; 20(4): 373–381.

Section 17.2   Develop the Search Strategy

Jahoda, Gerald 1974.5. *Reference question analysis and search strategy development by men and machine*. JASIS. 1974.5; 25(3):139–144.—A good analysis.

Marcus, Richard S. 1979.4; Reintjes, J. Francis. *Experiments and analysis on the computer interface to an information retrieval network*. Cambridge, MA: Massachusetts Institute of Technology. Laboratory for Information and Decision Systems; 1979.4.133 pp. (ERIC: ED 190 104).

Section 17.2.4   Free-Text Searching

See also Chapter 18, other studies, Blair 1985.3.

Evans, Lynn 1975.4. *Search strategy variations in SDI profiles*. London: Institution of Electrical Engineers; 1975.4. 129 pp. (OSTI Report 5229. Available from British Library, Lending Division).

O'Connor, John 1973.11. *Text searching retrieval of answer-sentences and other answer-passages*. JASIS. 1973.11; 24(6): 445–460.

O'Connor, John 1980.7. *Answer-passage retrieval by text searching*. JASIS. 1980.7; 31(4): 227–239.—Presents a fairly sophisticated algorithm.

Section 17.3   Execute the Search Strategy

Marcus, Richard S. 1981.7; Reintjes, J. Francis. *A translating computer interface for end-user operation of heterogeneous retrieval systems. I. Design. II. Evaluations.* JASIS. 1981.7; 32(4): 287–303/304–317.

Marcus, Richard S. 1983.11. *An experimental comparison of the effectiveness of computers and humans as search intermediaries.* JASIS. 1983.11; 34(6): 381–404.

Meadow, Charles T. 1982.9; Hewett, Thomas T.; Aversa, Elizabeth S. *A computer intermediary for interactive data base searching. I. Design. II. Evaluation.* JASIS. 1982.9; 33(5): 325–332/1982.11; 33(6): 357–364.

British Computer Society. Query Language Group 1980; Salter, J. *Query languages: a unified approach.* New York: Wiley; 1980. 88 pp. (Also London: Hayden; 1981. 105 pp.)

Sections 17.5   Edit Search Results and Send Them to the User
and 17.6   Check Whether the Answer Was Helpful (Evaluation 2)

Lancaster, F. Wilfrid 1970.9; Jenkins, Grace T. *"Quality control" applied to the operations of a large information system.* JASIS. 1970.9; 21(5); 370–371.

Section 17.7   Interaction

See also the references on search term weighting given earlier under automated information storage and retrieval and the references given in Section 17.3.

Oddy, Robert N. 1977.3. *Information retrieval through man–machine dialogue.* J. Doc. 1977.3; 33(1): 1–14.—Reviews: CR 1977.12:#32,338.

Vernimb, Carlos 1977.11. *Automatic query adjustment in document retrieval.* Information Processing and Management. 1977.11; 13(6): 339–353.

CHAPTER 18   DESIGN AND EVALUATION OF INFORMATION SYSTEMS

This listing emphasizes references that deal with methodologies for or results of testing the performance of information systems, especially their ISAR system component. References that emphasize objectives and performance measures are listed with Chapter 8. More comprehensive references are listed with Chapter 6.

Methodology for testing and evaluation

King, Donald W. 1971; Bryant, Edward P. *The evaluation of information services and products.* Washington, D.C.: Information Resources Press; 1971. 306 pp.—Reviews: LJ 1972.4.1:1250. LQ 1973.1:80.—This is a classic.

Lancaster, F. Wilfrid 1977. *The measurement and evaluation of library services.* Washington, D.C.: Information Resources Press; 1977.—Reviews: LJ 1978.1.15:146. SL 1978.4:186. IP 1978: 54.—This is a very useful compilation and review of work both on testing methodology and on testing results.

Cleverdon, Cyril W. 1970.3. *Progress in documentation: evaluation tests of information retrieval systems.* J. Doc. 1970.3; 26 (1): 55–67.

Swanson, Rowena Weiss 1975.5. *Performing evaluation studies in information science.* JASIS. 1975.5; 26(3): 140–156.

Reports on Actual Studies and Experiments in the Testing and Evaluation of Information Systems

Cranfield II and Related Studies

Cleverdon, Cyril 1967.6. *The Cranfield test of index language devices.* Aslib Proceedings 1967.6; 19(6): 173–194. Reprinted in Saracevic, T., ed. 1970. Introduction to information science. New York: Bowker; 1970: paper 58, p. 608–620.—Reviews of the underlying report: CR 1969.1:#15,947–15,949. JD 1967.12: 338.

Swanson, Don R. 1971.7. *Some unexplained aspects of the Cranfield tests of indexing performance factors.* Library Quarterly. 1971.7; 41(3): 223–228.

Harter, Stephen P. 1971.7. *The Cranfield II relevance assessments: a critical evaluation.* Library Quarterly. 1971.7; 41(3): 229–243.

Keen, E. Michael 1973.4. *The Aberystwyth index language test.* J. Doc. 1973.4; 29(1): 1–35.

The Comparative Systems Laboratory at Case Western Reserve University

Saracevic, Tefko 1970. *Selected results from an inquiry into testing of information retrieval systems.* Saracevic, T., ed. 1970. Introduction to information science. New York: Bowker; 1970: paper 61, p. 665–681.—Review of the underlying report: JD 1969.6: 177.

Saracevic, Tefko 1967.3; Rees, Allen F. *Towards identification and control of variables in information retrieval experimentation.* J. Doc. 1967.3; 23 (1): 8–19.

MEDLARS Evaluation

Lancaster, F. Wilfrid 1969.4. *MEDLARS: Report on the evaluation of its operating efficiency.* American Documentation. 1969.4; 20 (2): 119–142.

Retrieval Tests with the SMART System

See the books by Salton listed in Part 1 of the bibliography and references on SMART listed with chapters 16–18

Other Studies

McCarn, Davis B. 1967; Stein, Charles R. *Intelligence system evaluation.* Kent, A., ed. 1967. Electronic handling of information. Washington, D.C.: Thompson; London: Academic Press; 1967: 109–122.—In addition to performing a retrieval experiment, this study looked at the incremental value of the information system studied over other information sources consulted by its users in terms of additional relevant documents found and in terms of additional substantive data gleaned from such documents.

Blair, David C. 1985.3; Maron, M. E. *An evaluation of retrieval effectiveness for a full-text document–retrieval system.* Communications of the ACM. 1985.3; 28(3): 289–291.—A good study in a real-life environment.

Myers, Marcia J. 1983; Jirjees, Jassim M. *The accuracy of telephone reference information services in academic libraries: two studies.* Metuchen, NJ: Scarecrow; 1983. 270 pp.—Reviews: LJ 1983.5.15:984.

Design Characteristics of Information Systems

Fugman, Robert 1985.3. *The five-axiom theory of indexing and information supply.* JASIS. 1985.3; 36(2): 116–129.—A good summary of ISAR principles with a view to design.

Wilson, Patrick 1968. *Two kinds of power. An essay on bibliographical control.* Berkeley, Los Angeles, CA: University of California Press; 1968. 155 pp.

Bates, Marcia J. 1976.10. *Rigorous systematic bibliography.* RQ. 1976.Fall; 16(1): 7–26.—A summary of and introduction to Wilson's book.

Author Index

A page number marked by an asterisk (*) contains several references by the author.

A

Allen, F. 412
Allen, T. 406
Altman, E. 410
Aslib Research Department, 408
Atherton, P. 417
Atkinson, M. 412
Atre, S. 403
Austin, D. 413, 414
Austin, J. 413
Aversa, E. 420

B

Barr, A. 402
Bates, M. 409*, 418*, 422
Batten, W. 400
Beasley, K. 410
Becker, J. 400, 401
Belkin, N. 406
Benenfeld, A. 412
Bernados, J. 418
Bernier, C. 417
Berthelot, A. 414
Bingham, J. 407
Blair, D. 421
Bliss, H. 404
Bommer, M. 408
Bonczek, R. 403
Bookstein, A. 416
Borko, H. 417*
Borkowski, C. 417, 418*
Branstein, D. 408
Braunagel, J. 418
Brenner, C. 414
Brill, N. 419

British Computer Society, 420
Brookes, C. 400
Bryant, E. 420
Bryant, P. 412

C

Cannell, C. 419
Carlson, E. 403
Carmon, J. 419
Cash, W. 419
Cepanec, L. 418
Chafetz, M. 407
Chapin, N. 412
Chapman, S. 417
Charniak, E. 402
Childers, P. 402
Churchman, C. 407
Clague, S. 414
Clark, E. 410
Cleverdon, C. 421*
Coates, E. 404
Cohen, P. 402
Cohen, S. 406
Connor, J. 407
Cook, K. 411
Cooper, M. 418
Cooper, W. 410*, 411, 414
Craven, T. 413
Cros, R. 414
Crouch, W. 419
Cuadra, C. 399, 409, 411*

D

Date, C. 403*

423

Subject Index

This subject index serves also as a key to abbreviations. It should be used in conjunction with the table of contents, which serves as a classified index. Cross-references are introduced only as space permits; cross-references that can be inferred from the term itself are not given (for example, there is no cross-reference Polyhierarchy to Hierarchy). Page numbers 399 and above refer to the bibliography.